'Travelling outgrows its motives. It soon proves sufficient in itself. You think you are making a trip, but soon it is making you—or unmaking you.'

Nicolas Bouvier, *The Way of the World*

'how was I, out of all this, to make a book?'

Graham Greene, *Ways of Escape*

CONTENTS

PART ONE
THE QUEST(IONS)

PART TWO
THE TRAVEL WRITING TRIBE

PART THREE
ACROSS THE BORDER

PART ONE

THE QUEST(IONS)

1

THE LONG WHITE TRACK

This is what I remember:

A long white track through the fields. A cock pheasant, lumbering into flight on frenzied wings. At a field corner, an old barn, built of rusted iron sheets and flamboyantly collapsed, its roof-ridge warped like the spine of a Chinese dragon. And at the end of the track, the house: the house from the book.

It was an afternoon of absolute stillness in late April, with deep shadows in the curves of the countryside. To the west a thin streak of blue showed where the River Fal was creeping into southern Cornwall with the flooding tide. I had come to conduct an interview, a 1,200-word profile for a regional magazine: local author with a new book out; *tell our readers what you love most about Cornwall!* But he was a writer in the genre that was my abiding literary obsession, and I was excited at the prospect of talking to him.

He came to the door with a spaniel eddying around his feet: 'Yes, yes, come in; we'll get a drink and then we can go to my office…'

Philip Marsden. *A travel writer.* In the flesh.

* * *

I read my first travel books in my late teens, five of them in short succession, though I can't recall in which order: Eric Newby's *A Short Walk*

3

in the Hindu Kush; Wilfred Thesiger's *Desert, Marsh and Mountain*; Paul Theroux's *The Happy Isles of Oceania*; Nick Danziger's *Danziger's Travels*; and Nicholas Crane's *Clear Waters Rising*. It was like finding a way through the back of the wardrobe. This was what I had been looking for as a bookish boy who was also a surfer and kayaker and cross-country runner. I had already dallied with Ernest Hemingway and Joseph Conrad, but this was better still: books by writers who seemed to be hardy outdoorsmen (and they were all men, though I scarcely registered the fact at the time) but who were as scholarly as they were intrepid. With books like these I could gaze at lapis-blue tilework under vast Central Asian skies in the company of a guide who knew the difference between Seljuk and Timurid architecture, but who would, with the next breath, be setting out to cross an uncharted desert with little more than a leaky waterskin and a handful of dates. What was more, travel writing seemed to have both a busy present and a limitless past (I was eighteen, a trainee chef from the far west of Cornwall in the late 1990s, and Eric Newby and Wilfred Thesiger seemed to represent some distant classical epoch—though both men were, in fact, still alive and publishing at the time).

As Lonely Planet guidebooks and long-haul flights began to frame the geography of my winters, my fascination with travel writing grew. I didn't realise as much at the time, but I was reading at the tail end of a remarkable, quarter-century-long commercial boom for the genre. The 'travel' section in the bookstore was bloated with new titles and reissued classics: William Dalrymple and Robert Byron, Sara Wheeler and Freya Stark. Soon the collection of travel books in my bedroom far outstripped the bank of novels on the shelf above. I had to hammer up new planks to make space for them. I took to lingering in the corners of second-hand bookshops, leafing through foxed pages and finding travellers from other eras: Peter Fleming and Ella Maillart, Peter Mayne and Fitzroy Maclean. And I took unconsciously to aping their pose and their prose in the diaries I scribbled as I rattled around the backpacker circuits of Asia.

It was a literary love affair, and an enduring one. But as love affairs are wont to do, it developed its distress points over the years. I began to notice comments in the review sections of the weekend papers about travel writing 'falling out of commercial favour', or, worse yet, becoming an 'unfashionable genre'. I hurried back to the bookshops to check. At first there seemed little cause for concern. But then the dedicated sections really did begin to shrink, and before long the travel shelves in my local WHSmith had contracted to a mean three feet of guidebooks and celebrity jaunts. Even as a confirmed aficionado I could sometimes see why. As the chilling aftereffects of the 'war on terror' unfolded across what had once been prime travel writing territory, the globetrotting escapades of the 1950s, and even of the 1990s, began to look like unwitting elegies at best, and appalling self-indulgences at worst.

And there was more. In my first flush of infatuation with travel writing I had read the genre uncritically under its official designation: nonfiction. But by now I had heard the dark stories of fabrication, of invented encounters and counterfeit characters. Worse yet, I began, in my mid-twenties, to dip tentatively into the body of strictly academic literature that came under the designation of 'travel writing studies'. This was a rather esoteric field, little known beyond the confines of the campuses. But it had its own journals and conferences; and it was worlds apart from the genre that was its object. I began to supplement Thesiger and Thubron and Theroux with a little of Mary Louise Pratt and Edward Said. If the earlier encounter with travel writing itself had been a magical passage through the wardrobe, then this was the discovery of something nasty in the woodshed—for as far as some of the scholars were concerned, travel writing had uncomfortable questions to answer.

Travel writing, both old and new, was hopelessly entangled with the history of European colonialism, their argument went. It was a genre that rolled along tracks laid down in an imperial epoch. It departed from traditional centres of power and travelled with scant real respect or regard for those through whose homelands it passed. Some of the more radical scholars seemed to suggest that the entire genre was irredeemable, its very exercise tantamount to an act of ideological violence, no matter how superficially sympathetic the writer. One of the most critical scholars, Debbie Lisle, had described her own first encounter with the genre, just a few years before my own, and with one of the very same books: Paul Theroux's *The Happy Isles of Oceania*. But there was no beguilement here; Lisle found the book 'boring, nasty and offensive in equal measure [...] Intuitively, I knew this wasn't just a bad book; there was something *wrong* with this book and something *wrong* with travel writing in general.' It was, Lisle felt, a genre that 'encourages a particularly conservative political outlook'.[1]

I wasn't entirely convinced. I *loved* travel writing, didn't think of myself as sympathetic to conservative political outlooks; and I often found myself bristling defensively at such scholarly assaults. But I knew that there was something in the critique that couldn't be dismissed out of hand. And that book collection on the much-extended set of shelves in my bedroom? It was certainly very male, and very white.

I kept reading, into my thirties, long beyond the first flush of youthful infatuation. I was still haunting the dusty corners of those second-hand bookshops—where titles from the 1980s and 1990s now seemed as much like artefacts from another age as those from the 1930s and 1950s. From time to time I would find myself grumbling with fellow aficionados about the relative dearth of decent new travel books, and worriedly wondering how a promising young travel writer might get started in an age of dwindling advances. But I read more critically, and as I did so I felt an occasional twinge of conscience—and not simply at the unsettling possibility that the writer might have made it all up. What if Debbie Lisle was right: what if there really was something *wrong* with travel writing?

People have been asking the melodramatic question, 'Is travel writing dead?' for the best part of a century. Evelyn Waugh was already answering in the affirmative in 1946—prematurely, as it happens:[2] Bruce Chatwin was six years old at the time; Paul Theroux was five. But when I heard the question now, I did sometimes find myself wondering. Could travel writing *really* survive—ethically as much as commercially—into the unfurling twenty-first century?

This all goes some way to explain why I was so delighted when a magazine editor asked me to interview Philip Marsden.

* * *

Philip Marsden was one of the young British travel writers who appeared at the close of the 1980s, a contemporary of the likes of William Dalrymple and Sara Wheeler. He started out writing about Ethiopia, but it was his second book, *The Crossing Place*, published in 1993, which properly marked him out. It was an account of a journey through the Middle East and into the Caucasus amongst the scattered

Armenian people. It came with the sort of elegantly restrained prose, scholarly grasp of history and authorial self-effacement that had somehow become the unofficial last word in highbrow British travel writing. There was more of the same in the books that followed: *The Spirit-Wrestlers* (1998); *The Chains of Heaven* (2005); and also *The Bronski House* (1995), which tested the limits of the genre, combining first-person travel with a novelised memoir of a Polish family. He was one of the travel writers that reviewers always took seriously.

He lived with his wife Charlotte—also a writer—and their two children in an old farmhouse at the end of a long white track in Cornwall.

* * *

Marsden's office was a neat little outbuilding at the edge of the fields, slate-roofed, built of local stone. Inside there were threadbare rugs and shelves laden with books. I glanced along them as we went in, and spotted Graham Greene and Colin Thubron, along with heavyweight tomes on Russian history. Robert Macfarlane and Kathleen Jamie were there too, and a hardback copy of Tim Winton's *Land's Edge*. A gap in the rear wall opened into a shadowy space filled with more books.

He sat in a creaking office chair by the window with light and birdsong coming in through the open doorway: a tall man in a crumpled blue shirt a couple of sizes too big. He was in his mid-fifties, but could easily have been a decade younger. The youthfulness wasn't simply down to his crop of thick dark hair or his boyish complexion; it was his energy. He fidgeted as he sat, sipping from a glass water flask of the kind that people carry on Chinese trains. His accent was clipped, but he spoke with an unfettered enthusiasm. He said 'exactly' a lot.

Marsden was brought up in a village in the Mendips, but Cornwall had been a constant presence throughout his life. His maternal grandfather had owned a cottage in St Mawes—a place for family holidays across the generations. Later, after a degree in anthropology and a stint working at the *Spectator*, he came to the cottage alone each winter to work on books about Ethiopia, Russia and the Middle East. And then, married and with a family on the way, he had moved permanently to Cornwall.

I asked which writers he had taken as models, penning his own early travel books in the St Mawes cottage while the winter westerlies whipped across Falmouth Bay.

'To begin with,' he said, 'there was that generation, the 1980s generation—you know, the generation above me; Thubron, Chatwin, Theroux, Redmond O'Hanlon...' He paused with a sheepish smile—'All blokes!'—then went on: 'Particularly Thubron and Chatwin, in different ways; they were the big formative influences...'

Thubron and Chatwin. Something struck me here. 'Radically different in their... sort of...' I wasn't quite sure how to put it; '... their approach to...'

'To the truth?' he grinned.

'That's the word I was dancing around!'

'You're right. But *In Patagonia* just opened my eyes to what a travel narrative could do. It articulated that sense of moving through a landscape. It just flowed with that lovely sense of movement, of one thing leading on to another—like all good stories and all good journeys. He made a lot of it up, of course, but it just showed what you could do with the travel form, and I loved that.'

In the early years of a new century, Marsden had seemed for a while to be drifting away from travel writing. There was a novel, *The Main Cages* (2002), and forays into narrative history with *The Barefoot Emperor* (2007) and *The Levelling Sea* (2011). This might have made perfect commercial sense: many of his fellow 'Class of 1990' travel writers were beginning to step sideways into other fields as the genre slipped from the forefront of literary fashion. But then came the book that had prompted my magazine assignment: *Rising Ground: A Search for the Spirit of Place* (2014). It might have been about a walk through Cornwall rather than an expedition to some far-flung land, but it was, unmistakably, a travel book in the proper sense. There was the narrative of a journey—on foot, down the tapering length of the peninsula from Bodmin Moor to the end of the land. There were the forays into history and biography, the unplanned human encounters, and the wrestling with a 'bigger theme'—in this case the idea of a 'sense of place'. All of the requisite ingredients of what we might call the 'classical travel book' were here.

'Exactly!' he said. 'That's right; you're absolutely right! And it *is* a classic travel book in its form. It's interesting that Rob—Robert Macfarlane—says that he's a travel writer too...'

Robert Macfarlane: a name that would come up again and again during the encounters on the journey which—though I didn't yet know it—would result from this clear Cornish afternoon. It was a name always spoken with respect and admiration, but also with an occasional puzzlement as older writers tried to figure out why their own travel writing tradition had given way to a slew of books about domestic explorations—the so-called 'new nature writing' of which Macfarlane was the figurehead. Marsden's own most recent book had itself ended up filed in amongst the myriad accounts of meadows and badgers and birds. I asked if he had any idea why this publishing industry shift had occurred.

He twisted in his chair and half-turned to the window for a moment. 'It's after the idea that one thinks about these things. The first part— why did travel writing die?—I think it has something to do with the hype of the 1980s, a reaction against it. Also, a lot more people began to travel independently. With such a glut of books, some of the freshness was lost. As to the other part of your question... I find that as a writer you just write the book that needs writing—you can't choose where bookshops end up putting it. But I think that there *is* something common to travel writing and nature writing. Much of it comes down to the use of the first person. It *can* smack of self-indulgence to a lot of people—I'm mean, *I'm* shy about the first person. But I've learnt that, actually, it's not about *me*. The 'I' is not the writer—it's just a figure wandering through a landscape.

'I love that thing that travel writing does, and in a way nature writing does too, of taking the reader on—I know it sounds trite—a voyage of discovery. It's all about the process of finding out about the world, of uncovering connections. The writer is learning about something and is filled with the thrill and urgency of that discovery. You just tell that story, and that can be a wonderful thing for a reader to share.

'This is a fundamental difference between academic writing and travel writing. In a travel narrative, you don't start off as an expert saying, "This is how it is." You're saying, "This is what I found."'

* * *

We talked on—about *Rising Ground*, and about his earlier books, and more about what connected and separated travel writing and nature writing. He came back, again and again, to the power of the first-person narrative, always fidgeting in his creaking chair, sipping from his flask, and saying 'exactly'.

He also told me about the idea for his next project.

'My plan is to sail from here to the Hebrides, via Ireland, and to write about boats and sailing in terms of the journey. But the real idea of it is to write about mythical islands. There's a great tradition of that, especially off the west coast of Ireland, but actually all over the world, and the idea is to use that to show how we project ideas onto places, so much so that sometimes the places don't exist at all...'

He was on his feet now, and I noticed for the first time that the desk behind me was cluttered with books on the sea and sailing, and on islands in human culture, face down and folded open, or bristling with page markers.

'I'm really excited about it.' He lifted an anthropological treatise with a particularly indecipherable title—'This sort of thing!'—then turned to fossick along the shelves, rocking a book forward here and there. A fresh surge of enthusiasm was upon him, and suddenly I was similarly excited at the prospect of his coming journey—or rather at the prospect of the book that he would write about it.

'Are you a fan of Raban?' he asked, still at the shelves. '*Passage to Juneau*—have you read that? It's a brilliant book; actually a much better book than *Coasting*...' Then he turned again and started to rummage through the piles on his desk.

'Have you read Tim Robinson, by the way? His immersion in one particular place—a thousand pages on Aran! He finds a story in every stone... there's a lovely phrase...' He was leafing urgently through a paperback copy of Robinson's *Connemara: Listening to the Wind* (2006). 'Here it is! "The drive beyond opens as promisingly as a nineteenth-century novel, skirting a little water-lily lake and disappearing around a bend between banks of rhododendrons..."' Marsden looked up from the book, his eyes glittering. 'You just need one phrase like that and you're there, dropped into the place in an instant!'

This, then, was the beginnings of a travel book, the writer at work, already voyaging long before the point of departure. It was thrilling.

'It *will* be a travel book, then?' I asked.

'Oh yes, and I really look forward to those chance encounters with people, where you can sketch people's stories. It's just such a joy to be able to do that—one of the great pleasures of writing about travel is not landscape or history or architecture: it's people. At the heart of any idea about a place is the people who live there, or who have lived there. So yes, it will be a travel book...'[3]

* * *

Afterwards we went out into the thinning sunlight so I could take photographs for the magazine. He stood with the house in the background, hands dicing as he shifted to the topic of the locality. The story of his family's recent move from the cottage in St Mawes to this old farmhouse, Ardevora, had featured in *Rising Ground*. It was a sturdy building with a pair of bulky yew trees rising to the right. The grass of the lawn badly needed cutting. Marsden was pointing left and right as I tried to catch a decent portrait shot.

'This is unlike anywhere else... oak woods coming right down to the water... yes, exactly... we've put in a wood, about five acres of trees. It's only in the last week that the cherries have leafed out... Yellow rattle—it feeds off rich pasture, it's the only way to get rid of it... exactly... put in a kilo of seed—it's just started to come up...'

By the time I drove away, back up the long white track, the sun was slipping far into the west and the tide had turned. The Fal was slithering back seawards, and I had more than two hours of recorded conversation to transcribe.[4]

* * *

Travel books abound with questionable coincidences and contrived 'chance encounters'. All I can say is that this really *was* a coincidence: two weeks later I met Philip Marsden again. We were on the same flight from Newquay to Dublin.

The little Aer Lingus plane was half-empty, and we sat together as it shuddered through the clear air over the Celtic Sea. He spoke every bit as enthusiastically as before. He was on his way to Connemara, scouting out the ground ahead of the coming sea journey.

He talked about the literature that he loved—'Are you a fan of Turgenev? *Sketches from a Hunter's Album* is just so...'—and for the briefest of moments he was actually lost for words. He spoke of how lucky he had been to get decent advances when he was starting out at travel writing in the 1990s—'I seemed to write more quickly then, too'—and of how he worried about the financial challenges for

11

young writers today. And he told me about his wife's formidable family—'They're the sort of people who make puns in Russian at the dinner table...'

At the other end I left him on a footbridge outside the terminal. I was bound for the buses and he was heading for the hire cars. We shook hands and he strode off, head up, glancing left and right. It was fanciful, I knew, but I had the idea that anyone who stopped to look might have been able to tell that he was a travel writer about his business. And there it was: a travel writer, a real, live travel writer, about his business in the twenty-first century...

* * *

Travel writing adores a quest. It's a venerable model for any writer, of course, with Odysseus signalling the way—a journey out or a journey back, with a prize at the end. But the purported moments of inspiration for the quests of contemporary travel writing can sometimes smack horribly of retrospective invention. Passing youthful encounters are inflated with spurious significance. 'Lifelong fascinations' with obscure historical figures are conjured from the ether. And pieces of brontosaurus skin materialise in the cabinets of elderly relatives.

If I was so inclined, I might make a lightning strike of that moment on the footbridge outside Dublin Terminal 2, though that would be to start off on entirely the wrong foot. But it really was the moment at which the kernel of a notion was set in place. As my red Bus Éireann coach rumbled westwards through the Irish Midlands, and in the weeks and months that followed, it grew into a full-blown idea.

I had been reading travel writing for all of my adult life. I had been enthralled and informed and inspired by it. I had been frustrated and troubled by it. And sometimes of late I had been worried about it. Travel writers were forever setting out *in search*. They went in search of nomads, or some similarly exoticised people. They went in search of long-dead adventurers and vanished empires. They sought out the *heart* or the *spirit* or the *meaning* of any number of outlandish locales.

But why not twist the quest back on itself? Why not hunt out travel writers themselves, just as Philip Marsden had tracked down Spirit-Wrestlers and Armenians? Why not seek out the high priests and priestesses of the passing generation, and the younger writers trying to carry the genre forward to unknown destinations? And why not, at the same time, properly wrestle with the critiques and the controversies? If I did *that*, then maybe I could scratch the itch in my conscience that reading travel writing sometimes caused. Maybe I would be able either to answer confidently back, or to nod in grim affirmation with the more condemnatory denizens of travel writing studies. Maybe I would even know what to say the next time someone asked, 'Is travel writing dead?'

I would do it, then.

It was a journey that would bring me face-to-face with writers whose work I had known and loved since my teens. It would take me deep into the archives, amongst the yellowed raw matter of some of the greatest travel books of the twentieth century. It would also bring me to seminar rooms and scholarly gatherings. In time, it would raise unforeseen and uncomfortable questions that were often as much about myself as about the books I read. And if the journey began on a long white track in Cornwall, then it would end—in as much as these things ever have an ending—at a derelict chapel on a mountainside in Greece. But of course, I didn't know any of that yet.

Philip Marsden had said of travel writing that 'you don't start off as an expert saying, "This is how it is." You're saying, "This is what I found."' The same applies here. The narrator, the 'I' who appears in the first line of this chapter, does not know exactly where he is going, and he has been considerably transformed by the time he reaches his destination. I set out on a journey in search of travel writing, and this is what I found.

2

NAMING FATHERS

The cathedral was like a freighter at anchor, riding high in the water, waiting for a cargo.

I pushed through the west door. The air was clammy and cool, with some scent that I recognised but couldn't place: dampness and candles and a suggestion of roosting bats. Beyond the choir, in a grey chamber at the heart of the building, the tomb of St Alban sat like a cold engine. An ancient place of pilgrimage, this; older than Canterbury. But I was not here to pay my respects to England's first Christian martyr. The object of my own small pilgrimage lay closer to the door.

It was a simple, dateless memorial, painted high on the second column on the left. Its faded black borders overshot the fluting untidily, and it had the look of an old fly-posted advert for a gig on a rain-streaked wall. It was hard to make out the words. I moved closer, shuffling between the rows of wooden seats. Somewhere deep in the building a side door opened and a file of choirboys hurried through, tugging white surplices over blue blazers.

I peered up. The first line of the memorial was in Latin, with scabby fragments of English below: 'In this Inn a Travailer… rich in nothing but in memory…'

An urgent shuffling from behind the rood screen and a single, preliminary blast from an organ pipe, like the siren of a ship readying to sail.

Near the centre of the memorial a name, clearly legible: 'John Mandeville'.

The organ sounded again, and from the belly of the building evensong erupted, freighting the great space with sound.

* * *

I had begun with the books. I knew, from Philip Marsden's example, that this was how a travel writing journey ought to start, long before bags are packed and tickets booked. I did my reading at a desk on the upper floor of a university library in the English Midlands, a place full of the furtive rustle of quiet study and the occasional industrial rattle of roller stacks on the move. The view to my right was cut into thin strips by a bank of window-mounted solar panels. Between them I could make out a city sinking into winter and a quartet of wind turbines turning in the milky distance.

I arrived early each morning, to be sure of my seat by the window, securing myself behind a small stockade of books. I'd combed the library shelves for scholarly works on travel writing: strident postcolonial critiques; esoteric monographs dissecting some obscure subset of the genre; edited collections from the big names in the field; minute discussions of *gender* and *alterity* and *Orientalism*. These books came with greasy laminate covers. Their thin white pages were marked with fierce underlinings and cryptic doodles—the footprints of those who had travelled this way before me. On my laptop I had a folder full of PDFs—articles downloaded from the digital journals, *Studies in Travel Writing* and *Journeys*. And I had a black, hardback notebook, folded open at my right. At the back I'd made a list of the writers I hoped to talk to and the archives I planned to visit. I began to fill the preceding pages with my gleanings: *Mary Louise Pratt notes... Holland and Huggan say...*

Sometimes, by late morning the scholarly discourse got too much for me. I always made sure there was a remedy for this amongst my piles of printed material—an actual travel book, an old favourite from my own collection. I'd take it downstairs, find a seat in the noisy campus café, and for an hour before lunch I'd be gone from the Midlands.

> *I am a stranger in these parts and Tangier feeds on the flesh of strangers...*
> *It was in the citadel of Feroz Shah Kotla that I met my first Sufi...*
> *I had left Geneva three days previously...*

NAMING FATHERS

Ever since childhood...
Dear Xan...

* * *

It seemed sensible to start with a survey of my quest-object's history.

Travel writing is the oldest of all literary traditions, they say. Norse sagas are simply accounts of voyages, after all. The Book of Exodus is a journey narrative with its nature writ large in the very title ('the going out'); Xenophon's *Anabasis* likewise ('the journey up'). And wasn't Herodotus the original travel writer, 'encountering and constructing difference', as the scholars might put it, in the exotic lands of Asia Minor? Even further back, all the way to Mesopotamia in the third millennium BCE, the opening of the *Gilgamesh* epic features what looks a lot like a portrait of the travel writer: 'He went on a long journey, was weary, worn out with labour, and returning engraved on a stone the whole story.'[1]

And further back still, it only takes a small imaginative leap to go beyond the beginnings of the written word, to some prehistoric campfire where a returned prodigal told their tale. From the very moment that language grew strong enough to bear the weight of memory, the travel narrative has existed.

But something wasn't quite right here. None of these ancient artefacts was a perfect fit for the position of travel writing urtext. They seemed instead to belong to the baggy category of *almost*-travel writing—along with narrative history books, ethnographies, even novels that take as their setting a place foreign to most of their readers. People have been writing about *journeys*, and about foreign lands, for a very long time, certainly. But was an ancient chronicler of myths and troop movements really a travel writer? Didn't this stuff belong to a broader 'literature of travel' rather than within an actual genre of 'travel writing'?

What I needed was a definition.

I scoured the academic accounts. The scholars usually began by declaring that travel writing defied easy characterisation. They tended to emphasise this point with a quote from an old book review by Jonathan Raban, which had it that travel writing was 'a notoriously raffish open house where very different genres are likely to end up in the same bed'.[2] But then, having made their excuses, the scholars almost always turned in a neat delimitation. For Tim Youngs, the genre consisted of 'predominantly factual, first-person prose accounts of travels that have been undertaken by the author-narrator'.[3] For the old-school American critic, Paul Fussell, it was 'a sub-species of memoir in which the autobiographical narrative arises from the speaker's encounter with distant or unfamiliar data, and in which the narrative—unlike that in a novel or a romance—claims literal validity by constant reference to actuality'.[4] Carl Thompson, describing what he called 'the modern travel book', wrote of 'the first-person, ostensibly non-fictional narrative of travel'.[5] And Jan Borm, tackling the question of definitions head-on, eventually settled on this:

> [Travel writing is] any narrative characterized by a non-fiction dominant that relates (almost always) in the first person a journey or journeys that the reader supposes to have taken place in reality while assuming or presupposing that author, narrator and principal character are but one and the same.[6]

It was quite simple, then. As far as these academics were concerned, travel writing was a first-person narrative of a journey, featuring a narrator who shared at the very least a name with the author. And, perhaps most importantly, readers supposed that the journey described had really happened. This was why Philip Marsden's *The Crossing Place* was travel writing, but Cormac McCarthy's *The Crossing* (1994) was not, for all that they both described a journey. It also explained why I felt that instinctive reluctance to admit *Gilgamesh* and the *Odyssey* as travel writing. And for all that Xenophon and Herodotus had made their own forays into Persian realms, they didn't write in the first person. What gave travel writing its strange fascination, as well as its awkwardness and its tension, was the idea of an *actual* journey, bound directly into a text that overtly claimed the status of eyewitness testimony.

So where did *this* begin?

The answer, as far as one influential scholar of travel writing, Mary Baine Campbell, was concerned, was with a Galician nun named Egeria.[7] Details of her life are scant, but sometime in the late fourth century, Egeria set out from Spain to make a pilgrimage to the Holy Land. And she penned an account of her journey in idiosyncratic

Latin, addressed to her fellow-sisters back in the nunnery. Travel writing has been an excessively male genre for much of its history, but its earliest European practitioner and her original intended audience were women.

The first part of Egeria's untitled account is missing, and it begins with a tantalisingly decapitated sentence: '... were pointed out according to the Scriptures'.   Then comes a description of movement through a landscape:

> In the meanwhile we came on foot to a certain place where the mountains, through which we were journeying, opened out and formed an infinitely great valley, quite flat and extraordinarily beautiful, and across the valley appeared Sinai, the holy mountain of God.[8]

There is something here. A certain style, grandiose and restrained at the same time. It could almost be Wilfred Thesiger. It offers a vision of heat coming off broken stone under a high clear sky, and in the wide flat valley, a witness. She has little to say about the actual experience of travel (other than occasionally to note that certain monks were 'friendly'), and an exhaustive account of liturgical matters in Jerusalem takes up the second half of the manuscript—which ends, as it begins, mid-sentence. But still, this is it: *a factual, first-person prose account of travel that has been undertaken by the author-narrator.* We're off!

Lone pilgrims to Jerusalem streak through the hazy centuries that follow Egeria's journey. And then, in a new millennium, missionaries and traders fling themselves further afield—to the court of the Mongol emperor, or to India. Sometimes they return with first-person stories to tell. William of Rubruck: a portly Franciscan from Flanders, traversing Mongol China, grumbling misanthropically about the filthiness of the lodgings and the ugliness of the local women like some thirteenth-century Paul Theroux. Friar Jordanus from Catalonia: off to India at the dawn of the fourteenth century, with an eye for passing marvels like a medieval Bruce Chatwin. And of course, Marco Polo.

A certain uncomfortable pattern was appearing here: the traveller-writers seemed always to go eastwards, out from Europe into the elsewhere. The adumbrated histories of travel writing that I read often carried a suggestion of European exceptionalism. For sure, people from all corners of the earth had always made journeys. African traders traversed Saharan salt routes; Indian pilgrims headed for the Himalayas; and at about the same time that Egeria was bundling her bedroll and her rosary in some damp Galician chamber, a party of Austronesian-speaking Southeast Asian sailors were making their way 4,000 miles across the Indian Ocean to settle in Madagascar.

But these were unrecorded odysseys. When it came to writing it down and bringing it back, perhaps there really was something particular to Europe. Maybe it was to do with the fact that the ultimate pilgrimage destination for early European Christians—unlike the focus of an Indian *yatra*, or arguably even the Muslim *Hajj*—lay entirely beyond their own cultural common ground. En route to Jerusalem, Egeria would have encountered plenty of *difference*. Could this repeated experience have fostered a particular cultural inclination to the writing of travel? At least one of the PDF articles I had downloaded made such a suggestion: the allegedly unique nature of Christian pilgrimage from Europe to the Middle East, helped 'to explain the emergence of the travel account as a personal testimony of the sufferings and adventures of the self-chosen journey'.[9]

But something wasn't right here. 'What about Yijing?' I muttered, frowning over my laptop.

From the fourth century—at about the same time that nuns and monks from misty Celtic fringes were getting increasingly serious about visiting the Holy Land—similarly pious travellers were striking out from the opposite end of the Eurasian landmass, heading for sacred sites equally as far removed from their own homeland. These Chinese Buddhist pilgrims forged west for the Indian wellspring of their religion, taking the same routes around the Taklamakan Desert that would later be traversed in the opposite direction by William of Rubruck and Marco Polo—and later still by Nick Danziger and William Dalrymple. Or they sailed southwards, through the straits and channels around Indonesia, encountering difference at every turn. Sometimes they brought back polished narratives of their journeys.

Faxian, Songyun, Xuanzang, Yijing: in an era when all that Dark Age Europe can throw up is Egeria with her chiselled prose and biography extending no further than a name, these men are bathed in light. They have precise dates and places of birth, family histories and detailed résumés. They have opinions. They have personas. And sometimes they deliver accounts of their journeys in the first person.

Yijing, born in 635 CE, was principally concerned with gathering Sanskrit texts during his epic, quarter-century journey. Like Egeria, he gives a great deal of attention to ecclesiastical matters in his write-up. However, he also provides a personal narrative—brief, but very lively—of his adventures.

Like so many others since, Yijing is inspired by reading the accounts of previous travellers. He gets dumped by his would-be travel buddies before he even hitches his first ride out of China, wavers briefly but then sets out alone. There are various encounters and misadventures along the way. At one point, crossing the thickly forested Rajauli Hills of Bihar at dusk, a feverish Yijing finds himself left behind by the party of merchants he has joined. As darkness falls, brigands emerge from the bushes:

> [T]hey came and glared at me, and one after another insulted me. First they stripped me of my upper robe, and then took off my under garment. All the straps and girdles that were with me they snatched away also. I thought at that time, indeed, that my last farewell to this world was at hand, and that I should not fulfil my wish of a pilgrimage to the holy places. Moreover, if my limbs were thus pierced by the points of their lances, I could never succeed in carrying out the original enterprise so long meditated. Besides, there was a rumour in the country of the West [India] that, when they took a white [i.e. fair-skinned] man, they killed him to offer a sacrifice to heaven. When I thought of this tale, my dismay grew twice as much. Thereupon [after the brigands had abandoned him to his fate] I entered into a muddy hole, and besmeared all my body with mud. I covered myself with leaves, and supporting myself on a stick, I advanced slowly.[10]

This bit of resourceful improvisation to hide his pale flesh pays off, and eventually Yijing stumbles into camp, where the merchants are starting to worry about his absence. They dunk him in a pond to wash off the mud and leaves, and give him a replacement robe. A few days later he reaches the great Buddhist monastery at Nalanda. In moments like this, Yijing's account reads a lot like a 'modern travel book'.

There was nothing exceptionally European about the travel writing impulse, then. The issue was simply one of legibility. Yijing's *Record of the Buddhist Religion as Practiced in India and the Malay Archipelago*—which I only knew from reading around the history of Southeast Asia—wasn't translated into English until 1896. Most of the other ancient

Chinese journey narratives, as well as the *rihlas* of Arab wanderers like Ibn Battuta, and various other non-European travelogues, remained untranslated until at least the nineteenth century. The average European armchair traveller was no more able to access them than Yijing and his brother monks were able to read the account of Egeria's pilgrimage to Jerusalem.

The scholar Steve Clark has called travel writing 'a one-way traffic'.[11] Really, though, it was a *series* of one-way streets, running parallel to each other without intersection for most of human history. My own journey would, inevitably, be along a single street for the most part. I wanted to examine travel writing not as some essential impulse, but as a literary tradition with a distinct heritage, a genealogy, common points of reference and influence. I ought at least to remind myself from time to time that the other streets existed, but what I needed for a starting point was neither Egeria nor Yijing. What I was really looking for was the beginnings of travel writing in *English*.

A wraith had been hanging around the desk for some time, leering suggestively from the fourteenth century. I closed my laptop, returned the books to the stacks, and drove south down the M1 to a cathedral on a Hertfordshire hilltop.

* * *

When I think of Sir John Mandeville, I see him as he appears in the engraving that illustrated one of the many medieval editions of his book: a scissor-legged, wasp-waisted dandy with lugubrious eyes, posing in a narrow chamber with a sword he looks scarcely strong enough to lift. And yet, by his own account, in 1322 this knight, 'born in England in the town of Saint Albans' left his homeland and embarked on a thirty-four-year journey to the very ends of the earth. And when he returned, like Gilgamesh, he set down the whole story.

Mandeville's 'little treatise' was penned, its author avows, in 1356. The first version may well have been written in French, or perhaps Latin. But it was swiftly translated into English, purportedly by the original author himself, 'that every man of my Nation may understand it'. It quickly worked its way into wide circulation around Europe, and within a century of its first appearance translations existed in at least ten languages, from Czech to Gaelic.[12]

Mandeville's itinerary crosses Europe, following the course of the Danube then striking for Constantinople some 600 years ahead of Patrick Leigh Fermor. From there the chapters skip southwards to the Holy Land along Egeria's old pilgrimage route. But this is only the beginning, for the book then launches itself eastwards, describing a meandering passage through India, Indonesia and China, and into all manner of unidentifiable lands beyond.

The *Travels* was not, properly, a first-person narrative—and certainly not in the detailed, personal manner of Yijing's brief travelogue (or indeed of Mandeville's travel writing contemporary, the Moroccan globetrotter Ibn Battuta). But a sly 'I' intruded here and there to remind readers that this was all eyewitness testimony:

In the land of Prester John there are many marvels. Among others there is a vast sea of gravel and sand, and no drop of water is in it. It ebbs and flows as the ocean itself does in other countries, and there are great waves on it; it never stays still and unmoving. No man can cross that sea by ship or in any other way; and so it is unknown what kind of land or country is on the far side. And though there is no water in that sea, yet is there great plenty of good fish caught on its shores; they are very tasty to eat, but they are of different shape to the fish in other waters. I, John Mandeville, ate of them, and so believe it, for it is true.[13]

But of course, as this tale of delectable fish hooked from the depths of a shifting sand desert plainly suggests, it wasn't really true at all. Mandeville's book wasn't actually an eyewitness account; it was a hoax, a blend of shameless plagiarism and pure imagination. The author had probably never been as far as the banks of the Danube, still less to the court of the Great Khan of Cathay.

The itinerary for the first part of the *Travels* was cadged from a thirteenth-century pilgrimage guidebook. The second part—the wandering route to the Far East—was lifted, in places virtually word for word, from the narrative of Odoric of Pordenone, an ill-humoured Franciscan missionary who really had travelled to China just a few decades before Mandeville's purported journey. The hoaxer then adorned this framework with all the flotsam and jetsam he could glean from the tideline of Europe's collective imagination. His book was a compendium of fabulous beasts and uncanny races first recorded by Herodotus and Pliny then rehashed in medieval 'wonder books'. There were dog-headed men, fish-guzzling cyclopes, maidens with snakes in their vulvas, and much, much else besides. The author also threw in a lengthy treatise on Prester John, the great chimera of the medieval church, a mythical Christian king ruling a lost land amidst the heathens, somewhere between Ethiopia and the Mongol court.

Throughout this fabulous cavalcade of ideas and images, Mandeville inserted subtle rhetorical touches, designed to reinforce the notion that this was all perfectly true. The cleverest and most convincing of these were the little admissions of the limits of his own experience. When it came to the 'Earthly Paradise', he wrote, 'I cannot speak properly, for I have not been there; and that I regret.'[14] It made the rest of the account seem all the more reliable.

For the angry empiricists of the nineteenth century, John Mandeville was the ultimate travel liar—though one Victorian critic, William Minto, in recognition of his enormous influence, called him 'the father of English prose'.[15] For some modern scholars, meanwhile, he has been rehabilitated as a proto-novelist, or an arch satirist. But ultimately, what makes his work look most like travel writing is that crucial common element of the scholarly definitions I had collected from the library. In the fourteenth century, and indeed long, long afterwards, the *Travels* was frequently read as an account of a journey *that the reader supposes to have taken place in reality*. 'Mandeville must be received as truth (where he is so received)', writes Mary Baine Campbell, 'because he sounds like truth.'[16] Christopher Columbus had a copy with him for reference when he first crossed the Atlantic in 1492.

There was something else too—something new. Egeria and Yijing alike had travelled as pilgrims; their written accounts were secondary to the religiously inspired journey itself. The medieval friars, meanwhile, were missionaries or emissaries. And Marco Polo was a trader. Like the memoirs of retired diplomats, their narratives were an incidental by-product of professional travel. But Mandeville's purported journey had no obvious practical purpose. The author seemed to have travelled not for trafficking alone. His stories appeared to be knowledge gathered for its own sake. If he went elsewhere it was simply because elsewhere existed—and because it was interesting. *That*, surely, was true travel writing.

Mary Baine Campbell—who, though she generally stuck to the more distant past, had quickly become one of my firmest favourites amongst the travel writing scholars—put it plainly. 'Mandeville-the-narrator', she wrote, emerged from his fabulous mishmash of borrowed styles and sources 'as a pure wanderer, and travel as an activity in and of itself [...] Thus, if we are naming fathers, we can call Mandeville not only the "father of English prose" but the father of modern travel writing.'[17]

* * *

I sat for a while in the gloom at the back of the cathedral. The nave was empty, row upon row of folding wooden seats like war graves. The disembodied evensong came washing through. I tried to snatch at the memory the musty scent of the place had set dancing. A crusader castle? A maharaja's palace? A cave temple on a limestone island in a boiling sea? But it skittered away.

St Albans was an irresistible starting point for a journey in search of travel writing. In the dark heart of the cathedral was the martyr's grave, the object of singularly focussed journeys since the age of Egeria. But this other memorial, just inside the door, catching the last shards of coloured light through the stained-glass window in the western wall, was for a man who went out for no discernible reason at all, other than that he wanted to write a book about it—even if his going out was all a fantasy.

The hoax went beyond the pages of the book, for no knight by the name of John Mandeville was ever born at St Albans. There has been much debate and a good deal of inspired detective work down the decades. Suspicions of original authorship have long been directed towards a shady medical practitioner who lived, died and was buried in Liège in Belgium. But no one really knows for certain who it was that plagiarised guidebooks and monkish itineraries and made of them something more than the sum of their parts. And no one knows why he did it.

The scholar Iain Macleod Higgins noted of Mandeville's *Travels* that its author 'may have been an Englishman called John Mandeville, and he may even have been a knight [...] [B]ut the work's chivalric guide is not a real person; he is a textual figure written into others' writings and sometimes depicted as doing their deeds. The author is not so much dead, then, as deeply and probably irretrievably encrypted.'[18]

The dog-headed men and all the other wonders and grotesques had their titillation value. But surely *this* was what had compelled generations of scholars and readers, myself amongst them, to keep picking at Mandeville's *Travels* like a scab: the fiendish three-part riddle of the thing—journey, writer, book—and the tantalising possibility that the encrypted author might be retrievable after all.

I shifted uneasily in my seat and looked up at the memorial. Exactly when it was created is unclear, though it was certainly there by 1657 when an amateur alchemist named Elias Ashmole made note of it.[19] Sometime during the preceding three centuries, with Mandeville's work at large in countless editions, fuelling the futile search for Prester John and carried in the luggage of the pioneers of European empire, the monks of St Albans must have wondered why no trace of him existed in this, his supposed home town. They decided to set things right.

It was almost dark now, and a fresh shuffling signalled that evensong was at an end. I could still just about pick out the words in the gloom: 'In this Inn a Travailer...'

A travel writer had a great and terrible power: he could conjure himself into existence.

3

A LETTER TO THE EDITOR

Exmouth Market on a winter's day, sunlight slanting in against the northern side of the street. Women in heavy coats hunched over coffee cups outside the cafés. The buildings, with their high white windows and book-sized bricks, framed a sky so sharply blue that it looked as though it might shatter when an aeroplane scratched across London from the east.

A narrow brown door beside a pizzeria. I pressed the button for the top-floor property, and heard the lock snap open like a gun. A twist of stairs, and at the top a gust of overheated air as an inner door opened. Barnaby Rogerson, publisher of Eland Books, appeared in bare feet and a crumpled collarless shirt.

'Come in! Come in! Tea?'

The office was hoisted into the roof space, and the windows looked out onto the slates and dormers across the street. The place had a glorious scholarly clutter. Books slumped drunkenly against one another on the shelves. Galley proofs hung about the room like winter laundry, and a lurcher dozed mournfully under a desk. Rogerson was the only person there. He clattered at a sink by the window, then carried a heavy teapot to a table in the middle of the room, pushing papers and envelopes and books aside to make a space.

'Lapsang okay?'

* * *

If the encrypted figure of John Mandeville is the progenitor of English-language travel writers, then the idea of an English-language travel writing genre, and within it a canon, surely has its proper beginnings two centuries later.

Sometime in the 1560s, a teenage boy visits an older cousin in his lawyer's chambers in the Middle Temple, London. The boy is from a hilltop village in Herefordshire, but he resides now at Westminster School along with thirty-nine other Queen's Scholars. Perhaps today he has walked from the school, along the Thames to the Inns of Court.

There's a vision here—a panelled room and a leaded window giving out onto Elizabethan London. But I find it somewhat confused with my memory of the Eland Books office in Exmouth Market. Certainly there is a table, crowded with papers. Amongst them, lying open, are 'certeine bookes of Cosmographie, with an universall Mappe'. These catch the boy's attention. His cousin notices his interest, and begins an impromptu geography lesson:

> [H]e pointed with his wand to all the knowen Seas, Gulfs, Bayes, Straights, Capes, Rivers, Empires, Kingdomes, Dukedomes, and Territories of each part, with declaration also of their speciall commodities, & particular wants, which by the benefit of traffike, and entercourse of merchants, are plentifully supplied. From the Mappe he brought me to the Bible, and turning to the 107 Psalme, directed mee to the 23 & 24 verses, where I read, that they which go downe to the sea in ships, and occupy by the great waters, they see the works of the Lord, and his woonders in the deepe, &c.[1]

A travel writer might make a legend of such a moment: Paul Theroux watching passing trains as a child; Nicolas Bouvier 'stretched out on the rug, silently contemplating the atlas'.[2] The exposure to these 'things of high and rare delight' certainly made an impression on the boy. But it wasn't wanderlust that they prompted. Instead, he resolved to make it to Oxford University where he would 'by Gods assistance prosecute that knowledge and kinde of literature, the doors whereof (after a sort) were so happily opened before me'. He didn't decide to become a travel writer, then, but a travel publisher.

The boy's name was Richard Hakluyt, and after his time at Oxford, ordination to the clergy and a stint as a junior diplomat in France (the furthest he would ever travel in person), he realised his ambition.

There had already been one collection of travel accounts published in English—Richard Eden's *Decades of the Newe Worlde*, which first appeared in 1555, and then again, expanded as *The Historie of Travayle into the West and East Indies*, in 1577. But this had mostly been made up of translated accounts from Spanish conquistadors. Hakluyt's *Principal Navigations, Voyages, Traffiques, and Discoveries of the English Nation*, meanwhile, was explicitly intended to present a national literature of travel. He included a few translations, as well as vintage texts— Mandeville's amongst them, still received as the truth it resembled in the late sixteenth century. But Hakluyt also gathered contemporary journals, and solicited new travelogues from 'the chiefest Captaines at sea, the greatest Merchants, and the best Mariners of our nation'.[3] The collection was first published in 1589. A second printing, swollen now to some 2,000 pages, appeared in 1600.

The edition I had explored lay like a motherlode, deep in the stratified roller stacks of the university library. There were twelve volumes on a low shelf, each as deep as a house brick. When you opened them, the pages crackled like dried kelp and turned up inky engravings of bearded and be-ruffed figures, meetings with 'the Great Turke', journeys 'into Barbary' and all manner of 'True Accounts'. On the shelf above lay the similarly voluminous *Hakluytus Posthumus or Purchas his Pilgrimes*, the 1625 work of Hakluyt's mentee Samuel Purchas, another stay-at-home editor-priest who claimed never to have travelled more than 200 miles from his Essex birthplace.

By the turn of the seventeenth century there was a steady flow of new material for a travel editor's consideration. Walter Raleigh had crossed the Atlantic; Francis Drake had circumnavigated the globe; and new East and West India companies were receiving their royal charters in all the major maritime nations of Europe. Hakluyt was no disinterested literary observer of this action. His publishing projects were intended to encourage it. His opus, he hoped, would stir the English nation from its 'sluggish security' to race against the Spanish, French and Dutch for exclusive trading rights and territorial acquisitions in far-flung corners of the globe.[4] He had a financial stake too, but it had little to do with the paltry book sales of a largely illiterate age. In 1606, three years before his death, Hakluyt became one of the first directors of the Virginia Company of London, the royally sanctioned joint-stock company, charged with establishing English colonies in North America.

Richard Hakluyt had drawn together the scattered and disparate travel accounts of the previous centuries and made of them a recognisable genre—though it wouldn't be known by the term 'travel writing' for several centuries. And right at the very outset, he had made its queasy connection with European colonialism overt.

* * *

I wanted to meet a latter-day Hakluyt—though preferably not one with a financial stake in colonial adventures. I wanted to talk to someone who called travel books into being from behind a desk, who cast an appraising eye over raw manuscripts and decided whether or not they had a shot at entering the canon. But when I began to search for likely candidates, I found that they were almost as hard to come by as pieces of brontosaurus skin. Dedicated travel lists had been dropped by the big publishing houses years ago, and the smaller publishers that had once made travel writing their mainstay seemed mostly to have moved over to novelty gift books and business manuals. It was an alarming discovery. As far as the publishing industry was concerned, perhaps travel writing really *was* dead. There was, though, one honourable outlier, still going strong in the twenty-first century. And so, on a bright clear winter's afternoon I walked from King's Cross Station to Exmouth Market and presented myself at the office of Eland Books.

The Eland output is familiar to anyone who regularly lingers around the 'travel' shelves. Half an inch taller than most trade paperbacks, every cover follows the same stylish template: a vintage image; title and author's name in a dignified serif font on a cream-coloured oblong like the business card of a private banker; and the publisher's own moniker set vertically in burgundy and gold at the top-left corner. The text inside almost always belongs to a book that was originally published elsewhere: the backlists of Norman Lewis, Martha Gellhorn and Dervla Murphy; 'lost classics' of travel writing from the middle decades of the twentieth century; and rescued memoirs of improbable lives in unlikely places. There are over 150 titles on the Eland list, including many books that I treasure: Jonathan Raban's *Old Glory*; Nicolas Bouvier's *The Way of the World*; Peter Mayne's *A Year in Marrakesh*. But more than that; the existence of this curated catalogue, its cool constituents instantly recognisable amidst the gaudier covers of the new releases, creates a suggestion of literary respectability. It declares that a travel book can indeed be a 'classic'.

Eland was founded in 1982 by a sometime magazine editor, journalist and publisher's rep named John Hatt. Working in Southeast Asia, Hatt had stumbled upon Norman Lewis' 1951 travelogue, *A Dragon Apparent*, and was astonished to find that it was out of print. When his enthusiastic championing of the book was rebuffed by existing publishers, he decided to take on the task for himself.

Hatt's timing was fortuitous. Travel writing was just entering its sustained purple patch, and soon there would be other lists dedicated to reissuing old titles into the contemporary slipstream of Chatwin, Thubron and Theroux: the Penguin Travel Library, Century Travellers, Virago Travellers, Picador Travel Classics. Each series had its own distinctive livery. None of them was quite as stylish as Eland, however—and none of the others still exist today.[5]

At the turn of the twenty-first century, John Hatt decided to move on from Eland. He no longer needed the income it provided, having earned a considerable windfall by selling a website offering cheap air fares which he had originally cobbled together as a side project after the launch of Eland's own rudimentary home page in 1996. There was an obvious irony here: a publisher of travel writing making a fortune from the internet and budget flights—two factors sometimes cited to explain the supposed demise of the genre. Barnaby Rogerson and his wife Rose Baring—former guidebook writers looking for a more settled family existence—took Eland on.

* * *

Rogerson filled the teacups. The lapsang souchong was thinly golden.

His connection with Eland was older than his own role as publisher, he said. As a student at St Andrews in the 1980s he'd written a fan letter—'in purple ink'—to John Hatt.

'Most people would have put it straight in the bin, but he wrote back and invited me for tea.'

They'd kept in touch, and over the years Rogerson would sometimes send in suggestions from amongst the out-of-print travel books he'd encountered during his work on guidebooks to Turkey and North Africa. But still, I suggested, the year 2000 had not been the most promising moment to take on a press that specialised in travel writing.

'Exactly!' he said cheerfully. 'I remember a lot of people saying, "What on earth are you doing wasting your life doing this?" The answer is that if it had been successful there would have been no room for someone like me, who remains an enthusiastic amateur. And actually, by being in a declining market we've been able to grab lots of books that commercial publishers just don't think are worth keeping in print anymore.'

He talked rapidly, flying off the mark with complicated replies before I'd even imprinted a question mark in the air, and sometimes carrying himself straight off the end of his sentences into space. But he knew exactly what he was saying, and occasionally, when I mentioned a particular author, he would cut in, gently interrogative: 'What do you make of his writing?' I'd hesitantly offer a response, hoping it was the right one, relieved when it was.

'So, obviously you were a professional travel writer yourself,' I said.

'Guidebooks; I was doing guidebooks, so I've never really been a travel writer. I'm *not* a travel writer.'

'Okay, can I ask you to expand on that?' I said. 'How do you define a travel writer, and how do you define travel writing, then?'

He was off with his answer in an instant. 'Very simple: a travel writer is someone who's published *one* book of travels that has got a commercial audience, that is not self-published. So it's a straight sort of market thing; it's having got a book out there that's got a readership.'

That was a simple enough definition; I wondered if his characterisation of travel writing itself would diverge from my collected scholarly definitions.

'Travel writing,' he said, 'very simply, has to be a direct observation by the narrator or the author, and by its nature it's probably about abroad—or some sense of being sufficiently an outsider, even if it's the next-door village or something. So it's not an inside account; it's some sort of understanding that you are describing this community from outside, and coming back and writing it up and having it published and read.'

Not so different, then, I thought with relief.

He went on. 'I think the best travel writers are people who don't consider themselves travel writers, who've just done one or two books in an otherwise full life. The bleating about, "Oh there's not enough money for travel writing"—I think actually it's making for better books...'

I had not expected *this*.

On my way into London I had reread an article Rogerson had penned a few years earlier. Its title was 'Where Travel Writing is Now' and it read like a threnody for the genre. He listed the high-profile travel writers of the previous decades who had vanished or turned to writing fiction or history. He added some rough figures to the oft-mentioned declining advances ('a period when "fifteen [thousand] is the new fifty", which has now seeped down towards six'). Here he did make a connection between literary travel writing and the work on guidebooks which had once 'acted as a forcing house for talent, employing, training and feeding new writers, editors and travellers'. But now this industry—the Lonely Planets, the Rough Guides, the Footprint Handbooks and others—he wrote, 'is virtually silent, like some old cotton mill in Bradford'. The article seemed to have little doubt about the prognosis: 'The role of the professional travel writer will soon be at an end.'[6]

The piece brought an awful pang. It was like one of those travelogues where the author sets out in search of some venerable nomad society but finds only gimcrack shanties on the edges of the towns—and maybe one emblematic old man, still minding his goats a few miles out into the desert. I'd arrived in Exmouth Market primed for gloom, and now I found myself protesting at its absence.

'Okay,' Rogerson said, offering a small concession when I repeated the lines from his own article back at him; 'it's fantastic if a young writer, like yourself, can get given anything between £4,000 and £40,000 to go and study something for a couple of years. But you've then got to deliver; you've got to deliver the book you planned; you've got to get it out of the way; this has got to be over and achieved, a bit like a job, rather than...' He tailed off for a moment, then started again with a flourish: 'The best books fall into people's hands; they're books that have to be written because the experience is so strong and so profound.'

He gave examples from the Eland catalogue: Irfan Orga's *Portrait of a Turkish Family*, the memoir of an exiled Turk, written in England in the 1950s ('not really a travel book, I suppose, by my own definition, but it's useful for this'); and *Forgotten Kingdom* by Peter Goullart, an account of a decade working as a trader in southwest China, written after the author had fled the communist takeover of 1949.

'These were books that were oscillating inside them and had to come out,' he said, 'rather than somebody dutifully delivering a project every five years...'

He seemed to be suggesting that no one ought, ideally, to be able to *choose* to be a travel writer, to take travel writing as a vocation. I was somewhat distressed by the idea. Norman Lewis and Dervla Murphy were mainstays of the Eland list. These were surely amongst the most obvious examples of professional travel writers, people who had honed the mysterious business of reporting their journeys to the level of a highly polished craft. I pointed this out.

Rogerson did not miss a beat. 'I accept that,' he said, 'and they're great, and I wouldn't want them diminished at all, and there *are* some people who aspire to follow in their footsteps.'

'But it's very difficult for them to do so...' I said.

Later, when I transcribed the recording of our discussion, I realised that I had been scrabbling around, looking to find the thing I had expected. I was trying to prompt him to say what I had *thought* he would say. Perhaps I had already drafted the encounter in my head: an old travel writing hand, gloomily decrying the demise of this vital genre. But the conversation was on tape, irrefutable, and Rogerson was firm on his point.

'You know, you can't in the end decide whether supporting a young professional travel writer is as important as allowing for someone who's had natural experience of the world and engaging with people.' He motioned to the space I had cleared on the table alongside the teapot, 'Not with their little black notebook and their recorder like you've got, and like I use, but actually in the normal drift of their life, and producing something good at the end of it. We know that in the end *that's* what we really want.'

This, he explained, was why the emphasis at Eland had subtly shifted over the years. These days, additions to the list were most likely to be what Rogerson called 'anthropology-lite'—and this applied as much to the select smattering of new titles that they published, as to the treasures retrieved from travel writing's past.

'I'm not interested in books that have a fit young man with his shirt off on the cover, doing something tough in the jungle. Or mountain books, or exploring deserts—either ice or sand deserts—really. But I'd be fascinated if someone had spent, for instance, six months work-ing in the leather tanneries in Fez and had got to understand how you learnt the craft, if you married within the guild, or if you were born to it, how it happened. That would immediately excite my interest, to the extent that if someone sent me an email, I'd say, "Yes, send it!" And I probably get about three emails a day about books that are cer-tainly never going to be published...'

* * *

Rogerson went to the sink to refill the teapot. Under the desk at the back of the room the lurcher thumped its tail hopefully for a moment, then resumed a mournful repose. I got up to look at the cover proofs of new editions hanging from the shelves while the kettle boiled. Amongst them was *On Persephone's Island* by Mary Taylor Simeti.

'That's a good example of a blended one-off,' Rogerson said over his shoulder as he spooned in more lapsang souchong. Originally pub-lished in 1986, it was the memoir of an American woman who married into a Sicilian family. 'She'd got an outsider sensibility because she was an American scholar, but she'd also got that long access. I'm astonished a book like that was allowed to fall out of print.'

Behind the dangling proofs, the shelves were loaded with old books, travel titles dating from the mid-twentieth century and beyond. The office had the air of a cache, a vital repository in a declining monastery that might end up walled off and forgotten when the last monk departed.

Back at the table I asked, a little nervously, what might happen to Eland itself, should Rogerson ever decide to move on or retire.

'I would be very, very reluctant to just see it bought by some large company and then just disappear, and be asset-stripped,' he said. 'I know that if an accountant took over they'd sooner or later just con-centrate on the twelve books that actually make money.' He was, though, blithely unconcerned about the future. 'My daughters have said, "One thing we do know, dad, is we don't want to run a small literary list", and I think that's fantastic! But there will be some nutty nerd out there who'll write me a letter in purple ink in a couple of years' time...'

* * *

Outside, the mania of a cold rush hour was building in the blue gloaming. I made my way back to King's Cross along with the rest of the clip-clopping crowd.

If I'd expected to find an air of gloom about the future of travel writing anywhere it had been in the Eland office. But Barnaby Rogerson, all enthusiasm and bonhomie, had merrily refused to play the role of eulogiser for the genre. Travel writing of some sort would always be needed, and would always exist, he'd insisted, even if the old figure of the professional travel writer—the guild-member, the endogamous tribesperson—was endangered. There was reassurance to be had here, then. But still...

That figure of the writer: it was surely central to so much travel writing—and certainly to my own quest. I'd never been particularly interested in books featuring 'a fit young man with his shirt off on the cover' either. But I hadn't entirely left the idea of the travel writer as hero behind in adolescence, no matter how many defenestrating biographies I might have read. And soon I would be meeting some of those writers in person. But before I describe my encounters with the members of the travel writing tribe, I must pause to look at that other body of literature: the one that had generated so much of my own unease around the travel genre—the postcolonial scholarly critique.

4

IN BERLIN

A rainy Friday in Berlin. Outside, the arrow-straight avenues of Dahlem have vanished behind grey cataracts, and the windows of the humanities building at the Freie Universität are clouded with condensation. The lobby is slowly filling, and the sound of the buses, churning the surface water on Habelschwerdter Allee, fades behind a buzz of polyglot chatter. There is a register to sign, and name badges to collect. New arrivals shed overcoats and rattle dripping umbrellas, and the air thickens with a fug of wet clothing and coffee. Some people excitedly greet acquaintances from previous international colloquia; others stand alone, earnestly perusing the printed programme. No one, as far as I can see, is wearing a necktie.

I am here in Berlin for a two-day academic conference on 'travel writing and gender' at a German university. This is not the very first such event I have attended, but as at the previous conferences I feel like an interloper amongst the professors and postdoctoral researchers. When people ask me where I'm from and what I 'work on', I'm never quite sure what to say. They are always interested, enthusiastic even, when I try to explain myself, but I can never quite get past the idea that I'm at risk of being discovered and thrown out. It's a natural enough reaction, I suppose. As someone who comes to travel writing first and foremost as what academic discourse sometimes calls a 'naive reader', and—God help me!—a practitioner of sorts, there's good reason to be scared of the scholars.

* * *

In 1978, just as the late twentieth-century resurgence of travel writing was getting underway, a book appeared in a parallel universe—the gradually emerging field of postcolonial scholarship. Its title was *Orientalism* and its author was the Palestinian-American academic, Edward Said.

To call *Orientalism* a seminal work doesn't even begin to explain its impact. It's not that the ideas it contained were entirely new; similar theories had been quietly developing amongst other literary critics and historians for several decades. But never had they been presented with such brio—or in such baroque and sweeping style. If Said had a counterpart in travel writing itself, then it was surely Patrick Leigh Fermor.

In brief, Said's thesis was that 'Orientalism' was not simply old-fashioned scholarship of 'Eastern' subjects; it was the entire academic, political and imaginative approach of the imperial 'West' to 'the Orient' (for Said the Orient was mainly the Middle East; but his ideas could be applied to everything as far as the South China Sea, and indeed beyond). That approach had a purpose: it was an overarching 'western style for dominating, restructuring, and having authority over the Orient'.[1] It wasn't necessarily that the West *lied* about the East—though Orientalism certainly contained plenty of myth and misinformation. Rather, it chose its component parts according to an agenda, picked them carefully to make a pattern. And by creating its own image of the Orient, Said's argument went, the West controlled it. The 'Orient' as constructed by Western literature and scholarship was a 'stage on which the whole East is confined'.[2] Knowledge was power, after all, and if the knowledge was created on your own terms, then the power was limitless. Orientalism was the intellectual underpinning of European colonialism, and although the original political apparatus of empire had been dismantled, its ideological and imaginative framework remained intact, ensuring that old and insidious power structures endured.

A 'colonial discourse' such as Orientalism could be made of everything from 'the most formulaic and bureaucratic of official documents' to 'the most non-functional and unprepossessing of romantic novels', as a subsequent scholar, Peter Hulme, put it.[3] 'Literary' writers were certainly identified as arch actors—with Kipling and Conrad, inevitably, coming under particular scrutiny. But travel writing too was an obvious accessory. Travellers in foreign lands would always tend to 'fall back on a text', Said wrote. They would remember what they had read in a travel book as they tried to make sense of it all, because 'people, places, and experiences can always be described by a book, so much so that the book (or text) acquires a greater authority, and use, even than the actuality it describes'.[4] A British traveller arriving in colonial Southeast Asia, for example, already 'knew' that the natives were 'indolent'—because that was what he or she had been told by the books read ahead of the journey.[5] The traveller's own observations— and any subsequent writings—were thus predetermined to confirm that judgement. Travel writers, then, created the places they wrote about, and in doing so confirmed what they themselves had read.

I first read *Orientalism* in my early twenties. Like many others before me, I found it revelatory. I already had—or thought I had—a firm sense of the iniquity and moral untenability of European colonialism. But now, for the first time, I understood that it was not simply about physical violence and tangible injustice and exploitation; it was also about *ideas*. And given the way that texts talked to other texts, those ideas could have a potent afterlife—particularly in travel writing, and well beyond any deliberate intention of the authors. Even if you rejected the notion that the Orientalist discourse itself was still at large, informing everything from foreign policy to Hollywood movies, then at the very least the endurance of its mechanism was impossible to deny. A British tourist arriving in Southeast Asia in the twenty-first century was still primed by the guidebooks and travelogues they had consumed in advance. And their own observations were still predetermined by those texts. That the judgements were likely to be ostensibly more positive—*exotic, vibrant, spiritual, timeless*—really wasn't the point.

It was in Said's immediate train that travel writing studies as a distinct academic endeavour emerged. Peter Hulme examined European encounters with the Caribbean; Mary Baine Campbell looked at the way medieval European travellers saw and wrote the wider world; Sara Mills appraised nineteenth-century British women travel writers. And then, in 1992, came the big one, Mary Louise Pratt's *Imperial Eyes: Travel Writing and Transculturation*.

Pratt was second only to Said himself in the development of contemporary scholarship of travel writing, and she gave the field much of its critical lexicon. There was the 'contact zone'—'the space in which peoples geographically and historically separated come into contact with each other and establish ongoing relations, usually involving conditions of coercion, racial inequality, and intractable conflict'—in other words, the historical working environment of the travel writer.[6] There was 'travellee', the people already there in the contact zone when the traveller arrives, the locals travelled past and written about, represented in the travel books. There was the 'monarch-of-all-I-survey scene', a 'brand of verbal painting whose highest calling was to produce for the home audience the peak moments at which geographical "discoveries" were "won"'.[7] This was the familiar scene in which a travel writer crests a ridge, looks out on the land beneath him (and it is usually a him) and describes it lavishly. There was 'auto-ethnography', where a colonised or subjugated people took hold of the subjugators' own methods and ideas to represent themselves. There was 'transculturation', 'anti-conquest' and more besides—language which seemed thoroughly opaque from the outside, but which had become so ubiquitous that it no longer even required a citation in scholarly works on travel writing.

At first Pratt and the other tough new critics looked mainly at the travel literature of the passing imperial epoch. But soon they began to examine the newer books—and in much the same critical light. Some of them were positively fire-breathing in their condemnation. Looking on disdainfully at the various high-profile travel writers—Bruce Chatwin, Redmond O'Hanlon, James Fenton and company—who graced the pages of the literary magazine *Granta* during the genre's 1980s boom, one professor, Charles Sugnet, had dismissed their output as 'a highbrow version of the Banana Republic catalog'. It was, he wrote, a 'curious fusion of the 1880s and the 1980s' which kept 'all those *Granta* travel writers up in the air, afloat over various parts of the globe, their luggage filled with portable shards of colonialist discourse'.[8]

* * *

I had arrived in Berlin the previous morning. On the train from the airport a grey-haired German man was explaining the complexities of the city's rail network in perfect English to two young Scotswomen.

'We can talk in French too, if you prefer,' he said, and the women giggled nervously. When he learnt that they were from Scotland he said, 'Ah, so; you are having to follow England with Brexit.'

I got down at Alexanderplatz. It was a still day under a pale sky, but leaving the station I felt the deepening cold of the coming winter. I'd never been here before, so on the flight I'd tried to audit the personal literary references that I might unwittingly fall back on when I viewed Berlin: John le Carré, mostly. I spent the afternoon wandering the city centre, guarding against sneaking visions of furtive Englishmen in homburg hats, then rode the S-Bahn to a far southwestern suburb and checked into a guesthouse that smelt strongly of furniture polish. In the morning I walked up Habelschwerdter Allee in the rain to join the scholars.

* * *

At 9.55am the conference organisers—two women called Gigi and Lenka—shepherd everyone into a lecture theatre, a grey room with long benches. People scatter themselves around it, singly or in little clusters. The opening keynote is delivered by Carl Thompson, one of the big names of travel writing studies. His books have been amongst the pile on my desk by the window in the university library for months.

Thompson's talk is called 'Beyond Gender? Gendering and Ungendering Early Nineteenth-Century Travel Writing'.[9] It's the sort of title that invites ready pastiche, fosters an idea of wilful opacity in the academic discussion of literature. But there is nothing opaque about Thompson's delivery.

The significance of gender, he says, pacing the space at the front of the hall, can sometimes be overemphasised in studies of travel writing. There is 'a slight myopia' in the relentless scholarly focus on the marginalisation of women as travel writers; by focussing on it, he says, we risk inadvertently perpetuating it.

His clothes—chinos, a blue shirt, a knitted grey waistcoat—are slightly crumpled. He looks more like someone who works outdoors—or who works with wood, perhaps—than a desk-bound academic. He has a greying, gingery beard and wiry red hair pulled back into a tight ponytail.

Thompson talks about travel writing before it came to be known by that name. In the early nineteenth century what we would now think of as travel books had come under the designation of 'voyages and travels', he says, and if travel writing today has a faint air of literary disreputability, dismissed as mere entertainment, this was not always the case. Two centuries ago it was a 'knowledge genre'. If this is so, then old arguments claiming that the women travel writers of the nineteenth century were marginal figures, working in a marginal genre, don't make a great deal of sense. Thompson has unearthed an 1835 review of a travel book about Chile by Maria Graham from the *Edinburgh Magazine*. The reviewer, with lordly condescension, expressed his alarm that women authors had moved beyond the composition of 'trashy novels and poetry' to write more serious 'travels'— too serious, as far as the reviewer was concerned, for mere women! So much for a 'subordinate genre'.

I sneak glances around the room to see who else is here: a few enthusiastic students from the Freie Universität who've come in during their midterm break; a lot of young women; a diverse crowd, generally, and all adhering to the resolutely informal dress-code of academia. They look singularly unthreatening, and when it comes time for the questions, they are all careful—in their global array of accents—to thank the speaker profusely for his contribution.

After the opening session everyone peels off into separate seminar rooms for the panels: three twenty-minute papers apiece, read back-to-back with questions at the end; a dozen listeners nodding enthusiastically and scribbling notes as the speakers scroll through their PowerPoint slides. In the session I join there is a talk by Barbara Schaff, a professor from the University of Göttingen, on the way that publishers and editors shape authors as 'discursive constructions'. An Indian scholar, Diviani Chaudhuri, speaks about Agatha Christie's Syrian travelogue, *Come, Tell Me How You Live* (1946); and a tall Canadian called Lucas Tromly—the most smartly dressed man at the conference by a mile—introduces his concept of 'echotourism', a catchy new name for the old travel writing trope of journeying in the 'footsteps' of a literary predecessor.[10]

At lunchtime people stand around in the lobby, talking noisily and eating salad from tiny plates. The conversation is enthusiastic, and not in the least bit rarefied. Everyone has tales of the delayed Ryanair and EasyJet flights or tricky train connections they've endured to reach Berlin. No one seems to know what to do with their empty plates and coffee cups. They hold onto them long after they've finished eating, their gesticulations restricted. A few leftovers get spilt.

Then it is time for the second keynote, this one from Churnjeet Mahn. Here's another name I know from my reading in the library— this time manifest as a Scotswoman dressed entirely in black. She speaks like the lead detective in a gritty crime drama. Her talk is about 'sexuality and dissent in travel writing' and she runs through some intriguing examples of 'queer travel writing' in a voice of weary authority.[11]

In the evening there's a conference dinner in a Chinese restaurant. The rain has stopped now, and the pavements are clean and dry under the streetlights. Dahlem is a leafy area. Long, straight streets lined with trees just coming into autumn colour; houses with half-timbering and hipped roofs behind white fences; expensive cars in darkened driveways, and no sign of a student population. The restaurant stands incongruously alone at a residential intersection. For a moment the vision of the furtive homburg-sporting Englishman resurfaces, waiting in a lonely dining room for a clandestine meeting with his source. But I wrestle myself back up from the textual fallback, and once we're inside the restaurant things are anything but bleak. I sit with a merry Israeli historian whose research specialism is 'girlhood', and her husband, who says he usually tags along when she travels to conferences. People are still asking me 'What do you work on?' But the wine makes it much easier to answer, and I'm no longer worrying about being thrown out. Everyone laughs a lot. After dinner no one seems quite sure how to get back to their various hotels, and the conference organisers have to guide giggly groups to the S-Bahn and U-Bahn stations.

From the outside, it's easy to assume that the academic study of travel writing amounts to nothing more than the ferocious postcolonial critique. But there's plainly much more to it than that. No one here in Berlin seems to be on the attack—though Mary Louise Pratt's terminology certainly echoes loudly around the seminar rooms. And the truth is, I love all this—love having the chance to talk daylong about travel writing with people who recognise its complexities, understand the way one book talks to another, the way ideas transmit from text to text and the way history and point of departure might impact how an author views and writes the world. Above all, I love spending time with other people who think that travel writing is something *worth* studying.

* * *

The conference continues the following morning. There is another keynote—on 'vagabondage' reimagined as a mode for women's travel writing—from an Irishwoman called Dúnlaith Bird who speaks with soft, half-whispered enthusiasm.

At one point, hurrying along a corridor between sessions, Churnjeet Mahn falls into step alongside me. The previous day, during the questions that followed her keynote, I voiced a half-formed idea. The queer travel writing she discussed seemed to earn that designation through its sensibility or its subject matter. A gay man, for example, wouldn't automatically produce queer travel writing, just by the fact of his sexuality, I said, tentatively; he might well write a book that wasn't discernibly 'queer' at all. Mahn seemed to agree, so I continued. In that case, perhaps someone whose own identity *wasn't* queer might, in theory at least, be able to produce a text with 'queer' qualities. I glanced around the room at this point to check that I wasn't saying something stupid. It didn't seem like I was, so I went on: well, then, what about 'women's travel writing'? Was *that* an automatically ascribed category, and if not, could anyone, regardless of gender, produce a piece of 'women's travel writing'? Might *I* be able to do so myself? No one had a clear answer at the time, but now, as we stride towards a panel on 'British Women Travellers', Mahn comes back to it.

'I was thinking about your question,' she says, 'and I think it would depend on whether you could pass.'

I'm not sure what she means. 'Pass?'

'Could *you* write a piece of women's travel writing—it would depend whether you could pass.'

'As a *woman*?'

'Exactly.'

The last panel of the conference has the feeling of the early hours of the second morning of a very heavy weekend. The coffee is beginning to taste like charcoal. My notebook is full of excited squiggles that I'll struggle to make sense of by the time I get home: 'cites Pratt's notion of a modernist myth of travel mobility as freedom'; 'argues that the "consolidated vision" is present in Thesiger's books'; 'how do picturesque and sentimental interact with the Other?'

And then we're done, and once again, the organisers have to guide people to the correct stations for their homeward journeys.

Riding the train back to the airport, I know that I'm coming away with more questions and more anxieties than I had at the start—about the identity, position, point of departure of the travel writer, and more besides. It's always the same: the more I read, talk, think about travel writing, the more questions there are. Looking for answers is always a fine motivation for a journey, but I have a very long way to go.

PART TWO

THE TRAVEL WRITING TRIBE

5

BELATED TRAVELLERS

He was right on time.

A cold day in late January. In the piazza of the British Library, swaddled figures cut left and right, clutching takeaway coffee cups in gloved hands. At three o'clock on the dot, as we'd arranged, Nicholas Jubber came jogging down the library steps. He was somehow smaller, sprightlier, than the photographs in his books suggested, with thick black hair, glasses, and a neat goatee beard. We shook hands and he fumbled to clip a bicycle helmet to his backpack. He must have been my own age, or thereabouts, but he looked younger—like an earnest undergraduate, briefly escaped from his studies.

He nodded back towards the library with its layers of Uluru-coloured brick: 'It tends to get a bit hectic in there around three, as everyone's attention starts to flag.' He'd been in the reading rooms, doing research for his next book—another travel writer caught during the desk-bound first leg of a new journey.

'It's about the relationship between Europe's epic literature and Europe today,' he said, as we hurried west through the pedestrian crossings. 'There's a nice café just up here...'[1]

* * *

My wrangles with the scholarly definitions had helped me to work out just what sort of people I wanted to meet during my journey. I had decided to stick mainly to British travel writers. Not only did this help to narrow a dauntingly wide field; it seemed to be an approach with reasonable methodological justification too. British travel writing had its own distinct literary heritage—one which stretched back through Freya Stark and Robert Byron, into the nineteenth century and beyond. It had its own particular historical contexts too: those of empire and its dissolution—helpful if I hoped to map connections and spot patterns. I wouldn't be too strict about it, if an author was based in Britain—or at very least was published in London. But I had to have parameters of some kind. I'd also decided that to qualify, a writer needed to have penned at least two books in the genre. Barnaby Rogerson of Eland felt that one book was enough to make a travel writer. But I was looking for a little more proof of commitment, and a deeper familiarity with the practices of travel writing.

Having figured all this out, I needed to choose who to speak to first. My first thought was to go to some grand figure from the genre's upper echelons. It made sense—start with the past, a view from the heights. But a niggling unease arose. Wouldn't it be better to confirm the relevance of my own quest early on—to check that travel writing wasn't, in fact, *already* dead, that I wasn't simply travelling amongst ghosts? Perhaps I should begin instead with a new writer in an old tradition.

In the end I decided to have it both ways—to start with two writers, one from each end of the pack. Choosing a grand veteran was easy— I'd known exactly who that would be right from the get-go. Finding a suitable candidate with a career that had begun in the twenty-first century was a little trickier. But then I thought of Nicholas Jubber.

* * *

The café was in the Quaker Centre on Euston Road, a bright space that sold books as well as coffee. We sat in the corner by the children's play area.

It took me a while to work out who it was that Jubber reminded me of. It wasn't simply the thick dark hair and boyish complexion; it was the fidgety energy, and, once we began to talk, the sheer passion for travel writing. He was two decades younger than Philip Marsden, but they had a good deal in common.

His life as a travel writer had begun, he told me, when he went to Jerusalem to work as a teacher after studying English at Oxford. He had been there a bare two weeks when the second Palestinian Intifada broke out.

'I'd become very interested in travel writing, probably a couple of years before I went out there, so it'd been in the back of my mind that I'd love to write a travel book. But the first travel books that I'd read were by Wilfred Thesiger, and so I thought that it would be impossible to have the sort of experiences that you could possibly make a book out of—because, you know, the standard of experience seemed so high.'

Wilfred Thesiger—a name that was to crop up again and again on my journey.

'I mean how could you possibly explore anything in the way he has?' Jubber said. 'Also, there's a certain feeling of an end of an epoch about Thesiger's books, that this is the last word; people say this is the last word on Arabian travel. It was only slowly that I realised that what was happening, what I was experiencing, was obviously very different—a much more urban setting for a start, and it was the twenty-first century. But it was a whole new story, really, in the Middle East and its relationship with the West.'

Jubber's time in the Middle East produced his debut, *The Prester Quest*, published in 2006, about a journey from Jerusalem to Ethiopia in pursuit of the myth of Prester John—a myth foisted on the world in significant part by none other than Sir John Mandeville. Next came the gloriously titled *Drinking Arak Off an Ayatollah's Beard* (2010), following in the footsteps of the Persian poet Ferdowsi through Iran and Afghanistan. And in 2016 he'd published *The Timbuktu School for Nomads*, which found the author at large in the Sahara Desert and seeking connections with the sixteenth century.

The books were quirky, self-deprecating, and each markedly different from the last in form and theme. But they all seemed to belong to what we might call the 'classical tradition' of British travel writing practice: an underpinning scholarliness; a deep engagement with the relevant literature; a concerted effort to get to grips with the most relevant language (Persian and Arabic here) ahead of the journey; and then a lengthy, immersive and by no means risk-free journey into what William Dalrymple has called that 'particular quadrant of the world— the area roughly between Athens and Calcutta' (with an added North African annexe in Jubber's case).[2]

This was the very approach that had so beguiled me as a reader of travel writing in my late teens and early twenties. It was what had attracted me to books by Philip Marsden and many others. It implied a serious commitment, a formidable outlay of time and effort, and a certain intellectual seriousness no matter how light the mode of delivery. (Every book he'd written so far, Jubber said, had involved 'more than a year's worth of journeys'—and that without counting the library time and language-learning in advance.) But it was an approach that seemed to have gone out of fashion since the 1990s—or simply been made unsustainable by the contraction of the publishing economy. In fact, Jubber was almost the only British travel writer I could think of who'd started out writing in this mode since the beginning of the twenty-first century—and who had stuck with it. Three books down, and now on to his fourth. It suggested an impressive tenacity. But it must, at times, have been disheartening.

Towards the end of *The Timbuktu School for Nomads* there was a memorable passage about travel writing itself:

> Like nomadism, the travel book is marginalised, and often misunderstood [...] But what literary genre bears no scars? The travel book is the hunter-gatherer of literature, picking up whatever it can to sustain itself. And in this divided world of ours, is the attempt to connect, to explore a culture outside of our own, truly redundant?[3]

It was a rallying cry. But it also hinted at the frustrations of a travel writer who had, perhaps, started out on his journeys just a little too late.

* * *

One idea that cropped up again and again in the academic discussions of travel writing that I'd read in the university library was that of 'belatedness'. Travel writing, the argument went, had long been suffused with a discomfiting sense of being a genre out of time: the nagging suspicion that all the truly worthwhile journeys have already been done—quite possibly by Wilfred Thesiger. Wherever they went, travel writers knew in their hearts that they had turned up a generation, or a century, or a millennium too late. And, wittingly or unwittingly, the pose that they struck in foreign lands was often prompted by this sense of inadequacy—'what might facetiously be called "the 100-years-too-late" school of travel writing', as the scholars Patrick

Holland and Graham Huggan put it.[4] This was categorically not a commercial thing; it had nothing to do with publishing fashion, and it was nothing new. It had been going on since at least the eighteenth century when the snootier Grand Tourists began to worry that Italy had already been overrun by the masses. Maybe if Egeria had had more to say about herself she might have announced that heavy pilgrim traffic had already ruined Mount Sinai.

'Belatedness' was supposedly what generated the aura of melancholy, which certainly features in some travel writing. It was allegedly what prompted its obsession with history. And it drove its tendency to what the scholars called 'anti-tourism'—the incessant avoidance of beaten tracks, the humourless insistence that the 'tourist is the other fellow', as Evelyn Waugh put it.[5] Tourists, one academic wrote, are 'an unwelcome reminder to self-styled "travellers", of the modern realities that dog their fleeting footsteps'.[6]

For the more hostile scholars, attempts to overcome belatedness were often behind the worst of modern travel writing's alleged faults. They were what made it an inherently conservative genre; they were what bound it up so inextricably with colonial heritage and empire nostalgia. 'In short,' as Debbie Lisle—the critic who had suggested that there was something fundamentally *wrong* with travel writing—would have it, 'travel writers maintain their relevance in a globalised world by mimicking their colonial forebears.'[7] If the encounters in travel writing seemed often to be with the most exotic and most 'othered', the least modern and least mobile of people, it was a strategy—an unconscious one, perhaps—to keep them, quite literally, in their place. It let the travel writer, and by extension his or her readers, feel that he or she was still the boss, just like the colonial travellers who went before.

This idea of 'belatedness' had an effect on me that I had encountered before with canny scholarly concepts. It was instantly compelling, irrefutable almost. And yet it left me with a frustrating, indefinable unease; a sense that it was somehow flawed, if only I could work out why.

Nicholas Jubber struck me as the perfect travel writer to talk to about belatedness. He'd pretty much raised it himself, with that curious comment about Wilfred Thesiger's 'standard of experience'. I asked if he had read much travel writing scholarship.

'*Is* there a lot of scholarship on travel writing?'

'There's *quite* a lot,' I said, 'and you'll probably have a sense of where it goes if you know that it really starts from Edward Said onwards.'

'Ah...' He bowed his head wearily. 'Okay, I see, yeah... maybe I don't want to see it...'

I gave him a brief précis of what I'd read myself, the sort of things I'd picked up at conferences. He took out a reporter's notepad and wrote down the names of a few of the travel writing scholars I mentioned in a small, neat hand, words trailing across the page like strings of little black bubbles. He said he'd look them up when he was back in the library.

The fact that Jubber was largely unaware of the scholarly field seemed to confirm an impression that had troubled me ever since I had first begun to delve into the academic discussions: the idea that travel writing studies and travel writing itself belonged to separate states, with very little traffic across the frontier. That blistering critique of the '*Granta* travel writers' of the 1980s by the American professor Charles Sugnet had appeared in a strictly scholarly journal, published by a university press. I don't suppose many subscribers—or indeed contributors—to *Granta* itself ever knew of its existence. I wasn't sure who this reflected worse upon—the scholars or the travel writers.

But once we began to discuss the matter, it quickly became clear that Jubber was perfectly familiar with the sort of accusations that scholars might level at his genre. I wasn't sure whether this was through an innate self-awareness, or simply because he was a well-read Oxford English graduate—perhaps a little of each. And as he began to engage in a defence of travel writing—a passionate, enthused defence, patting at the table and swaying in his chair—I found myself listening sharply, for his championing rested above all on the possibilities of the first-person narrative, the self-same element that had so enthused Philip Marsden.

'There's a sense you get with the travel book that's like being backstage, seeing how it all works, how it all goes together, seeing the perspective of the person who's gone out there. Because there's *always* going to be a perspective; there's always a perspective of the person who's putting it together—and somebody is *always* going to be putting it together.'

He paused here for a moment, and I had the sense that he was decid-ing whether to share something. 'I was actually told by my agent...' He began, then paused again, then went on, quietly and hesitantly, dropping down from the earlier impassioned heights. 'When I was writing my last book... that it might well be easier to sell if it was done with the authorial presence more in the background...'

This was remarkable. I couldn't imagine *The Timbuktu School for Nomads* as anything other than a traditional travel book.

'Why did you decide to not take that advice?'

He laughed. 'I'm probably not very good at taking advice! I wanted to write a travel book, and I was conscious that I wouldn't feel like I was being particularly honest. I felt like I was telling the story that I was trying to tell more authentically by making my presence felt.'

The first person, he argued, was actually the only obvious way to reveal the *limits* of a writer's authority, the deficiencies in their know-ledge or skill. If this was true—and it certainly seemed very convinc-ing—then perhaps it was actually the *most* ethical way to approach any nonfiction narrative. It did have its own problems, however, Jubber acknowledged, which was where the self-deprecation he routinely deployed in his own books was so important.

'I'm very aware that the travel book is basically a very narcissistic genre. I mean, people talk about the travel bore, and it could go really badly—writing a three or four-hundred-page book all about your travels is clearly a sign of an egomaniac! So to make that palat-able really, and for there to be any justification in presenting that to the general public, it feels like there needs to be some kind of self-deprecation in it.'

I'd known of the scholarly debates around travel writing for years. But it was really only now, listening to Jubber discussing all this, that it struck me how incredibly fraught a genre it could be for any conscien-tious author—even one who'd never read the academic critiques. I wasn't sure how many readers, casually picking up a travel book, would recognise the underlying anxieties. How much easier—and less time-consuming—it would be simply to sit at home and write a novel! And the tricky balance to be struck with the first person was just the start; it was representing other people, other cultures, that was the greatest source of anxiety.

'That's the really heavy burden,' Jubber said. 'How do you know that you're getting it right? And it's impossible of course, and you *can't* get it right, because there are always alternative perspectives and inter- pretations. But what you can do is try to learn the languages as well as possible, read *hundreds* of books about the places you're travelling to, immerse yourself in the journey and work really carefully on what you're writing.'

There was something reassuring about this, and I knew that it was what I had wanted him to say. It also confirmed that sense of a ten- acious commitment to the genre, come what may. But I knew too that I had to push him a little further on the question of belatedness.

In the middle of *Drinking Arak Off an Ayatollah's Beard* there is a memorable scene: Jubber passes himself off as a Muslim pilgrim to sneak into the shrine of the ninth-century Imam Reza in Mashhad in Iran. It seemed like a deliberate reference to Robert Byron, consider- ing the same exercise at the same spot seven decades earlier in *The Road to Oxiana*.[8] But it also reads like an overt acknowledgement of belatedness, an attempt to re-enact—*100 years too late*—the escapades of the travellers who came this way in the past, when the going was good—at least in terms of travel writing material. The travel writing scholars who followed Edward Said's lead would likely spot a further troubling significance here too, for, as one of their number, Sara Mills, had written, 'The westerner in disguise is a figure of great textual power since it demonstrates great knowledge to a western audience, and at the same time it asserts even greater power over the people of the colonised country since they are represented as being fooled by the disguise.'[9]

I reached for my notebook where I had copied the passage, and read aloud, with Jubber nodding self-consciously across the table:

> With the world becoming so much more accessible every day, it's great to have a few spots that are still, officially, off-limits. When you sneak into a shrine like Imam Reza's, you get a tiny whiff of what it must have been like for travelers of the past—men like Sir Richard Burton, steal- ing into Mecca disguised as an Afghan...[10]

He grimaced. 'Oh right. So the academics, the travel writing hound- ers, would have a field day about this!'

We grinned at each other nervously for a moment.

But then, as he began to reflect on the passage, its significance seemed to dwindle. There *was* a thrill in the dressing up, he said, in playing at being Burton, Lawrence, Thesiger. What was more, he'd had a passion for student theatre during his time at Oxford, had even performed at the Edinburgh Festival. But in the end, he had only put on the disguises when his local companions had told him to do so: 'They were simply saying, "Do this because otherwise you're going to get killed and this is the safest way to go, and if you look more like us you're not going to stand out as much."' Travel writing might be suffused with the play of what the scholars called 'intertexts'—the influencing books that had gone before—and laced with threads of old discourses. But a narrative was still determined by what actually happened on the ground—or it was supposed to be, in any case. And looking back, the figure that Jubber cut in the scene didn't seem quite so much one of 'great textual power' as it might have done had he been writing in a different style and a different century. Pushed, pulled, tugged by his companion, 'sucked' into a 'whirlpool' of humanity within the crowded shrine, there's a sense of uncertainty, a loss of control rather than authority.

'Actually, I think that probably I feel slightly differently now from when I was writing the passage about Imam Reza,' he said. 'Certainly, it feels like there are more journeys that would be very hard to undertake now than they were even ten years ago. So I think belatedness is probably a sort of academic misunderstanding of the way the world works.

'The world is constantly evolving so there are always going to be journeys to do. There are always going to be things that are new, things that have changed, things that have evolved, and there's always the opportunity to try and track that. That's one of the virtues of the travel book—to try and track the way the world changes. If you read Thesiger's *Arabian Sands*, and then you read Jonathan Raban's book about Arabia,'—he meant *Arabia: Through the Looking Glass*, published in 1979—'those are completely different places, and yet they were both travelling in the same region. The travel book is an authentic calendar of the way that the world evolves.'

* * *

It was dark outside now, and beyond the café windows the traffic on Euston Road was slowing to a rush-hour crawl. Jubber needed to be heading home. As he buttoned up his jacket and shouldered his backpack, the bicycle helmet clattering against the table, I told him who I was going to see the following day. His eyes brightened enviously for a moment.

'I'm in awe of people like him,' he said, 'and the breadth of the world that they've been able to explore through all those books.'

The author I'd named had been a travel writer for five decades. Jubber, meanwhile, was eleven years into his own career.

'In another thirty-nine years am I going to be able to come and find you and still refer to you as a travel writer too?' I asked.

He smiled ruefully. 'If I could just carry on doing the journeys and writing about them, and I could do that for fifty years, I would be absolutely thrilled. But do I really believe that I'm going to be able to carry on doing it over fifty years and have a readership that would be big enough for publishers to keep publishing me? I don't know, and I think that's the factor—more so than danger and politics or anything—that's the factor where it's harder for travel writers of my generation.'

There was a sense of 'belatedness' here, certainly—but perhaps not quite the one the academics had in mind.

* * *

A Friday afternoon in June in the last year of the twentieth century:

A meeting room in a high-rise hotel on the corner of Chestnut and 36th in Philadelphia. The campus of the University of Pennsylvania sprawls over the leafy blocks to the south, and there are scholars at large amongst the business travellers in the hotel. A three-day academic conference on travel writing is underway. There are panels to be chaired and papers to present—papers with such titles as 'Gendering the American West: Feminized Landscapes and Phallic Intrusions' and 'Exploring Liminality: The Spatial Politics of Travel and Gender Identity in Lady Mary Wortley Montagu's Turkish Embassy Letters'. Professors and graduate students have travelled in from Kansas and North Carolina, even from Munich and Oxford. The hotel is offering rooms at preferential conference rates.

This is the professional scholarship of travel writing two decades in from the publication of Edward Said's *Orientalism*—not quite a discipline in its own right, but travelling with a distinct head of steam. By this stage, some scholars are already recognising a problematic absolutism in the cruder redeployments of Said's ideas, or perhaps simply wearying of relentless negativity. They are exploring other, less condemnatory angles, seeking out examples of travel writing that subverts or reverses standard power dynamics, hunting for nuances and contradictions that the more hostile commentaries might overlook. But on this summer afternoon in Philadelphia as the 1999 'Writing the Journey' conference gets underway, the postcolonial critique still dominates the scholarly discourse.

This particular afternoon session, however, is focussed rather more on the aesthetic than the political features of the travel genre. There are three papers to be read, under the banner of 'The Journeys of Thubron and Raban'. The first speaker gets to his feet. Perhaps he is particularly nervous. Perhaps he feels a certain sense of unreality, for this is a highly unusual situation: the subject of his paper is sitting in the audience.

Two decades later Colin Thubron chuckles—though not unkindly.

'It was some absurd thing about "Time and temporality in Colin Thubron's look at Russia" or something,' he says.[11] 'It was perfectly complimentary, but it was absolute rubbish! It was somebody having to create something out of something. The author himself was not meant to exist...'

But Colin Thubron did exist.

* * *

The dampness that had lain across London the previous day had deepened. The daylight was already shortening in the early afternoon when I found my way to a quiet avenue in the west of the city. I walked slowly along the wet pavement, counting off the house numbers. The buildings were tall, set back from the road, with brickwork the colour of Tibetan hills.

Colin Thubron met me at the door. Like Nicholas Jubber, he was smaller than I had expected, his face less equine than photographs on the dust jackets of his books suggested—though the thicket of ash-blond hair was the same. He was dressed for a day indoors, in corduroy trousers and carpet slippers. His accent, with its blurry consonants, was decidedly that of a man schooled at Eton. But there was an unexpected diffidence and concern, as if *I* were the one doing *him* the honour. He was utterly charming.

His home was an apartment across the two lower floors. Tall, well-lit rooms; a wall of books, and the windows opening onto a garden, liquid green in the premature gloaming.

He introduced me to his wife, Margreta de Grazia, a Shakespearean scholar, of the University of Pennsylvania. They had married late, and there was a certain unabashed sweetness between them. He called her 'darling', and she displayed a tender concern for his comfort. This was not the domestic environment I might have expected of a man who delivered ascetic books about the bleaker parts of Russia and Central Asia.

De Grazia brought us coffee and shortbread biscuits, and left us to talk in the living room.

There was one question I was desperate to ask before we properly began. Thubron's travel books had been great landmarks on my own reader's itinerary. *Behind the Wall* (1987), *In Siberia* (1999), *Shadow of the Silk Road* (2006): they came with delicately worked prose, crystalline sketches of human encounters, and with the authorial persona edged to the very margins of the page. Like Nicholas Jubber, he was firmly committed to that classical practice: the language-learning (Russian, Chinese); the deep reading for months, even years in advance of departure. The books he produced were things to be eked out sparingly like expensive chocolates, but I'd long since emptied the box. His most recent travel book, *To a Mountain in Tibet*, had been published in 2011. It was uncharacteristically slender, uncharacteristically personal, and with a distinct hint of valediction. He was in his late seventies now, after all. But in recent interviews I'd spotted hints about a planned trip to the Amur River, the cold watercourse that marks the eastern border of Russia and China.

'Is that on the cards still?' I asked.

'Yes.'

'And will you write about it?' Later, when I listened back to the recording of the conversation, I could hear a pleading hint in my own voice here.

'Yes.'

'You will?'

'It needs an awful lot of preparation,' he said, 'so it won't happen until the spring of next year—and it would only be something political that stopped it, unless I had some health problem—because I've got to get my Russian better...'

I realised I had been holding the air high in my lungs. I breathed out. I had wanted to know if I was talking to a retiree. If so, it would have shifted the significance of the whole conversation. But more than that, it seemed to matter for travel writing in general. Many of best-known figures amongst the older generation of travel writers seemed to be fading from the scene. Paul Theroux had published what appeared to be his own valedictory book of foreign travels, *The Last Train to the Zona Verde*, in 2013.[12] Jonathan Raban, meanwhile—with health problems and perhaps a fickle muse—had edged quietly towards obscurity. But here was Colin Thubron, and the carpet slippers counted for nothing. If *he* was still out there, stalking the banks of the Amur River, then travel writing was alive and kicking—for the time being at least.[13]

* * *

Colin Thubron was born in the summer of 1939. Part of his childhood was spent at a family home in Sussex, but a certain internationalism arrived early. His father was a military diplomat, serving in Canada in the aftermath of World War II, and for four years the young Thubron had travelled to join his parents after each term at prep school. These journeys were made aboard a Boeing 377 Stratocruiser—a lumbering, snub-nosed pioneer of mass air transport, tracing the cupola of the North Atlantic from Shannon to Reykjavik to Gander. The excitement of both journey and destination was tremendous, and the boy—already an aspiring poet—wrote verses about the Canadian prairies.

Eton followed prep school, and here Thubron seemed to have the archetypal pedigree of an old-school British travel writer. But he hadn't gone on to Oxford or Cambridge. The problem, he explained, was that he couldn't pass his O-level maths exam.

'I took it about three times, failing by a wider margin each time,' he said. He then failed the entry exam for a scholarship to study English at King's College, Cambridge. While pondering what to do about this growing tally of educational miscarriages, he came up for national service, and here he failed yet again—the medical, because of a knee injury.

'I was moving some furniture for my sister's dance...' He paused and laughed softly. 'She was having a coming-out dance, or some dance—yes, it was her twenty-first. I put the knee cartilage out.' He appealed the military examiner's decision, and failed here too. 'I felt rather humiliated, because my father was a military man, and so he'd already sort of got me some commission in the Third Hussars, I think, some quite scandalous way of going about such things...' In the end, Thubron went into publishing as an apprentice at Hutchinson, in a London on the cusp of the 1960s.

Coming-out dances and commissions in the Third Hussars: to me this was all as alien as the Amur River.

I had heard the story about the transatlantic Stratocruiser flights before. It was the answer that Thubron always gave when asked about the genesis of his travelling life. But he hadn't written *Mirror to Damascus*, his first book, until he was twenty-seven, after several years in publishing and a brief foray into filmmaking for the BBC.

'Twenty-seven is young,' I said, 'but not *that* young for somebody who has said he was writing poetry as a small child.'

'True.'

'So where did that desire, not to travel, but to travel *write* begin?'

He paused and smiled, tilting his head in thought for a moment. He was sitting with his back to the windows, and the thin green light from the garden made a halo of his hair.

'You know, you get asked these questions,' he said, 'and you find that you produce a sort of an answer that you're a little bit used to, that becomes the one you believe in, and when you have to seriously think about it, these things may not be true.'

The love of travel itself had indeed begun, he was certain, with those end-of-term flights to Canada. But the roots of the travel *writing* did lie elsewhere. As a young apprentice publisher he had encountered *Venice* (1960) by Jan Morris (still James at the time, of course), Patrick Leigh Fermor's *Mani* (1958) and the books of Freya Stark: 'This was rather the aristocracy of travel writing one was suddenly being given.'

Then, already under the effect of these authors, there had been a caravan journey with his parents, from Turkey to Egypt.

'It's a journey I wrote about—a short book, never published, luckily; terrible, tremendously overwritten. It was a first effort, which may have had some promise—probably sort of did. That's where it came together, and I don't know quite why; it just seemed automatic that I would have to write about this.'

His first published works, emerging in a sudden flurry in the late 1960s, had all been about the Middle East: *Mirror to Damascus* (1967), *The Hills of Adonis* (1968) and *Jerusalem* (1969). In the mid-1970s he published what he called his 'first mature book', *Journey into Cyprus* (1975), after which he turned away from travel writing for a while, making his first experiments with fiction, and taking commercial writing commissions for Time-Life.

But elsewhere something remarkable was happening. In 1975, just as Thubron stepped temporarily away from the genre, Paul Theroux had published *The Great Railway Bazaar*. This is the book usually credited with launching the sustained travel writing boom of the late twentieth century. It sold 1.5 million copies.[14] Two years later Bruce Chatwin's *In Patagonia* (1977) appeared, as did Patrick Leigh Fermor's *A Time of Gifts* (1977). Something had begun—spontaneously it seemed. As the 1970s moved towards their close, Peter Matthiessen's *The Snow Leopard* (1978) emerged glittering from the Himalayas, Robyn Davidson proved that desert journeys were not the exclusive preserve of writers like Wilfred Thesiger, and Jonathan Raban discovered that travel writing offered as much scope for fine writing as fiction. By the time Thubron returned with *Among the Russians* in 1983, travel writing was a very different beast from the staid and sometimes rather conservative creature of the 1960s.

'You'd have thought I'd have had my eye on the market,' he said. 'But I really didn't; I never really had my eye on anything. I don't think I'm worldly wise in that way. And when I wrote the Russian book— indeed, Paul's book had come out, and *In Patagonia*... yes, they were all out.

'In retrospect I realise that I had a tremendous advantage. The Russian book was published at the peak of the travel writing revival— or not even revival; the surge in its popularity. And all through the 80s it went on. It was always Jonathan Raban, Bruce and Paul who again and again were cited through the 80s as *the* travel writers. It was as if publishing had discovered that travel writing could be a literary genre. I was lucky, you know, because by the late 80s people were adding me to the list, and Redmond O'Hanlon. I suppose there were five of us by the end of the peak period.'

In 1983 *Granta* magazine—object of the scholar Charles Sugnet's ire—had confirmed the genre's remarkably fashionable standing with its seminal 'Travel Writing' edition. Thubron and Chatwin and Theroux and the other young bloods were shuffled in with older stalwarts who found themselves suddenly and unexpectedly at the frontline of the literary zeitgeist: Norman Lewis, Martha Gellhorn and Jan Morris. Big reviews and big advances for travel writing followed, and by the close of the decade a whole new generation—Marsden, Dalrymple, Wheeler and countless others, now forgotten—were beginning to emerge. For me—and no doubt for Nicholas Jubber too—it all seemed scarcely imaginable in the second decade of the twenty-first century. But Thubron, looking back from the heights, could detect a certain absurdity.

'I think to some extent it was publishers' fashion. They tend to jump on bandwagons. But I do think *The Great Railway Bazaar* had an extraordinary impact. It was a new kind of travel writing, of course, or it seemed to be—a bit hip and fun,' he said. 'I was incredibly lucky to be the beneficiary of it all—not that my books ever sold like Paul's did, but you did well enough. I was suddenly being paid more for what I wanted to do than for Time-Life.'

* * *

I asked—as I had asked Nicholas Jubber—whether Thubron had read anything of the scholarly critiques of travel writing.

'A *little*, mainly because my wife is an academic.' He'd read Mary Louise Pratt, 'and one or two others'.

'I could *see* the point,' he said of the critique. 'I could see where it comes from, which is fair enough, and particularly for the sort of paternalistic tradition from which I come—we're all sort of upper-middle class; we're all educated in a certain way; we're almost all white; we inherit a certain tradition, even now, a certain sense of Englishness or Britishness. They're all dangerous things, suggesting that we take certain attitudes to people, even if we think we're not doing it.'

But he was sceptical about the more extreme deployments of such an argument: 'It risks consigning all human contact to silence or paranoia,' he said. 'If you follow this, there would be no contact; there would be a wall between us, and however inadequate the interactions, they've got to be there; one's got to try to understand the other.

'This critique is always, to my mind, *always* about the imposition of power. Who has the power—it always comes up. And there's no acknowledgement that travel writing can be an exercise not in power, but an attempt at understanding, and empathy. It can be from a position of some humility in some cases, from people who think this culture has something to teach them, and that *will* come up in some travel writing. Again, that can be seen as very condescending in certain ways itself. But it's much more fraught in practice than these stay-at-home academics imagine, I think.' I thought again here of Nicholas Jubber— pushed, pulled, *sucked* into the Imam Reza shrine.

To be fair, some of the more recent scholarship I'd encountered did draw attention to travel writing's empathetic qualities, and even when the postcolonial critique was in its pomp in the 1980s and 1990s, there had been plenty of scholars who were willing to acknowledge the possibility and seek out examples of sensitive encounters with what they called 'alterity' or 'otherness'. But it was also true that there were some critics who seemed to come close to damning the entire genre as ethically irredeemable. Thubron, however, saw travel writing's greatest possibility—its ethical redemption even—in the first-person form. Here it was again—the same redeeming feature that Jubber and Marsden had both described.

'I think that there's a possibility in travel writing that people can be more aware because of that "I" figure; be more aware of your own culture, be more aware of its inhibitions, its effect, what you are automatically feeling about these people, and be quite self-reflective about it. You might just catch yourself. I do it a little bit in China: this is me, I realise; this is one culture looking at another—which is what travel writing is. It can acknowledge those shortcomings that the academics impugn travel writing with so much. It has the possibility within itself, within the genre, of acknowledging that this is so, which academic work itself doesn't do; it plays God; it says, "This is how things are."'

Thinking back on this later an idea struck me: perhaps literature scholars should start using the first person more often in their own work.

Thubron told me about the 1999 conference at the University of Pennsylvania, his wife's institution. In the evening, after he had sat in and heard his own recent writing on Russia examined in academic fashion, he had delivered the keynote address.

'It was very peculiar for a travel writer actually to be getting up and speaking to these scholars about it. And I realised that I was confusing to them, because here I was talking about the practice of travel writing, a certain amount about travel writing history and so on, and they didn't know what to make of me. I was meant to be a text; I shouldn't be a person. They were quite respectful, but I realised that they didn't know what to do with me…'

* * *

Margreta de Grazia appeared from the garden where a proper dusk was now lowering. Thubron sprang from the sofa: 'Hello, my love!'

A young woman was hovering at the living room door—the house-keeper: 'I'll just see if she wants to come in. We can go downstairs; there's a study downstairs we can use. Karina, love, do you want to come in here?'

I got up to make way for the vacuum cleaner.

We had already been speaking for an hour and a half, and I worried that I was taking too much of his time. But he was quite unconcerned. 'It's been very enjoyable,' he said.

The downstairs study was as uncluttered as Thubron's prose. There was a small daybed and two desks, slotted against one another at right angles, looking out to the garden through a basement window. Old photographs of a man and of a woman, together in a hinged frame, looked down from a chest of drawers—his parents, I supposed. Books were meticulously filed on the shelves, with new copies of his own works in amongst those of others. There were guidebooks too—I spotted the Lonely Planet guide to Bali and Lombok.

He had laid out a stack before I arrived—his own travel books, to give to me should I need them. But I already owned them all, so he went rifling along the shelves to see if there was anything else he could offer. He pulled out an old *Granta* travel writing collection—'You're welcome to have that copy if you wish; it's alright, I have two!'—and then reached for the latest volume of the magazine and handed me that too. It featured a series of essays pondering the question 'Is Travel Writing Dead?' I wasn't the only one wondering about that, then.

'I wonder, as somebody looking back on fifty years of travel writing, what *you* think its prospects are?' I asked.

'I wish I knew,' he said. 'It's so hard to tell. If I look at my contemporaries for a moment, I'm wondering if their careers or mine would be possible if one was literally starting up now.'

When it came to the world itself, however, belatedness had nothing to do with it. 'As one area falls off the map another becomes accessible,' he said, just as Nicholas Jubber had done. The old, informational approach of a writer going off into the wilds and bringing back knowledge of places quite unknown to his readership—the approach most likely to raise the ire of hostile scholars, with its obvious colonial parallels—*was* likely to fade away, he suspected. 'But I think there's a huge future in travel writing, simply because it's so flexible.'

He pointed to the new edition of *Granta*, with the names of several younger writers on the cover alongside his own: Rana Dasgupta, Mohsin Hamid, Samanth Subramanian.

'You'll find various reactions to this in that book,' he said. 'The voice of those once written about is coming back and writing about us, which is another element that's beginning to happen—these writers who are coming from somewhere else and who will give a different slant on it and another energy. I think that's another sort of element to which travel writing as a genre is immediately accessible. It can change itself to suit anybody that wants to write about what it means to be somewhere else. I think the future's there for travel writing, it's just not going to be travel writing as you and I perhaps recognise it.'

* * *

Outside I wandered slowly along the damp streets. I had come to Nicholas Jubber and Colin Thubron—both British travel writers with that formidably committed approach, but two literary generations apart—seeking reassurance, hoping to find that I wasn't too late. Both had been quite clear on that count: the world was still very much waiting to be written about, shifting and transforming with each season—

though travel writing might need to do a little shapeshifting of its own if it was to catch up.

I found myself on Holland Park Avenue. A genteel part of the capital, this, with broad pavements and tidy shopfronts. Between a pizzeria and an artisan butcher's shop stood a branch of Daunt Books, glowing like a jewel box in the greasy darkness. I went inside, and headed for the travel section.

6

THE TRAVEL WRITER WHO DISAPPEARED

Nice: a pale city by the sea; narrow balconies and mustard-coloured stucco, and a faint perfume of cigarillos in the shade on the narrower streets. The Avenue Jean Médecin was full of people tugging trolley cases. They gave the place an air of stifled mania with the whirring and clicking of their little plastic wheels over the joints in the pavement. An old man swam a slow backstroke in the dancing water off the Promenade des Anglais, and a quartet of young soldiers—two boys, two girls—patrolled in square formation under the ornamental date palms. They wore dark glasses and their guns looked like toys. Back from the seafront, on Cours Saleya, they were setting up trestle tables for the Monday flea market: battered chinoiserie and cracked porcelain cats; old maps of Algiers; vast quantities of tarnished cutlery, laid out carefully as if for some interminable banquet. A vendor sat on a packing case behind his stall, playing a flamenco guitar.

I went to the station and caught an eastbound train. There were glimpses of the Mediterranean to the right, and then we were in Monaco, across an unmarked border. I got down, and the train went on to Italy.

I sat in a café and scribbled in my notebook: 'A bustle of people pulling wheeled suitcases... narrow balconies, mustard-coloured masonry and stucco. A scent of cigarillos on the street in the morning...'

An elderly American man and an elderly English woman bickered viciously at the next table. He was heavyset, dressed in chinos, a baggy blue jacket and a sunhat. He looked a little like Paul Theroux. She was thin and wore pink and turquoise jogging gear. Their dialogue came so fast and harsh it sounded as though it had been scripted.

'I rarely get to see the real you,' he said.

'Count yourself lucky.'

'You're a real *bitch*, you know that?'

'I certainly *am*.'

'You're a delight.'

'Don't start sucking up to me now I'm famous.'

'Your *dog* is famous.'

'No, *I* am; they want to make a programme about me...'

Down at the harbour men in paint-splattered overalls were getting the yachts ready for the coming summer. The water was clear and there were small fish shoaling in the splintered sunlight. The hills rose steeply inland, with the town stepped up their lower slopes.

It was early afternoon now, and time for my appointment. I found the building, on a quiet street near the station. I pressed the bell. The speaker was broken, but the door clicked open and he was waiting in the hall outside his apartment on the top floor.

'Tim?'

'Nick?'

* * *

When I began to read travel writing in my late teens, one book made a particular impression. The cover showed a photograph of a dun hillside slanting away to a plain, and beyond it a ridge of ribbed brown mountains streaked with the shadow of late afternoon. In the foreground a party of men dressed in turbans and *shalwar kameez* strode into the distance, stirring up a smudge of yellow dust. The image stirred up something inside me too when I first saw it, and the contents matched its promise: an account of an eighteen-month journey 'Beyond Forbidden Frontiers', from Europe, via Afghanistan, all the way to China, complete with illegal border crossings and escapades in disguise. To an impressionable youth it wasn't the writing itself that was compelling, or even the subject matter, so much as what the book seemed to say about the figure of the travel writer: a hero, with his name in the very title—like Odysseus; like Gilgamesh. It was published in 1987.

I wasn't the only one taken this way. There seemed to be a battered copy in every backpackers' guesthouse in northern Pakistan and north-west India at the close of the twentieth century, title page stamped like a passport with the names of travellers' book exchanges all across Asia. And then there was a striking reference in a lightweight travelogue called *The Wrong Way Home* by the Australian author Peter Moore, published in 1999. Passing through Pakistan, loosely concerned with tracing the old 'Hippie Trail' of the 1960s and 70s, Moore and a fellow Australian called Keith donned turbans and *shalwar kameez* and got themselves briefly smuggled into Afghanistan. It was a moment not unlike Nicholas Jubber's clandestine foray into the shrine of Imam Reza, but Peter Moore did not hark back to Richard Burton or Robert Byron. Instead, he invoked a romantic hero who had travelled this way little more than a decade earlier: 'I got to dress up and pretend I was Nick Danziger…'[1]

* * *

'Oh God!' said Nick Danziger, grimacing and setting down his tea mug. I had mentioned the reference in *The Wrong Way Home*.[2]

We were sitting at the scrubbed wooden table in the little kitchen at the back of his apartment in Monaco. The window on my left gave out onto a view of an olive-green hillside hemmed by tower blocks. A framed panel from *Les Aventures de Tintin au pays des Soviets* hung above the old-fashioned white ceramic sink. There was a sound of drilling from somewhere outside.

'It's obviously awkward when people come up to you and say, "Oh you know…"' He grimaced again. 'I've had, "My son was going to go into banking until he read your book!" And you think, oh my God! Do I celebrate that? Or do I, you know… um… yeah…'

More than any of the other travel writers I had arranged to meet, I had been apprehensive when I first contacted Nick Danziger. It wasn't so much that I was hobbled by teenage hero-worship; I was long past that now—or so I hoped. Instead, it was the impression created by everything Danziger had done in the three decades since *Danziger's Travels*. His career seemed to have been defined by an utmost serious-ness. It was rather intimidating.

But in person he was anything but intimidating. He was in his late fifties, though like the other travel writers I'd met, he seemed somehow younger than his years, lightly built, with a buzz-cut head and hooded eyes. His accent was flat, neutral—certainly *English*, but without any indication of class background or geographical provenance, beyond the faintest hint of London. He was, I realised, the first person I'd spoken to so far on my journey who did not sound particularly posh.

He *was* serious—strikingly so. None of his answers to my questions were pat replies polished on literary festival stages, and when he finished making some important point he would lean forward and say, with real concern, 'Do you see?' or 'Does that make sense?' But all this was leavened by an air of great kindness.

The story of how he came to be sitting in this apartment in Monaco was one of the various remarkable things about Nick Danziger. He was born in London to wealthy parents—his father an American film-maker; his mother a British actress. But he grew up mostly in Switzerland, before going to study at Chelsea School of Art in the late 1970s. After graduating he successfully applied for a travel grant from the Winston Churchill Memorial Trust. It was supposed to fund a trip to Guatemala, but when political turmoil there made that impossible, he set out overland for China instead. *Danziger's Travels* was the result, a bone fide bestseller.

More books, photography and documentary-making followed, but Danziger was never a detached observer. In Kabul in the early 1990s he had stumbled upon a group of orphans, housed amongst mentally ill adults in an asylum. He started a project to establish a proper orphanage for them, and then to rehome them with local families. By 1996 there were only three children still waiting for fosterers, but the Taliban were about to take over the city and time was running out. Danziger decided to adopt them himself.

'Back then the UK government didn't recognise single-parent adoption. So I was stuck in Peshawar for over four months trying to find a country that would take us,' he said. One place that would, as it turned out, was Monaco. And not only that—as a single parent Danziger qualified for government housing. This was a government-subsidised apartment, perched high above the harbour and full of light.

'It's pretty amazing,' he said. 'The government here has really, really looked after us.'

The adopted children were all grown up now, but Danziger had since married a Belgian woman, a former ICRC delegate, and had three more children. His wife was away on an assignment at the moment, but the kids would be home from school later in the afternoon. Danziger was going to cook crêpes, he said, and I was welcome to stay and join them.

* * *

Going back to a book is like going back to a place.

Before I flew to the shores of the Mediterranean to seek out its author, I had reread *Danziger's Travels*. There was much that I remembered from two decades earlier: the route of the journey, many of the incidents, even some individual phrases. But there was much that came as a complete surprise. It was as if I'd returned to a foreign city having learnt the local language in the years since my previous visit. What was most surprising was what the book *lacked*.

Travel writing is often suffused with references, overt or covert, to the wider genre. You come almost to expect it as a reader, to be reassured by some cosy nod to Robert Byron or Peter Fleming. It helps to confirm that what you're reading really is travel writing. It might be Sara Wheeler flinging out mentions of Christopher Isherwood, Gavin Young and Paul Theroux left, right and centre as she travels through Chile. It might be Jason Elliot's quiet cap-doff to Patrick Leigh Fermor, in the form of an opening chapter to *An Unexpected Light* (1999) disguised as a letter to a friend. Or it might be another hugely successful travel writing debut about a journey eastwards across Asia, which appeared just two years after *Danziger's Travels*: William Dalrymple's *In Xanadu* (1989), a book so conscious of the literary tradition to which it belongs that it occasionally sags under its weight.

I've been doing it here myself too, naturally enough.

This is where the postcolonial scholars so often find reason to point a finger at travel writing. This is where Edward Said's idea of travellers 'falling back on a text' comes into play. And this is where travel writing supposedly struggles to free itself from its colonial heritage. A travel writer in the twenty-first century offers a nod to a writer in the 1980s; the writer in the 1980s offers a nod to a predecessor in the 1950s, and before anyone realises what's happening, they've all been hauled back to the colonial nineteenth century in a tangle of intertextuality. This tendency was particularly obvious in travel writing about Afghanistan, according to the scholar Corinne Fowler. British accounts of that country from both travel writers and journalists were, she convincingly argued, largely trapped in a continuous feedback loop, with contemporary authors forever falling back on colonial-era texts for their points of reference. Fowler also spotted a pattern of modern travel writers in Afghanistan conjuring up a sense of impending danger where no actual threat ever materialised. But grounding the ominous atmosphere in 'internalised cultural references'—as often as not a quick quote from Kipling's poems 'Arithmetic on the Frontier' and 'The Young British Soldier'[3]—gave it a gloss of legitimacy, while 'the provision of key details' provided 'an historical alibi to acquit the protagonist of the charge of irrational paranoia should the anticipated harm fail to be inflicted'.[4]

It came as a shock, then, when I went back to *Danziger's Travels* and discovered that I could not find a single reference—not even a heavily veiled one; not even a *suspicion* of one—to the travel writers who had passed this way before (Marco Polo excepted). There weren't many traces of 'internalised cultural references' either. I started trying to explain this, sitting in Danziger's Monaco kitchen with the light coming in through the window and the drilling still going on outside.

'One of the things that struck me,' I said, 'something that I had obviously missed when I first read it, partly because I was very young, partly because I didn't know travel writing as a genre...'

He cut in: 'Well *I* didn't when I set off on that journey either...'

'That's precisely what I was going to say! I was so struck by the fact that it is almost entirely without any acknowledgement or reference to travel writing.'

'I hadn't read travel writing,' said Danziger.

'Right!' For someone concerned by the criticisms levelled at the genre, this was rather exciting.

'I mean, Tintin was probably my inspiration,' he said.

Danziger *had*, he said, begun to read other travel writers in the years after *Danziger's Travels* was published. Wilfred Thesiger's *Arabian Sands* (1959) had been one of the first he'd encountered ('What an incredible journey!').

'Now I would say I'm better read, and better researched when I go to places. But I think there's something of getting a balance and not referring back constantly. Times move on. And I think it's also very British, if you look—the references. You know, I didn't have that classic British education either. A lot of those travel writers had a certain upbringing and a certain education, which I didn't fall into; that wasn't my background; whether it's liberating or not, I didn't have that.'

There was something else too, he said: 'When people say, "Oh, you know, cultures should be left as they are"—well, most of the people I come across, even today, they *want* roads and they *want* electricity because it takes them to clinics when they're ill, and to medication. So again, I'm probably slightly away from that sort of British nostalgia of what the world was once like. It's not where I'm coming from.'

Nick Danziger was not your typical travel writer.

* * *

After *Danziger's Travels* there was another book, *Danziger's Adventures*—a collection of travel pieces from around the world published in 1992. Then, in 1996, nine years after his debut, he published *Danziger's Britain*. I remembered seeing it under 'travel', back when that fiefdom occupied a fair chunk of bookshop territory. The familiar author's name, a stark monochrome cover and an arresting subtitle: 'A Journey to the Edge'. But for a long while I had shuffled on along the shelves. I was reading travel writing then for vicarious encounters with the exotic, and when I flicked through the photo sections in *Danziger's Britain* I saw things that were insufficiently unfamiliar. He'd even visited Cornwall.

I did read it later, though. It was striking: a series of written portraits of marginalised communities in post-Thatcher, pre-Blair Britain, in Leicester, Glasgow, Belfast—and yes, indeed, Cornwall. The photos, I saw at second glance, were striking too: black and white; in shabby living rooms and derelict places; intimately engaged with their subjects. What was most remarkable, though, was the shift from *Danziger's Travels*. The striding romantic hero of the first book was gone. There was still a first-person narrator of sorts, but when the book ventured into dirty bedsits and cold housing association flats its mode was quietly observational. Great swathes of the text were given over to the words of the people it portrayed. The travel writer himself had begun to disappear.

The idea for *Danziger's Britain*, he said, had begun to emerge during the lectures and discussions that came with the publication of his previous books.

'I realised at one point at the Royal Geographical Society in London, that actually the gathered audience could see what I was seeing in Mongolia a few miles down the road.'

But why, I wanted to know, had the hero-narrator of the earlier books disappeared? He still made occasional earnest interjections in *Danziger's Britain*, but the book's focus was solidly outwards. 'Were you uncomfortable with the heroic role of the travel writer?' I asked.

'Well, you know, vanity is such that...' He laughed, a little nervously, and paused. 'I mean I *was* slightly uncomfortable because obviously I think about all the people I leave behind... and, you know, I guess part of it is age. Now I'm a bit more diplomatic.'

This was not entirely out of the ordinary; other travel writers had made similar shifts in focus over the course of long careers, I said. But Danziger seemed to have done it in double-quick time—and in a period when commissioning editors were surely eager for more tales of derring-do in far-off lands.

'I realised, I think, that other people's stories are a lot more important. So I think it's a value thing...' He seemed, for some reason, to be wriggling slightly under my questioning. I pressed again.

'I know,' I said, 'but lots of people would have a consciousness of that. The other people I've talked to have mentioned that, but they haven't necessarily actioned it.'

'You know I look at other people's lives and I think they're the real heroes...'

'I hear that, but I'd just like to dig around in your own process of coming to that point, because I think that's the most interesting thing about you really, Nick—that rapid movement, that rapid trajectory. I'm just curious.' I could hear myself. I had not been this robust with the other travel writers I'd met. And yet all the way here—EasyJet flight to Nice, train along the coast, walk uphill from the harbour— there'd been that faint trepidation. Perhaps it was Danziger's unexpected air of gentle approachability; perhaps it was the intimacy of this little kitchen, with a bread-maker stacked atop the dishwasher and children's drawings on the wall.

'Well maybe...' he said. 'I'd become much better read. So that's one thing.'

The books he had in mind, though, were not by Wilfred Thesiger. They were George Orwell's *Down and Out in Paris and London* (1933), Jack London's *The People of the Abyss* (1903)—travel writing, more or less, according to the scholarly definitions of the genre, though not of the most obvious kind—and Hubert Selby Jr's *Last Exit Brooklyn* (1964), a novel. So, unlike *Danziger's Travels*, *Danziger's Britain* did have conscious, deliberate intertexts. And rather than drag it backwards into a mire of hoary tropes, they had driven its determination to give voice to its subjects.

* * *

The final thing I had wanted to understand, coming here, was what had happened after *Danziger's Britain*. It was the last full-length book that Danziger had written. But he had not retired or crept off into academia: he'd been busy taking photographs and making documentaries. In this he had been thoroughly successful, but as a travel writer, he had disappeared—and well before the contraction of the bookselling economy and the shift in publishing fashion which saw many of his peers vanish too. I wondered why he had stopped, having come up with a formula in his final book that seemed to do exactly what he wanted to do—letting people speak who did not normally get to do so, and reinforcing the message with intimate imagery. The answer was unexpected.

'What I did in *Danziger's Britain*, where I was taking notes—it was so intense that I couldn't actually do the writing and the photography at the same time. At one point I decided I'm going to take the notes, do the writing side, then I'll go back to the communities and do the photography.' It had simply taken too much time, too much energy, he said, to be a readily repeatable formula.

'Like now: I'm fully concentrated on what you're saying; I'm analysing, and you're probably listening to me. If I had a camera, I'd want to compose that image so that you've got the right expression, the right moment. I know for a fact through what I've done that sometimes when I'm really concentrated, what you're saying to me is disappearing. So that's what's difficult. If I want to listen to you I need to be fully focussed on what you're saying.'

I thought back to a spring afternoon in Cornwall, and to a vision of myself, fumbling with the settings of my camera while Philip Marsden waved his hands about and talked of estuarine oak trees. I'd only been after a usable shot for a magazine, but if it hadn't been for the fact that I'd left my recorder running I'd have had no idea afterwards what he'd spoken about.

Danziger mentioned Thesiger again: 'The quality of the photographs is far superior to anything I did in *Danziger's Travels*...'

I cut in: 'But I'm sure you're aware of the criticism of his photography?'

The people in Thesiger's famous images, beautifully composed though they were, often had the quality of pinned butterflies in a Victorian museum. They did not shift on their own terms the way people often seemed to do in the photos from *Danziger's Britain*.

'Yeah, yeah...'

'That the people don't have agency, in the way that the people in yours maybe do?'

'Yeah, so that's what I'm getting to! I cannot think of someone who's produced both to a level.'

It was a problem, he said, even when working on magazine photo-essays, still more full-length books. That morning, before I arrived, he had been preparing extended captions for a series of images of women in the Caucasus.

'I can't just write "ninety-year-old woman, lives on her own". There's more; there's a paragraph, which gives you a better idea of who this individual is in the picture. I want the story as well, and I miss things. Like one of these, I didn't know what had happened to the husband; if I'd only been doing the writing I think I would have not missed that.'

This was why, in recent years, Danziger had often chosen to work on joint projects with other travel writers—Rory MacLean in particular, but also Tahir Shah and Philip Marsden. Covering the lives of people in war zones and refugee camps, sometimes following individuals over many years, Danziger had taken care of the imagery and left the recording of the words to others. It was necessary, he said, to do the job properly.

He leant forward across the table. 'I think it's really important with my work that it's not seen as, "Oh, she's from Afghanistan, she's from Sierra Leone, she's from Gaza, she's from wherever", because actually no; it's Dzidza, it's Mariatu, it's Mah Bibi—they are *women*, they are *individuals*, rather than labelling a country or further stigmatising. I try to say to people that with the stories that I have—I go to a lot of primary schools—it's not important where you go; it's what you do. And I think that goes back to the Britain thing. You don't have to go very far. Can you see what I'm trying to get at? So it's not the idea of "let's go and do a travel book about Mongolia..."'[5]

The telephone rang down the hall. It was Danziger's children, on their way home from school.

'Does all of that make a bit of sense?' he said when he came back to the kitchen. It did, but I wanted to push it just a little further. Even if Danziger, with or without a writing accomplice, gave all the focus of his craft to the people in front of the lens—or across the table—there was still a presence, a storyteller; privileged, educated, a white European male. Danziger's name had been there in the title of his book about Britain (though he did have a reasonable excuse at that stage, with two similarly titled books behind him: 'It was a genre, I was stuck with it!'). Was there any way that the task could be handed over entirely to the people the travel writer met?

'Well that's what I do!' he said brightly. Danziger was a very busy man, and amongst his many other commissions he had, for several years, been running workshops in Myanmar, teaching local people the techniques of documentary-making in the name of human rights advocacy.[6]

This all sounded very admirable, but I wondered if the people who attended these workshops would ever be able to take their stories to an audience.

'Okay, so that's really interesting that you should say that—and then I have to get on with crêpe-making!' Danziger said. 'I feel that I've given some the tools to tell their stories, which they can do, often adequately, and often not only very well but better than I can do. But then how do they get them known? So now my next workshop in Myanmar will also include a section on how they get their stories out there…'

'And how *do* they get their stories out there?'

'Well in Myanmar, for example, the last workshop I had, we asked them to produce short films, three minutes long. So out of the three films, one was seen 250,000 times on Facebook, and the other has been taken up by the UN and a university in Australia for a curriculum. So, you know, I'm constantly trying.'

If he kept on trying, the travel writer really might disappear altogether.

* * *

He started making the crêpes—'No, no! Stay! I said you could!'

Nick Danziger, Afghanistan-bestriding backpackers' hero, was very deft with a whisk and a mixing bowl. He cracked the eggs one-handed. The kitchen was small, and I moved to the other side of the table to give him space. The telephone kept ringing—the children coming in from different angles. I was still thinking about Danziger's own visits to other government-subsidised flats, in the Britain of the early 1990s.

'I think it was in *Danziger's Britain* you make that point, quoting George Bernard Shaw—about no Englishman being able to open his mouth without some other Englishman hating him—and that you in a way were able to sidestep that because of your internationalism…'

'Totally!' He cracked another egg into the bowl. 'I mean, you know, with *Danziger's Britain* I got a lot of access to a lot of those communities because they didn't see me as particularly posh.'

It was true. I had no trouble at all imagining Colin Thubron visiting a bleak tenement in Siberia or China, but it was somehow harder to imagine him on a British council estate.

'I was amazed when I started reading travel books,' Danziger said, 'including Wilfred Thesiger. I mean, I was *horrified*, to be honest with you. They're *all* public school-educated, you know, top-flight… I mean, I went to an international school, but it's like, hang on a second! What is it that's produced this? Do you know what I mean? And India! They all go to India at some point!'

He saw his own identity, he said, as neither British nor American (though he had inherited American citizenship from his father) but European.

The door clattered open and the children came in. Danziger called down the hall: 'Come and meet Tim; come and have a crêpe!'

Sam and Freya, twins aged eleven, and thirteen-year-old May, were willowy, French-accented and precocious—though Danziger had to remind them to speak English from time to time. They jostled with each other to tell stories of their own travels with their parents in Asia and Africa while their father dished up the crêpes.

State schools here in tiny, wealthy Monaco were well integrated, Danziger said. 'You have the children of people who own three smart cars, and the children of the people who clean the streets together.'

Sam piped up: 'But there is also ISM; you can have sushi in the canteen there!' This was the local international school, serving a transient expat population. One of the students there, met at an inter-school sports day, was the son of a famous Formula One racing driver, Sam said, sounding thoroughly impressed by this fact.

'Yeah,' I mumbled through a mouthful of crêpe, 'but *your* dad is *Nick Danziger!*'

Danziger, standing at the stove, angling the frying pan over the flame as he poured in more crêpe mix, rolled his eyes and grinned: 'Oh God!'

* * *

That evening, back in Nice, I wandered in the tight alleys of the Vieille Ville. I ate a bowl of mussels in a café, then sat for a while, scribbling more notes: 'kitchen, view to mountain between tower blocks, drilling outside, Tintin picture on wall, bread-maker on the dishwasher…'

We had covered many topics in our conversation, but I kept thinking back to one little cluster: Thesiger, schools, accents. My flight back to the UK was booked for the following morning, and I knew where I needed to go next.

7

A CLASS OF THEIR OWN

The box file came open like an oyster: a hard black bivalve debossed with gold leaf, and the diaries inside like living matter. I lifted them out gingerly. One had its long spine bound together with sticking plaster; another had a cover of pale leather so soft that it seemed ready to melt through my fingers. In the neighbouring office an archivist rustled at some careful task, and the world beyond the high windows was full of a jet, howling out of Heathrow. But I was alone in the reading room.

I placed the first diary from the box before me. As I read the label pasted to the cover, birds took flight in my belly: 'W. Thesiger, Rub' al Khali 1945–46'.

* * *

Nick Danziger spoke of him as one of the very first travel writers he had ever read—*after* his own first book was written. Nicholas Jubber made that curious comment about the unattainable standards of his experience. Other writers I spoke to mentioned him too. It seemed that you couldn't discuss British travel writing without Wilfred Thesiger's bony figure appearing over the crest of a distant dune.

He had been part of my own private travel writing canon from the very beginning. In my late teens I had sometimes even called him my hero: a craggy superman bestriding deserts and mountain passes, seemingly insensible to all physical hardship and yet capable of writing with great elegance about the places he had visited. Later, of course, the veneration shaded into discomfiture as I began to encounter critical scholarship around travel writing. Here, surely, was the epitome of the elite traveller, obsessed with the aesthetic qualities of otherness and determined to fix the places he visited in a changeless past, railing against globalisation and proclaiming *his* Bedu ruined by the arrival of the motor car in the Middle East. Here too was a traveller almost deliberately condemning his successors to an insurmountable belatedness: 'I went to Southern Arabia only just in time', he had written, and many of those who followed seemed to believe him.[1] The accounts that others had written of Thesiger's life—with all its chauvinism and hypocrisy—had further helped do away with any lingering adolescent hero-worship. But the books remained, and the idea of reaching out and touching the diaries he had written during his journeys was thrilling.

* * *

Wilfred Thesiger was born in 1910 in Addis Ababa where his father—younger son of the second Baron Chelmsford and brother to the future Viceroy of India—was British consul-general. Thesiger was schooled in England—Eton and Oxford—and then began a lifetime of travel. There were journeys in Ethiopia and Sudan, journeys which, perhaps self-consciously, seemed to belong to the Victorian age rather than the middle decades of the twentieth century—with their long trains of laden mules and legions of local servants. Then there were years in the Arabian Peninsula, ostensibly surveying for the Middle East Anti-Locust Unit, but generally wandering the deserts at will. He crossed the Rub' al Khali, the 'Empty Quarter' at the core of the peninsula, twice—in 1946 and 1947. After leaving the desert he spent six winters in the marshes of southern Iraq, shifting in the hotter part of the year to the mountains of Kurdistan, Afghanistan and Pakistan. Later, he returned to the continent of his birth and stayed with an irregular household of hangers-on on a hilltop in Kenya. But between these spells abroad he lived in his mother's flat in Chelsea and strutted around London with a bowler hat and a furled umbrella.

Thesiger was not like Colin Thubron or Philip Marsden: men who were writers foremost and for whom the journey itself was a conscious first draft. He did *not* travel to write, but that is precisely what gives his work its lustre. His first book, *Arabian Sands*, was published in 1959; *The Marsh Arabs* came five years later. They seem to be things received, not made, their stentorian prose emerged from the desert like scripture. The journeys and the texts that describe them are somehow indistinguishable. They are books made of a native metal. Or so I thought.

Thesiger died in August 2003—not on an African hilltop or an Afghan mountainside, but in a nursing home in Surrey. I remember hearing the news the morning after a late shift in a Cornish restaurant kitchen, lying in bed with the heat of the day already rising and the *Today* programme on BBC Radio 4 stitching strange patterns into the fabric of my half-sleep. I had a month in the mountains of Morocco planned for the coming autumn. 'The explorer Sir Wilfred Thesiger has died at the age of ninety-three...' the announcer said in the eight o'clock bulletin, and I came to instantly and wished that I had had the chance to meet him.

Thesiger left the bulk of his papers—diaries, letters, manuscripts—to his old school. And so, on a bright Monday morning somewhere between winter and spring nearly two decades later, I drove into the frantic metropolitan thermosphere that lies to the west of London to spend a week in the Eton College Archives.

* * *

The reading room was on the first floor at the back of School Yard—the broad quad at the heart of the College. It was a small square space with a table at the centre. I had it to myself. The shelves around the walls were loaded with bound blue volumes of *The Eton Chronicle*, and books with such titles as *The Elevens of Three Great Schools* and *The Eton Boating Book*. Every half hour the bell in College Chapel rang. There was a great thud behind its tolling, like the beating of the *bedhug* drum at a Javanese mosque.

The room had a distinctive smell. For me, the aromas of individual reading rooms always have incongruous associations, based on the materials I have read within them. That of the Royal Geographical Society map room—mainly industrial cleaning products, I think—is the smell of the high passes of the Himalayas in the 1860s. In my mind, the colonial offices and royal courts of Southeast Asia during the years of the Napoleonic Wars have the aroma of the Asian and African Studies Reading Room in the British Library—made up of furniture polish and overheated photocopiers for the most part. And now I know that the smell of the Eton archives—cleaning products again, with an added hint of something educational, rather like Plasticine—will forever be that of Wilfred Thesiger's wild campsites.

I began with his earliest diaries. In 1930, a twenty-year-old Thesiger had been invited to join the official British delegation to the coronation of Haile Selassie in Ethiopia—the country of his own birth. This was the royal progress of an exceptionally well-connected young man, and the first entry, for 16 October, read: 'departed Victoria 1.50 PM. Introduced to HRH on the train'.[2] The HRH in question was not the Ethiopian Emperor, but the Duke of Gloucester.

Thesiger wrote in a cramped but consistent hand, always filling the recto page of the little burgundy notebook with his daily entries and leaving the verso empty for later insertions and amendments—a nice professional touch, that. But I was disappointed to discover that most of the entries were perfunctory notes. Perhaps I'd been hoping to find the resounding prose and crystalline images of the later books.

The diaries did fill out somewhat after Selassie's coronation, when the young Thesiger headed off on his first safari, into the home country of the Danakil people, having rebuffed various would-be European companions and equipped himself with a vast retinue of local staff. This was a safari of the old-fashioned sort, and the slaughter that ensued was appalling. Wild pig, lesser kudu, waterbuck, crocodile and oryx were gunned down in vast numbers. On 28 November, Thesiger wrote: 'Hit a hyena with the 400. Lots of blood and looking very sick, but it got into the reeds and we lost it.' Why would you want to shoot a hyena, I wondered?

He didn't shoot any people, although as he travelled out of the Danakil lands and into Oromo country the diary took on a distinctly ominous tone:

> Dec. 5 [...] Have an unpleasant feeling of being in a hostile country. No Gallas [the colonial name for the Oromo people] even come into camp or bring presents. We are constantly being watched from the hilltops but they always vanish as we approach.[3]

If this had been a published piece of travel writing I might have raised an eyebrow here, suspecting the wilful inflation of a sense of threat for dramatic purposes. But this was not a crafted book; this was the daily journal of a twenty-year-old travelling without compatriots in a foreign land. I underscored the line about 'being watched from the hilltops' in my own notebook—Mary Louise Pratt's famed concept of the monarch-of-all-I-survey mode in imperial travel writing nicely inverted, there!

In the end no disaster befell the young traveller, though he had some important reflections to make at the end of the journey: 'Forgot to order curry powder, a serious mistake…'[4]

This journey and this diary were Thesiger's beginning, equivalent to Colin Thubron's family trip through the Middle East and the resultant manuscript. But there was absolutely no hint of writerly intent here, no flash of lyricism or self-reflection. I thought for a moment of my own earliest travel diaries—covering a five-month backpacking trip through India, also written at the age of twenty. They featured no massacred wildlife and no hostile tribespeople watching from the hills, but the entries were full of impressionistic detail.

* * *

At lunchtime they evicted me from the archives for an hour, and I went out into the cold sunlight. The high sky was crayoned with vapour trails, and a stiff breeze blew down Eton High Street. A pair of old men, wrapped in winter jackets, were gazing at the glossy images in the window of a wedding photographer's studio. A few boys from the College came past, rook-like figures in pinstriped trousers, black tails and white ties. Most walked with a slight stoop—adopted, perhaps, out of self-consciousness on the first day in the uniform, and then made a habit. Two of them stood in the queue at the Budgens supermarket where I bought a sandwich for my lunch. They looked like members of a hill tribe, spotted amongst the townsfolk in a weekly bazaar.

At the southern end of the High Street a bridge arched across the Thames, and beyond it Windsor Castle leapt suddenly into view, startlingly close; a great battleship of a thing, far bigger than I had ever realised. The willows beside the river were showing their first buds, and the water was busy with ducks. Heathrow lay within earshot to the east, and the planes came up like missiles in the space between college and castle.

* * *

In the afternoon I came to the black box containing the five Arabian diaries, covering the years between 1945 and 1950 when Thesiger had stalked back and forth across the sands.

It was the possibility of viewing these that had thrilled me most of all. *Arabian Sands*—the book he wrote about this period, and which I had first encountered in a battered Everyman edition in a second-hand bookshop in Penzance—thrilled me as much on each rereading as on the very first. It had been written a decade after the journeys it described, but the sound, the scent, the sensation of individual moments came off the page with every detail complete. I could easily forgive any uncomfortable Orientalist traces, for *Arabian Sands* seemed to represent the very essence of travel writing: a work of perfect recall; the author as camera with all hifalutin literary performance stripped aside. And now the original accounts of the journeys that had made the book lay before me.

I opened the first diary:

May 3rd. Read "Sons of Sinbad" by Villiers. Good.

May 4th. Went round the suqs. Interesting and unspoilt but very expensive.[5]

The flock of desert birds in my belly settled slowly back onto their perches.

I went on through the entries. The lettering was faint in places, but the names of places and people were always blocked in in capitals in the first instance. As in the earlier diaries, the left-hand page had been left blank, but there were few later additions and only a smattering of ethnographic gleanings.

I found the original account of the first meeting with Salim bin Kabina, one of the two teenagers whom, it seems perfectly reasonable to say, Wilfred Thesiger loved in some way during his time in the Arabian Peninsula. The diary entry was dated 1 February 1946: 'Wandered round collecting with SALIM bin Mohamed an Imami boy.' 'Mohamed' had been later crossed out with red biro, and 'KABINA'

written in above. 'He is about 17 and is to be circumcised shortly [...]
Collected a stick insect, a butterfly and several different grasshoppers.'
The following day he added another cursory note: 'Collected with
SALIM bin Mohamed in the morning. Enlisted Salim at 2 $ a day.'[6]

In *Arabian Sands* there was no mention of any two-dollar daily wage,
and no mention of any 'enlisting' either; instead bin Kabina simply
'announced that he was coming with me'.[7] Thesiger had once told the
writer Michael Asher that 'There was no question of bin Kabina being
a servant or being paid. He wouldn't have risked his life for me under
those circumstances. The last thing I wanted was a master-servant relationship with the Bedu.'[8] What was more, the scene in the book
unfolds as Thesiger and his party 'worked day and night in relays' to
water their camels at a meagre well. There is categorically no wandering around in pursuit of butterflies.

There was something else too. In *Arabian Sands*, bin Kabina speaks
here—an impassioned tale of hardship.[9] It is the first of many times that
his words are heard. Indeed, the whole book brims with dialogue
between Thesiger and his companions—each a distinctive personality
speaking with his own voice, and all of it with the authentic cadence of
a verbatim account.

I went forward and back through the journal, peering more closely
at the faded entries now, and scanning both right- and left-hand pages.
There was not a single line of recorded speech. The flutter in my belly
reconfigured as a dull ache.

* * *

Each morning that week I came in to the College. I collected my visitor's
pass on its red lanyard from the porter's lodge by the gate, then crossed
the cold, scrubbed stones of School Yard, passing the central statue of
Henry VI with his orb and sceptre, the College Chapel rising like a petri-
fied stegosaur to the right. The Chapel bell thudded out the half-hours,
and the minutes between were marked by the passing planes.

I saw little of College life, though one day a boy in sports gear came
and sat at the far corner of the reading room table and fiddled with his
mobile phone for half an hour with a book open before him. Once I
heard a voice in the corridor: 'Her horse has been *terribly* ill; the vet's
been called, but he's had to be called again today...' I only know that

these words were spoken because I reached for my notebook the moment I heard them.

At lunchtimes I sat in my car in the visitors' car park and ate my sandwiches, and every day I saw variations of the same family group arrive. A large car would nudge into one of the parking spaces, and three figures would emerge with deliberate slowness. There would be a man and a woman in their forties, gym-slim and expensively clothed. With them would be a boy, ten or eleven years old, as often as not dressed in the peppermint shorts and blazer of a prep school. Somehow, the woman always seemed to be the least engaged member of the group, clutching a large mobile phone in long fingers as they made their way unhurriedly across the car park towards wherever it was that prospective new boys were presented. Only the men talked to the boys. Once I saw a father drop his hand gently onto his son's shoulder as they passed out of view.

Wilfred Thesiger suffered horribly at his own prep school, St Aubyn's in Rottingdean—a mild, damp, English Channel setting not dissimilar to that of Rudyard Kipling's 1889 short story, 'Baa Baa Black Sheep'. By his own account he was an awkward boy—an awkwardness he liked to ascribe to his early years in Addis Ababa, outside conventional British society, and to the fact that his father had died when he was just nine years old. He was preyed upon by a violent headmaster, Robert Vaughan Lang, who would strip him naked and thrash him with a riding whip until he bled. In old age, speaking to his official biographer Alexander Maitland, Thesiger seems to have made it clear that the abuse was overtly sexual too, though 'He denied being upset by Lang examining and touching him.'[10] It has always struck me as odd that anyone should make light of such experiences, and odder still that anyone might be ready to take Thesiger's own blithe dismissal of their significance at face value. After all, the strange course of his life certainly suggested a man in some way damaged. Maybe it had everything to do with Thesiger's class: the aristocratic ancestry; the elite education; the priceless social connections. Would a biographer tackling a subject from a less rarefied background be so ready to glide past a tale of child abuse?

Whatever happened at St Aubyn's, Thesiger was happy at Eton. It was, he claimed, the place where he 'learnt responsibility, the decencies of life, and standards of civilised behaviour'.[11] The fact that he chose the school as the final repository for his papers suggests some urge to return. Perhaps he never really left. In Arabia and beyond, his preferred society seems always to have been a small group of young men and boys, possessed of some elite and initiated status, perfectly isolated from the great plurality of town and village, free from obvious familial and economic responsibilities, and with an inevitable homo-eroticism latent, if not manifest. And between these terms abroad with the boys—until he was sixty-three years old, when finally she passed away—he always came home to his mother Kathleen.

* * *

At the end of each day in the Eton archives I drove two miles north, under the shrieking motorway and past the rows of Polski skleps, chicken shops and halal butchers, to a narrow white bedroom in a cheap guesthouse beside a primary school in Slough. When I got in on the second evening, a bare-chested man with a Liverpool accent was stalking the breakfast room, looking for a fork so he could eat his instant noodles.

* * *

I worked my way into the diaries from the 1950s. These were red notebooks, small enough to fit into a pocket, and the words inked on the covers were at least enough to set my belly-birds briefly aflutter: Hunza, Chitral, Nuristan. The entries, however, were always cursory and functional.

I found Thesiger's own version of his encounter with Eric Newby and his travelling companion, the British diplomat Hugh Carless, in the Panjshir Valley in Afghanistan in 1956. This meeting produced perhaps the most famous—and funniest—closing line in British travel writing. At the end of *A Short Walk in the Hindu Kush*, Newby describes the supremely hardy Thesiger watching in disgust as the lesser travellers (who have actually just endured some fairly horrific high-altitude con-ditions) prepare for the night by inflating their airbeds. 'God,' he says, 'you must be a couple of pansies...'[12]

But there was no trace of this incident in the diary:

31st July [...] I stopped at SHANAIZE having just run into Hugh Carless and Eric Newby. They have been trying for the past 20 days to

91

climb the 20000 peak ['Mir Samir' was inked in later here]. They got to within 300 feet of the top. Too small a party and the locals would not carry on the mountain. They could not get their camp high enough. Spent the night together in an apricot orchard above the village. Cool.[13]

Further up the valley, Thesiger detected a certain trail of offence amongst the local women: 'I suspect Newby had been trying to photograph them.'

I went back to the Arabia diaries too. Going through them a second time I noticed something peculiar. They spanned the entire five years Thesiger had spent travelling in the Arabian Peninsula, but they did not cover the two crossings of the Empty Quarter, the central journeys recorded in *Arabian Sands*. The Eton archivist could not explain this anomaly.[14] I did, though, find the letters Thesiger had sent to his mother as soon as he completed the crossings.

On 26 February 1947 he wrote to her from the Omani coast:

Dearest Mother

I have got back to Salalah after accomplishing all and more than I had hoped to achieve [...] I have just finished what is I think the hardest journey yet done in Arabian exploration and one of the longest.

Here there *was* a little more colour, and even a few faint hints of the familiar prose style:

The sands were unbelievable. Mountainous dunes rising 700 [feet] from the gravel floor below so that I had a constant delusion of being among mountains, and the salt flats show blue like lakes far below [...] we rode night and day to get across before our camels failed us or our water finished. Yet hard work as it was I loved it, and am more than ever bitten by the sands. They are wonderful and supremely lovely.[15]

Still, it was a flimsy foundation for a book, and towards the end he lurched off abruptly to respond to his mother's own domestic concerns—'What wicked weather you seem to have been having. It is a relief to know you had plenty of coal in.' He also asked her to tell his brother to 'chase the RGS over my articles. They won't get any account of this journey if they don't publish the other ones.' Was *this* writerly ambition, or simply an explorer's self-importance?

* * *

The empty space between Thesiger's Arabian diaries and the book that covered the same territory was far wider than I had ever expected. I had borrowed a copy of *Arabian Sands* from the Eton library by this stage—a fine first edition, heavy as a bag of sugar in my hand—and reading even a few lines of it only made the chasm yawn wider. So in the second half of the week, I abandoned the diaries and called up other black boxes—those containing the papers around the production of the book itself.

The story goes that Thesiger had never intended to pen a book. But in the mid-1950s the literary agent Graham Watson convinced him to try to write in detail about his journeys in Arabia, and in doing so discovered a formidable talent. In the winter of 1956–7 Thesiger had locked himself in a hotel room—in Copenhagen, of all places—and produced the first draft. It appeared in print two years later. *This* journey was not a business of desert wells and Bedu encampments. It was a course plotted between the smoky offices of publishers and agents, ringing with the rattle of typewriters. There were no more battered diaries, sitting stolidly inside their box files. Instead, there was a mille-feuille of bundled correspondence, drafts and typescripts in creamy envelopes, and a folder of photographs for possible inclusion. There was something more forceful about these images—some instantly familiar, some unknown—as loose prints rather than as plates stitched into a book. Here was the arresting portrait of Salim bin Ghabaisha, the second of Thesiger's beloved teenage companions in the desert, his tousled head coquettishly tilted, the camera thrust so close that his face has fallen slightly out of focus. On the reverse the word 'MUST' was underscored in Thesiger's hand.

The first things I looked at closely were two tatty school exercise books, identified in the archive catalogue as 'early chapter notes' for *Arabian Sands*. The moment I opened them I realised that I had been on entirely the wrong track, trudging dutifully through the diaries. My journey was in search of travel *writing*, after all.

There was none of the professional order of the diary entries here. The exercise books were a maelstrom of fragmented thoughts, images and instructions, shot through with a rainbow of coloured biro. They were undated, but I had the sense that they had been present throughout the writing of the book—and they gave a powerful impression of chaos and confusion. At times they appeared to feature the earliest tentative jottings; elsewhere they suggested notes for revisions to an existing text; and in yet other places they included tormented labours over a single passage.

The first legible entry—scrawled inside the front cover of the first exercise book in a hand far less controlled than that of the diaries, and later scribbled out with red ink—seemed like a belligerent yell: 'Kill a camel and drink from its stomach, or shove a stick down its throat and make it sick and drain this through cloth.'[16] It was followed by a quote from the apocalyptic Isaiah 32 about 'the shadow of a great rock in a weary land'.

There were all manner of fleeting impressions—'The wind like opening an oven door'; 'Wondered if we should die of exposure'— and an occasional hard-headed calculation: '16 chapters at 8000 words = 128000'. There was a long list of numbered 'incidents', all later crossed out, and a list of 'memories' likewise; and what seemed at times to be ethnographic notes gleaned from some other text. In places he seemed to be trying out a précis for an individual chapter—and these suggested less a travel book than a sort of popular ethnography, detailing marriage customs and history, and devoid of any personal stories. Occasionally—frustrated by the writing process, perhaps—he launched into a private tirade:

> Value of Freedom [...] We think that Communism can be stopped with wars and raising the standard of living. Balls [...] We are obsessed with comfort [...] I know that you can do with very little. Modern life cluttered up with inessentials. Takes you 2 hours to get up in the morning.[17]

And later:

> [...] welfare state, the very name is damnation [...] alien world [...] aircraft, cars [...] wireless, television, tarmac ribbon development, neon lighting, Rock and Roll. Indifferent what happens. A malignant growth which we call progress.[18]

This was the screed of a man ensconced in a comfortable Copenhagen hotel. Sometimes there were little notes-to-self of the kind that writers often scribble. One of them brought me up short: 'Get al Auf to describe Bedu life.'[19] I reached for the first edition of *Arabian Sands*. Al Auf was the guide on the first crossing of the Empty Quarter, a figure of great wisdom in Thesiger's description, and a man who speaks often and with apparent authority in the book. But could I be sure that they were really his own words?

At one point in the second exercise book Thesiger spent half-a-dozen pages fiddling with a single passage: 'We had come here dropping the weary miles behind us like beads on the rosary of time, to this high place on the threshold of the sands to look upon this vision of the dawn...'[20] In the pages that followed he worked over it again and again with a palpable frustration, the phrases shunted back and forth along the thread of the paragraph: *beads upon a rosary of time... threshold of the dawn... seeking the desert shrine... colours of the opal... rosary of time...*

I reached for *Arabian Sands* again, and found the ultimate iteration in chapter 11:

> We reached the Aradh at one o'clock and camped two hours later in a shallow watercourse on the limestone plateau. We were across the Sands.
>
> The valleys when I woke at dawn were filled with eddying mist, above which the silhouettes of the dunes ran eastwards, like fantastic mountains towards the rising sun. The sky glowed softly with the colours of the opal. The world was very still, held in a fragile bowl of silence. Standing on this far threshold of the Sands I looked back, almost regretfully, the way we had come.
>
> We reached the Hassi three days later [...][21]

Thesiger's seemingly effortless blend of lyricism and restraint had not come easy, it seemed.

I turned to the first handwritten manuscript. I knew that Thesiger had sent his drafts to his friend Val ffrench Blake for feedback, but I was unprepared for the extent or the stridency of the input. Every page swarmed with ffrench Blake's livid marginalia in green ink, and his systematic underlining—straight for 'cliché', squiggly for 'faulty construction'.[22]

In the first version of the book's opening Thesiger had written: 'The wind wipes out their footprints as the waves wash out the vessel's wake', and ffrench Blake's green pen had come thrusting in: 'Just too many Ws. Wind, waves, and wake OK; but not wash and wipe as well. It's too purple and will alarm the sensitive reader.'

It went on, page after page: 'No, too clumsy'; 'Very clumsy'; 'A clumsy sentence'. Where Thesiger called the Bedu 'laughter-loving', ffrench Blake cut him down ('awful travelogue word!'); and where he talked of mountains 'stripped of earth' and 'crumbling away' he was curtly told that 'Earth is made by the rocks crumbling away. Check your geology.' Ffrench Blake demanded that Thesiger up the sense of jeopardy in the sections about crossing the Empty Quarter, and called for climaxes where chapters tailed off weakly. Elsewhere he strode in to save Thesiger from himself, as when the explorer claimed never to have had enough interest in technology to listen to a wireless: 'Don't say it! It makes you sound a philistine or a prig...'

Val ffrench Blake—a military man and occasional writer on the training of horses—had first met Thesiger at Eton, a younger boy in the circle of a teenager who was, by many accounts, a bully. Ffrench Blake himself described the schoolboy Thesiger as 'a thug'.[23] Was some kind of revenge being played out here, I wondered? It didn't matter, for he was a magnificent editor, and under his lash Thesiger's distinctive style began to emerge.

Alongside the annotated manuscripts there were letters from Graham Watson of the literary agency Curtis Brown, the man who had supposedly first inveigled Thesiger to try his hand at travel writing. The letters spanned three years, and they confirmed what the exercise books suggested: the writing process had been an almighty struggle. More than once Watson had to deliver a pep talk to his client, beset by crises of confidence in the Copenhagen hotel room. There were stern orders too, to 'loosen up, take the reader into your confidence'; much enthusiastic agreement with ffrench Blake's criticism; and word that the publishers at Longmans were worried that the working title—'The Weary Land', presumably from that quoted verse in the Book of Isaiah—might have 'a somewhat sedative effect'. There were also warnings about the astronomical typists' bill that Thesiger was running up with his densely handwritten drafts ('they say that the writing is particularly difficult and they are having to charge by the hour').[24]

At one point, with Thesiger apparently lost in the weeds, Watson suggested a total change of direction:

> I am not sure that you would not be better advised to abandon any idea
> of a day by day account pinned to an individual journey and write

instead a generalised study of the area [...] There is no reason therefore, to my mind, why you should not devote individual chapters to
their way of life, or their marriage customs, or life in the desert, or
their historical origins [...][25]

This seemed strangely familiar. Nicholas Jubber's agent had also
suggested abandoning the travelogue for a more formal ethnographic
account. Happily, the advice went unheeded here too, and eventually
Arabian Sands was published. On 26 October 1959, a relieved Watson
wrote to Thesiger again:

You must be permanently a delicate shade of pink, glowing with satis-
faction at all these wonderful reviews. I imagine that they are spurring
you on to new thoughts and that you are already sharpening your pen-
cils [...] We want the definitive book on the Marshes; we want a book
about Abyssinia; we want a book—at least I feel there is one there—
about your wanderings in Kurdistan and adjoining part [...] I believe
that you would now find that such writing would come much more
easily and much more enjoyably now that you have mastered so
superbly well the craft.[26]

He was off at last, but what a struggle it had been! Thesiger had filled
his first travel diary three decades earlier, but only now was he a travel
writer.

* * *

One evening, after they closed the archives, I wandered through the
quiet lanes west of Eton High Street, past the various school houses
with their signs for the lodges of housemaster and dame. It was damp
and still, and I came out into the expanse of playing fields and turned
south. In the bare branches of a tree beside a muddy path hundreds of
green ring-necked parakeets—descendants of escaped pets, somehow
established around the western fringes of London—were chattering
furiously. I walked on. Windsor Castle surfaced like a submarine
ahead. On the bridge over the Thames a group of Chinese tourists were
taking selfies in the fading light. I stopped nearby and watched the
planes coming out of Heathrow in the darkling sky.

This place—castle, airport, college—seemed like the nexus of
something. The British Establishment? A faded empire? Travel writing
itself? Thesiger was by no means the only travel writer schooled here.

Later, I made a list in my notebook of all the significant male British travel writers I could think of from the last hundred years, alongside their places of schooling. Nick Danziger was right: almost every one had been to what are now called 'independent schools'—and generally to the more prestigious amongst them. Marlborough, Lancing, Rugby and Ampleforth all featured. But one place was dramatically dominant on the list: Eton seemed to have produced travel writers like nowhere else. I made another column beside the first list. This one featured an even greater single-institution dominance. Over and over, travel writers turned out to have degrees from Oxford; and down the decades, from Peter Fleming to Rory Stewart, Eton–Oxford was the paramount combination—just as it was for British prime ministers. This, then, was an elite genre, for all its occasionally disreputable literary status.

I walked back north along the High Street towards the visitors' car park in the gloaming. All of this—this place—prompted strange sensations.

Travel writing seems at times to belong more firmly to the upper tiers of the British class system than any other genre, and its pages are full of signals to that effect. Even in recent British travel books, passing mentions of boarding school are not unusual, and the genre is suffused with casual classical references. When Thesiger described his first beguiled encounter with the beautiful seventeen-year-old bin Ghabaisha, he declared that 'Antinous must have looked like this, I thought, when Hadrian first saw him in the Phrygian woods.'[27] This was not the sort of learning that you got at a county comprehensive or a technical college.

If Thesiger had come from a different background he would never have had the chance to travel to Haile Selassie's coronation in the party of the Duke of Gloucester, and without that peculiar blessing known for some reason as a 'private income', he might at some point have faced the need to get a real job. But more than that, without a certain inherited assurance, would he—or any of the other great travel writers before and since—have taken so naturally to going forth and declaiming authoritatively in foreign lands? Would he even have had a natural interest in books by other people about such places? Who exactly was that 'we' that Graham Watson had spoken of in his letter to Thesiger after the publication of *Arabian Sands*, craving definitive books on

Abyssinia and the Iraqi marshes? Not quite a royal 'we', but perhaps some distinctly elite collective. During my conversation with Colin Thubron, he had talked of 'certain assumptions' which a travel writer, until very recently, could hold about his readership: 'that they would share, more or less, your kind of knowledge, a certain knowledge of history and even classical history and biblical history...'

Discovering travel writing as a trainee chef in Cornwall, I had somehow been blind to all of this. I came from Penwith, the crooked westernmost extremity of mainland Britain, an almost-island where the land was circumscribed but the horizons were limitless, where a dippy 1960s egalitarianism had actually put down roots, here and there, amongst a society of farmers' daughters and artistic drifters come to rest; and where it was perfectly possible to grow up *completely unaware that class existed*. I tell people this and they never believe me; but it was only after I had backpacked around India and Pakistan, circuited Southeast Asia, read a thousand books and finally found myself in my mid-twenties, forty miles west of Oxford in an old arts school strapped to a teacher training college and given university status, that I discovered that where you went to school and what your parents did for a living actually had some bearing on your social standing—and perhaps on the sort of books you might like to read and aspire to write.

What was I doing here?

8

LUCKY MAN

He slapped the edge of the garden table and the teacups rattled on their saucers.

'Do you know the last thing that Wilfred Thesiger said to me before he died, when I went and saw him?'

The house stood on a high ledge of land, and beyond the broad lawn the countryside tumbled away to the southeast. It was still, and the afternoon sunlight came through a thin wash of white cloud high up. A peacock cried somewhere in the valley—an absurdly exotic sound here, as if the *Asr* prayer call had just erupted from one of the granite outbuildings.

'It was almost the last sentence he said—and one of the better things that ever happened to me. I was showing him pictures of the Tuareg. I'd just been travelling in the Sahara—forty days and forty nights on my own—and I went to see him and show him the photographs.' He slapped the table again and leant forward, adopting a theatrically husky tone: 'And he said, *"My boy, I envy you the Tuareg..."*'

He lifted his hands and eyed me. '*He* envied *me* the Tuareg!' Then he returned to his impersonation, drawing his mouth downwards to stretch his own round, ruddy-cheeked face into a simulacrum of Thesiger's craggy visage. '"*I didn't spend long enough with them; very little time with them. I envy you the time you've spent with them.*"'

He sat back, grinning, and appraised his own anecdote: 'Wow!'

I didn't know quite what to say. 'Well... that's pretty good...'

He waved a hand as if to dismiss it. 'I mean he *did* go to the Tibesti Mountains, but he was mostly with Nuer and other people. So yes, that *was* good.'

This is what he was like.

* * *

I had driven along deep lanes to get here. The countryside in the southern lee of Bodmin Moor had the neatness of early spring. There was a fuzz of new green at ground level, but the trees were still bare, and the tangled jungle of high summer had yet to sprout at the verges. Smooth blue tarmac between high hedges; unsigned junctions under hunchbacked sycamores; and on the high ground at the edge of the moor, a blaze of gorse flowers the colour of turmeric. So this, I thought, is what he's been coming back to. From Borneo and the Amazon and the Sahara; for sixty years this is the landscape he has returned to.

Most of the travel writers I had spoken to were writers first and foremost. But in the long centuries between Sir John Mandeville and Robert Byron, much European travel writing was a by-product of exploration. This is what had filled the massed volumes of Hakluyt and Purchas. For Europeans it was the 'Age of Discovery', and beginning with the letters and journals of Christopher Columbus at the close of the fifteenth century, proper first-person narrations of journeys into territories unknown to both author and audience became the order of the day.

This newly dominant mode brought with it stronger elements of authorial persona and sentiment. Columbus' faint intimations of the true nature of his discovery, prompted during his third voyage by coastlines that ran on forever and river mouths debouching far more silty water than any island could ever harbour, have the quality of an unspeakable horror apprehended: 'I have come to believe that this is a mighty continent which was hitherto unknown...'[1]

The proto-travel writing that had gone before, in gazetteers and early guidebooks, had been dominated by the blunt assertion of facts—even if those facts ultimately turned out to be nothing of the sort. But now facts were shading into *experiences*, and as the travel writing scholar Mary Baine Campbell brilliantly points out, 'The difference between a journey of forty [miles] and a "two-day journey" is the difference, writ small, between geography and the novel'—or, indeed, the travel book.[2] It was, she writes, in the literal self-centredness of the writing of explorers like Columbus 'that the travel memoir was born'.[3] (Of course, Yijing, Faxian and the other traveller-monks of China had been merrily deploying this very mode in the write-ups of their journeys to India fully a thousand years earlier—but no one in Europe would get to read their accounts until the nineteenth century, and there could be no cross-fertilisation of eastern and western travel writing traditions.)

But if the psychological, and indeed aesthetic, elements of travel writing were already latent in these voyage narratives, there was still no requirement to make them the *purpose* of the journey and its book; that stuff would have to wait until the twentieth century. In exploration the physical journey is unique, unrepeatable. There is no need to justify it with philosophical pondering, literary showboating or an explicit 'inner journey'. There is certainly no opportunity to follow 'in the footsteps' of some more illustrious predecessor. And as long as they have found something to explore, explorers are rarely troubled by a sense of belatedness.

It went on this way for many centuries, through Francis Drake and Walter Raleigh to James Cook, even while the Grand Tour got underway at home in Europe. Deep into the nineteenth century, the best-known travel writers were primarily explorers with geographical or scientific motives. Alfred Russel Wallace; David Livingstone; Henry Morton Stanley: their first and most important audience was usually the Fellows of the Royal Geographical Society rather than the ranks of the Victorian reading public. Indeed, those who travelled with RGS sponsorship were explicitly expected to deliver a formal account to the Society before they ever penned a book for popular publication.

It was with all this in mind that I had first contacted Robin Hanbury-Tenison. His were books about journeys, rather than journeys about books. Their dust jackets routinely proclaimed him 'the doyen of British explorers'. He had completed a certain number of 'firsts'—crossings of this, traverses of that. His travel was not the business of stepping solo aboard a long-distance train with nothing more than a notepad; he had commanded actual *expeditions*, where teams of porters shouldered crates of surveying equipment into trackless forest. Where Colin Thubron was a Fellow of the Royal Society of Literature, Hanbury-Tenison was a Fellow of the Royal Geographical Society—like Richard Burton, Charles Darwin and Ernest Shackleton before him.

But since my strange foray into the Eton archives, I had another reason for coming here. Robin Hanbury-Tenison belonged squarely to that travel writing class apart, a member of an old landed family with an Eton–Oxford pedigree. He was a generation younger than Wilfred Thesiger, but they had much in common.

* * *

He was out on the track to the house with his wife, Louella, painting a fence. I rolled to a stop and wound down the car window.

'You go on up,' said Louella, 'I'll finish up here'; and he swung himself lightly into the passenger seat.

'Straight on and then right.'

Green wellies, a checked shirt with a frayed collar, a quilted gilet and a flat cap over snowy white hair—the weekend attire of the sort of countryman for whom 'town' means London rather than Bodmin. He was eighty, but—and this hardly seems worth noting at this stage—he didn't look it.

The track bent past a bank of pale azaleas and opened into a skirt of gravel fronting a solid granite house.

'It's in the Domesday Book,' Hanbury-Tenison said, springing out of the car as lightly as he had leapt in.

Inside, the décor was somewhere between a farmhouse and a stately home. The kitchen had a low ceiling, a scent of baking and a working clutter of envelopes and Tupperware. Two square-headed terriers shuffled sluggishly over the tiles.

'What breed are they?'

'Westies. Always Westies.'

There was a stuffed woodcock in a glass case, and in the lavatory by the back door a photograph of a shooting party on the gravel outside the house—Labradors and more quilted gilets. In the sitting room grand portraits glowered down like exiles from a bigger building. Copies of his books were strategically placed here and there.

Because it was such a fine warm afternoon we sat at a wooden table in the garden. Seated on a bench across the grass was a life-size model of a white-haired man in a flat cap.

'Is that supposed to be you?'

'Yes! It's great for security. Often people come round when we're not in, and they say, "I spoke to the old chap; he didn't say much!"'

Every utterance was halfway to being a joke, and if he hadn't been the doyen of British explorers, I could well have imagined him as a regular on the clubby panel of some long-running BBC Radio 4 comedy show. He dished out self-aggrandisement and self-deprecation in equal measures, but he knew exactly what he was doing.

'You should always be interesting in life,' he said. 'It's very selfish to be uninteresting, in a way. You have to give of yourself. I always think of sitting next to a really boring person at a dinner party—it never bores *me* because I talk about myself, which is absolutely insufferable! My family tease me mercilessly about it and say, "You never listen to anybody; you only talk about yourself!" Well I'm sorry, but I find that the most interesting subject if I'm with somebody who's deeply boring!' He grinned broadly. 'I don't know why I'm saying all this—and on record!'

Later, when I transcribed my recording of the conversation, I found that the comic performance masked a remarkable coherence of speech. More than anyone else I'd interviewed, he spoke in fully formed sentences. He could throw in a lengthy subclause and pick up the original thread effortlessly at the other end.

* * *

The lawn was a perfect platform, set on the hillside like one of those infinity pools you see in magazine images of tropical spa resorts. Beyond its cusp was a view to sheep pasture and conifer plantations. Hanbury-Tenison had bought this place with its attached acreage of rough grazing in the early 1960s.

'Very important, I think, a taproot,' he said.

'Could you tell me something about that?'

'Well, there are two sorts of explorers really. We're all running away from something, but some are running away without any idea where they're going. The better sort of traveller, I think, has a deep taproot which brings them back to where they came from. I've always been deeply rooted here in Cornwall—or certainly for the last sixty years. And so, when I've been travelling with very remote tribal people and they say, "If life is so jolly good here, why don't you stay with us?" I'm always able to say, "My tribe lives somewhere else, and I'm closely bonded with that, and although I deeply respect what you do, I would find it just as difficult to live with you as you would find it to live my way of life." And we settle for that, which is a little different from people who think they can actually change their culture, which is very difficult to do. I find it easy to *blend* into other cultures, but to assimilate completely would be quite alien to me.'

'You said that you think the better kind of travellers have that sense of rootedness?'

'Well, not better, but *my* sort...'

'I'd like to ask you a bit more about that,' I said. Which sort, I wondered, was I? I thought for a moment of Nick Danziger, with his Monaco housing association flat, American passport and European identity.

'I've never really thought about it very much, that particular question.' Hanbury-Tenison struck a pose of theatrical thought. He did this often: claiming never to have considered a particular point before cheerily delivering what sounded like a very well-formed response. He took a sip of tea before he continued. I had now drunk tea with a fair few travel writers, but this was the first time it had come in a proper china service.

'When I say better, I mean *better balanced*; people who have a root. I think it's a better way to be, because there are a lot of people who are very lost today, whose culture, particularly in the West, has been undermined and who don't really believe in any of the values they were brought up with. They're constantly seeking eternal truths elsewhere.' He paused again, considering something. 'I'm sure there are many old retired hippies living very happily in Kathmandu, who went out on the Hippie Trail in the 1960s and never came back. But for me that's rather sad. The best of all worlds is to believe in your own culture—which I do.'

During my conversation with Barnaby Rogerson, back in the overheated Eland office in Exmouth Market, he had said something similar of Colin Thubron and Wilfred Thesiger: 'they never doubted their own culture; there's not a shadow of a doubt'. It also recalled something written by Jonathan Raban—a writer whose own sensibility seemed to have drifted, along with his place of domicile, from England to the western coast of the United States: 'Four hundred years of imperial existence had given the travelling Englishman a very clear idea of where he stood in the world—bang at its moral centre.'[4]

* * *

Robin Hanbury-Tenison seemed never to have had Wilfred Thesiger's horror of the internal combustion engine. In 1957, fresh from Oxford and a decade ahead of the hippies, he and a friend drove a second-hand jeep from London to Sri Lanka ('Pure running away. Escapism… a very silly thing'). The following year he and Richard Mason decided to take another jeep across the widest point of the South American continent from east to west through 6,000 miles of forest, swamp and mountain ('That *was* a first'). A few years later there was a traverse of the same continent by smoother, though still motor-powered, means, north to south by river boat; and shortly afterwards a role in a major expedition by hovercraft through northern Brazil and Venezuela.

It was during the latter trip that Hanbury-Tenison first began to worry deeply about the fate of what came to be known by those who campaigned for their rights as 'tribal peoples'—those inhabitants of places such as the Amazon still following ostensibly 'traditional' ways of life. He was not the only one thinking this way, and the following year, 1969, an eye-catching feature headlined 'Genocide' by Norman Lewis—stalwart of the Eland list today—appeared in *The Sunday Times* magazine. It detailed the persecution of the Indigenous peoples of the Brazilian Amazon. Shortly afterwards, Hanbury-Tenison became one of the founders of the charity Survival International.

Throughout the next four decades he travelled incessantly—a mix of research trips for Survival, extended horse-riding journeys, eye-catching stunts (attempting to water-ski across the English Channel in his eightieth year to raise funds for Survival, for instance) and the stuff of serious exploration, not least heading a huge RGS-sponsored scientific research trip into the forests of Sarawak in 1977, which he wrote up in the book *Mulu: The Rain Forest* (1980).

His approach was that which had dominated British travel writing in the nineteenth century—a journey beyond roads, beyond maps even, followed by a report and a lecture to the RGS as the official

107

culmination, with the popular travel book a mere by-product. Not any more, though.

'We're a dying breed,' he said; 'a dying breed.'

* * *

Hanbury-Tenison was the third son of a long-established landholding family. He grew up in an isolated house in the lake-blotched country-side of County Monaghan—a fragment of the old Protestant Ascendency, a day's walk inside the border of the new Irish Republic. His military father was mostly absent, and he seems to have been a rather lonely boy.

'I've long held a theory that most of the great explorers and travel-lers throughout history have had *troubled childhoods* of some sort.' He put a peculiarly breezy inflection on 'troubled childhoods', as if he were simply saying 'blue eyes', or 'blond hair'. He shrugged. 'Perhaps everybody has a troubled childhood; I don't know. But it's a very notable feature if you research the great explorers that most of them— or a very high percentage—had no father and a very domineering mother. And I think a lot of it is trying to please *mother*.' The inflection was even more peculiar here: a clipped emphasis—'*mmm*-uthah!' A comic concept, a joke word.

'I think that a lot of the motivation to cross the last blue hill comes from showing off as a child, which you do as a reaction to being some-what put upon, bullied, small, weedy, despised, and having to try and prove that you really are better than that. And half of that motivation is to please your *mother*.' Again, that strange emphasis.

'It's funny you say that...' I had been thinking about Thesiger's letters from the desert to his own mother, I said. 'He was clearly very eager to please her a lot of the time. And you'll find it with all sorts of people—people who are less explorers than writers, people like Robert Byron, and Patrick Leigh Fermor as well.'

'Good.' Hanbury-Tension nodded briskly. 'I'm glad that you agree with me. And you actually have brought up names other than the ones I would have brought up.'

'Who else did you have in mind?'

'Well, Younghusband, and... my bloody memory! The greatest explorer of them all—who Younghusband said was the greatest; the great Victorian one with the strange name...'

'Oh,' I said; 'Ney Elias?' The name had emerged from some deep recess.

'Ney Elias! Well done!' He eyed me quizzically for a moment, and I had the sense that I was being reappraised. I had, I think, just gone up in his estimation—though perhaps he didn't see a twenty-year-old chef, reading books about Victorian explorers of Central Asia in the weary afternoon hours between kitchen shifts.

'Thank you! Well, Ney Elias never wrote a book because his mother didn't think that gentlemen wrote books...'[5]

* * *

After prep school, Hanbury-Tenison, like Thesiger and so many others, had gone on to Eton and Oxford. I mentioned my recent experiment, listing notable travel writers with their places of education, and the striking dominance of the Eton–Oxford combo.

'Well done!' he said. 'That's a good piece of research!'

'I was hoping that you'd give me an explanation.'

'Well, I hated my time there,' he said. 'I was very unlucky. I went into a bad house in an era in which, just after the war, it was really *Tom Brown's Schooldays*. I mean, the *cruelty*! People talk nowadays about bullying, child abuse and all the other things, and one reads what sad people are accused of having done—and some, like Jimmy Savile, were obviously absolute monsters. But seriously, the sort of thing that people get frightfully upset and all hot under the collar about now *pales* to what one went through at Eton in that particular era.' He chuckled, sitting in the thin sunshine on this high Cornish hillside, though it didn't seem much like a laughing matter to me, even seven decades later.

'The fact that it was all totally unjust and you hadn't actually done anything to deserve the punishment being inflicted on you was very awful, and really made one not particularly want to live. But one got through it. One showed off a *bit* and became a *bit* cocky and rebellious, and I really think that's where it started.' He meant the travelling, the attention-seeking.

In more recent years, despite his unhappy memories of the place, Hanbury-Tenison seemed to have developed a new affection for Eton. He'd sold off his vast collection of artefacts, gathered during a life of travels—'The next generation aren't going to be interested in having father's old blowpipes around the house!'—and it had all ended up in the school museum. He was planning to leave his papers to the archive there too.

'It *is* a very good school,' he said. 'Of course there is the dreadfully unfair and unattractive arrogance and self-confidence that goes with being an Etonian—I mean you *know* you're better than anybody else. But then I always say that everybody knows they're better than everybody else. If you find any culture that is strong anywhere in the world, those people will not just believe, but they will *know* that they are the only true human beings and that everybody else is subhuman. Try going and travelling in China—I don't know if you have?'

I was still keen to pursue an idea about Old Etonian travel writers having some particular predilection for 'tribal cultures' in other parts of the world, and the possibility that this had something to do with their schooling.

'You do have elements of ritual there that are very tribal...' I said.

'Yes, yes, never thought of it...' Again, I wasn't quite sure I believed that he had never considered this.

'You have elements of costume which immediately set you aside from other people...' I said.

'So Etonians are looking like a Maasai!'

'Well, it turns heads...'

'In Eton High Street, yep! It's a lovely idea,' he said. 'I'd never thought of it, but I think you're probably right.'

* * *

According to Hanbury-Tenison's autobiography, *Worlds Apart* (1984), it was at Oxford—for him a far happier place than Eton—that he decided, during a late-night conversation in lodgings with two friends, to become an explorer.

'*Is* that true or is it just a story?' I asked.

'No, that's true! Entirely true. There was a Damascene moment at three o'clock in the morning when Richard Mason and John Hemming and I—all for *totally* different reasons; mine were purely for showing off; theirs were, I think, much more respectable reasons—decided that we were going to become explorers.' And because they all came from a particular background, with a particular family wealth and at a particular moment in twentieth-century history, that's what they all became.

'I suppose your generation, from that background, were in an unusual position,' I said, 'because had you been born just twenty years earlier...'

'I'd have been in the war...'

'... And if you'd been born a little bit before that you'd have been in colonial service, most likely...'

'Or the First World War, or I'd have been a district officer. I'd certainly have been a district officer. I'd have loved that—been quite good at it too...' But that was not the era into which he was born—not quite.

'It does seem like a strange sort of moment where you could have your cake and eat it,' I said, 'coming out of that heritage and with that background.'

'Yes. Any of us could have walked into any job at that point; we were deeply privileged. But we—certainly in my case—didn't want to do it unless we wanted to do it, and I *didn't* want to do it! It's rather horrible, but in a funny way I did have the best possible life. And it's grossly unfair.' He paused for a moment, looked upwards, then smiled.

'Do you know, I have been astonishingly lucky in my life in the things that I've done. The classic clichéd joke when you get an OBE for travelling, is that everybody knows what OBE stands for—and I *have* been supported by "Other Buggers' Efforts" more than anybody I know. And I've been married twice, totally happily. I've never had marital dramas. Very tragically my first wife, who I loved dearly up until the very end, died at forty-four, and I've been very happily remarried for longer than I was to her now. I've had more than two silvers—they were golds! And *that's* incredible luck, because marriage isn't necessarily an entirely judicious step. You get married because you fall in love, and that isn't necessarily a very balanced thing. And how lucky to find that you've actually married the right person—*twice!* I mean, that's pretty rare.'

A lucky man, smiling in the spring sunshine on a high hillside.

* * *

Hanbury-Tenison's first book, *The Rough and the Smooth*, was an account of the two South American crossings, by jeep ('the rough') and by water ('the smooth'). It was published in 1969—not exactly a Thesiger-level delay between the start of his travels and the launch of his travel writing career, but still more than a decade after the first of the two journeys the book described. The original plan, in fact, had been for Hanbury-Tenison's fellow jeep-driver, Richard Mason, to write an account of that expedition.

'Of course!' he said, when I asked about this; 'He was much more intelligent than me!'

But Mason had died before he had a chance to write the book, so in the end it was Hanbury-Tenison himself who, somewhat reluctantly, took on the task.[6]

'You didn't have any inclination or any sense that you were going to write books, in that first decade of travel?' I asked.

He paused for a very long time, touching his fingers to his chin. 'I wonder...' A light aircraft—the kind that carry travellers to airstrips carved out of the forest in the Amazon—buzzed slowly overhead.

'It is interesting, because I'd never really thought of it that way'— this time I *was* convinced. 'I certainly didn't have any confidence in my ability to write, but I had a great sense that it was *what you did*. I keep banging on at young people who are going exploring or travelling, and I just tell them that there's only one thing that matters, and that's your diary. Nothing else matters; it's the *only* thing that matters. You're knackered, tired, the end of the day, everybody else is tucking up in their hammocks or switching off or doing stuff, or you're on your own, or whatever. You sit up for another hour by candlelight—which attracts every kind of mosquito—and you write at least two pages every day, otherwise you *didn't do it*; otherwise it didn't happen; otherwise it'll all be forgotten tomorrow. I don't know who told me that; I suppose it was my *mother*.'

Hanbury-Tenison *had* kept his diaries, and in the late 1960s a New York literary agent, Julian Bach, suggested—much as Graham Watson had to Wilfred Thesiger in the previous decade—that he draw on them to write a book.

'I said, "I don't think I'm capable of writing a book", and he said, "Don't be silly, Robin; with your background, as an Etonian, and being at Oxford, you can write a book! Of course you can; don't give me that! Now, we just need to talk about the shape of the book..." And he was so adamant about it that I thought, well, perhaps I *can*, with that background. But it hadn't actually occurred to me until he spelt it out.'

He was not, by his own account, a high literary writer like Colin Thubron. But there was a polished fluency and rattling good pace to his twenty-odd books—some about his own remarkable journeys, some compendiums of the adventures of others. He was still at it now, working on the final proofs of a book that had grown out of a recent return to Sarawak.

'I think it's good stuff. I'm told it's the best thing I've done; my publisher says so.'[7]

* * *

It was growing cold now, and we moved into the deep conservatory that ran along the side of the house. Somehow I hadn't noticed earlier just how small he was, but as we stood up to go inside I realised that he had the stature of a schoolboy. There was a tall dresser of blond wood against the wall in the conservatory, with a china dinner service neatly arrayed on its shelves like the gleaming crockery displayed in village homes in Ladakh.

We talked about the founding of Survival International—a peculiar saga of the elite of late 1960s London, gathering in one another's flats to drink wine and express outrage over Norman Lewis' *Sunday Times* piece: 'Teddy Goldsmith had turned up by then, and he said, "My brother Jimmy might be able to get some money to do something." And Jimmy put on a lunch at the Clermont Club with John Aspinall and Lucan and all the usual suspects, and we raised £2,000 for tribal people—primitive people as they were then called...'

Hanbury-Tenison had spent half a century deflecting the various criticisms that could be levelled at the charity—paternalism and a colonial urge to place exotic cultures in a human zoo, troublesome terminology or the indulgent fighting of a lost cause. There were polished answers to all this—convincing answers too, for Survival had grown out of its early idealism into an adaptable, realistic and self-aware endeavour that worked hard to put the voices of the people it championed at the fore. There were also polished answers to the question of whether exploration still had a purpose.

'The travel writing explorers of the past have been amateurs.' I attempted a challenge. 'Is there really a position, is there a scope for someone who isn't a...'

'Would you call someone like Alexander von Humboldt an amateur?'

'I think they were generalists, weren't they? And Alfred Russel Wallace...'

'Alright, okay, they were amateurs; but they were incredibly well informed. Get your twenty-year-old Humboldt today, who is obviously extremely bright—he'll probably have a university degree...'

'He'll probably have a PhD in biochemistry or something like that...'

'Okay, he's got a PhD in biochemistry and he's interested in the biochemistry of the coral reefs that are dying in the Great Barrier Reef; he'll go and take his PADI, his diving course, and he will do some extremely adventurous stuff finding out how it works. That's exploration!'

'I suppose so.' I could see I wouldn't get very far with this.

Hanbury-Tenison grinned at me and raised his eyebrows. 'I think it's alright! I'm making it up as I go along, but it sounds okay!'

Louella came into the conservatory with an azalea flower, cut from the drive, and Hanbury-Tenison sprang to his feet to show me his library—shelves packed with hardbacks in a dark dining room. He pulled books out here and there: Danziger, Dalrymple and, of course, Thesiger. It was time for him to reprise his impersonation.

'You know, Wilfred came on my Mulu expedition? He actually broke in, because there were terrific restrictions. The Malaysians wouldn't allow him, and so he just rolled up. We were frightfully pleased to see him, and we said, "Well, what do you think of the rainforest?"' Hanbury-Tenison cleared his throat and stretched his face into a severe frown—'And he chewed a bit and said, "*I prefer an environment where water is better appreciated...*"'

* * *

After I had threaded my way back through the mesh of tight lanes below the moor to the junction with the A30, I turned west.

Somehow—and I didn't quite understand why—lucky, jocular, *charming* Robin Hanbury-Tenison had dispelled some of my unease at the image of British travel writers as an Etonian horde.

At one point during our conversation, he had told me how, as a somewhat directionless youngest son of a landed family at Oxford, his older brother ('we practised primogeniture, so everything went to him') had ordered him down to London to visit Sir John Hanbury-Williams, chairman of the huge textile corporation Courtaulds ('a fairly distant cousin, but close enough to be approachable, apparently'). Hanbury-Tension had done a gravelly impersonation of Sir John which sounded much like his impression of Wilfred Thesiger: *"Let me tell you, if you join up when you leave Oxford, when you come down, if you start at this company there's no reason you shouldn't be sitting here in thirty years' time."* He'd chuckled and shaken his head at the recollection.

'I can remember thinking I don't *want* to be sitting there! I don't *want* to be chairman of Courtaulds! I would be stinking rich, but that's not what I want to do! I absolutely *knew* that I didn't want to do it.'

I found that I was grateful for this resistance, that he had chosen his particular path—and that Robert Byron, Peter Fleming, Wilfred Thesiger, Colin Thubron and all the rest had done likewise. If an Old Etonian was going to put his privilege to use, then surely becoming a travel writer was one of the more benign things he could do with it.

* * *

The westbound A30 was empty of traffic, a thin lode of native copper shining under the slanting sun. There was haze over the china clay workings above Goss Moor, and the wind turbines at Carland Cross were motionless and huge. Some kind of gravity was always with me when I drove this way.

A glimpse of the sea to the north. Carn Brea to the south with the rusty bracken on its slopes blazing in the last of the light. And beyond the slip road from Camborne, a brief sighting of hunched western hills, plum-coloured in the cold evening.

Towards the end of Philip Marsden's 2014 travel book, *Rising Ground*, there's a glimpse of this same sea-girt bank of hills: 'Up ahead was Penwith, the last piece of land before the ocean. Above it the sky hung dark and heavy, as over an island.'[8] A view from without. That line sets up a strange turbulence inside me, because for my whole life I have been looking back in the opposite direction, from within.

Postscript: In March 2020, Robin Hanbury-Tenison fell seriously ill with the COVID-19 coronavirus. (Just a few weeks earlier he had published his latest book, Taming the Four Horsemen, *a discussion of radical solutions to the global threats of war, famine, environmental catastrophe—and pandemics.) He seems to have contracted the disease in France, where he had been on a skiing holiday. For five weeks he lay unconscious in hospital in Plymouth. Medical staff did not expect him to survive. But he did survive, and he was home on Bodmin Moor in time for his eighty-fourth birthday. A lucky man, once again.*

9

THE TRAVELLEE-READER

Two days after my meeting with Robin Hanbury-Tenison and sixty miles to the west, I walk up over the high country from the south on a bloodless afternoon. The black earth along the path is dry underfoot and the rough ground lies bleached by the passing winter. Tresses of moor grass like shredded paper; last year's bracken, crackling in the thin breeze. This is a journey that needs no maps.

I cross the last shoulder of land where it slants down from the crown of Watch Croft, and home ground opens below: a ledge of stone-stitched pasture half-a-mile deep between the moors and the cliff, dotted with huddled grey hamlets. I can see my washing, treading the air on a slack line in front of the field shelter.

I perch myself on the drystone wall that marks the edge of the moors, take out my notebook, and try to fix the country on the page: the Atlantic, blotched with silver, rising on the vertical as if someone has hitched the belt of the horizon up an extra inch; the dark pubic tangle of withies on the parish boundary; the fields on the slope like shingles on a roof; and the old lynchets, faint as veins under a green skin. But it is a lost cause. A storm-surge of privately signified images rushes up to meet me, limitless small intimacies and names and personal histories. In a few moments I am word-blind, monarch-of-all-I-survey but incapable of commanding any of it.

* * *

The first time I read Philip Marsden's *Rising Ground*—the book which prompted the magazine assignment which, in turn, precipitated this entire journey—I remember skittering excitedly to paragraph ends like a child with an adventure story, as the book's trajectory veered west through Cornwall. But there was something else too, an apprehension almost, and when the narrative did finally reach that 'last piece of land before the ocean', Penwith, my home-place, there were sensations that I can't properly describe, and for a long while didn't fully understand. More than once I stopped reading, unnerved as by something uncanny, realising that the author had passed within hailing distance of my own home or had met someone I'd known my whole life.

So many of the academic discussions of travel writing I'd encountered—particularly those 'undertaken in a pronounced spirit of critique', in Carl Thompson's words—dwelt on the representation and status of what Mary Louise Pratt had called the 'travellee', the local people that the traveller-writer passed during his or her journeys.[1] And it was here that the more censorious scholars often found fault. Travel writing persistently failed to show genuine solidarity with the travellee, they argued. It hyped their 'otherness', and reproduced imbalances of power when it encountered them. It kept them in their place, as immobile representatives of their own cultures, even when the portrayal was ostensibly sympathetic.

I'd read enough bad travel books to know that this was undoubtedly sometimes true. But weren't the scholars at times guilty of the very thing they critiqued? At first I'd wondered if I was imagining this. But no; it was there alright, buried a layer or two down in the discourse, as when the academic Steve Clark wrote of travel writing, 'customarily only legible to one culture, intrinsically commentary upon rather than dialogue with'.[2]

Customarily only legible to one culture… As if there could be no traffic across the frontier; as if the travellee couldn't ever read the traveller's account—perhaps couldn't read at all. 'Home' and 'elsewhere' were firmly delineated; the idea of the travellee as powerless and mute was quietly reinforced. Wasn't this what travel writers themselves were accused of doing? And why did I feel a flicker of personal affront when I spotted this latent inference in the scholarship?

There are no officially designated zones in which travel writers may operate. Their elsewhere can be *anywhere*, and it does not begin at the tideline on Chesil Beach any more than it finds its frontier in the Straits of Gibraltar or the Bosphorus. And if a travel writer can travel anywhere, then surely the travellee can be *anyone*. Scholars did seek out examples of 'writing back', pleasing inversions where a travel writer from a place or culture more typically written *about* grabbed the lens and twisted it towards the traditional centres of power. There was also Pratt's concept of autoethnography—'a selective collaboration with and appropriation of idioms of the metropolis or the conqueror', in which the cannier travellees adopt the travellers' language and style and use it to self-represent, perhaps with resistive or subversive intent, gaining agency in the process.[3] But these scholarly notions still seemed to rest on a firm sense of 'here' and 'elsewhere', connected only by Pratt's fraught 'contact zone'. And, perhaps more importantly, they still didn't ask how it actually *felt* to be on travel writing's receiving end.

But there *was* one scholar who had properly considered that question. Her name was Wendy Bracewell. She was a professor of South East European History at University College London, and she'd made a study of travel writing *within* Europe in the eighteenth and nineteenth centuries. She'd focussed mainly on the Balkans, and she'd found, of course, that there have always been plenty of travellees to whom the traveller's text *is* legible—either in the original or in translation. Bracewell had uncovered the angry responses they'd penned when they felt that they and their home-places had been maligned: reviews, essays, private and public correspondence, even book-length counterblasts. She called these ripostes 'counter travelogues' or 'travellee polemics',[4] and she'd discovered an 'extraordinary outburst' of them all over Europe in the late eighteenth century, with aggrieved travellees popping up everywhere from Ireland to the Adriatic.[5] As Bracewell pointed out, reading travel writing is to share the writer's gaze, but 'reading foreign travel accounts of one's own society means finding oneself simultaneously displayed as the object of the narrator's description and analysis'. This is the unsettling experience of what she called the 'travellee-reader'; and the lot of the travellee-reader is to be 'doubly written into these texts'.[6]

Doubly written. When I first ran into that phrase, in the dense thicket of an academic collection called *New Directions in Travel Writing Studies*, it sent a prickle of recognition crawling over my scalp. Finally I understood why Philip Marsden's *Rising Ground* set up that strange roil in my chest. When he approached Penwith, the last, crooked joint of Cornwall's long, arthritic finger, I, as reader, *had* to share his gaze, peering in from the east, even though I was already there ahead, waiting to be travelled past. It demanded the impossible: it meant being in two places at the same time. I had been doubly written.

Marsden certainly wasn't the first travel writer to describe Cornwall. They'd been coming this way for hundreds of years, and they'd often dwelt on its perceived difference from the rest of the country. Part of this was simply down to geography: a long peninsula stretching westwards as if trying to distance itself from the English centre, almost entirely bounded by water—the Atlantic on two sides and the deep cleft of the River Tamar on the third. But there was also a meaningful historical distinction. Cornwall was one of the parts of mainland Britain—along with Scotland and Wales—that had not been thoroughly anglicised when the border was fixed at the River Tamar in the tenth century by the early English king Athelstan. At that time— and indeed for a good while afterwards—the land west of that border was still largely occupied not by Anglo-Saxons but by Britons, speaking their own entirely distinct Brythonic language. The second syllable of the name—Corn-*wall*—shares an etymology with Wales: *Wēalas*, an Old English word, usually translated as 'strangers' or 'foreigners'—or, in this context, *un-English* (the Cornish word for Cornwall is *Kernow*). Some sense of that distinction lingered down the centuries, even as the Cornish language withered away, leaving the place as 'a kind of halfway house between English county and Celtic nation', in the words of the historian Bernard Deacon.[7] By the Victorian era, tourist literature was referring to Cornwall with a certain arch ambiguity, half ironic, half serious, as 'West Barbary'.[8]

In the week following my visit to Robin Hanbury-Tenison, I went into the public library in Penzance to look more closely at what the travel writers of the past had written about Cornwall—and to watch my own reaction to their representations—as a 'travellee-reader'.[9]

* * *

The Cornish reference section was in a high white room upstairs, with the heads of the cordyline palms around the car park shimmying at the windows. The books slumped against one another in glass-fronted cabinets along the inner walls, the massed literature of a region: parish histories; biographies of local worthies; gazetteers of prehistoric monuments; and scholarly studies of the Cornish diaspora. I worked my way along the shelves, plucking out the travel books—aged hardbacks with cracked spines and slack bindings—then carried them to a desk.

The first was *A Tour through Cornwall in the Autumn of 1808*, by the Reverend Richard Warner. Warner was an amateur antiquarian and enthusiastic voyager on foot, author of a dozen travelogues about journeys through various regions of Britain. He was not in the least bit impressed by the Cornish scenery. Cornwall, he assured his readers, 'can offer no claim to the praise of the picturesque or beautiful'; the whole place was, he felt, 'deformed'.[10] This was no surprise; Warner was a protégé of William Gilpin, who first popularised the idea of 'the picturesque' in Britain. Gilpin himself had ventured no further into Cornwall than Bodmin, declaring it 'a barren and naked country, in all respects as uninteresting as can well be conceived', before retreating rapidly eastwards.[11] Places likely to attract the admiration of modern travel writers as 'rugged' and 'wild' were often judged in a more critical light by their eighteenth- and nineteenth-century predecessors. For Cornwall as for Connemara—and indeed Tibet—the commonest travel writing epithets had once been 'dreary' and 'dismal'.

What really caught my attention, however, was the way Warner's gaze fell upon the locals, the Cornish travellees—for the good Reverend clearly found them far more visually appealing than the countryside in which they lived. At Mousehole, a couple of miles from my desk in the library, he declared that 'The broad and muscular outline of the male, and the luxuriant contour of the female form, here, evince that the climate, food, or employment of the people, (or perhaps all together,) are highly conducive to the maturation and perfection of the human figure.'[12] This made me snigger, naturally. But there was some other faint feeling too. A 'denial of coevalness' was one of the crimes of which travel writers were often accused: a placing of the travellee on some other temporal or civilisational plane, subordinate to the writer and his or her readers.[13] And amongst the means by which 'coevalness' was denied were 'unilateral observation of the "natives"; classification of their habits and practices; [and] taxonomic descriptions'.[14] Warner was certainly doing that; he was sizing these people up as specimens, ascribing them generic characteristics, pinning them to the page like butterflies. This was the emerging ethnographic language of the nineteenth-century scholar-adventurer; but it wasn't being applied here to travellees in Asia or Africa; it was angled towards my own predecessors in Penwith.

I moved on to the next book, *A Londoner's Walk to the Land's End* by Walter White. This was a proper Victorian travel book, with a memorable opening:

> 'How far might you be going?' asked the coastguard, as we stood chatting on the top of the cliff that overlooks Lulworth Cove, on a sunny afternoon at the beginning of July, 1854.

> 'As far towards America as a man can go on foot,' was my answer.[15]

White crossed into Cornwall by boat to Torpoint, for there was no bridge over the Tamar in those days. It was a powerful moment of arrival, entry into a new land. Arriving on the western shore, he shouldered his pack and set off inland: 'A few minutes take you clear of the houses, and then at once you are struck with the difference between the county you are in and the one you have left. It is obvious. The generally soft features of Devonshire are exchanged for a landscape of a stern and unfinished aspect.'[16] This was nonsense, surely. That fleshy underbelly of eastern Cornwall has the same wooded combes and swollen pastures that run back eastwards through the South Hams; the harder stuff lies far to the north and west. Was Walter White falling back on a text here, seeing a difference in the landscape simply because he had been primed for it by Gilpin, Warner and all the other authors that went before him?

As he moved westwards, passing Truro, Walter White began to detect a physical change in the human geography too: 'the eye, feature, and expression, are Celtic'.[17] Somehow this pleased me; somehow I didn't want to allow the possibility that he might have seen this difference only where the books he'd read had told him to expect it.

* * *

I worked my way through the little stack of Victorian travelogues. Here was Wilkie Collins, better known today as a novelist, but proving himself a decent travel writer too in 1851 with *Rambles Beyond Railways*: 'I doubt whether Cornwall will not gain by comparison with foreign countries, as an unexplored region offered to the curiosity of the tourist.'[18] A frown and a mutter of complaint here. *Unexplored?* Unexplored by whom? Not by the 'pleasant primitive population' that Collins encountered on his journey, obviously.[19] There was a clear inference: Wilkie Collins was writing for people who weren't in Cornwall; he was not writing for *me*.

I had reached the dawn of the twentieth century now, and here was *Days in Cornwall*, by Charles Lewis Hind, a London art critic. It began: 'Having decided to walk round, down and through Cornwall, I fold the map, draw a deep chair to the fireside (the place is London, the month November), and begin by recalling a few impressions of past wanderings in the Duchy.'[20]

Another promising start for a travel book, this. In spite of myself, I felt the reflexive loosening of the shoulders, the settling into a seat that comes with the beginning of a vicarious journey to a far-off land. Hind had hooked me with a nifty bit of rhetorical strategising—as the scholars might say. He was establishing that Cornwall was elsewhere, and that London was the point of departure—both the centre of power and, with that cosy hearthside seat, the place of safe domesticity.

But how did that make you feel if your own positioning of London and Cornwall was reversed? When the author described the very moors that I would drive home across once the library closed, and said that 'this was Cornwall—interior Cornwall, land of the undying Celtic race who always go forth to battle and who always fail', a place 'still peopled with the progeny of the prolific Pan, speaking ever in the wind, among the reeds, and beneath the branches of the swaying trees', I rolled my eyes, but also felt... what *was* this?[21]

Hind seemed more determined than any of the earlier travel writers to ramp up the exoticism, to make Cornwall a profoundly othered place. He commanded a fine array of travel writing tricks, and when he found a lack of difference on the ground he could simply conjure it out of the ether:

> [A]s everyone knows, the Cornish language is dead [...] And yet, perhaps, who knows? In solitary huts on moor and mountainside, when none of the 'foreign' English are near, Cornish cronies may still chatter

> to one another in their ancient language [...] Perhaps strange tales of
> [...] Cornish witches and pixies, and the doings of the little people are
> told, in a strange tongue, in moorside cottages, on dark nights, in wild
> Western Cornwall.[22]

This was a brilliant stroke. Hind was amongst travellees of his own
nationality, speaking his first language as their own. Finding this perhaps a little disappointing, he had suggested an occult otherness which,
in its very obscurity, was doubly exotic. It was utter nonsense, of
course: even by the time of Reverend Warner's visit a century earlier,
the last scraps of spoken Cornish had probably gone. But it didn't matter; Hind only needed to make the suggestion, early on, and its effect
would linger throughout the book.

A moorside cottage in wild Western Cornwall—that could be *my*
house. This feeling, high up in my chest, behind the breastbone: an
unstable emulsion of outrage and pride.

* * *

Here's the thing: travel writers from without are *not* the only ones who
construct difference. People from Cornwall—the Cornish travellees,
no less—sometimes work to emphasise an aura of difference too. I did
it myself: bristled slightly when referred to as 'English'; lapsed readily
into pub-bore mode on the subject of Cornwall's historical distinction.
This could all be faintly ridiculous, I knew, and I tried to keep my
tongue somewhere near my cheek as I did it. But my feelings about
westernmost Cornwall as a physical place were deadly serious, and I'd
always enjoyed knowing that this matrix of tawny moor and stony
pasture, of sea and hills, is positively strange to many outsiders.

Some scholars might suggest that this was simply an example of
people from a periphery internalising the sense of difference foisted
upon them by powerful stories from the centre: a myth of romantic,
'Celtic' Cornwall cooked up in London then sold back wholesale to
the very people it had exoticised. But surely it wasn't quite as simple
as that. As the historian Bernard Deacon had written of Cornish identity, it 'may indeed borrow from dominant discourses but the content
of the resulting identities cannot simply be "read off" from such discourses'.[23] Either way, the point was this: the travellee-reader was not
necessarily insensible, or entirely resistive, to a traveller's construction

of difference. If you want to feel that your home-place is somehow different, is *special*, it can be affirming to have a travel writer confirm (or indeed construct) that difference for you. Was *this* the crux of the uncanny sensation of being doubly written into a traveller's text: a mix of validation and violation, a guilty pleasure in being associated with the exotic?

I needed to check my own privilege here, of course. I might come from the exact same place as the men and women to whom Warner had 'denied coevalness'. But we were separated by two centuries. They were, in truth, far closer than I to that essentialised image of the mute and powerless travellee latent in some of the scholarly accounts. They probably *were* less equipped to receive Warner's text and to produce a travellee polemic in response. They didn't have my ease of mobility. They were almost certainly far less able—and this was an awkward admission to make—to slip their Cornishness off and on like a coat as they crossed the River Tamar. They didn't have the *luxury* of revelling in their own exoticness without consequence. But none of that made my own reaction to being 'doubly written' somehow inauthentic. If anything, it proved the point: the travellee could be *anyone*.

There was something else too, some other layer of personal conflict when I read travel writing about home: a recognition that when it came to describing this place that mattered most, I would always be hope-lessly hobbled. A travel writer from without, be it Philip Marsden or Wilkie Collins, would always do it more assuredly.

I reached for *Rambles Beyond Railways* again, and there at the start of chapter 12, I found Collins and his fellow traveller, the artist Henry Brandling, at nightfall on the coast between St Just and St Ives:

Imagine three or four large, square, comfortless-looking, shut-up houses, all apparently uninhabited; add some half-dozen miserable little cottages standing near the houses, with the nasal notes of a Methodist hymn pouring disastrously through the open door of one of them; let the largest of the large buildings be called an inn, but let it make up no beds, because nobody ever stops to sleep there: place in the kitchen of this inn a sickly little girl, and a middle-aged, melancholy woman, the first staring despondently on a wasting fire, the second offering to the stranger a piece of bread, three eggs, and some sour porter corked down in an earthenware jar, as all that her larder and cellar can afford; fancy next an old, grim, dark church, with two or three lads leaning against the churchyard wall, looking out together in gloomy silence on a solitary high road; conceive a thin, slow rain falling, a cold twilight just changing into darkness, a surrounding landscape wild, barren, and shelterless—imagine all this, and you will have the picture before you which presented itself to me and my companion, when we found ourselves in the village of Morvah.[24]

It was a description of the place I had looked down on from the edge of the moors a few days earlier, hunched over my notebook, knowing neither where to start nor where to stop. It was a description of home. I might take exception to Collins' unrelenting negativity—equal to Paul Theroux at his most caustic—but there was no doubt that his was the better piece of travel writing. Of course it was: *he* was the stranger here.

10

BESIDE THE BLACKWATER

Afterwards—after what I'm about to relate here—Cara said, 'How are you going to write that chapter?'

We were driving north through the Knockmealdown Mountains, somewhere near the Waterford–Tipperary border.

'What do you mean?'

'Isn't it going to be a bit weird, when you've met all these other travel writers on your own, and then suddenly with this one I'm there too, and you have to explain who I am?'

Cara is my partner. Because this latest stage of my journey had taken me to Ireland, her home country, and because it was a weekend and she wasn't working, I'd asked her to join me. She'd driven us down from Galway, and she was at the wheel again now, heading back. The encounter had been a delight, and a privilege, and I was glad that she'd been there to share it. But I hadn't stopped to think of the practical consequences.

She was right: it *would* be a bit weird—though I wasn't exactly sure why. I *had* travelled alone to all my previous encounters. But was there something else going on? Had I, unconsciously, constructed a persona for myself as the narrator of my own journey—one which owed something to the solitary, self-contained figure I knew from Colin Thubron's books, or the elegantly unanchored protagonist of Bruce Chatwin's *In Patagonia* and *The Songlines*; a figure incompatible with allusions to domesticity?

I looked out at the bank of Sitka spruce rising at the roadside. Overhead the sky was freighted with summer storm clouds.

'Could you just leave me out?' Cara said. 'Pretend I wasn't there; don't mention me when you write it up.'

The very suggestion was appalling.

'God no! No! That would go against everything I've been trying to do, right from the start. I'm being really careful not to invent anything...' I hadn't, perhaps, stopped properly to think about why I was doing this either, but it seemed important, seemed to have something to do with the unease that had arisen as I worked my way through Wilfred Thesiger's diaries, back at Eton.

She shrugged over the steering wheel. 'You wouldn't be making anything up, though, would you? You'd just be leaving something out.'

She was right again. What was more, I wouldn't be the first to do it.

When I read travel books I sometimes catch a faint hint of a hidden presence, a guide or local fixer, like a cough offstage. And even when companions are acknowledged, they sometimes vanish into the authorial shadow without ever properly materialising. The 'we' of Patrick Leigh Fermor's books on Greece is sometimes so singular that it sounds like a royal we. And when Graham Greene travelled to Liberia in the 1930s to write *Journey Without Maps* (1936), he briefly admitted that he had been accompanied by his twenty-five-year-old cousin Barbara, but then proceeded to mention her so infrequently that the book often seemed to be the tale of an Englishman trekking without compatriots in the West African forest.

But following the precedents of other books was no justification; following the precedents of other books was one of travel writing's biggest problems, as far as the critical scholars were concerned.

Cara shrugged again. 'You could just try it; see if it works.'

'I don't know...' I frowned sceptically from the passenger seat. 'I'd have to somehow let readers know what I was doing, what was really going on.'

'Well,' she said, 'that's what you'll have to work out how to do, then.'

* * *

The little town of Lismore stands on the banks of the River Blackwater, before it makes its abrupt, right-hand turn towards the Celtic Sea. This is a lush part of Ireland, far removed from the flayed western seaboard. In summer Lismore sits amidst thick hedgerows and deep silage grass. The Knockmealdown Mountains rise in a lavender line, ten miles to the north.

There is a castle, standing over the swift-flowing Blackwater, and a main street of hanging baskets and pastel-coloured shopfronts. Halfway along that main street is an arch of ivy-strangled stone. It is inconspicuous between the buildings, though it makes for an unkempt note in a tidy town. If you are expected, the metal gates will have been left ajar. Beyond: a weedy path between high walls. You step forward uncertainly. Low stone buildings appear ahead. The path narrows and the weeds grow taller; brambles and ragwort and crooked, wind-seeded ash saplings; a second gate of rusted metal. It seems as though no one has passed this way for years, and you wonder if you have made a mistake, thinking to turn back. But then a dog barks, and suddenly a figure with short grey hair is before you on the path, attended by two grizzled brown terriers. She is very old, and little higher than your shoulder, but broad and imposing nonetheless. She swings her right arm through a low haymaker into a crushing handshake.

'*Lovely* to meet you,' she says, with the first of the almighty emphases that sweep through her speech, then thrusts a piece of paper into your hand—a flyer for an upcoming demonstration in Dublin demanding 'Freedom & Justice for Palestine'. Dervla Murphy.

* * *

When I was in the first flush of my youthful obsession with travel writing, Dervla Murphy's books were always there in the travel section—paperback editions, all with the same cover layout, but each with a distinct pastel colour scheme, like the shopfronts of a small Irish town. I'd enjoyed her accounts of journeys in the Indian subcontinent and Africa; enjoyed the unfussy prose and the humour. She seemed to be the originator of a breezy subgenre involving intrepid women on two-wheeled modes of transport.

But it was only later—at around the same time that I finally picked up *Danziger's Britain*, no longer demanding of travel writing an instant hit of exoticism—that I began properly to appreciate her work. The change came when I read *A Place Apart*, her 1978 account of a visit to Northern Ireland at the height of the Troubles. It was not simply a jaunty journal of a bike ride (though her mode of transport was, as usual, an old Armstrong Cadet man's bicycle named Roz). Instead, it was a stark panorama of communal division, observed at the level of shabby sitting rooms and sectarian pubs. The whole thing was a thoroughly journalistic undertaking, but its author's sensibility was in no way that of a journalist. It was angry and opinionated, ready to call out wickedness wherever it appeared, but always seeking the humanity in ostensibly bad people. In places it was downright terrifying—though its own narrator, a middle-aged woman wheeling an antiquated bicycle—never seemed frightened.

After that I'd looked at Dervla's books with a different eye. There was, it seemed, something transgressive about them. It was not simply that she was a woman in a male-dominated genre; nor that she seemed simply to *go*, brazenly, without ever needing to contrive a quest object for justification. It was, I think, that she spoke her mind, and in doing so revealed that travel writers, like journalists, weren't really expected to parade their opinions quite so strongly.

She'd published more than twenty travel books across half a century, and was just about the only person who'd been at it longer than Colin Thubron. Her most recent book, in 2015, had been *Between River and Sea*, an account of a visit to Palestine and Israel very much in the mould of *A Place Apart*. But somehow the idea of actually meeting her seemed fantastical—almost as fantastical as the idea of meeting Ella Maillart or Freya Stark in the twenty-first century. She was of a great age, and reputedly something of a recluse, closeted away in County Waterford. But then I'd asked Barnaby Rogerson if she ever received visitors. (For most of her career, Dervla had been published by John Murray, but after Murray's was bought by a conglomerate in 2004, she'd decamped to tiny Eland Books.)

'She does, actually,' he'd said, 'but you'll have to bring her some beer.'

* * *

I handed over the bag of bottles.

'*Thank* you.'

The two terriers—their names were Pepper and Wurzel—clattered ahead into the nearest building on unclipped claws. I asked, as I had of Robin Hanbury-Tenison, what breed they were.

'Don't ask rude questions! They are *dogs!*'

Clearly pedigree counted for little hereabouts.

The place could hardly be described as a house. It was a yard, surrounded on all sides by walls of grey stone. Piles of firewood and old junk stood here and there amongst the stinging nettles, and rough pathways ran between small buildings—a study, a bedroom, a bathroom in a far corner, like the freestanding *bales* of a Balinese family compound. The yard had once been the town market. Dervla had bought it from an artist friend, and turned it into a home. Before that she'd lived in a nearby bungalow, inherited from her parents. She was born in 1931 in the maternity home at Cappoquin, four miles west along the Blackwater, and had never called anywhere but Lismore home. Rootedness amongst travel writers, once again.

Dervla Murphy's had been a neat inversion of a time-honoured career path for Irish writers: she had never felt the need to go into exile, but she had spent most of her life writing about anywhere but Ireland. 'There was nothing in Ireland that I felt I had to get away from, either as a person or a writer', she had once written; 'On the contrary, it was the place I had to get back to, wherever I went.'[1] And yet she was hardly a quiet conformist. In 1968 she had deliberately chosen— chosen!—to have a child as a single mother in rural Ireland. While her exact contemporary Edna O'Brien was penning scathing fictional critiques of conservative Irish society from distant London, Dervla was blithely overturning its norms on the banks of the Blackwater. Later, she took her young daughter, Rachel, through the Karakoram and across the Andes, with similar happy disregard for convention.

* * *

She led the way through a small kitchen into a den full of light and books. Shelves rose on three sides, packed with faded hardbacks arranged by the geography of her own journeys—Pakistan, South Africa, Madagascar and more. Four faded kilims hung from the banister of a narrow mezzanine at the shadiest end of the room. At the other end clean light fell through skylights onto a worn wooden table.

She cracked open the beer bottles, filled pint glasses, and settled herself onto a daybed in the brightest corner, a bulky figure in a shapeless blue cardigan with an old green sleeping bag over her knees. Pepper scrambled up onto her lap.

'You have this reputation for being reclusive,' I said, 'but I get the impression that you're not really.'

She cackled. Her eyes were narrow horizontal slits in the ruddy breadth of her face, and when she laughed they almost disappeared.

'Well, I think that's only because when I'm actually writing a book I go into *purdah*.' She put a lovely emphasis on the word, making it sound like something rich and sweet and creamy. 'I lock the gate and I take the phone off the hook and I don't open the post until I'm finished with the book. I would be off the scene from the point of view of having people just visiting for supper, or for a weekend. So that's why I've got that reputation. But as you say, it's not really deserved, because when I'm not in purdah then I do love having people here. Reclusive suggests I'm a sort of hermit, *permanently*, *constantly*'—the adverbs always got a great push on the first syllable—'but it's not so.'

Dervla's ancestry lay in the old-established Dublin middle classes, with their bookishness and genteel poverty and men who'd spent time in British prisons for their politics. Her father had come to Lismore as the county librarian, and his only child grew up with the naive sophistication that comes of a book-filled house in the deep country. By the time she was ten, Dervla knew that she wanted to be a writer. She also knew that she would never marry, and that one day she would cycle to India.

She'd made her first solo international bike trips in her early twenties—to Wales and England, then two forays into continental Europe. These journeys had produced a smattering of published articles, and, in 1954, a rejected travelogue about Spain. It was only in 1963 that she finally set out cycling to India. Her debut, *Full Tilt*, an account of that journey, was published two years later.

Full Tilt, like many of her other early works, was essentially a journal, written along the way—cut to book length later, 'but *absolutely* not rewritten,' she said, when I asked. But for the later, more serious and political projects, she'd moved away from the diary format. These books brimmed with dialogues, some with significant public figures. But I'd read somewhere that she never took notes during interviews. My digital recorder was rolling silently on the table between us, and now and then I would scribble a little note, matching a gesture or an expression to a phrase. Without these aids I simply couldn't see how I would ever be able to reproduce an extended conversation. Dervla, however, seemed to do it without difficulty.

'You must have a formidable capacity for perfect recall of the conversations,' I said.

'Oh, that was something dating from Northern Ireland, *A Place Apart*, because that was the first time I found myself in the situation of definitely not going in to talk to anybody with a notebook in hand. And of course I've never used one of *those* gadgets'—she pointed, somewhat disapprovingly, at my recorder. 'But it was absolutely essential not to misquote anybody, because everything was so sensitive. So what I did was develop through sheer force of circumstances the skill of really concentrating on every word and every nuance of the voice and so on, and the moment I left that meeting with the person, or a little gathering or whatever, immediately I'd go and write it down before there was any other discussion, any other experience, not even cycling off around somewhere else, just hiding myself. I remember several times just going to the loo, pretending that I had some internal problem and hastily, in the loo, writing something vitally important. It was sort of a little recording machine I cultivated in my brain. Of course, I kept trying to perfect it after that, because I realised how useful it was. I used it in Siberia or South Africa or wherever I went.'

It was striking, I said, that her most recent books—*A Month by the Sea* (2013) and *Between River and Sea* (2015)—had featured more of these extended human encounters, more use of that internal recording device, than almost anything else she'd ever written. They were formidably committed works, and not what you might expect from a travel writer in her eighties.

She cut in: 'Well, you see, I don't consider either of those books a travel book. I wasn't *travelling* on the West Bank; I was living there.'

'So if they're not travel books, what are they, Dervla?' The outline of another private question was beginning to form here. These books certainly matched my collected scholarly definitions, but if they *weren't* travel books, then what was this thing that *I* was planning to write?

'Well, as you say, they're journalistic records of living in a certain place—West Bank, Gaza,' she said.

'So can you define what a travel book is, then, if your last ones are not travel books?'

'*Well…*' She drew the word out, took a mouthful of beer and looked up. 'You know, in the old-fashioned travel book there's an element of adventure. You're not going around on clearly marked roads with signposts from one safe lodging to another. You never know when you get up in the morning where you're going to be in the evening—or are you going to get there! *That's* what *I* call a travel book.'

She certainly wouldn't call *my* project a travel book, then.

'But if that is your definition, then a big chunk of your books have not been travel books…' I protested

'That's why I often think it's silly just to describe me as a travel writer.'

'So what are you then?'

'I suppose a sort of commentator, and to that extent a journalist, of course.'

Outside, a thin rain had begun to fall. The junk and the nettles in the lee of the compound walls faded behind a sad smear of moisture. Dervla began to talk about a visit to a literary festival in Key West on her way to Cuba, a decade earlier. She'd appeared on a panel with Peter Matthiessen and Barry Lopez, and two younger travel writers.

'The debate was about to what extent is a travel writer allowed to invent things, and to what extent should he or she stick to accurate descriptions. There were five of us, the two famous oldies, and then there was myself, almost as old, and then there were two younger ones—when I say younger now, I mean under forty-five sort of age. And it was really interesting how the thing divided up, because the three oldies were absolutely adamant that you do *not* invent; and the two younger ones thought you were perfectly entitled, if that was making a more entertaining narrative, to invent.' She chuckled.

I'd never really had any doubts about the essential veracity of Dervla's books. She'd always seemed more likely to downplay the drama of her real experiences than to add invented spice. But I wanted to be certain.

'Have you had that across all your writing—that sense of needing to be accurate, of wanting to honour? Was that always there just automatically from the start?'

'Oh yes,' she said. 'I think it's purely a generational thing. *Absolutely*. My parents would have been *very* precise in that way.'

'But even though you'd be intending to record what really happened, do you think it's ever really possible to do that?'

Dervla seemed quite untroubled by the question. 'Oh, I'm sure human beings always sort of tweak things in their minds without intending to.' She straightened up a little on the daybed. Pepper grumbled and resettled himself on her lap. Dervla looked left and right across the table. 'The three of us could see the same thing and write down a completely different record of it…'

* * *

Dervla went out into the drizzle to use the toilet on the far side of the compound, and while she was gone I turned in my chair and scanned the wall of books behind me. It was a formidable array—a mix of vintage travel titles, heavyweight history and political treatises. There were slogan-bearing cards leaning here and there against the serried spines like placards from a whimsical demonstration: 'Books don't need batteries'; 'A weed is a plant out of place'. When she returned I asked which travel writers she'd had as her own models, starting out.

'Well, I'd never read much,' she said, then waved a hand at the book-armoured walls of the room. 'I mean, these that are *real* travel books—I read them because they were review copies. Paddy Leigh Fermor and Freya Stark would have been the two that I read before I started off myself, and that was for the quality of the writing.' Stark and Leigh Fermor—along with Jan Morris—had provided Colin Thubron's first encounter with travel writing too.

Dervla went on. 'I mean, I could see no point in reading travel books about places that I was going to or wanted to go to. You know; you just go there and find out for yourself. Not even *remotely* interested in somebody else's view of it. But really the history of course, that's a *completely* different thing; the history of the region that I was going to, or if it were a politically agitated region, then reading about the contemporary background. But travel books as such, I can never understand why anybody reads them, actually!'

This was quite a thing for a woman who had made her living by writing travel books to say. There was, though, a certain twinkle—there's no other word for it—in her deep-set eyes as she spoke.

* * *

In the weeks before I travelled to Lismore, I had, I knew, found quiet reassurance in the prospect of talking to Dervla Murphy. For one, the surfeit of male voices I had recorded so far on my journey was troubling me. A woman travel writer of Dervla's standing would do something to redress the balance. But since my visit to Eton there had been something else too. Her upbringing might have been separated from my own by half a century and 150 miles of seawater, but I somehow found it more comprehensible than that of some of the other writers I had met. I wondered if she might be able to answer a question that was really about myself—though I wasn't entirely sure how to articulate it. I began to talk about the long list I'd made of Eton- and Oxford-educated travel writers, and about the genre's alleged colonial heritage.

'Isn't that *interesting*?' She said this often, and I was never quite sure if she wasn't quietly humouring me. The twinkle was quite distinct.

'It's been making me wonder if maybe travel writing just comes naturally to people of that background,' I said. 'This is why I cling on to you, Dervla, because, to be honest, you're one of the only significant people with a big body of travel writing who doesn't really come from that background.'

'I'd never thought of that!'

'Had you not?'

'*Never*! I see what you mean though. It is *interesting*!'

'So you're a bit of an oddity—you're not a man for a start!'

She put down her beer, fumbled in the folds of the sleeping bag, and held up a paperback copy of Isabella Bird's *The Yangtze Valley and Beyond* (1899). Tucked inside was the handwritten draft of the introduction she was penning for a new edition.

'Well, yes,' I said, 'but weren't most of those earlier women travel writers a bit posh too?'

'Not really. I'd say they're all like myself; they're of the educated middle class.'

But why, then, were there so comparatively few women working in the genre, I asked, and virtually no working-class travel writers?

'Doesn't occur to them,' Dervla said. 'I think that's it.'

'But it occurred to *you*. And you're a woman; you're Irish and you're middle class—in terms of background and culture, solidly Irish middle class, and you just took to it completely.'

'*Absolutely*, yes.'

'With no sense that this was something that you weren't allowed to do as a middle-class Irishwoman. I wonder why that is, and why there weren't more of you.'

'Cannot imagine!' She pushed Pepper to the floor, disentangled herself from the sleeping bag and got to her feet. She was round-shouldered and had the swaying gait of one with troublesome hips and knees, but she moved swiftly about the place. Pepper scrit-scratted over the bare floorboards to get out of her way as she made for the kitchen.

'You know, the colonial thing is interesting, isn't it?' she said from the doorway. 'And I would have had *absolutely* the reverse, coming from a family, very active in my parents' generation, of Republicans, anti-colonial.'

'I wanted to ask you about that, because you come so strongly from that background, but then, in your early books anyway, your travel writing in a way would belong to the British tradition...'

'Well, there was no Irish one to belong to!' she chuckled.

'And when you were cycling to India you used the British consulates along the way...'

'*Absolutely*!'

'And in Baltistan your epigraphs are all from colonial texts...'

'A-ha!' She waggled a crooked finger. 'But that's interesting, you see, because supposing I were, as my parents were and my father and grandfather were, a fluent French speaker; supposing I were a fluent French speaker—wouldn't I have had these quotes from French travellers instead? The English language just restrained me to what was written in English.'

'And I suppose there'd just be more British consulates than Irish ones,' I said, a little sheepishly.

'Of course! Now—lunch!'

As befitted a woman who had cycled to India with minimal planning, and who had taken a five-year-old to the Upper Indus Valley in the dead of winter, Dervla Murphy had a way of making big problems seem small.

* * *

Lunch, laid out with mismatched bone-handled knives amongst the papers on the table, was a hearty soup of red lentils. 'You needn't worry about anything here; you just get a plate of food thrown at you,' Dervla said, as she set down cheese and a loaf of cakey Irish bread. 'I usually make my own bread, but I've run out of spelt flour so this is bought bread, of which I'm ashamed.'

She did not eat anything herself, though she opened another bottle before settling back into her spot on the daybed. The soup was delicious.

'Dervla,' I said, through a mouthful of bread and cheese, 'is it true that you only eat breakfast?' I'd read this somewhere.

'Yep.'

'So you don't eat at all during the day?'

'Nope.' She raised her glass and sloshed the sudsy ale from side to side. 'Drink!'

She woke at five in the morning, ate a huge breakfast, and needed no more solid food for the coming twenty-four hours. It was a particularly convenient routine, she said, when working on a book.

While I ate, she talked on, always with great sweeping emphases on odd words, always with that glint in her eye, and always with dog and beer in easy reach. There were strong thoughts on international development agencies ('It's a filthy racket, the United Nations'), contempt for contemporary Irish politicians ('I hate the background that Coveney comes out of; this smug Catholic righteousness') and disillusionment with modern journalism ('The BBC has gone so down, it really has'). Amongst the few reporters she had any time for were the veteran Middle East correspondents Patrick Cockburn ('Brilliant!') and Robert Fisk ('One of the few sources of reliable information the public gets'). I dared to suggest that some might consider Fisk's streak of anger to be unjournalistic. 'I've contempt for that,' Dervla snapped.

I asked again about the other travel writers she admired.

She repeated the name of Freya Stark. 'And Mary Kingsley. Who else?—well really she and Isabella Bird, really they'd be the main influences.'

'They're all women—is there a distinct difference between women's travel writing and men's travel writing?' This was something I was going to have to tackle at some point, I knew, but I wasn't sure that

Dervla—transgressive, outlying Dervla—was necessarily the right person to discuss it with.

'I don't think so.'

'But it's curious that those three travel writers you mention are all women.'

'Well, I suppose in Victorian times when Isabella and Mary Kingsley were functioning, I suppose that would be the sort of affinity I'd have with them. When I set off for my first cycle tour around the continent, I was eighteen or nineteen. I mean, the whole locality here were absolutely *horrified*. Might as well have been a hundred years earlier, me going into the jungle of somewhere or other! So I suppose that would be the link that I'd have had with them at that stage.'

'So the fact that they're women is crucial, but not so much in the writing? It's the act of going?'

'*Exactly*. Yep.'

I wondered if there were any more books to come, and she pointed, somewhat dismissively, to a slew of papers along the top of the shelf under the window to my left.

'There's a book half written up there.'

'What's that one about?'

'Jordan. It won't be finished.'

It was meant to be the third leg of her exploration of the scattered Palestinian community, but, she said, the pain of her arthritis made sitting at her desk for long stretches impossible. There would be no more periods of purdah.

I looked again at the papers, overlapping like roof tiles above the Tibet section of Dervla's library. 'Could you not—you'll probably slap this down—but could you not get help in with that, if you're able to write longhand, could you not get...' But I didn't finish the thought: Dervla was glowering at me fiercely.

'You know,' she said, 'at 85 you can't teach an old bitch new tricks!'

She went back to the kitchen and returned with the steaming soup pan, and for just a moment there, bending over the table, she could have been any octogenarian Irish farmer's widow: 'A little more now. You couldn't be full! Have some cheese! You'll have some, good man. I just throw in everything that's around, I don't do recipes! And at the end a dash of Yorkshire Relish...'

I saw, with a small pang, that she had a red alarm button, of the kind that my grandmother had worn in her last years, on a piece of elastic around her wrist.

* * *

The most important question I'd had in mind, coming to visit Dervla Murphy had not been one that I could actually ask her: what would she be *like*?

When a travel writer is a distinct persona, the central character of their own books, surely it's worth wondering whether this figure is truly *them*. Readers are always sniffing out autobiographical ciphers in works of fiction, so why not consider the opposite scenario: that the central figure in an autobiographical work might be a piece of fiction? The figure that emerged from Dervla's books—all of them, from the very first—was unmistakable: opinionated, brooking no nonsense, perturbed by nothing, apparently insensible to hardship yet with a certain self-deprecating streak, and plainly inviting the epithets routinely awarded to many of the women travel writers of an earlier age: 'doughty', 'indomitable', 'fearless'. So far, Dervla Murphy in the flesh was indistinguishable from the Dervla Murphy of the books. But I wanted to explore the idea, and so, when the soup was finished, I made an attempt.

'In a travel book the central character is the writer,' I said. 'So you have the central character, the narrator, and the author, who in a novel might well be three different people, but here they're all called Dervla Murphy—or Colin Thubron or whoever it might be. But to what extent do you end up fictionalising yourself?'

'Oh,' she said, without missing a beat, 'I think that's probably inevitable. As we said earlier, if we all went through the same experience we'd all describe it differently, and to that extent I'm sure everybody fictionalises themselves in writing their travel books.'

'But I wonder if that idea of the fearless but also self-deprecating and also humorous character—how much of that is really you, and how much of that is a sort of literary persona that you adopted in the first book and then were kind of stuck with?'

'Um...' Now, for the first time, she did pause. 'I don't *think* it was adopted, because, after all, from the age of ten I had had the plan to cycle to India. You know, it wasn't a sort of new idea that I had become this person who would cycle to India. It was absolutely *baked* into me by twenty years later when I did...'

'But Dervla,' I said, '*that's* the significance...'

Before travelling to Lismore I had read, for the first time, *Wheels Within Wheels*, Dervla's 1979 account of her life up to the point at which—aged thirty-one—she clambered onto her bicycle and started pedalling towards India. It had originally been written as a private memoir, meant to be put aside for her daughter to read in adulthood. But when her publisher, John 'Jock' Murray VI, discovered its existence she had unsentimentally handed it over. It was startling. And harrowing.

By the time Dervla was three years old, her mother had already been crippled by rheumatoid arthritis, unable to walk, to wash or dress herself, even to brush her own hair. At fourteen, Dervla—an intellectually curious child—had been pulled out of school to become her mother's full-time carer. Those early solo bike trips to the continent had not been liberal indulgences, but meagre consolations, offered by parents who had themselves studied and travelled abroad in their own twenties without grim responsibilities to haul them back. As her mother's condition worsened and began to affect her sanity, the young Dervla's horizons narrowed, then vanished altogether. There was other pain amongst all of this too. Her first lover, an older Englishman in some kind of exile in rural Waterford, had fallen ill and taken himself away to die. And then, suddenly in the winter of 1961, her father too had died. Dervla was left alone to cope with her mother's bleak final eighteen months of life.

I said that I had only recently read *Wheels Within Wheels*. 'What really struck me about it was that when you set off, cycling to India, this was just *months* after emerging from all of that.'

'Oh yes, *literally* months.'

This was what had astonished me, for there was not the faintest trace of any of it to be found in *Full Tilt*. 'So that journey, this fully-made tough woman, toting an automatic pistol, shooting wolves and being completely unfazed by all these things that happen—you must have still been psychologically in a process of coming out of everything you'd been through in the previous years?'

But she shook her head. 'You see, I don't think so. Because I think the last—what would it have been? Can't even remember myself now—eighteen months or so, between my father's death and my mother's death...'

'But it was more than eighteen months Dervla; your horizons had been very much...'

'Oh, before that, yes, my whole adult life, from the age of fourteen to thirty.'

I realised that I was the one who sounded pained. Dervla was as cheery as she was on every other topic.

'Anyone reading *Wheels Within Wheels*,' I said, 'would think she's going to kill herself in a minute...'

Dervla laughed.

'But seriously!'

'Well, I very nearly did, *absolutely*.'

'But...'

She shook her head firmly. 'No, no; as soon as my mother died—finished.'

'Is that really true?'

'That is *absolutely* true.'

Some of the academic work I'd read argued that travel writing by women was more likely than that by men to feature a pronounced 'inner journey'—some process of healing or transformation running parallel to the record of the temporal voyage. At times the academic texts lapsed to bold assertions on this matter: the scholar Sara Mills stated quite bluntly that women's travel books 'are far more self-revelatory than men's'.[2] I wasn't entirely convinced. Hadn't Graham Greene, ignoring Cousin Barbara in the forests of Liberia, been the one to pioneer the deployment of Freudian self-analysis in a travel narrative? And hadn't even some of the bearded imperial explorers of poles and peaks waxed lyrical on their own psychological responses to physical hardship? It was certainly true, however, that the idea of a journey of recovery was a very well-established trope in more recent travel narratives by women. Internationally, Elizabeth Gilbert's *Eat, Pray, Love* (2006) and Cheryl Strayed's *Wild* (2012) had surely been amongst the biggest-selling of all the books ever to be filed under 'travel' since the start of the twenty-first century. And the recent run of British nature writing was full of healing journeys too—Helen Macdonald's *H is for Hawk* (2014); Amy Liptrot's *The Outrun* (2015); Katharine Norbury's *The Fish Ladder* (2015). If Dervla had been setting out to write an account of her transcontinental bike ride today, it would surely have to come out themed like these books. I said this, and she roared with laughter.

'You see, I've no time or use for inner journeys or healings,' she said with a gravelly cackle; 'I really haven't. You know, you get up and go and do what you've been wanting to do for twenty years and you don't sit around, you know, having deep thoughts about it. You just go and do it.'

'So... I'm sorry, I have to push you a bit...'

'Push me!' She grinned, eyes twinkling.

'Your mother had passed away literally just a few months before you set off...'

'Four months.'

'There you are! And a year earlier you'd been in a horrendous state.'

'A very bad way. But I don't actually remember that eighteen months between my parents' deaths. It's a blank. I mean, I do *vaguely* remember that I was drinking neat whisky and chain smoking. Otherwise I *genuinely* don't remember, it was so bad.'

But the moment her mother died, the trauma ended, she insisted. There was no inner journey in *Full Tilt*, because there had been no process of recovery to document. It had been instant.

'So you would genuinely stand by the idea that the Dervla Murphy central character who appears in *Full Tilt*, and gets older but stays basically the same through all those books right up to Gaza and Palestine—that genuinely was you; you emerged as that person and set out cycling?'

'Well as far as I know I did!' she said. 'You don't have much time for much else when there are no paved roads and you're cycling to India; you don't have time to introspect, I can assure you of that!'

I'm fairly certain that I believed her.

Later, when I wrote up my notes, I realised halfway through that I was referring to her as 'Dervla'. Usually I baulked at this chummy business of discussing writers on first-name terms: Paddy, Bruce,

Willie. No matter how friendly the encounters had been, the other travel writers I'd met had to be a surname on the page: Thubron, Danziger, Jubber. I stopped, and started writing 'Murphy' instead, but it sounded ridiculous. Dervla, quite simply, was Dervla.

* * *

It was time to leave. The rain had eased off, and the mist at the windows had cleared. Through them, tucked away in a corner, I could see an old white road bike, rusting amongst the woodpiles and nettles. Surely this wasn't *the* bike, left so unceremoniously to moulder?

I pointed through the glass. 'That's not Roz, is it?'

'Oh no, that's a later one. Roz is in the county library headquarters to be looked at by tourists,' Dervla said. 'She was in use in Dublin for short cycles around the city in her retiring years, and, as I say, now she's a tourist attraction. When they begged me to let that happen, I said okay.'

'Well, seeing as you're supposedly so reclusive yourself...'

'Yes, let Roz do it—she can take the shit!'

She walked out to the inner gate with the dogs to see me on my way. '*Do* visit again, if you're down this way,' she said. 'The both of you...'

* * *

'Well, that's what you'll have to work out how to do, then,' Cara said.

On the far side of the Knockmealdown Mountains the land flattened out and lost the benign fecundity of the Blackwater Valley. The sky was low and grey, and there was a strange airlessness. The roads were empty. We passed small grey towns beside rivers, and long empty fields. At one point, where the road bent through a block of forestry, there was a wrecked car at the verge.

What would it do to the substance of the account if I did as Cara had suggested? It would mean, for a start, that I'd have to excise the moments when I was silent and a pair of Irishwomen, two generations apart, discussed the merits of foreign beers, or the question of favourite countries. ('Couldn't say. What's yours?' had been Dervla's response; Cara had said, 'I suppose the country that would have your heart, it's India for me,' and Dervla had nodded: 'Yes, that's how Rachel is too...')

But was there more at stake than that? I'd asked Dervla about her third book, *The Waiting Land* (1967), an account of her stint in a UN-run camp for Tibetan refugees in Nepal. During her time there she had encountered serious institutional corruption, but, having signed a confidentiality agreement before she set out, she'd felt unable to discuss the matter in the book. I asked how she viewed *The Waiting Land* now, looking back and wishing that she had spoken out. 'Everything that's in that book really happened, but by taking out a huge chunk of the back story, is it in a way fictionalised?' I'd asked.

'Destroyed it,' she'd said, '*absolutely*. As you say, nothing is added, but an *awful* lot is subtracted.'

The travel writing scholar Carl Thompson, discussing the many instances of travel writers obscuring the presence of companions in their narratives, had noted that 'here the careful tailoring of the travel account clearly pushes the text in the direction of fiction, even if the writer does not perpetrate any outright inventions or falsehoods'.[3]

Something else too: Dervla talked about the necessity of changing names and disguising identities when writing about encounters in politically troubled places: 'And then of course I have the terrible problem of the person I'm writing about becoming identified in my mind with their invented name, and I can't remember their real name when I want to send them a card for some reason!'

Dervla had found this very funny, but it left me uneasy. If I wrote Cara out of my account of the visit to Lismore, might I end up inadvertently redrafting my own memory?

All this was pointing in one irresistible direction. I needed to confront the original travel writing controversy, the thread of contention that ran all the way from Sir John Mandeville to Bruce Chatwin. I needed to visit the troubled frontier between fact and fiction.

We were on the motorway now, racing north towards Galway in a lowering evening, and Cara was saying something about our trip to Lismore. I turned away from the window. 'What did you say?'

'Honestly, I think that was the nicest soup I've ever had.'

11

FLYING PIGS

The voice behind my right shoulder said, 'This is Katrin.'

A slim, fair-haired woman, standing in the light of an uncluttered room in an English village. I think I must have made some small exclamation of surprise, though I don't really know what it was that surprised me—that she was real, I suppose.

'It's a bit odd,' I said, uncertainly, 'meeting someone in real life that you've already met in books.'

Katrin smiled. 'Ah!' she said, 'But I'm a *character* in the books...' Her accent was English. Why did *that* surprise me?

The voice behind my right shoulder again, speaking from the shadow of the hallway; decidedly *not* English, pitched somewhere in the coastal waters off the eastern seaboard of North America. A voice that sounded like a wry smile. 'We *both* are,' it said.

* * *

Several months had passed since my visit to Dervla Murphy. I'd been reading more travel books—old favourites and new titles, viewed now with a more critical eye—and I'd continued to fossick in the back catalogue of travel writing studies. Its lexicon—'traveller and travellee', 'contact zone' and all the rest—was now as familiar as the place names of Central Asia, learnt from travel books.

In the high summer I'd spent a month in Indonesia. I'd watched over my own shoulder as I filled my journal each night, obeying Robin

Hanbury-Tenison's strictures. For the first time I found myself wondering why I was recording certain things and not others. What unseen forces were guiding my pencil across the pages of the notebook? And how might I twist the shape of the journey if I were to translate the rough diary into a polished travel narrative?

I knew that on my return I wanted to consider the question of travel writing's troubled relationship with 'truth'. It was, I'd realised, much more complicated than I'd first assumed. John Mandeville was simply a 'travel liar': he said he'd been where he'd never been, talked to people he'd never met. It was easy enough to mark him down as a fraud, his work as a hoax, and then to move on. But it was seldom so simple. My unease during the visit to Eton wasn't all down to class anxiety; the slight disconnect between the raw records of Thesiger's journeys and his books had left me discomfited too. Thesiger *had* been where he said he'd been, had talked to the people he said he'd met. And yet, somehow... And then there was my own encounter with Dervla Murphy, and the challenge I'd created for myself in writing it up. My collected scholarly definitions all mentioned some kind of factuality as an identifying feature of travel writing. But if this was a nonfiction genre, it seemed to be one haunted by fiction.

I went back to the academic literature, hoping to find out more. But, to my surprise, when I searched the library catalogue I discovered that this was one issue that scholars tended to avoid. They had pored over the questions of power and colonialism, dissected countless texts in search of some unique essence in 'women's travel writing' and discussed 'ethics' at length. But no one seemed to want to ask uncomfortable questions about the slippery veracity of travel narratives. The few journal articles and monographs dedicated to 'travel lies' that I managed to dredge up focussed on the distant past—on John Mandeville and his ilk. Perhaps some kind of politeness was at play. If a travel writer had been dead for six centuries, and if he claimed to have met a dog-headed man en route to supper with Prester John, it was probably quite safe to call him a liar. But if he was only recently deceased—or indeed was still at work—and if all he'd done was claim to have found a clump of mylodon hair in a cave—well, you were edging towards potential libel.

I'd be no braver than the scholars, I realised. I'd asked Colin Thubron about his own trustworthiness as a narrator during our conversation, and he'd declared himself reliable by the 'abysmal standards of the genre'. But I couldn't very well accuse someone of *lying*—least of all someone who had invited me into their home and given me tea and biscuits.

I settled down to read through my meagre haul of scholarly texts on travel writing and untruth. There was *Travelers and Travel Liars, 1660–1800*, an old book by Percy G. Adams.[1] It was a brisk run-through of Patagonian giants and mythical maritime passages, written in a sprightly style uncommon amongst more recent academics, and it showed how the travellers of old had incited the lies of their peers with their own fabrications. Elsewhere, in an edited collection, there was a chapter by Daniel Carey, looking at the way *Gulliver's Travels* had cannily satirised the unreliable travel braggarts of the eighteenth century.[2] And there was an article by Kirsten Sandrock on 'Truth and Lying in Early Modern Travel Narratives'.

Sandrock claimed that 'medieval travel narratives were still allowed and quite possibly expected to invent parts of their material', and that it was only sometime between the late fourteenth and the early eighteenth centuries that 'the generic conventions of travel writing changed fundamentally' as readers began to expect—and indeed demand—the truth.[3] Surely something wasn't quite right here. Wasn't it simply the limit of readers' credulity that had shifted? Just because dog-headed men are literally incredible to us, it doesn't mean that they were to a medieval audience. Columbus had carried Mandeville's *Travels* as a guidebook, after all.

Still, the article was useful: Sandrock quoted another scholar, Siegfried J. Schmidt, arguing that readers of overtly fictional stories had learnt to replace the 'fact convention' that governed their daily conversations, their reading of newspapers and, indeed, their reading of nonfiction books with an 'aesthetic convention' that gave the creative vision of the writer free rein, that licensed the literally unbelievable. Peter Hulme, a senior scholar of travel writing, had said something similar: 'We read books either as fiction or as non-fiction.' It was a binary distinction, and, Hulme felt, a 'contractual point'.[4]

But what happened, I wondered, when a reader came upon an unstable text? What 'convention' applied when you picked up a book that messed with your expectations, that wasn't fiction but which plainly played fast and loose with the facts?

And that's when I knew exactly who I needed to speak to next.

* * *

Rory MacLean had been amongst the first rank of the second generation of contemporary travel writers who appeared at the opening of the 1990s. By the time I discovered the genre, his books were already prominent on the shelves of the travel section. His 1992 debut, *Stalin's Nose*, was an account of a journey around Eastern Europe just after the fall of the Berlin Wall—a journey made in an old Trabant in the company of an aging aunt called Zita and a pig called Winston. Other books followed: *The Oatmeal Ark* (1997), an exploration of MacLean's own Scottish ancestry; *Under the Dragon* (1998), about Burma; *Next Exit Magic Kingdom* (2000), an odyssey through Florida; and more—*Falling for Icarus* (2004), *Magic Bus* (2006), *Berlin: Imagine a City* (2014). And he was very much still at it today.

I originally came to these books with a certain youthful fundamentalism. I could see that they were finely written. 'But,' I remember spluttering to myself, 'this didn't *happen!*' And in the case of *The Oatmeal Ark*, narrated partly by ghosts and partly in the third person: 'This isn't a travel book at all!' It was only later—about the time that he published *Magic Bus*, I think—that I realised this was the point. MacLean never pretended to be recounting the hard facts; he made a journey, then worked creatively, to a greater or lesser extent, with whatever it was that he brought back. *Stalin's Nose* begins with Winston the pig falling out of a tree and killing the narrator's uncle.

Since then, I'd enjoyed his books enormously—though it was never an uncomplicated enjoyment. There was sometimes a disconcerting sense of giddiness as I read, as if the solid earth was shifting beneath me, ever so slightly. It was the needle ticking back and forth uneasily between my 'fact convention' and my 'aesthetic convention', I suppose. In fact, the way MacLean messed with expectations meant that I sometimes found myself particularly destabilised when I *couldn't* spot him obviously inventing—as in *Next Exit Magic Kingdom*.

Introducing a new edition of MacLean's 2004 book, *Falling for Icarus*, Robert Macfarlane had cast about for an appropriate comparison. 'I would pause over Bruce Chatwin as a possibility,' he'd written, 'but then probably stretch far further back: to John Mandeville, to St

Brendan and to Marco Polo.' What a compliment! Mandeville and his ilk, Macfarlane wrote, with an echo of Kirsten Sandrock, 'returned bearing tales that were not to be submitted to the usual tests of verifiability and falsifiability, but in which the actual and the miraculous rubbed shoulders'.[5] If I was going to talk to someone about fictionalisation in travel writing, then who better than a writer who did the same thing, openly, in our own era?

* * *

MacLean lived in a little village somewhere near the Dorset–Somerset border. I drove there on a damp afternoon, tracing a route across a map marked with improbable names: Hazelbury Bryan, Beer Hackett and—I am not making this up—Mudford Sock.

Summer had departed without ceremony, leaving wet tarmac, low scudding skies and roadside trees waving hysterically in the moderate westerly. The village itself was a place of steeply pitched roofs and scrubbed yellow stone. It looked like a film set.

They'd laid out lunch on a wooden table in the front room of the cottage: bread from a bakery in the neighbouring village, thinly sliced ham and cheese, and a salad of roasted squash. I was still a little disconcerted by the existence of Katrin, MacLean's wife, who features in several of his books. I'd *known* she was real, of course. But still, it was peculiar to find her, sitting to my right at the table, loading my plate with roasted squash and listening as I explained my journey. MacLean chuckled at the thought of Old Etonians and Thesiger's stiff propriety. No veneration of the departed greats here.

'I have a theory that there are two kinds of travel writer,' he said; 'the lean ascetic ones, and the garrulous ones who like to eat.' His accent was Canadian, mostly, but with other traces, and he talked with a soft, half-whispered enthusiasm. It took me a while to work it out: he sounded like the best sort of children's storyteller.

'Which kind are you?' asked Katrin, across the table.

'Oh,' said MacLean through a mouthful of buttered bread, 'the lean ascetic kind!' and he laughed. Like his speech, his laughter—and there was a lot of it—was somehow both forceful and soft.

Afterwards we went upstairs to talk in his office.

'Look!' he said, reaching across to his desk as I settled into my seat and switched on my digital recorder. He lifted a small, hard object like a battery. 'I've just rediscovered this film, photographic film, Kodak film from I think about 1967. And I exposed half of it and then I thought, "Oh, well, I'll wrap it up and expose the rest later," and I never did! And what I love about it is the latent images that are there. *What did I photograph? What is on there?*'

'Can you remember?'

'No, I *can't*! You know, they're probably terribly boring and naff photographs. But I just *love* the potential there. I must never process it of course…'

He sat across from me in a low easy chair beneath a ceiling-high bookshelf, hands pressed between his knees. He was tall—taller than me, I'd noticed when we were standing downstairs. But folded into the low seat, rocking slightly, eyebrows lifting and falling above his glasses, half-smile always in place, he seemed to shrink—not to the form of a child, but to that of an imp—an imp feigning absolute innocence.

* * *

Rory MacLean was born in Vancouver in 1954. He went to school at the elite Upper Canada College—the Canadian Gordonstoun, more or less. His father was a newspaper publisher, and his English mother had once worked as a secretary for Ian Fleming. But MacLean didn't really seem to have a classical travel writer's pedigree. He'd gone on to film school, and then, after a series of jobs on movie sets in Canada and the UK, he'd found himself in Berlin, working with the director David Hemmings on the David Bowie vehicle, *Just a Gigolo*. The film itself might have turned out rather a flop, but for MacLean the experience was the start of something.

'I was pulled out of Canada—borderless Canada, the Great White North—and then thrown into the island city of West Berlin surrounded by three quarters of a million Red Army soldiers with the Wall,' he said. 'I'd never seen anything like it. It shook me to the core.'

For a decade afterwards he worked in the film industry, and on the side he rattled out dozens of unsuccessful film scripts on a Smith Corona typewriter.

'That's how I taught myself to write—writing film scripts for films that would never be made. I also think that's why I feel quite at ease with handling dialogue, and so therefore, I think, with handling character as well. Because movies—indeed all narratives—are based on dialogue.'

It seemed obvious now, though I hadn't spotted it the first time I read *Stalin's Nose*: it was a scriptwriter's book; the whole thing was driven by dialogue. Perhaps I'd been distracted by the pig.

MacLean said that he had not noticed the popular and commercial excitement around travel writing while he was living in London in the 1980s.

'I wasn't aware of that,' he said, 'because—well, first and foremost, I'm not English, and for the most part it's an English tradition. Of course there were, there are, Scottish, Welsh, Irish travel writers— and Dutch and American travel writers too. But it has been a mostly English genre.'

He did, though, go to hear Colin Thubron give a lecture at the Institute of Contemporary Arts in London, about his book *Among the Russians* (1983). Thubron had spoken of visiting countries viewed from without as objects of fear, and of overcoming that fear through under-standing. 'That really struck a chord with me: to understand the world one can try to "people the map", while also writing about something you feel passionately about. And that obviously includes questions about yourself.' MacLean still had the notes he had scribbled during Thubron's lecture all those years ago. Sometime later, he won a travel writing competition in the newly launched *Independent* newspaper. The commission to write *Stalin's Nose* came soon afterwards, and the film scripts were forgotten.

'Famously, Bruce Chatwin said "I don't believe in coming clean",' I said.

MacLean rocked back in the easy chair and roared with laughter— roared, but softly, somehow.

I went on. 'I know you're always very overt, you make it clear right from the outset that you are not a "straight" travel writer. You say that in lots of places, but without really going into any further detail. So I wonder if, like Chatwin, you do come clean...'

He raised his eyebrows. The light coming through the window behind me caught on the lenses of his glasses.

'You know,' he said, 'with *Stalin's Nose* I thought, this is a chance for me. I've been given a chance to write a book about something I really care about, and a part of the world I'm fascinated by, at a turning point of history—the fall of the Berlin Wall. The forgotten half of

Europe can be discovered again by a Westerner—quote, unquote "discovered again". And it felt like such an opportunity, such a privilege. I simply wrote the book that I wanted to. Perhaps because I wasn't aware of a tradition of travel writing, I didn't think, "Oh, well, I've got to stick to the absolute observable facts of the experiences that I alone have had." It didn't occur to me. I just thought, "This is probably the only book I'll ever have the chance to write," and I just felt my way through it. I think that's the right word: I *felt* it.

'I made the trip. I travelled from Berlin to Moscow; I went to all the places I wrote about; all the people who are in the book are real people and I met them. But then, if you like, when I sat down at my desk it was like starting a parallel journey. The experience and memories of the actual journey were drawn together and distilled, creating two realities—one on the road and the other on the page. It was... it was...' He half turned to the bookshelf, as if the answer might be there somewhere. 'It was... would *freer* be right? It was... it was as alive as the real journey. And I just loved it. I just loved the experience, this ability to remake this journey. Does that sort of answer it?'

I wasn't quite sure if it did, but I went on anyway. I'd been rereading *Stalin's Nose*, I said, and I'd spotted something else that I'd missed the first time around, besides the dominance of dialogue. 'I might be mistaken about this, but although it's a first-person narrative, I don't think you're ever referred to by name in it.'

'No, I'm not!' he said brightly. 'I don't name myself. So from the beginning I was as much of a character as any writer creates a character. So yes, I was never "Rory" travelling.'

'Well, that's what I thought,' I said. Something had occurred to me. It was a silly question, perhaps, but it seemed worth asking: 'Were you actually not a travel writer at all? Were you just tagged as a travel writer because it wasn't a particularly classifiable book?'

The glasses glittered; the eyebrows rose and fell. 'But it *is* a travel book! I start in Berlin and end up in Moscow.' It was with words like Moscow—'moss-*cow*'—that his Canadian accent came through most strongly. The fact that he wasn't *British* struck me again.

'I'm a foreigner travelling through these lands, observing them as an outsider, as a young man in 1989, 1990, from the point of view of someone living in London, as I was then. From the beginning, travel writing has been the individual going out from his or her home country to a foreign place, observing and then bringing back their subjective experience—claiming it's objective, but bringing back their subjective experience and sharing it at the RGS or wherever, and saying, "Golly, this is how it is!"'

But that had never been quite the way he worked, I pointed out; and his wasn't quite the tradition of his contemporaries. It wasn't William Dalrymple emulating Robert Byron and Peter Fleming, or Philip Marsden following Colin Thubron's lead.

'But at that time I'd never *heard* of Peter Fleming!' he protested. 'I doubt I'd read Robert Byron in 1989. I *had* heard of Colin...'

'But you clearly weren't trying to write *Among the Russians*.'

'No, because I *couldn't*. I wasn't able to do that. That's a rich tradition, but that's not *my* tradition.' He paused and said, 'How can I put it?' There were often these little halts, these little questions of his own discourse, angled in the direction of the window or the bookshelf. 'I don't quite know how to put it, Tim; it's just the way I wanted to write the book.'

I felt a little guilty. MacLean was forever having to answer these questions.

'I understand it's provocative,' he said, 'and I understand that there's lots of arguments saying that my approach is unacceptable, in the argument of subjectivity and objectivity. But it's an old argument; you know that. Individuals maintain that they have an objective view of the world, but of *course* it's subjective; they come back with a totally subjective view.' He laughed again. 'I'm just making a point of that by incorporating fictional elements or using fictional devices within a non-fiction book. So I see my books, if I'm forced to define them, as nonfiction, but having extensive use of fictional devices. I think it sits more comfortably in the American genre of creative nonfiction. That's how I see it. It's essential I make the trip; I *must* make the trip; I must meet the individuals who I'm going to write about. Perhaps those individuals will be transformed into composite characters in places; perhaps I'll shift dates; but I will *never* shift the inner meaning of an individual; I always will be true to the individual, and reflect as honestly as possible a people, a society, a time—because I want the reader to *empathise*. I want the reader to identify with the character, and to feel what it was like to grow up in Nazi-controlled Berlin or to live under martial law in Burma, for example.'

There was another impetus at play too, he said: 'I think it's part of this ongoing rebellion against the audacity of individuals who claim they're being objective. And I've never accepted that. Of course, they're doing their best to be objective, but their observations will inevitably be subjective, which is why I start all my—quote, unquote—"nonfiction" travel books with an incident that is patently not literally true, like a pig falling out of a tree, or a ghost speaking in the first paragraph. That's a signpost; I'm saying please suspend your disbelief.'

* * *

The afternoon rolled forward, and the light from the window dimmed and brightened like a lamp fed by a fluctuating current as the squalls rattled by. MacLean seemed to grow ever smaller in the easy chair, as though I might eventually be able to pick him up and place him on the desk like a talisman alongside the undeveloped film. He threw back his head and laughed with soft force so often that the room, high and pale and clean, seemed to fizz and pop with it.

He talked about his methods as a writer on the road. During the research for *Stalin's Nose*, he said, he had felt self-conscious about taking notes in front of people—though he'd always told them he was writing a book. Like Dervla in Northern Ireland, he'd made frequent dashes for the toilet to scribble down the most important points of a conversation.

'I think I gave Canadians certainly, and maybe Brits as well, this reputation throughout Eastern Europe of having really weak bladders!' he said. At the end of each day these first scribbled notes were written up longhand into a fuller journal, and then reworked into a first draft back at his desk when the journey was over.

'That reworking once one's back at home, that's the flying, that's the magic. Lawrence Durrell has this wonderful quote in *The Alexandria Quartet*, from the first book, *Justine*, about the role of the writer, the role of the artist, and he talks about the sackcloth covering that is reality, and how the writer or the artist has to see through the sackcloth covering to the cloth-of-gold underneath, the meaning of the pattern. And I guess that's also why it is, for me, so important that one acknowledges the subjectivity, acknowledges that this is a creative work, that it is *a* truth not *the* truth.'

He told me about an organised debate on fictionalisation in travel writing he had taken part in a decade earlier, at the Royal Society of Literature in London, with another Rory—Rory Stewart, author of *The Places in Between* (2004), an account of a winter walk across Afghanistan.

MacLean had explained his own way of working to the audience. 'Of course, I approached with a very convivial, collegiate manner: "We're in this together, we're travel writers!"' He paused and grimaced. 'He didn't see it quite that way.'

Stewart—a former diplomat, rumoured secret service operative and future Conservative Party leadership candidate—had argued, with all the relentless assurance of an Eton College debater, that staunch empiricism was the only way to do travel writing properly.

'And I was saying, "That's not right, this is the twenty-first century, come on, Rory!" But he was saying, "No, no; don't make anything up." And I thought, come on! You walked across Afghanistan; it took six weeks; you don't talk about going to the loo!'

'No travel writers ever go to the toilet,' I said.

'Unless it's to write notes!'

I found a recording of the debate later online. I'd half expected to come down on Stewart's side of the argument. I'd loved *The Places in Between*. And for all that I also loved MacLean's books, there was still a lingering unease at the idea of a travel writer licensed to invent. But in the end I listened with some kind of horror as Stewart declared a dubious array of imperial spies and colonial administrators, penning missives to the mother country at the height of the nineteenth century, to be the honourable apogee of travel writing. Thesiger, as far as he was concerned, was 'about the end of it', and the subsequent 'falling away' into 'decadence' had come 'because the stakes of empire have been lost, because the standards of espionage have been lost' and because 'the extraordinary moment in which they operated at the end of the nineteenth century' has been lost. Rory Stewart had roundly bulldozed Rory MacLean's puckish, soft-spoken contribution with all the might of the British Empire. Suddenly a fact-convention-defying pig in an old Trabant seemed much less ethically troubling.

* * *

Amongst the smattering of scholarly texts that addressed fictionalisation in travel writing, I had, to my surprise, found a couple which argued for a 'fictive mode' as an ethical approach. Rory Stewart would doubtless have been outraged at such decadence, but in a funny way, the argument made sense. One scholar, Claire Lindsay, had looked at fictionalised accounts by Luis Alberto Urrea of migrants trying to cross the US–Mexico border—accounts which imagined the experiences of travellers unlikely ever to write books of their journeys. Sometimes Urrea had used a second-person address—*you* do this, *you* do that—in his efforts to establish what Lindsay called 'affective identification' with the ill-fated migrants.[6] It was a little blunt, perhaps, like grabbing the reader by the nape of the neck and shouting 'Look!' But it certainly suggested greater empathy than the passing glances of some more conventional travel books. Another scholar, Corinne Fowler, following Lindsay's track, declared that in such works 'it is a fictive mode that encourages the reader to identify with the subjects of the travel account'.[7] I wasn't really sure that the examples they gave properly counted as travel writing, but their argument could certainly apply to Rory MacLean.

Under the Dragon, MacLean's third book, published in 1998, was an account of a journey through Burma. This was where I had first met Katrin—or at least the character that bore her name. On one level the book was a fairly straightforward travel writing quest, with little obvious invention—as the narrator and his wife went in search of an obscure type of woven basket. But threaded crossways through the travelogue were four discrete chapters, intimate and unhappy life stories of four Burmese women. Occasionally these stories glanced briefly off the narrator's own journey, but for the most part they stood alone. There was no overt trace of the authorial research that must have gone into them. And they were, clearly, in some way fictional. But they did—undoubtedly, powerfully, movingly—'encourage the reader to identify with the subjects of the travel account'.

I tried to explain all this now. MacLean giggled as I gabbled out the inelegant phraseology of travel writing studies: 'affective identification'; 'traveller and travellee'.

'I don't know what that means! Do I have to fill in a form to understand this correctly?'

'Basically,' I said, 'their point is that by embracing fictionalisation it becomes much easier to promote solidarity. And it strikes me that

that's very much what you've been about really, certainly from *Under the Dragon* onwards.'

He thought about this for a moment.

'I guess that the *travellee...*' he paused and dipped his head as if I'd forced him to take something he didn't really want. 'I don't like the word—but I do make the trip for the travellee as much as for myself. I see myself as a conduit between a reader and, say, a peasant farmer in rural Burma or a Scottish immigrant to pioneer Canada. I try to link the two worlds. I try to be the eyes and ears of my reader, to let observations and impressions pass through me to him or her. In that way—and this is very important to me—I'm not proclaiming, "Look at me, aren't I clever, I've climbed the Atlas Mountains or paddled to the source of the Limpopo." Rather I'm saying, "Look with me, look *with* me at these individuals, these societies, these forces which are so much greater and more interesting than I am."'

This made good sense. But Lindsay's and Fowler's approving assessments of the 'fictive mode' had left me with certain unanswered questions. What was the process? Where was the craft? How had the writer accessed those lives? If the only place he'd accessed them was inside his own head, then this, surely, wasn't travel writing at all. And even when there was no such outright invention, I sometimes felt a certain unease with travel writing in which the author stepped out of the narrative altogether to present a purportedly journalistic account of the lives of the travellee: Katherine Boo's *Behind the Beautiful Forevers* (2012), for example. I couldn't put my finger on it, but something there made me uncomfortable. If travel writing was a kind of larceny, at least when Colin Thubron entered a Soviet housing project you could see the theft taking place. At least *you* can see *me*, stepping through the hallway of a house in an English village, startled at the presence of a woman from a book. Nicholas Jubber had said something about this too: *it was like being backstage.*

'But what about the actual process and what goes into it?' I asked. 'Thinking about *Under the Dragon*, I wonder how you went about creating those lives. Where are the actual travellees behind them, if you know what I mean?'

MacLean nodded. He knew what I meant. 'That was a very difficult time in Burma. The individuals who were courageous enough to meet

159

me, and Katrin who was travelling with me, they took a lot of risk, and I had to protect them. I say this at the beginning, which again, like the earlier books, is a sign going up, saying "fictional elements here, dear reader, be aware!" So I do change location; I do change the sex of some of the people; I do have composite characters...'

'That's what I was wondering,' I said; 'whether they're just a distillation of various stories picked up, or whether there are more detailed encounters behind, for example the first woman, Ni Ni.' This, of the four portraits, was the one that I had found most affecting: the story of the succession of small misfortunes that ruin a life and end with death in an HIV refuge. 'Clearly it has to be fictionalised to a degree.'

'Sure.'

'But I was wondering, was Ni Ni drawn from a specific person whose life story you had a great deal of access to?'

'I had access to *parts* of her story. The real Ni Ni had ended up in an HIV-positive care home in Yangon after her time in Bangkok. And so, if you like, for the research, that was my starting point—in Yangon, me finding that woman, hearing her story. So she *is* a composite character, because it's combined with other stories of women of the same social class, the same difficulties, the same general trajectory of life. That woman did die, like Ni Ni dies. So they are all based on real individuals—no, on *actual* individuals, met.'

Actual. MacLean had given me a word I'd been seeking for a long time now: a clear, unambiguous descriptor for the hard, resistant realities that a writer ran up against during a journey; a word distinct from the slippery, chimerical concept of 'truth'. I was sitting in an *actual* cottage, in an *actual* village, talking to an *actual* writer. That much was beyond dispute.

* * *

MacLean's most recent book had been *Pictures of You* (2017), a collection of ten stories divined from the Archive of Modern Conflict in London, a strange private collection of images and objects—some 8 million of them.[8] It wasn't really travel writing at all, and it pressed further into fictional realms than almost anything he'd done before, though it was, again, all about 'affective identification'—with a Black woman in the racist Midwest of the 1950s; with a young girl in communist China; fictional stories inspired by nameless faces in the Archive's collection. But what, I asked, about fictionalising *actual* people?

MacLean shot me a look of horror over the top of his glasses. 'But I would never fictionalise an identifiable real person!' he said. 'That's not respectful. I wouldn't do that.' It was a clear and unambiguous statement. 'I respect the individuals I meet, if they're identifiable. But if they somehow aren't—because I have, for example, in *Magic Bus*, the central character, Penny; she's a composite character...'

'I wanted to ask quite bluntly whether she was real or not.' *Magic Bus* was a whimsical retracing of the 'Hippie Trail' from Europe to India. Reading it, soon after it came out in 2006, I had realised for the first time that I was *supposed* to know that MacLean wasn't strictly relating the actual facts.

'She's another composite character,' he said. 'To create the portrait of her, I took elements from three different women—a Londoner, a Welshwoman and a Canadian from Vancouver Island. All were the same age; all had done the trail at about the same time. Of course I could,'—he sighed theatrically—'I *could* have reported that Judy had made the journey this way, and Mary did it that way and somebody else did it a third way. But how prosaic! How boring that would be! And much more importantly, their separate stories would not have evoked sufficient empathy. The reader would not have truly *felt* what it was like to be alive at that time, to embrace such 60s optimism. The reader wouldn't *feel* what it was like to be—quote, unquote—a "hippie chick" crossing Afghanistan in 1967, believing that by changing herself she could change the world. So once again, I took the three actual individuals and made one composite character.'

'Did they know what you were doing when you spoke to them?'

'They knew I was writing a book.'

'Okay, but they're not... the elements of those three women are not identifiable?'

'I don't *think* they are. The names are changed, the details are changed; I don't think they are.'

'So it would be different if you'd actually met a woman called Penny in Istanbul?'

'If there had been a real Penny. I *did* meet one of them in Istanbul— she was one of the three. But she wasn't called Penny; Penny's an invented name. But of course, if there *was* a Penny who I met in

Istanbul and we did the trip together, I wouldn't stick bits on her and still call her Penny. That would be disrespectful; that would be manipulative. I would never do that.'

'I wonder where the line lies though, Rory.' This, perhaps, was the ultimate question about fictionalisation in travel writing.

'That's a very good question, because in *Under the Dragon* I write about my meeting with Aung San Suu Kyi—a real person. I quote her. I don't put any words in her mouth that she didn't say to me. But in the previous chapter there's a composite character; in a subsequent chapter there's someone who was actually in another part of the country. So I can't tell you where the line lies; I can't answer that.'

Maybe there *was* no answer—unless you wanted to follow Rory Stewart. And though I might have been inclined to do so when I set out on my own journey, I was no longer sure that I did.

* * *

Outside an early dusk was threatening, and suddenly MacLean noticed the time. 'It's five o'clock! My goodness, I've got to go to Pilates!'

This was my cue. The idea had formed some way back in the conversation—a mischievous one. He *had* come clean, cleaner than I'd ever expected, really. But I wanted to push my luck a little before I left.

'I said at the beginning I wondered if you'd come clean. So, Rory, that pig...'

'What, Winston?' he said, with studied innocence. He was taking it a little too far now.

'You know which pig I mean!' I said sternly.

'Well, there *was* a pig, there *was* an aunt, there *was* a Trabant—not necessarily all at the same place at the same time, but they did exist...'

This was a polished answer; he'd given it in other interviews. I cut in, still stern: 'I've heard you say that before...'

He stood up, and suddenly he was a tall man once more, no longer an imp. 'I can show you a picture of the pig—and the aunt!'

This was unexpected. It was as if I'd met John Mandeville and he'd offered to show me a Polaroid of the dog-headed men. 'My goodness!' I said. 'I would *love* to see a picture of the pig...'

But, of course, it couldn't be as simple as that. MacLean looked around the room, at the tall bookshelf, at the pale window, at the undeveloped film on the desk.

'I actually don't know where the pig is. I have to think. I can show you the publicity pig?' I frowned fiercely, and he grinned—'But no, you want the real pig. I have him lying beside Zita's—her name was Ruth—her fireplace, and it's printed on a mat. Where the hell is it? It's here somewhere...'

But suddenly I wasn't sure that I did want to see the photo after all. MacLean was still scanning the corners of the room—or was he just pretending to do so?

'I can show you a picture of Zita, a beautiful picture of Zita, of Ruth, in a 1950s gown.' But he couldn't find that picture either.

'She was an Austrian, from Carinthia. She had one brother who'd been a Communist, another who'd been a Nazi,' he said, as he continued his show of scanning the room. 'My uncle—Peter in the book— met her in Carinthia at the end of the war when the Cossacks were being taken away, during all those terrible events. He was a Grenadier Guardsman and about to be seconded into British intelligence. In *Stalin's Nose* I flipped his allegiance, making him a Russian, and retold those stories that he had been willing to tell me. But with Zita, nothing was changed. I pulled her back on the page. As Katrin will attest, she is totally underwritten.'

He trotted downstairs and called to Katrin. 'Do you know where the picture of Winston is?'

Katrin started rooting through the drawers of a sideboard under the window. 'It's here somewhere...'

But now I was quite certain that I did not want to see the picture. 'Stop!' I said, with some distress.

MacLean gave the broadest of all his impish grins. It was gloomy, now, in the downstairs room, but somehow the rims of his glasses were still glittering. 'I think Tim doesn't actually want to see it,' he said.

'I don't!' I said, urgently, though I couldn't for the life of me work out why.

* * *

Signals—was it really as simple as that? Was that the difference between a 'travel liar' and whatever more honourable thing Rory MacLean might be? Was that all you needed to do—signal clearly what you were about, and get on with it? I'd already done it myself, writing up my visit to Dervla Murphy, *signalling* that I was leaving my companion out of the story. It seemed almost too easy, but I couldn't think of any reasonable objection, either. And MacLean was right, too, about the absurdity of believing in the possibility of a truly objective account. *Travel writers never go to the toilet...*

But still, even if Rory Stewart's argument for empiricism—or pseudo-empiricism, really—was not one I wanted to associate with, I did still like the idea of reliable travel writers. Colin Thubron was still my touchstone. In the end there was only so much of that discombobulation between the conventions, fact and aesthetic, that I could take as a reader. I was very glad that Rory MacLean existed—but I was also glad that there was only one of him.

* * *

Driving back, I somehow went astray in the weave of B-roads around Yeovil. It was almost dark now, and homebound traffic was roaring against me in a blur of cold lights. A lay-by appeared ahead. I *signalled* left...

The car rolled to a stop. I flicked on the courtesy light and reached for the road atlas. As I tried to work out where I was, certain familiar words seemed to jump at me from the map: 'John Mandeville', 'Chatwin' and a mocking 'Honest!' I shook my head and blinked, and the words resolved themselves as Hardington Mandeville, Chetnole and Holnest. The next junction, it seemed, would lead me to the A303.

I stepped out of the car into the wet twilight. 'No travel writers ever go to the toilet,' I muttered, and made for the bushes. Behind me, the evening traffic snarled past. It was cold, and there was a sudden fierce pungency in the air. On the other side of the strip of roadside trees, beyond a short incline, I could make out a wide field. The soil was churned over, and scattered across it, moving ponderously in the dusk, were pale, lumpen shapes. Pigs!

I edged forward onto the slope, fascinated. Wet twigs and bleached Coke cans snapped and crackled under my feet, and the roar of the traffic faded slightly. I could see more clearly now through the mesh of branches. There were corrugated shelter arks scattered across the field, stretching into a pig-speckled distance.

One particularly large boar was rooting in the mud close to the edge of the trees, away from the rest of the herd, nose buried deep, driving forward with little flicks of its head. I took another step, slithering a short way down through the litter and leaf mould. The pig must have heard me, for it raised its snout and turned to face me head on. From this angle, it looked as though it was smiling. I ducked under a low branch and moved closer to the fence line. The pig *was* smiling—or rather, it was *grinning*, impishly.

It *couldn't* be, could it? I stared into the half-light, the name forming as a hesitant whisper.

'*Winston?*'

And then, the pig winked. It winked, rose onto its hind legs with balletic grace, gave its suspended fore-trotters a sudden shimmy, and lifted clear of the ground like a rising moon. I followed its ascent slack-jawed. It soared vertically, trotters peddling gently at the evening air. I wanted to call out, urge it to come back—that pig had questions to answer! But it was too late. It executed a smooth about-turn thirty feet up, and sailed away across the treetops...

PART THREE

ACROSS THE BORDER

12

COLLATERAL DAMAGE

Long ago and far away:

The cabin was one of a dozen, ranged under the papaya trees inland from the Kamehameha Highway where it skirted the coast under the steep green bank of the Waianae Range. There was graffiti scrawled in black pen on the back of the door and sand between the floor tiles. Four sets of bunk beds stood around the single room—space for eight travelling surfers. Mine was the upper bunk to the left of the door. I was eighteen years old. I had an NVQ in catering and an A-level in sociology, and I'd saved for my month in Hawaii at £3 an hour in a pub kitchen.

There were half a dozen other Cornish surfers staying in the cabins, amongst the Australians and Brazilians and US mainlanders. Most were older than I was by a few years. One had attained the impossibly grand age of thirty. I don't think any of them had been to university, but they'd all surfed in Indonesia and Mexico and Western Australia. They worked in restaurants and surf shops, and on building sites and farms, and every winter they vanished for a month or two and came back with reef scars and sun-bleached eyebrows. My own first trip outside of the UK had been just two years earlier—on the ferry from Plymouth to Santander to represent Cornwall in a kayak race. But now everything and everywhere seemed possible.

We surfed in the mornings when the air had a sweet, peppery scent and the ribbed flanks of Ka'ena Point showed clear to the west. In the afternoons, when the trade winds came up, we shuffled to the Pūpūkea Foodland to buy bulk packs of instant noodles, or went bodysurfing in the shore-break at Ke Iki. After dark we'd sit around the table in the cabin, slapping at mosquitoes and flicking through old surf magazines. No one had a mobile phone or a laptop computer.

Sometimes a non-surfing backpacker on a round-the-world trip would move into one of the bunks in the cabin for a day or two. The backpackers talked about Thailand, and most of them seemed to be reading Alex Garland's *The Beach*. Someone lent me a copy, but I didn't understand what it was satirising, so I went back to the book I had brought from home: Wilfred Thesiger's *Desert, Marsh and Mountain* (1979). A belated traveller, already.

Even at publication, two decades earlier, most of the journeys that *Desert, Marsh and Mountain* described—précis of the earlier *Arabian Sands* and *The Marsh Arabs*, plus accounts of Thesiger's summertime forays into Central Asia—had belonged to a previous generation. And the whole thing was rank with dubious nostalgia. In the very first line the author made a belligerent point of calling Ethiopia 'Abyssinia' and Iran 'Persia'; and the epilogue, recounting his return visit to the Gulf states in the 1970s, was a sour screed against transistor radios, 'schoolboys in flared trousers', and what he saw as the inhabitants' betrayal of their own culture for 'the tawdriest and most trivial aspects of Western civilization'.[1] But somehow, stretched out on my bunk in a cabin on the North Shore of Oahu, I missed all of that. What Thesiger described seemed as immediate, and as attainable, as a surf trip to Indonesia funded by another six months of kitchen work.

* * *

My earliest encounters with travel writing were directly connected to the possibility of actual travel. I'd read Paul Theroux's *The Happy Isles of Oceania* (1992) because I was going to Hawaii. I was reading Thesiger because I had a hankering for the Hindu Kush. And the following summer I would sit out in the August sunshine and read William Dalrymple because I'd decided to go to India and Pakistan in the coming autumn, while my surfing friends went on to Bali without me (I'd catch up with them later in a squalid flat in Sydney, roll out my sleeping bag on the tiny balcony, and read Jason Elliot's *An Unexpected Light*, new in paperback).

But in the course of the next couple of years something shifted. By the time an older chef in another kitchen handed me a tatty paper-back with a red and white cover, saying 'Fucking good book, that— *The Songlines*,' I had no particular desire ever to go to Alice Springs— or to Patagonia, for that matter. And when I first picked up Patrick Leigh Fermor's *A Time of Gifts* it made no difference to me that the pre-war Mitteleuropa it described no longer existed. There was no surf on the Rhine or the Danube.

What was it about these books that kept me reading? What was it that made them more compelling than fiction? When I unearthed a forgotten hardback in a second-hand bookshop—Ella Maillart's *Forbidden Journey* (1937), say, or Peter Mayne's *The Narrow Smile* (1955)—why was there such a frisson? Certainly, for a budding auto-didact, authors like Leigh Fermor offered the chance to down great gouts of information with more than a spoonful of sugar to help their passage. But that wasn't the main attraction.

The only word I have by way of explanation is *promise*. The travel books *promised*, even the bad ones—with promise as an intransitive verb. It was there in their covers and their titles and their first lines. The promise, I think, came from the fact that no matter how unreliable the narrator or heavily fictionalised the narrative, these books had ulti-mately been made out of *movement*. The travel section of the bookshop seemed to jostle and fidget, while fiction stood in silent stasis.

But over the course of my current strange journey in search of the genre itself, an unease had arisen, a sense of jeopardy to which I had been blithely insensible at the outset. It had crept up on me with the shortening days of another coming winter, and it took the form of an awful question: when this was all over, would I still be able to read travel books—not as a critic or a scholar; not the way the people at the Berlin conference read them; but like a teenage surfer, with eyes for nothing but the promise?

* * *

Something else had surfaced with the alarming recognition that my own ability to read travel writing might be under threat: a sense that someone, somewhere, had been forgotten. It wasn't the travellees—travel writing studies had plenty to say on their behalf, and I was half a travellee myself whenever I read a travel book about Cornwall. It certainly wasn't the writers—they'd been speaking loud and clear. What was missing, I realised, was the boy with the book on the North Shore.

With this in mind I'd gone back to the university library once more, back to the scholarly texts in search of discussions of the *reading* of travel writing.

When it came to the study of historical travel accounts, there did seem to be space for readers. Scholars went digging around in the correspondence of aristocratic women to see how they had discussed the travel bestsellers of the eighteenth century. They examined reviews in inky periodicals, and deciphered scribbled marginalia. The concept of the 'travellee polemic' had emerged from this sort of exercise. But once the focus shifted to contemporary travel writing, readers—real readers, with their own ideas and opinions—seemed to vanish from the scholarly discourse. 'The reader' of my collected definitions of travel writing—the reader who supposes a journey 'to have taken place in reality'—was an abstract figure.[2] And when scholars discussed 'ways of reading travel writing', they were generally addressing their fellow academics, not 'the common reader'.[3]

But without readers there'd be no published travel books. I thought back over the travel writers I'd encountered so far. Thesiger and Hanbury-Tenison would have made their journeys regardless, and Dervla might at least have completed her first epic bike ride to India. But as for the rest, without the possibility of an audience, their travelling lives would have been very different. Readers shaped a travel writer's journey.

The scholarly tendency to ignore contemporary readers of travel writing puzzled me. But it was when the existence of an audience *was* directly acknowledged that I felt real discomfort: the more condemnatory scholars sometimes seemed to see readers of travel writing as complicit. Patrick Holland and Graham Huggan talked of travel writers pandering skilfully to the whims of a 'middle-class readership', and of travel books providing a refuge for the 'complacent, even nostalgically retrograde' values of their audience.[4] And when Debbie Lisle went to town on Paul Theroux, she confidently declared that a sneering description of a Mexican onion-seller in *The Old Patagonian Express* (1979) would 'resonate with readers'—all of them, apparently—because of their 'shared interpretations'. Worse yet, exposed to Theroux's customary causticity about Mexico, these readers would find that 'the heavy security presence at the US border' suddenly made perfect sense. Because of the book they had chosen to read, they would end up sanctioning 'the structures of power that justify America's most militarised and violent national border'.[5] Readers were implicated in the worst crimes of the writers. If travel writing was ethically problematic, Lisle seemed to be saying, then to read travel books with pleasure was to be found guilty by association…

Twenty years off and 7,000 miles out, an eighteen-year-old surfer looks up from *Desert, Marsh and Mountain* and says, startled, 'Are you talking about *me*?'

At least one academic had spotted this troublesome phenomenon. In *The Routledge Companion to Travel Writing* (2016), I'd found an essay by Robin Jarvis titled 'Travel Writing: Reception and Readership'. The questions of how, and why, people might actually read contemporary travel writing were not, Jarvis noted, 'questions that travel writing studies has so far considered worthy of serious investigation'. And when it came to the depictions of the travel writing audience, 'sweeping generalizations, often proffered without a shred of evidence, have long been par for the course'.[6] For Jarvis, the likes of Lisle, and Holland and Huggan, were guilty of something that another scholar, Jonathan Rose, has called 'the receptive fallacy', where a critic made the mistake of assuming that whatever a writer had put into a text—or whatever a scholar *thought* a writer had put into a text—was exactly what its readers received, accepted and absorbed, passively and uncritically, blocked together as if for mass indoctrination.[7] The receptive fallacy made no allowance for the existence of actual readers: individuals with diverse tastes and multiple points of departure, reading on trains and in libraries, in the corners of cafés and in hostel dormitories; roused by one book, repelled by another; reading from north *and* south of the border (*The Old Patagonian Express* existed in Spanish translation, after all). The result, Jarvis wrote, was that 'the reader has all too often become collateral damage in the war on travel writing'.[8]

I wanted to try and do something about that.

* * *

I set up the table in the corner of the hall—seven chairs and three packs of supermarket flapjacks and brownies—and waited for them to arrive.

It had snowed in the night. Outside, Covent Garden was dripping and greasy: a wrack of grubby slush at the kerbs; a unicyclist working a frayed hem of spectators in front of St Paul's Church; and girls in black leggings smoking outside the stage doors in the alleys off Drury Lane. But the hall—below pavement level, beneath the Crown Court Church—seemed not to belong to central London. There was a smell of cold metal and weak tea. Scuffed herringbone flooring, creaking radiators and pinned instructions: 'Please stack the small green tables here'. A place for village whist drives and school jumble sales.

They came in in ones and twos, bundled in scarves and heavy coats. Zillah, a neat, short-haired woman in her fifties, looking a little like a younger Dervla Murphy. David and Sandra, a merry couple in their sprightly seventies—he tall and lean, she twinkling behind her glasses. Roslyn, with a red hat and a certain air of detached amusement. Gavin, the youngest member of the group besides myself, in his forties, black hair in a ponytail. And Adam, a former schoolteacher with the look of a veteran rock climber. I went out to get hot drinks from a café across the way—flat whites for David and Sandra, a latte for Adam, black Americanos for Gavin and I, and 'anything herbal' for Roslyn—ginger and elderflower, as it happened. Then we sat around the table and talked about travel writing.

* * *

The idea of speaking to readers had seemed so obvious. But then I was faced with the problem of *finding* them. They were out there in their thousands, of course. But the moment you wanted actually to pin them down they turned instantly to quicksilver. This was when the receptive fallacy stepped out of the shadows, offering its easy alternative: *readers feel*, *readers accept*, *readers sanction*... I could see why some scholars had succumbed to its seductive solicitations. But no; I wanted actual members of the book-buying public. Should I stick up posters in libraries? 'Readers wanted!' Should I linger in bookshops? 'Excuse me madam,

I see that you've just bought a travel book...' But these didn't seem like practical options.

I went online and looked at the Amazon reviews of Paul Theroux's books. The bulk of them were positive, but there were plenty that seemed to agree with Debbie Lisle. One disappointed reader of *The Old Patagonian Express* suggested turning instead to Ella Maillart's *The Cruel Way* (1947) to 'see how one can be critical of the places or people one meets or visits, without insulting or being judgmental'.[9] Elsewhere, *The Happy Isles of Oceania* elicited some particularly hostile responses. One reader found that 'for all his criticisms of other people for being rude, racist, indifferent and obdurate, the clear impression from reading the book is that Theroux is the worst offender of the lot'.[10] In a short, angry notice, someone called 'C. Paddle' complained of Theroux's 'sweeping generalizations'—the very same phrase that Robin Jarvis had used to describe negative scholarly depictions of readers—and declared that 'As an Australian and a good friend of several Pacific Islanders, I was quite offended by this book.'[11] There was another one-star review that began with the same three words: 'As an Australian'.[12] Someone else took issue with the book, 'having grown up in Oceania',[13] and a reader from Hawaii was 'embarrassed that I had to share Oahu' with Paul Theroux. A jolt of recognition here—these were travellee polemics! They were the digital equivalent of the combative responses from eighteenth-century travellee-readers that the scholar Wendy Bracewell had uncovered. But still, these were just textual traces, and I had no idea who had really written them. I wanted to *talk* to readers, face to face, as I had done with writers. And that's when I thought of the Globetrotters Club.

The Globetrotters billed itself as 'the travel club for independent travellers and travel enthusiasts of all ages'. It had a quarterly newsletter and a monthly meeting in the basement of the Crown Court Church in Covent Garden. I'd given a talk at one of these meetings a few years earlier. I remembered the herringbone floor and hard seats, and the snippets of conversation thrown up above the general hubbub: 'You were in Ladakh last year, weren't you?' 'Two hours south of Tokyo...' 'Going to Sri Lanka, the north, you can go there now...' It seemed a likely place to find fans of travel writing, so I went back, and between a presentation by a man who'd been to Mongolia and a talk about

Arunachal Pradesh, I introduced myself and asked for volunteers. Now, a month later, six of them had turned up on a cold Saturday to talk to me about travel writing.

* * *

To start with, I asked the most obvious question: why did they read travel books?

At the far end of the table, David leant forward. 'Well, I think by definition, being Globetrotters, we're already nailing our colours to the mast and this is the icing on the cake—either to confirm what we thought about a place, or to discover about a place.'

The Globetrotters belonged to a particular subset of the travel writing audience, I'd already realised. These were people who *travelled*, who talked about Laos and Uzbekistan and Namibia as if they were high street shops. Their reading was likely to be directly connected to their own journeys, just as it had been for me in the early years. The scathing scholars might have expected a group of people with well-thumbed passports and subscriptions to *Wanderlust* magazine to be an absolute bastion of 'complacent, even nostalgically retrograde, middle-class values'. But at the Globetrotters meeting the previous month I hadn't been quite so sure. Compared with the tourist crowds on the streets outside, the audience had a faint air of make-do-and-mend, a suggestion of sensible economies and small sacrifices made to fund overseas trips—and maybe even of wanderlust satiated entirely vicariously. They were mostly middle aged—as might be expected of a group still committed to newsletters and monthly gatherings, rather than hashtags and online discussions. But not all of their accents or styles were those of Middle England—and they weren't all white. The receptive fallacy slunk off scowling...

Munching at the flapjacks and brownies, the rest of the group mumbled in agreement with David's reasons for reading. This was an interesting finding, right at the get-go. Way back at the very start of my journey—and that bright clear afternoon in Cornwall seemed impossibly distant now—I'd asked Philip Marsden about the supposed decline in the popularity of travel writing. He'd suggested that it might be because 'a lot more people began to travel independently'. If people could see Central Asia for themselves, the argument went, then why should they bother reading someone else's description of the place? But that certainly wasn't the case here.

'If you conceivably are going to Mongolia, for example, that wouldn't put you off reading a book about Mongolia?' I asked.

'No!' said David, through a mouthful of brownie.

'Does that apply to everyone?'

Nods all round.

'That wouldn't put me off,' said Roslyn.

The dynamic here was very different to that in my encounters with writers. Little conversational tangents opened up around the table without my input. It was good to be able to sit back for a few moments and simply to listen, to note the unbidden flow from one topic to another. In the one-to-one conversations that had gone before there was an intensity that I hadn't always recognised in the moment, a fraught compunction to direct the discussion, always to have a sensible next question primed, to keep pedalling at all costs. But here I could afford to freewheel. I helped myself to another flapjack.

Gavin and Sandra were discussing Colin Thubron's *Shadow of the Silk Road*. They'd both read the book during their own visits to the Central Asian regions it described.

'Other people on the same trip were reading it and they were all sort of talking about it,' said Gavin—though he added that he often avoided reading in advance about a place he was planning to visit.

Sandra said she'd turned to the book after finding herself on the road in Iran with an ill-matched travelling companion. 'I mean, we had nothing in common. But with Thubron, reading what he was saying, it was like having a conversation with him in my head. I sort of put him in place of the travelling companion I should have had. I've never had that experience before, and that was really good. Normally I read a book *after* I've been to a place, not before.'

Boom! Another finding! Zillah, sitting immediately to my right, was chipping in on the same point: 'I'd agree with that. Slightly coming back to Gavin's point about not wanting to frame or prejudge before you go to a place, but having come back from a place and then perhaps seeing what other people have written, or perhaps filling in some more colour about the place, or a bit more of the history.'

And for Adam it was the same. He *spoke* like a veteran rock climber too, with the syllables swallowed back hard: 'For me, sometimes because

I'm curious I do like to find out about what's beneath the surface and I find some travel books—not all—help you with that. But they *can* push you in a direction that is actually wrong, and you might be looking at certain things, and that's not actually what's happening.'

Edward Said's line about travellers 'falling back on a text' on first encounter with a new place, so that a travel book 'acquires a greater authority, and use, even than the actuality it describes'—it was a powerful concept in the criticism of travel writing.[14] But here were real readers, all apparently aware of the danger: a travel book could turn your head; it could skew your view, and if you wanted to see a place with your own eyes then it paid to be careful what you read.

Adam was talking now about stumbling upon an old copy of D. H. Lawrence's 1923 travelogue, *Sea and Sardinia*, in a second-hand bookshop in the Peak District.

'I never knew he did travel writing, but he wrote a few actually, about Italy, and I subsequently read them,' he said. 'I wasn't a great fan of D. H. Lawrence, but I quite like the way he writes. The other thing that I found out subsequently was that a lot of books that were written at that time were by wealthy people going on a European tour, and they didn't bother about how much it cost. But he writes down how much he's paid for his bowl of soup, and he travelled third class on the train, and I really like that. I think if he wasn't a writer he might have been in the travel business, because he had working-class roots; I really liked that.'

Adam had already visited Sardinia before he ever discovered the book. But he'd been back several times since, and now Lawrence's text was shaping his journeys. This was a trope from travel writing itself— the 'in the footsteps' mode. *This* certainly was a case of 'falling back on a text', and scholars had often indicted books that used such an approach for a particularly pronounced strain of retrograde nostalgia. But that didn't seem to be what Adam was about. He simply used the book to create an unusual itinerary.

'I mean, I found out loads about unemployment, about politics, about what's going on with jobs and people, being invited to people's houses because of this book,' he said. 'It was a hook. Not to underestimate the importance of the writing, but to me it enables you to meet with people really; I suppose that's what I'm saying. And something other than just going to the trademark famous places. You're standing in possibly a pretty obscure place where there's a very small plaque to Lawrence, which immediately starts this contact.'

The conversation moved along. The temperature in the hall was hardly higher than that out on the slushy streets, and everyone had kept their jackets and scarves on. Hands reached out across the table to the brownie and flapjack packets from time to time.

David described the pleasure of obscure books encountered by chance. He mentioned one from his own collection, Archibald Hamilton's *Road Through Kurdistan* (1937), the memoir of a civil engineer commissioned in the 1920s to oversee the building of a new highway in the mountains of northern Iraq. 'You can't resist a book like that, can you?' he said. I wasn't the only one, then, to take such pleasure in digging these things out of the second-hand shops.

I asked what people looked for in the persona of a travel writer—whether 'inner journeys' were important.

'Well,' said Sandra, 'I must admit I like as little as possible of the author.' She sat very neatly with her hands folded in front of her, her glasses catching the light.

'That's why you like Colin Thubron,' I said.

'Absolutely.'

Zillah was of a similar mind. 'There are some books where the focus is external, and there are other books where the backdrop is external and the focus is internal, and I suppose I'm more likely to buy a book where the focus is external,' she said.

None of them were particularly keen on high-altitude heroics and derring-do either—what Barnaby Rogerson had described as 'books with a fit young man with his shirt off on the cover'.

'I'm more connected with a regular bloke that I'd meet in the pub that's done this amazing round-the-world trip,' said Gavin, and everyone nodded, though Sandra leaned in, grinning and said, 'Levison Wood—you've got to excuse him because he's so damn good-looking; you just sit and look at the cover!' Everyone laughed.

During most of this Roslyn had been sitting quietly, smiling somewhat wryly from under the broad brim of her velvety red hat.

* * *

At the Globetrotters meeting the previous month various people had come to speak to me during the break, after I'd asked for volunteers. There'd been a busy hubbub in the hall, custard creams on chipped plates, and weak tea sloshed out into white cups on a green counter. Someone bemoaned the declining standards of the *Telegraph* weekend travel supplement, and someone else encouraged me to read his own self-published ebook about an overland trip in the 1970s.

And then, just as everyone was settling back into their seats for the second talk of the session—the one about Arunachal Pradesh—a rather elegant fifty-something Black woman had touched my arm and said in a conspiratorial half-whisper, 'I just wanted to say, about those travel books, I'll be of no use to you because I find that I can't read them. They're just all so horribly racist, as a woman of colour...' This was Roslyn.

It would be comforting to surround myself entirely with fellow aficionados, to seek uncomplicated reassurance that there were good reasons to read travel writing, that the genre was alright. But that would be far too complacent. If there were scholars who took issue with travel writing for its alleged racism and imperialism, then I couldn't pass up the opportunity to talk to a reader who had come to the same conclusion.

'Please,' I'd said, 'let me have your email address...'

* * *

I'd perhaps expected Roslyn to talk of Paul Theroux or V. S. Naipaul. But no; the last travel book she'd tried to read, she said now, was by Dervla Murphy. She couldn't remember the title, but she seemed to recall that it was about the Himalayas. I think it may have been *Where the Indus is Young* (1977).

Dervla—*racist*? I felt a faint tremor—not of outrage, as when I encountered some overstated scholarly brickbat, but of panic.

'I heard it being reviewed on the radio and I thought, I must read that. But alas, I couldn't finish it,' Roslyn said. There was something precise about her manner of speech, the words chosen carefully. 'I just didn't like it at all. I think I probably got through the first few chapters and I thought no, I just can't continue with this.'

Everyone else had gone very quiet. Things had narrowed down. I needed to start pedalling again. I was trying to think back to *Where the*

Indus is Young—if indeed that was even the book we were talking about. It was years since I'd read it, but I recalled an affectionate and finely written account in diary form of a journey through the far north of Pakistan in the dead of winter in the early 1970s. Some scholars, I said, trying to find the right line, had argued that woman travel writers—especially historically—tended to make a better job of their encounters with other cultures than their male counterparts.

'Well, that's why I was so disappointed,' said Roslyn, 'because I thought of her as someone who's an established traveller and she's travelled to these places. But the way she was describing her encounters with the locals, I just found deeply disappointing. I mean, obviously it's very Eurocentric, she can't be anything other. But I thought perhaps there might be something—that she could have that objective view. But it was the same sort of Eurocentric view that she brought to bear on the local people.'

I still wasn't quite sure what she meant. 'So your disappointment was compounded by the fact that she was a woman, would you say?' I asked, uncertainly.

'Well, it wasn't necessarily that she was a woman, but I thought that she could be a bit more sympathetic or objective about the local people. You know, typically it's the warm friendly locals—"Oh, they were warm and friendly and welcoming!" And I just found that so patronising and offensive, because I think most Europeans travel with that expectation. I mean, any programme that you watch on TV, any book that you read written from a Eurocentric perspective is about the warm friendly locals and the expectation that they're going to be friendly, they're going to welcome you into their homes, they're going to provide for you. And I just find that deeply problematic, that they can't move beyond that and have a relationship, a one-to-one relationship—you know, a human being relating to a human being without all that sort of baggage and that expectation.'

Ah, so...

It was too easy to point to some ugly traveller—Theroux at his worst, perhaps—and then to put it all down to personality, to point to the myriad other travelling writers less inclined to sneer and condemn. There have been countless counterblasts against Edward Said's concept of Orientalism down the decades, and the crudest of them

181

simply protest that 'orientalists' in the original, pre-Saidian sense were often committed lovers of 'the East'. The European gentlemen scholars of the nineteenth century who had made the study of 'oriental' subjects their specialism, who had translated Persian poetry, stripped old temples of roots and creepers, penned ethnographic treatises—they'd had nothing bad to say about 'the Orient'; they'd valued its traditions and cultures; Said was going after the wrong people. Kipling *loved* India...

To be sure, there were plenty of holes to be picked in the theories of Edward Said, but *this* was to miss the point spectacularly. Ziauddin Sardar, in a sprightly little reboot of Said's ideas, also titled *Orientalism*, published two decades after the original, had pointed out that just because Orientalism—or indeed the Western approach to any 'elsewhere'—could at times be admiring 'does not mean that it cannot, at the same time, be obsessed with the Other in a manner that the Other found denigrating, even in its admiring form'.[15] This was where you ended up with Wilfred Thesiger fulminating about Emiratis in flared trousers, condemning the Bedu for abandoning the 'traditional' culture that he claimed to revere. And when a travel book produced a warm portrait of a foreign place, full of apparently meaningful human encounters, it still paid to stop and to think: what did the portrait actually look like? Did it conform to certain expectations? Were the people—no matter how fulsomely and positively they were described—exactly as you expected them to be in such a place: poor, 'traditional', immobile? Was the book—subtly, even inadvertently—putting them in their place?

I'd thought I was properly sensible to this, and had been for years. And I was certain that there were plenty of travel books that *didn't* fall into this pattern—books by Jonathan Raban and Sara Wheeler, Dervla's own most recent books on Palestine certainly, and many, many others. And it was a *long* time since I'd read *Where the Indus is Young*. But if Roslyn's response—as a woman of colour, as she'd put it directly herself—had been so visceral, then I *had* been complacent. I hadn't always read carefully enough.

What, I asked Roslyn, would she hope to find in a travel book?

'An encounter with another human being, essentially, rather than, "I'm the sort of privileged European white traveller and I'm encountering a brown person in another country, and this is how we relate to one another",' she said. 'And this is why I find it really difficult to read these travel books, because almost all of them have that perspective. And I was so disappointed, really, that she was just as bad—"Oh yeah, I met the local people and they were really friendly." Not that there's anything wrong with that, but where's the one-to-one human relationship? That's the thing that I struggle with.'

* * *

We were almost out of time. Other club members were starting to arrive, setting up the hall for the main meeting—this month's speakers would be talking about Ireland and New Zealand. There was an inch of cold coffee left at the bottom of my cup, and a few minutes remaining in which to tackle the perennial question: what did readers *really* think about travel writers making things up?

'Was it Bruce Chatwin who wrote about Patagonia and there was a big controversy about it?' said Adam. 'Well, I remember reading that book and I really liked it, and then when this controversy came I didn't really follow it very closely, but I thought, is that going to change my ideas about the book? No, it's not actually, because it's a book. And so I know a lot of people got very excited about it. But to me, to a certain extent, I would go with it, because that's the writer's interpretation of what they've seen and the story that they're trying to portray.'

'I'm just wondering how much they can actually remember, for an entire book. Is all of it going to be factual? I can't see how that's possible,' said Roslyn.

'I agree,' said Sandra, across the table. 'I think you have to paint a picture sometimes, so somebody feels that they're on the bus with you.'

Next to her, Zillah nodded. 'And one of the days might have been raining all day, and they might sort of take the morning of one day and the afternoon three days later and put it together, and, well, actually it doesn't matter because the sun's come out in the afternoon in their book, when in fact it rained all week. That doesn't matter.'

Roslyn was speaking again: 'I guess there are things that really do need to be factual—if they went to a temple, what the temple looked like, you know, the interior of the temple. Those sorts of things that are very specific and very factual and should not be embellished. But the colour of someone's hat and whether it rained on Tuesday or whether it rained on Wednesday seems to be of no relevance, and sometimes you need that sort of padding anyway in a travel book.'

No one disagreed. I was surprised to find such pragmatism—especially amongst readers who were travellers themselves. Everyone seemed to have an innate understanding—and acceptance—of the trimming, the smoothing, the little flourishes which were part of a writer's craft.

But then I presented them with a list of specific examples of things that travel writers, in their practice, might do. And suddenly everything changed.

'So can you just put your hand up if you're okay with this?'

Everyone raised a hand to the possibility of the sort of condensing of timescales that we had just discussed. But there the ready acceptance ended.

'What about reordering events?'

Three out of six hands stayed disapprovingly lowered.

'David?'

'Well,' he said, 'it's a representation of the facts. That you'd be caught out in that particular lie—clearly you're not someone who can really be trusted to tell the whole truth.'

The shifting of events or encounters from one place in the actuality, to another in the narrative: every hand stayed down. 'Nobody's okay with that?'

'Well, culturally they might be different,' said Zillah.

'Tribally they might be different,' said Roslyn.

'In fiction I'd be happy for that,' said Gavin. 'You can make up your characters and put them wherever you want. But if you're believing in nonfiction, then no.'

What would they think, then, of the creation of composite characters? I was fairly sure I could guess.

'Only in fiction,' said Gavin firmly, speaking for everyone.

Adam nodded sharply. 'I think if you were writing a fictional book that would be fine, but not a travel book. I think that's not respecting people's individuality and character. I think that actually that's—well, not just patronising; I think that's poor practice to do that, actually.'

Travel writers were in trouble, it seemed. But then maybe so were the scholars. I couldn't have made a composite *reader* out of these six people—not now that I'd actually met them.

The possibility of hiding the presence of a travelling companion, got a couple of very reluctant half approvals, but no one was willing to sanction the masking of key practical details in a journey. And the idea of a fictionalised 'inner journey' simply baffled them.

What was going on here? They'd started out so tolerant, but now, presented with concrete examples of forays across the fictional frontier, they'd come over sternly conservative. It was as if readers—these readers, anyway—understood that there was some sort of liminal space between the fact convention and the aesthetic convention, accepted its inevitable existence; but the moment you pushed them into it they recoiled.

'The last one,' I said, grinning awkwardly like a politician in the face of a slow hand-clap. 'I'm pretty sure I know what you'll say to this, but who is okay—put your hand up—with outright fabrication? For example, putting yourself on a horse when you were actually walking, or putting yourself on a motorbike when you actually got a taxi, or seeing a tiger that you didn't actually see...'

All hands stayed very firmly on the table, folded in place.

Gavin shook his head in weary reprimand. 'That's fiction!' he said, and they all laughed.

* * *

Afterwards I wandered back through Covent Garden. There were only a few scraps of snow in the gutters now. The restaurants were crowded, and behind the Royal Opera House a busker was chugging through an earnest rendition of 'Mad World'. I went into the Stanfords bookstore on Long Acre. Books in bright piles, and the tropical fug of an overheated retail space on a cold day; middle-aged couples in new trekking boots peering at Lonely Planet guidebooks; and the distant hiss of the coffee machine from the café at the back of the shop.

Here at least, travel writing looked to be in rude health. There were new hardbacks from veterans and debut authors, and stacks of Eland titles in their familiar burgundy-and-cream livery. Every author I had spoken to so far was represented. Here, as amongst the members of

185

the Globetrotters Club, the connection between the reading of travel books and travel itself was obvious. At the downstairs checkout a tall man with glasses was waiting to pay for two books: Lonely Planet's China guide and *The Emperor Far Away* (2014), a recent account of journeys in China by David Eimer. I wondered if any small fictions might have crept into that book as its author crafted his narrative, and what the man with the glasses might say if he knew.

Talking to Adam, Roslyn, Gavin, David, Sandra and Zillah had suggested a tension between what many readers thought they wanted of a travel book, namely 'the truth', and what some travel writers seemed to think readers actually needed—a polished narrative with all its pace and balance, and perhaps even some 'greater truth'.

I was moving into a new stage of my own journey now—seeking out writers who might be shaping the future of the travel genre, while also tackling some remaining big issues—and big figures—of the past that I'd avoided until now. But at the same time the outline of another idea was forming. It wasn't only those who produced travel writing who would determine its future; it was also those who received it. The values and concerns of today's readers, surely, were not quite the same as those of thirty or a hundred years ago. The way people *read* travel writing would continue to change from generation to generation. This idea led me in turn to a new uncertainty. There were four figures ranged around a travel text—composite characters, if you like: the writer, the travellee, the scholar and the reader. And I wasn't quite sure where my own allegiance lay.

13

TO THE EAST

Norwich was cold, and its old buildings were made of fist-sized pieces of flint. Their walls looked like crocodile skin. I found the place he'd suggested for our rendezvous—a café with jungle print wallpaper beside the River Wensum—and sat in the back room, warming my hands around a coffee cup. There was a stack of old books in the window beside the table: *The Nature Notes of an Edwardian Lady*, three dog-eared *National Geographic*s; a battered Asian cookbook; and something called *Touch the Earth*, a collection of statements by North American Indians. Who had these belonged to before they became catering industry décor? I reached for the last title, and was reading the back cover—'We did not think of the great open plains, the beautiful rolling hills and the winding streams with tangled growth, as "wild". Only to the white man was nature a "wilderness"'—when I heard him clatter through the café door.[1]

'I'm a bit nervous, actually,' he said, taking off his jacket; 'I was thinking about it last night.'

This was a different kind of travel writer.

Patrick Barkham was a *Guardian* journalist.[2] But he was also the author of books that found themselves bracketed with the works of Robert Macfarlane in that most fashionable of recent literary phenomena: the so-called 'new nature writing'. Since the turn of the twenty-first century, this genre seemed to have ousted travel writing as the dominant mode of creative nonfiction in Britain. In 2008, *Granta* magazine had published its 'The New Nature Writing' issue, providing a quasi-official inauguration for the emerging literary trend, much as *Granta 10*, the seminal 'Travel Writing' edition, had done in 1983 for that then-ascendant genre.[3]

Over the last decade-and-a-half there had been dozens, probably hundreds, of books exploring facets of Britain's natural history and landscape. But reading them, something repeatedly struck me: these were almost always first-person accounts of 'a journey or journeys that the reader supposes to have taken place in reality'.[4] They often took the form of a quest—for a particular species, for a certain kind of geography. Many of them were rich with literary allusions, dense with research. They typically took the authors away from their home-places, their centres of familiarity, and more than a few of them seemed to be concerned with 'constructing difference'—or perhaps 'wildness'—even if they never ventured beyond British shores. It wasn't that the new nature writing had *replaced* travel writing, then; much of it *was* travel writing. British travel writing hadn't so much disappeared as come home and gone incognito, skulking around in the woods and the meadows.

Patrick Barkham's books in particular seemed to fit neatly with every scholarly definition of travel writing I'd collected. His first, *The Butterfly Isles*, published in 2010, described a summer spent travelling the UK in an attempt to see every resident butterfly species. His second, *Badgerlands*, was an account of the relationship between humans and badgers, hitched to a series of first-person forays and encounters. More recently he'd published *Coastlines*, about his explorations on foot around the British littoral, and now he was working on the final proofs of his fourth book, *Islander*, a journey around nine of Britain's offshore islands.[5] In these books he seemed notably more concerned with human encounters than many of his fellow nature writers, more engaged with the fraught business of representing the travellee. That was why I'd been keen to talk to him.

* * *

Barkham was tall and skinny, dressed in close-fitting clothes. His black hair was combed sideways across his brow, and everything about him was boyish except for the eyes behind his dark-rimmed glasses, which were those of a kindly, faintly worried old lady. His speech was peppered with the same kind of enthused emphases that I sometimes heard like an echo when I spoke to my brother on the phone. Norfolk was his own home ground, the place where he grew up and to which he had returned after living in London and overseas. He was raising a family here now.

'I do feel quite rooted,' he said, as he carried his own coffee cup gingerly from the counter. Rootedness amongst travel writers again— *very important, a taproot...*

Once we'd settled into our seats by the café window, I opened my notebook. I told Barkham that I was going to read a piece of his work from *Coastlines*, about Cornwall. He knew where I came from, and his eyes flared with alarm. 'Oh God!' he muttered. But I carried on anyway.

It was only afterwards that I wondered why, actually, I had felt confident enough here to critique a piece of writing in front of its author. I'd done the same thing with Nicholas Jubber, of course, but I hadn't laid out any passages from Thubron's or Danziger's books for live analysis. Did I feel less deferential because Jubber and Barkham were both closer to my own age than the other writers I'd met? In this particular case, was it because I had my own preconceptions about the views and values of a longstanding *Guardian* journalist, his likely receptiveness to ethical challenge? Or was it—and this made me squirm when it later occurred to me—because I had an innate sense that I could talk to Barkham on the level because we were somehow of a similar class?

That all came later, though. For now, I just folded back the pages of my notebook and read aloud:

We have a collective folk image of the Cornish coast from writers, painters and poets; from Daphne du Maurier, Virginia Woolf, JMW Turner, Patrick Heron, Sir Terry Frost; from numerous television dramas and travel supplements. And many of us, five million each year, visit and come away with our own vivid impressions of surf, sand and sky.[6]

'What was my reaction to that?' I asked.
'That they would all be outsiders, not indigenous?'

'Well, yes. But you also said "our" and "us", and "we come away". Quite explicitly in the construction of that you make Cornwall a place...'

He was already there ahead of me: 'To be visited...'

'Yes! Where none of the readers are going to come from! This is not for people from there.' Some things had changed little since Wilkie Collins' day, it seemed.

But this wasn't really about Cornwall. This was the nub of the thing, the uneasy issue at the very heart of travel writing itself.

'I suppose that's the ultimate challenge,' I said. 'When you're writing about elsewhere—and that can just as easily be somewhere just outside the M25 as the Himalayas—people do tend to live in that place. So I wonder if you think there's any way to acknowledge that the places you're writing about are elsewhere, but that there are people living within them. How do you do that?'

The café was filling around us. There was a clatter of cutlery against crockery, and a burble of voices.

'That was the main thing I was thinking about ahead of talking to you,' Barkham said, 'because I do think that's the ultimate question.' This, I suppose, was what had made him nervous.

'I do think there's been this massive loss of nerve, quite rightly, and a reflection on the colonial endeavour that is writing about other places. Bill Bryson did it here, didn't he, in a popular way? And we should have some of that I think, because I believe...' He paused and chuckled, though I wasn't quite sure at what. 'I believe that my perspective as an outsider is a valid one, and I feel from experience—and obviously this would apply to anyone—that when you first go to a place you've never seen before, you see it with a certain clarity and vividness. Later, you stop thinking about a place when you visit for the fifth or sixth time because you feel that you know it, probably erroneously. And therefore there is this validity to the initial journey, the initial impressions that you get, both in terms of describing it vividly or accurately for fellow outsiders who are readers, but also for people within that society: this is how people are going to experience your society, whether you like it or not.

'But I think the ways of making it a valid enterprise today have to be self-reflective; this postmodern thing of reflecting on the baggage that you're bringing to the encounter between you and this foreign place and its people. And also, you need to give voice to the people who are in that landscape and that place. I think I did that okay in *Coastlines*, but I'd say *Islander* is more about people than any of my previous books and has more of their voices in it.

'But with a book, when I'm writing from the position of a published author and I'm interviewing people who are *not* published authors and haven't got a platform and haven't got a right to reply, there is an asymmetry of power. I feel much more comfortable with the asymmetry of power with me in England, and I feel progressively less comfortable the further I go. With *Islander* I felt quite uncomfortable in the Hebrides where I was dealing with a culture that was actually deeply Gaelic, and so I didn't even have the first language. There's such a long tradition of English people travelling to the Hebrides in particular, and it's just as colonial as any piece of travel writing about Afghanistan.'

* * *

Barkham said that he'd been sending the draft chapters of his new book to each of the key people he'd talked to on his trip around the offshore islands of the United Kingdom. This was a technique that some professional anthropologists had begun to deploy following the discipline's postcolonial crisis of the 1980s, but I couldn't imagine many other travel writers doing such a thing.

'What kind of responses have you had?'

'It's been really interesting. It reminds me of just how travel writers, including myself—just how much we get wrong, simple details.'

He gave an example of an interviewee on the Isle of Man, an old Manx-speaker, and a misheard dialect word only picked up when Barkham sent his copy for feedback. The correction brought a surge of new insight about the island's Norse connections and maritime heritage.

'And so how much wider is my understanding, from just having made a simple mistake?' he said. 'That's a classic example of a literary outsider not getting something. And you see it with almost every piece of travel writing you read.'

'Did anyone come back, not on point of fact, but on the general presentation?' I asked.

He nodded. 'Yeah. Mostly it's been really good and positive—almost all, really—and so it makes me feel quite optimistic about the book. But in one case I had a really hostile response... hostile is the wrong word—critical.'

This had come when he sent his chapter about the Hebridean island of Eigg, with its distinctive settler community, to one of the people he had spoken to there.

'She got back to me and she was really critical of my portrayal of Eigg, and felt it was almost sensationalist, and like a tabloid, and I was perpetuating this myth that the island was a bunch of alcoholics.'

'So how have you responded to that critique?'

'It hit me quite hard,' Barkham said, 'because I felt that I'd done an honest and self-reflective and quite nuanced portrayal of this place, not as an idyll, but very positively, but also with this side to it that I was uncomfortable with, which was heavy drinking. I reflected on my own unease with it and the fact that I come from a very non-drinking culture and that was probably the source of my discomfort, not that anything outrageous was going on in particular. But I went back to it again. She'd very kindly gone through it and pointed out errors of fact, but also where she'd got really irritated with me, and you could see her irritation building; she was just like, "No! Not again!" by the end. And I've gone through it all and I have removed passages and looked again at my reflection and rewritten my reflection on what I'm seeing...'

This seemed a very unusual thing for a travel writer to have done—and very brave. But at the same time some niggling concern was forming. I tried to imagine what would happen if I sent an account of one of my interviews with travel writers to its subject for feedback, and received a similarly critical response. What if I sent Barkham my write-up of *this* meeting, and he didn't like it? I'd already scrawled 'eyes like a kindly granny behind his glasses' in my least legible hand at the bottom of a page in my notebook. What if that offended him? What if I pre-empted the offence and removed the description—which I thought was a good one—before I sent him the copy?

'Do you not think that there's now the beginnings of a danger here?' I said.

'Yes, absolutely...'

'Because you talked about the validity and the value of the outsider eye.'

'Yes. And I believe absolutely in defending that. It comes back to that whole thing—Michael Gove going on about experts, and this derision of professional people. I still believe that there's a validity in a person with skills coming and observing in a skilful way, just as you wouldn't suggest that a social anthropologist had no right to study a place...'

'Well,' I said; 'there *was* a sort of crisis in anthropology...'

'Yeah, I know, absolutely. And there's been a lot of reflection on that too, quite rightly. But no, I would defend the right to do that. I'm not asking them for *approval*. I am asking them for their criticism and comments.'

There was a very obvious question here: 'Do you think the portrayal of Eigg has been improved by engaging with her?'

He didn't hesitate. 'Yeah, definitely.'

* * *

I'd met Barkham before, in Cornwall the previous year when he came to speak at a literary festival. I had asked him then, as a reader who'd enjoyed his books and who had detected the undercurrent of ethical concern he was now explaining, if he would ever consider turning to travel writing about places beyond the territorial waters of the United Kingdom. Unlikely, he'd said. The challenge of language, the weight of colonial history, the sheer likelihood of getting things wrong: it was all too daunting. It would also be more difficult—often downright impossible—to engage with travellees for feedback on a draft if they were not literate English-speakers. I asked the same question again now.

'Yeah, I'd find that difficult,' he said.

This made me a little sad. Barkham was clearly ethically concerned—ethically troubled, even. He *did* doubt; he did *not* seem confident of his position bang at the moral centre of the world. I would have loved to have seen what sort of travel writing he might produce if he went to Afghanistan.

'I wonder', I said, 'if we are sort of ethically held back, because we're concerned, because we're engaged with these issues, is that ultimately a positive or a negative thing?'

'You could argue, certainly, that it's negative if it's us not being so global in our outlook,' he said.

I thought more about this later. The subtitle of Barkham's first book was 'A Summer in Search of *Our* Emperors and Admirals'; that of *Coastlines* was 'The Story of *Our* Shore'; and when *Islander* appeared the autumn after our conversation, it was subtitled 'A Journey Around *Our* Archipelago' (my emphases). The exclusive determiner on each cover stated quite baldly whom these books were for—and for whom they were *not*. Was ethically engaged, immaculately liberal Patrick Barkham—and with him all the other new nature writers—somehow an unwitting part of a wider cultural cringe away from the outside world, one which had political manifestations that were anything but progressive? It was an uncomfortable thought—but one which, in an unexpected way, might make for a good defence of travel writing about foreign places.

And then, as always, there was the slippery nature of 'power'. When Barkham handed over his draft chapters for feedback, he said, it was with a particular dynamic in mind.

'I think it's more important when there are asymmetries of power,' he said, 'and I think it becomes more problematic if you're submitting your words for approval to someone who's more powerful. Prince Charles is an islander. I could have tried to talk to him. I wouldn't be comfortable sending my copy to him for approval, because that would feel like submitting before power.'

I raised an eyebrow at this, and Barkham smiled ruefully: 'There's an inconsistency there isn't there?'

There was, but there was also an implication for my own project—if I were to follow Barkham's lead and to send my chapters out for feedback to the people they represented. The usual traveller–travellee power dynamic was reversed here: my travellees were all well-known, widely published authors, while I, the traveller, was the more junior researcher. It wasn't quite an imbalance on the scale of that between royalty and a journalist, but still. What if a senior writer took exception to my subjective depiction of their garden or home décor and asked me to change it? What if they asked me to remove parts of the dialogue that I felt were important? What if they pressed me to alter the *substance* of what had been said? Would there come a point where the text slipped out of my control, lost what I thought was its authenticity? In conventional travel writing, somehow ceding control to the travellee in this way might be judged by the scholars as a radically ethical practice. But the scholars didn't seem to have anticipated my own situation.

Barkham went on: 'When I say that I wouldn't check it with Prince Charles, it's that fear of having someone coming back to me who's going to try and coerce or influence or use their power to make me change my story in a way that I don't feel is true to the story. But you could argue that everyone in a sense could do that.'

'Was the woman on Eigg not, in a way, wielding power over you?' I said. 'Not the same power as Prince Charles, maybe...'

'Yeah, you're right. She was wielding "I'm the authority on Eigg here, and you're an outsider and you don't know." I'm accepting quite a lot of her critique, but I'm also saying that my position as an outsider still has some validity, not just in writing to outsiders but in interpreting your own community to you or giving you a picture of your community that's a fair one. Without getting too bogged down in what's right and what's wrong with the practice and the result, I think the only solution is to have that conversation, and to make sure that that's part of the process. It doesn't really solve anything, but I think you're potentially enabling yourself to write a better book in terms of one that's more accurate and more understanding of the place that you're representing.' He paused for a moment. 'But I agree that it's fraught with danger, and where you draw the line is a very difficult one. You could end up being completely emasculated as a writer if you take that to its obvious conclusion. And also we as a society end up being emasculated if we decide that the only person who can write about farming is a farmer, and the only person who can write about bereavement is someone who has been bereaved, and the only person who can write about hawks is a falconer, and the only person who can write about Eigg is someone who lives on Eigg—we're screwed at that point, aren't we?'

* * *

Afterwards I drove on eastwards. I'd come this far; it would have been silly not to go all the way.

The fields on either side of the road had been ploughed and harrowed. The earth, blanched by a drying wind, was almost white. I passed what looked like an old service station, but was in fact a Hindu temple, according to a sign in its car park, and then I was out in the Broads. A derelict windmill rose on the left, its sails thinned like the branches of a sickly pine tree. The road was long and straight and hemmed with yellow reeds. To the south a green flatness opened, puddled here and there with white water. I can't remember ever having had a more startled reaction to a landscape. I pulled into a lay-by and sat, slack-jawed as the wind from the passing vehicles buffeted the car. What did I previously know about Norfolk? I tried to remember if I had ever read a book set here. 'Flat' and 'big skies' and possibly 'Gypsies'—that was about it. It *was* flat, and the sky *was* big, but somehow not in the way I had expected.

I'd booked a room for the night in a guesthouse on the seafront in Great Yarmouth. The owner, Gary, was a hairless man with rolls of fat at his neck. He was keen to stress how busy he was, even at this lowest ebb of the season.

'Now listen: that's a double room I've given you, yeah? Only got two singles, got contractors in both. Now, the reason that's so cheap, yeah? It's on the corner; there's a nightclub; you might hear it, you might not, yeah? But that's good value, can't say that's not good value. That's cash only, yeah?'

It was cold outside, and a hard wind was coming off the slate-grey sea. I walked out across the wide beach to the water's edge. The sand was powdery, but with a hardened crust and a scattering of flinty pebbles. It was the kind of surface I imagined Wilfred Thesiger trekking across in the Empty Quarter. Short wavelets were growling angrily ashore and darkness seemed to be coming off the water like a contagion. I turned back towards the promenade.

Most of the businesses were still shut up for the winter. Boarded tea shacks and chip kiosks; a lap-dancing club looking terminally closed; a couple of amusement arcades, open, but with no customers amidst their angry yellow clatter. There were a few restaurants with menu boards by the steps: lasagne and chips, fish-fingers and chips, cod and chips; glimpses of empty dining rooms and worn velvet upholstery. I'd seen all this somewhere before. There was a suggestion of coming violence in the lowering light and the bitter wind. The town had the feel of a place battened down ahead of trouble. I turned inland on a straight street, and suddenly I realised where I had seen the empty restaurants with their lonely loitering waiters before: in Fuengirola during an off-season visit to the Costa del Sol. There was something very weird about this.

The air of impending trouble had a more human element in the working part of Great Yarmouth, away from the sea. Two policemen stood immobile at an intersection while shoals of wolfish teenagers swirled back and forth across the street. Great murmurations of starlings smeared the pale sky over the town.

* * *

The next morning Gary was stalking the breakfast room, peering over shoulders like an invigilator—'Extra sausage, yeah? All good, yeah?'

He came out to take my cash payment in the hall. I said I'd heard nothing from the nightclub, and he leaned forward, muttering conspiratorially. 'I'll tell you what, yeah? Couple of weeks ago there was a fucking riot. It was a Gypsy wedding, yeah? They came down, and they wouldn't let them in, but they was inciting the ones inside to come out, and there was a riot. The police took twenty minutes to turn up, yeah? I've seen the CCTV footage...'

I drove back on the long straight road and then followed a farm track into the Broads. I parked the car and pulled on my boots and walked out into the flatness.

I could say that there were windmills along the skyline like tarry black pepper-pots. I could say that I saw a bittern, rising heavily from a thicket as I approached, and that later a Chinese water deer fled along the path ahead of me at unreal speed. I could say that more than once I looked out and up, giddied by the vastness of the sky and the limitlessness of the horizon. But what chance, really, did I have of describing this eastern place in a way that wouldn't prompt in a Norfolk local the kind of eye-rolling that travel writing about Cornwall often caused in me? Very little, I suppose. And what had I taken from Great Yarmouth but run-down resort clichés and stories of Gypsy weddings? Hadn't I—like contemporary travel writers in Afghanistan—been cooking up an air of threat where no real danger ever materialised? A place *battened down*, peopled by *wolfish teenagers*. Were there internalised cultural references at work here too? Was I falling back on some forgotten text, even if it *was* what I saw and heard and felt?

And what about Gary at the guesthouse? I'd changed his name, because he had no idea what I was about and it seemed only fair. But what would *he* say if I sent him my copy for comment—about his portrayal and that of his town? (And would I ever remember what he was really called, without looking at my notebook?)

I was only passing through, rather than conducting serious travel writing research here, but Patrick Barkham had spoken of the validity of first impressions. The scholar Steve Clark had said something about that too: 'The traveller's comparative ignorance is the condition of freshness, wonder, power of insight.' Clark had also described the sort of travel writing 'customarily only legible to one culture, intrinsically commentary upon rather than dialogue with'.[7] But Barkham *was* attempting to make his most recent travel writing a dialogue rather than a mere commentary. And his end product *was* legible to the travel-lees he encountered—at least much more so than most of the other, older travel writing I'd considered. Barkham might have shied away from the problems that would come with writing about other countries, but it seemed to me that he was already travelling in the most daunting territory of all.

14

ON THE COUCH

This is what happens:

Another journey to London; another travel writer tracked down to the capital. You wonder what you can hang this on, how you can give this shape. Is there some appropriate place to visit, some memorial at which to pay your respects before you present yourself at the appointed hour? What little fragment of travel can you use to frame the encounter when the time comes to write it up?

You look at the map. The address the writer has given lies to the north of Regent's Canal, where London begins to rise from its riverine sump. Is there some unusual route you could take? Some appropriate angle from which to approach? You linger for a moment over the green birthmark of Hampstead Heath, then let your eye drift south into the veined grey. And there, amongst the Tube stops and national rail connections, you spot it: the Freud Museum. It's maybe twenty minutes' walk from where you need to be at two o'clock.

You've been thinking about 'inner journeys'. Surely Sigmund Freud's London home would be a fine place to start. Graham Greene had taken his approach to the writing of *Journey without Maps* from Freud, hadn't he? And there will be plenty of colour to fill your opening paragraphs: the couch, with its suggestion of Persian-rug-draped Orientalist fantasy; the assorted trinkets of a travelling life. Maybe you could even throw up a signal, *à la* Rory MacLean, and have the old man there himself, sitting in his armchair, analysing a travel writer. You are making the journey into a deliberate first draft. You start to write it in your head before you ever set out.

But when you get there, the museum is closed.

The street, Maresfield Gardens, is quiet. You stand, peering across the box hedge. The fretwork leaf of a cheese plant is pressed like a mask against an upper windowpane. There are two blue plaques, one for Sigmund and one for Anna, and two empty milk bottles on a ground floor windowsill. No one is at home.

You wonder what to do. The opening hours are posted by the gate, and you know that you'll be making another foray into the city soon. You could come back; write the thing up exactly as you had planned. Do the walk now, the museum visit later, and stitch the two together. There'd be no great mendacity here. A simple matter of craft. Travel books often have little notes about 'incorporating elements from earlier visits'. William Dalrymple had such a note at the start of *From the Holy Mountain* (1997). Even Colin Thubron—reliable, 'by the abysmal standards of the genre'—had done the same thing in *Shadow of the Silk Road* (2006). If you arrange your sentences with lawyerly care you might even allow yourself a technical exoneration.

But somehow you feel more uneasy about this than you ever did about placing a well-signalled pig in a Somerset field. You'll defer the decision, then, and get on with the walk in the meantime.

This is a cottagey quarter of London. The trees that line the streets are pollarded and leafless, starbursts of cold wood over the empty pavements. The houses could almost belong to a prosperous Leicestershire village. At one point, on Belsize Lane, you can hear nothing but muted winter birdsong. Then a huge black Jaguar slides past, a grand woman glimpsed in the passenger seat alongside a uniformed driver.

And a little while later, you are knocking on a grey door.

* * *

'You're always short of girls,' she said. 'I'm the honorary girl. I'm the honorary girl and they have to be nice to me. When I come into the greenroom at a literary festival they all stand up and say, "Here's Her Maj!"'

I'd expected her to be like this. A writer securely at the heart of things, a paid-up member of the literary establishment, and yet, somehow, operating with the air of a brazen interloper and not taking any of it entirely seriously. I was rather nervous.

The study was much as I'd pictured Freud's consultation room. There were faded rugs, worn leather furnishings and walls of books— hardback books of travel and exploration. An open fire crackled at the end of the room, and on the mantelpiece a collection of carved elephants was arranged by ascending size so that they marched out of an accelerated distance. It was the den of a Traveller with a capital T. I could imagine a bowler-hatted Foreign Office functionary, caught in some Cold War snafu, stopping in here for a snifter and a spot of advice from an Old Hand.

But the room's owner was no tweedy veteran of the Colonial Service. She had bare feet, painted toenails and short, iron-grey hair pushed back with an Alice band. She was sprawled in a deep leather armchair facing the fire, and she was waiting for me to ask her a proper question.

* * *

Sara Wheeler had been on my list of writers to talk to from the very start. How could she not be? She belonged, along with Dalrymple and Marsden and MacLean, to the first rank of the second generation of late twentieth-century British travel writers, and her third book, *Terra Incognita* (1996), about Antarctica, had been one of the biggest of all the 1990s travel bestsellers. She wrote with an understated lyricism about cold places, embraced inner journeys in a way that Dervla Murphy most certainly did *not*, and managed to be enthusiastic and authoritative about the history of Polar exploration while at the same time maintaining a healthy disrespect for 'men with frozen beards'.[1]

She was very much still at it too: *The Magnetic North* an Arctic counterpart to her earlier Antarctic book in 2009; *O My America!* in 2013. And I'd heard from Patrick Barkham and Rory MacLean that she was currently working on a new book about Russia.[2] She also seemed to be the quasi-official designated travel writer of the literary press. When a major new travel book or explorer's biography came up for review in the *Guardian* or *Spectator* or *Wall Street Journal*, Wheeler often seemed to have first dibs. She was a Fellow of this, a Trustee of that, and she'd chaired the judging panel for the Stanford Dolman Travel Book of the Year Award two years running. She had also frequently talked and written about 'women's travel writing'.

I knew that I needed to consider the matter of travel writing and gender. It came up again and again in the scholarly journals. It had been the central theme of the conference in Berlin. I *wanted* to talk about it. But, I realised, I had been putting it off, and the delay itself had stirred up a self-propagating anxiety. I was uncomfortably aware that Dervla Murphy was the only woman travel writer I'd spoken to so far.

The previous winter, just as I was starting my journey, Wheeler had published an article in the *Guardian* titled, 'Where Have All the Female Travel Writers Gone?'[3] In it, she listed notable women travellers of the past—Mary Kingsley, Gertrude Bell, Martha Gellhorn—then bemoaned the fact that a mere quarter of the submissions to the most recent Travel Book of the Year Award had been by women; 'we must do better', she'd written. It had begun to feel like an accusation, levelled directly at me.

* * *

'So what was your main question on that, Tim?'

I was trying to say something—clumsily pitched halfway between an observation and a question—about the prospects for a young travel writer having been rosier in 1992, when Wheeler published her first book, *Evia: Travels on an Undiscovered Greek Island*.

'It was tough *then*, Tim; it was tough then. I don't think it's tougher now.'

I started to protest: 'A lot of the people I speak to moan about how it was better in the 80s and 90s...'

But she was having none of it. 'That's always been, since the dawn of time. Travel writing has always come and gone like that, and I don't really see it's any different now from how it was then. That's my opinion.'

She did not, she said, believe in the possibility of an exhausted genre. 'Of *course* everything hasn't been done. It wasn't like travel writing only existed for places that no one had ever been to before in the whole history of the world. Absolutely not. I very much hold a candle for the survival of the genre, and I believe that there will be lots more men and women coming after me who will write brilliant things about observing countries. That's my opinion.'

That's my opinion. She said this a lot. She also used my name frequently and carefully, and said 'correct' whenever I offered an observation or checked a detail. None of this particularly helped me to relax.

Afterwards, listening back to the recording of the conversation, I tried to work out why I had started out so fumbling and ill at ease. I hadn't been like this elsewhere, even when star-struck at the prospect of meeting Colin Thubron. I think it was because I had a sense that this interview—the one that I had been putting off—was particularly important. It wasn't simply because Sara Wheeler was a travel writer of considerable stature; it was because she was a *woman* travel writer. Having spoken to so few of them, I needed to make this one count.

But I didn't seem to be making a very good job of it. Glancing down at my notebook I realised that almost everything I'd planned to ask her was connected to the issue of gender in travel writing. Wasn't this the problem? I seemed to be asking Wheeler to stand as spokesperson for the entire canon of women travel writers across history, instead of simply speaking for herself. If she was annoyed by this, wouldn't she'd be quite within her rights? So I asked about class instead.

Towards the end of *Terra Incognita*, after circuiting relatively happily through the Antarctic research bases of Americans, Kiwis and Italians, Wheeler approaches the British station at Rothera and finds a repellent temporary society of brattish food fights, lewd banter and 'British men doing what they did best—reverting to childhood and behaving like gits.'[4] Scholars of travel writing had spotted this moment during their musings on gender. Peter Hulme had cited it; so had Yaël Schlick and Tim Youngs.[5] It was an example of a woman writer *destabilising the masculine gaze* and drawing attention to *antiquated gender stereotypes*. But perhaps the moment had every bit as much to do with class as with gender.

Wheeler, by her own account, had grown up in an 'ordinary working-class environment' in Bristol, 'sheltered from the horrors of the class jungle'.[6] This seemed to make her something of an outlier in the upper echelons of British travel writing. I asked if, starting out, she had felt like something of an intruder.

'I think when I got into it I was very class-blind,' she said, 'and when I went to Oxford I had a terribly nice time, and didn't really notice that everyone was different—not *everybody*, but lots of people were different to me—and I ploughed on. And certainly when I started writing...' She paused. The leather armchair in which she was sitting was enormous, and she had folded herself up comfortably between its outsized arms. There were little daisy motifs on her blue shirt. 'My answer to your question is *no*, I did *not* feel that. It was only after I'd embarked on everything that I realised it was an issue. But by the time I realised it was an issue I was equipped enough to know that it wasn't an issue that mattered.'

* * *

I asked Wheeler about the books and writers that had influenced her at the outset—a safe, standard, gender-neutral travel writing question.

'Well, of course I looked a lot at the Victorian women. Mary Kingsley—an incredibly interesting writer in my opinion, underrated. Martha Gellhorn—later, war correspondent, but wrote a lot. There were a lot of things that she said, Martha Gellhorn, that really inspired me, on the social journalistic side. So Mary Kingsley, Martha Gellhorn, Freya Stark. A lot of stuff. There are more...'

A fortuitous breeze seemed to be blowing us in a particular direction. Back in Lismore, Dervla Murphy had recited a very similar set of names.

'Those are all women that you've mentioned. Is that deliberate?'

'Yes.'

'So you would deliberately make a point of citing them?' This was better. I'd stopped waffling now.

'Yes, I would. I would.'

'And why?'

'Because I believe that they are all unrepresented—*under*represented—and there's a reason for that, which is that the mainstream has sort of subsumed everything and put women under. And I think that's wrong, and I think women travel writers have been absolutely underrepresented and underappreciated, and I think that has a deleterious effect on young women trying to think about writing things today.'

The anxiety and guilt was back. Just how many women travel writers had I spoken to, again? Shouldn't I have tried harder? I started trying to explain myself.

'When I came to make a list of people I wanted to speak to…'

She cut in. 'You're of an age where you try and get a balance.'

'Well, I do. But it's very hard!'

'I understand that.' Wheeler was being very patient, and very kind, but it wasn't really helping.

'My criteria was that I wanted people—I had to have *some* kind of science to it—I wanted people who'd published at least two travel books…' I sounded a lot like someone failing to convince himself. It was true, though. The big names on my list—Colin Thubron, for example, and Sara Wheeler herself—had simply suggested themselves. I'd approached others because their work raised some specific, interesting issue. Of course, there were plenty of women travel writers whose books I knew and loved—Robyn Davidson, Alice Albinia, Freya Stark, Ella Maillart and many others too. But they'd stopped writing travel books years ago. Or had stopped writing travel books years ago and lived in Australia. Or had only ever written one travel book. Or were dead. Or were dead and from Switzerland. There *were* other names that I'd considered. But when I asked myself why I might include them and found that the main answer was 'because she's a woman' it had made me uneasy.

'I don't want to go to people just because they're women,' I said.

Wheeler nodded. 'No of course not. It's that terrible thing about positive discrimination, which I've had with loads of my friends in different professions. Actually you do a disservice. If you pick someone who's actually not up to it, all the enemies are going to say, "Ha ha!" So you do a disservice. I understand. You've just got to stay on the right side and do what you can without determining people to fail. That's what I've learned.'

'But this is why I have to talk to *you* about women's travel writing!' I was almost pleading now.

'Of course.'

I had, I realised afterwards, gone a very long way around just to ask for permission.

Wheeler had thrown her bare feet with their painted toenails up on the arm of her chair by this stage. I was still perched on the edge of the couch. I looked down at my notebook, and began.

* * *

'Some academics, scholars of travel writing, have for a long time attempted to identify fundamental differences about women's travel writing, and to establish whether women's travel writing is categorically different,' I said.

'Correct.'

The big text in this quarter of the travel writing studies library was *Discourses of Difference*, by another Sara—Sara Mills, published in 1991, a year ahead of Wheeler's own first book. Mills had examined women's travel writing from the nineteenth century, the age of high European imperialism. The argument went that even when they came from a dominant colonial nation, as members of a subordinated gender 'women travel writers were unable to adopt the imperialist voice with the ease with which male writers did'. Their accounts were often 'more tentative than male writing, less able to assert the "truths" of British rule without qualification'.[7] Mills didn't go as far as to claim the nineteenth-century travelogues about Asia and Africa by European women as outright anticolonial polemics. Instead, she suggested, they were unstable texts, poised between dominant ideas about femininity and colonialism and 'caught up in the contradictory clashes of these discourses one with another'.[8] She also believed that women writers tended 'to concentrate on descriptions of people as individuals, rather than on statements about race as a whole'.[9] This all sounded convincing enough, but I'd come away from *Discourses of Difference* with niggling doubts. Mills didn't provide many examples of the essentialised men's travel writing against which she compared her women's texts; its nature was simply taken as a given—and its nature seemed to be homogeneously egregious.

Elsewhere, Debbie Lisle, arch scholarly condemner of contemporary travel writing, had noted (of Robyn Davidson, as it happens) that 'The very presence of women in the genre destabilises the masculine gaze of the travel writer.'[10] No argument here; there was something of this at play when Dervla Murphy went striding through the Karakoram with a toddler in tow too. But was there really, fundamentally, something different about travel writing by women? This was what I needed to ask Sara Wheeler.

She stretched in her armchair and gave a little nod of acknowledgement. It was an old, old question. 'I would say at base I do *not* think so. But when you get above base, I think that women do have a separate way of looking at things. I can't help thinking about my own experience. When I walk into a house in the High Andes on my own and there's a woman there with a few children around the table, and I sit down, I can't help thinking that I get something that blokes don't get, because of course they're always a threat; do you know what I mean? Being a woman travelling on your own you have a massive advantage. That's my opinion.

'The question you're asking me about the point of view, from the one or the other, is a difficult one, but I think on the whole I would come down on the side that, yes, it is different and women do do things differently, do *see* things differently from men. And that's largely predicated on the fact that we're not competing, it's not competitive. It's like outside the cave, you know; I believe that. I think there's something in the DNA that's still within men—that you've got to be the guy who kills the mammoth outside the cave and drags it in. I think there are very fundamentally different ways in which men and women see the world that are exemplified in travel writing. So yes, I do think there is a difference, but I think defining that difference is quite hard, because I think it's quite DNA-based. I think we're still outside the cave when we're talking about that kind of thing.'

Still, I wondered. Wasn't there something else too? *My* only access to women's travel writing was as a reader.

'When it comes to women's travel writing being *women's travel writing*,' I said, 'obviously it has to be written by a woman. But do you think readers respond to it differently?'

Wheeler shook her head. 'No, actually I don't.'

I had to make a confession, then, and it was one that shamed me a little. I'd gone back through Wheeler's early books before coming to meet her, and in doing so I'd remembered an uncomfortable reaction I'd had at certain points on earlier readings.

'I remember in your Chile book, *Travels in a Thin Country* [1994], having these flickers of anxiety every time you hitch a ride with a truck driver…' I said.

She smiled knowingly. 'Right. Is something bad going to happen?'

'Yes!' She understood what I was talking about. I went on, tentatively: 'But if it was Philip Marsden hitching a ride with a truck driver…'

'You wouldn't.'

'It troubled me slightly, to be honest, that that response was there. But it made me think about the idea of women's travel writing being in the eye of the beholder to a certain extent. I wonder, then, if you're conscious of that? I know you've shied away from being called brave and so on, but when you're writing about hitching a ride with a truck driver you must have a sense that somebody reading this will wince, because you're a woman, in a way that they wouldn't do if you were a man.'

She gave a throaty chuckle and rearranged herself again in the armchair. 'I understand. If I might say, in this instance, I like you very much Tim, but I'm not too worried about your misgivings on that topic. I appreciate the fact that it's based on nothing but anxiety for my wellbeing, I appreciate that. But what can I do about that?'

* * *

We talked on. Wheeler told me about the forthcoming Travel Book of the Year Award, which she was chairing again. Once more, there had been a marked shortage of women writers amongst the submissions. She let slip that Patrick Barkham was on the shortlist, for *Islander*. We talked too about Dervla Murphy and women travel writers of earlier generations. Wheeler had never had any inclination to portray herself in their gritty image, even when trudging across the ice—or hitching lifts with truck drivers.

'I wonder if it's a generational thing,' I said. 'If you think back to all of the well-known woman travel writers, probably up to and including Dervla Murphy, a certain set of characteristics accrues around them. They're all *indomitable*, *doughty* and *a little bit crazy*. It goes back through Freya Stark to Isabella Bird and Mary Kingsley, all of them; they have that sort of persona. But by the time you started writing maybe you could just be a woman.'

'I think that's a good point,' she said. 'My brand is lipstick and all of that. I think that is probably a factor of the passage of time. They were honorary men; they all were—no sexual persona and no sense of any of that.'

'It's interesting that you say that not only is their gender pushed down but their sexuality is put aside. Dervla Murphy would very much be part of that,' I said.

'Absolutely.'

'But by the time you started, you could be a woman as a traveller and a writer, not just talking about gender, but talking about boyfriends and so on.'

'Correct, although I might say to you, Tim, in your work, that there's a lot of history of women of my generation talking about boyfriends that have not gone very well. I'm talking about Lucretia Stewart, who I think is a good writer, actually. She wrote about this affair she had somewhere or other—the Caribbean I think—and was absolutely pilloried. Dea Birkett, who I admire very much, she had this love affair in Pitcairn, and that was completely pilloried.'[11]

'Whereas it's not with the men...'

'No.'

I hadn't thought of this before, and I couldn't recall seeing it discussed by travel writing scholars—though it had been suggested that the old 'doughty and indomitable' archetype had developed as a way of deflecting suggestions of impropriety. A woman traveller—from Mary Kingsley to Dervla Murphy—might downplay the dangers of her journey because one of those dangers, as far as a conservative and patriarchal society was concerned, was sex.

'Why do you think people don't like it?' I said.

Wheeler snorted. 'We say "people", but we're talking mostly about critics and readers who are men. I think people don't like women writing about their sex lives; I think there's still some sense that that's a private domain.'

'Maybe that's also why travel in general...' I started tentatively. 'Because in travel itself there's a certain transgressiveness... So maybe there's a hint of sex about travel in itself...'

'Yes. But I think if you go too far as a woman—in my opinion, we have evidence for it—you get punished. And we hope that might change.'

I wondered, though. Did this really apply only to women writers? Scholars had often discerned metaphors of sexual conquest in the penetrating, acquisitive narratives of colonial explorers. But when it came to actual sex, there didn't seem to be a great deal of it in British travel writing—by anyone, man or woman. Going back to *Danziger's Travels* a few months earlier, when the author described his romantic encounters along the way it had brought me up short—not because I was a prude, but because it seemed so unusual in the genre. If writers like Wilfred Thesiger had presented themselves and their journeys as sexless, they may have had particular reasons for doing so. But perhaps they'd inadvertently created a model type.

'Actually,' I said, 'if you think about the classical form of travel writing, whether it's Colin Thubron on one side or Dervla Murphy on the other, you sort of expect them to be de-sexed, don't you?'

'Correct.'

'So whether it's a man or a woman, as soon as they have some kind of dalliance it's transgressive...'

'That's right. Maybe we'll go forward and make things different. Because it is odd. I mean the whole journey is supposed to be a metaphor for life, so if it's a metaphor for life it's going to be the whole emotional journey, which includes the sexual journey, and yet somehow...'

There was a long moment of silence. The fire crackled. I had fully recovered from my earlier befuddlement now. Talking about sex had helped, apparently. So I asked the same hypothetical I had put to Churnjeet Mahn in Berlin: could I, in theory if not in practice, produce a piece of 'women's travel writing'—or a piece of 'queer travel writing' for that matter?

Wheeler frowned at me. It *was* a daft question, and she didn't go straight to it.

'I could say I'm a woman travel writer and that doesn't make me inferior or in a separate category from men's travel writing in any way,' she said. 'And I like anything being categorised as "woman", so I'd always be very happy to be called by anyone a "woman travel writer", and any person who would think that that would mean I was inferior to a men's travel writer, I don't really care about their opinion and they can go and fuck themselves. As for your question. How *could* you? And that's no criticism of you. But how could *anybody*?'

'Ah, okay—but it's not a question of whether it's appropriate...' This was probably a bad idea.

'I understand,' she said. 'It's not about writing queer subjects, or as a woman writing about buying tampons or having men touching your knee; it's the sensibility. But why on *earth* would you ever want to pretend?'

'It's just an interesting question...' I muttered.

'It is an interesting question,' she said, with a shrug that suggested it was anything but, 'but, I mean, I could say the same thing...'

I didn't quite understand. 'What—dress up as a man?'

'I could go to Mount Athos, put all the kit on...'

I began to have a faint intimation that I'd been rather stupid.[12]

* * *

Outside, the light of the London afternoon had dimmed from dirty white to dull lavender, and a faint murmur of traffic and footfalls came through the window. It would soon be time for me to go. The open fire at the end of the room was still crackling perfectly. No one had stoked it or added more coal. I'd been fooled: it was a gas-fuelled imitation.

Wheeler was talking about the way that the best-known travel writers of the generation that preceded her own ('Colin and Jonathan and Paul') all also wrote novels—though not, she suggested, entirely successfully.

'They all think that fiction is a higher form of literature.'

'*You've* never written a novel though,' I said.

'No; I never will either. But they all think that fiction is a higher calling, and they don't realise that all their novels are pretty much not very good, while all their travel books are. They don't realise it because they think that in literary terms fiction is a higher calling, and that being a novel writer is of a higher echelon.' She laughed, swung herself upright in the armchair, and sketched the form of a ladder in the air, from top to bottom. 'It would go poetry, fiction, nonfiction, kids.' She laughed again. 'And I never feel that, partly because I don't think of myself as being amongst the gods, but actually I don't particularly believe it.'

'It's a funny thing,' I said; 'that idea of hierarchies.'

'It is, but it totally exists.'

Her mention of fiction brought up the perennial question. 'Where do you stand on the deployment of fictional elements?' I asked.

'Is it okay to make it up?'

'Yes.'

She shrugged as if it was the least consequential question of all. 'Yeah, I think it's fine to make it up,' she said.

'Really?'

'Yep.'

I couldn't recall the ground shifting beneath me when I'd read Wheeler's books—and I rather prided myself on what I thought was a keen ability to spot the points where a writer stepped from the straight and narrow. I was intrigued now. 'So *are* there fictionalised bits and pieces in yours?'

Wheeler seemed wholly unbothered. 'Yeah—although "fiction" would be a bit wrong. I suppose if you've got a huge great block of prose you can see that actually at this point I need some direct speech in here, like yeast, you know. So you might take a guy who you met elsewhere and bring him in.'

'How do you think readers would respond to that?'

'I *know*, because of speaking to them! They hate it, and they say, "I'm never going to read a word you write ever again!" So I should keep my mouth shut!' She laughed.

'Everyone does it, I suppose,' I said.

'To a certain extent. I mean, you ask Colin, who's a great friend of mine—Colin Thubron—and he'll say, "I never do that, ever," and I'll say, "Colin, I don't *believe* you."' Here it was again—that sense of Wheeler as a merry transgressor, confidently unbothered by niceties.

'Forgive me for saying so,' she said, 'but I feel that I'm creating a work of literature, so the demands of making it an acceptable work override, in my opinion, any question of verisimilitude. I take extremely seriously being faithful to my interlocutors—*extremely* seriously. And of course you have all the stuff in the introduction about people's names being changed and this and that or whatever, things being shifted around. But I'm not an *academic*; it's not a *report*.' She was sitting up straight now, and suddenly more exercised than she'd been talking about class or gender or sex.

'I'm trying to write a book that's going to *grip* people from start to finish, and I believe I'm allowed to do whatever I like—to do what*ever* I like—to be faithful to my material, to be faithful to the truth. Often the truth is truer than the truth. In other words, "He didn't say that then, did he?" *No!* But there's a truth that's truer than the truth, and I believe that it's my right as a writer to create that work. And then people can judge me!'

'You do have to smooth the edges off,' I said, trying to sound conciliatory.

She rolled her eyes. 'Colin would say, "No, I would never do that; I haven't got the imagination to do that; everything happened exactly in the order I say it happened." I say, "Colin, I don't believe you; it's not possible."'

There is a passage in Thubron's book about China, *Behind the Wall*, where, walking through a food market in Guangzhou, he finds a live barn owl for sale. Something—perhaps the fact that it is 'identical to the north European species'—stirs up an insurgent sympathy, and he buys it.[13] He hides it in his hotel room, then smuggles it onto a train. Later, when he thinks that his fellow passengers are sleeping, he releases it through the window into the night, 'like a giant white moth'.[14] It is a moment of strange magic—one of those indelible fragments that end up rattling around in your literary memory-drawer long after the books to which they belong have faded away. But it is also one of the very, very few moments in Thubron's oeuvre where I feel the faintest tremor in the ground beneath my feet as I read. It wasn't that I didn't *believe* it, exactly; but something in its dreamlike quality suggested that it belonged to some other category than the coolly observational bulk of the book. I mentioned this passage to Wheeler now. She threw her head back and roared.

'Bollocks did he do it! Absolute *bollocks*!'

* * *

Alright, then: the Freud Museum, Maresfield Gardens; a sign on the door reads, 'Come in. We are Open'.

Afterwards you will go outside and walk through a cottagey quarter of London, along quiet streets where you can hear nothing but muted winter birdsong. At the end of the walk you will knock on a grey door, and a woman in an Alice band will open it for you. But for now you enter another, airier hall.

Visitors stand around in silence with audio-guides pressed to their ears. They look like people stoically receiving bad news over the phone. Stairs bend towards the upper floor. By the window on the landing: a cheese plant.

You pass through into the study. The curtains are drawn, and the place has the muffled air of a house in mourning. The couch, hard against the wall to the right, looks like a Balinese *barong* lion, dumped in the corner of a temple complex after a ceremony. At its head, an upright green armchair. On the desk, a pair of tiny spectacles.

Visitors are hemmed into a strip at the centre of the room by a knee-high cable. Behind you a man's voice, American-accented, says, 'This is not how I pictured it...' A woman nudges you gently aside to take a photo with her phone. You step back and bend to peer at a large engraving of the Sphinx, and when you look up you find that you have the place to yourself for a passing moment. The other visitors have drifted off to watch the video on the upper floor.

And of course, it is as you expected, as you *planned*: the restraining cable has gone, and a familiar figure, bald and bearded, is sitting in the green armchair. Another man occupies the couch: a tall man, with watery blue eyes and fleshy cheeks. As you step closer he swings himself up to a seated position and smooths his necktie, then stands. His consultation appears to be at an end. 'Thank you, Dr Freud,' he says; 'this has been very useful.'

'You are most welcome, Mr Greene.'

The tall man nods at you in passing as he leaves the room. You turn, questioningly. 'Was that...?'

A small, wrinkled hand twists dismissively over a notepad. 'He needed some ideas for a book. He has already spent his advance—on drink, I suspect.' The accent is precise, clipped and high-pitched. He confronts the letter R with guttural aggression. 'Now, please.' He motions towards the couch. You look at it uncertainly. He motions again. 'Please. We haven't got all day. A Spanish tour group may arrive at any moment. Lie down.'

You do so gingerly, stretching out your legs, trying to keep your feet off the rug. The couch isn't very comfortable, but perhaps it isn't supposed to be. He is sitting directly behind you, out of sight. You place your hands on your chest and look up at the white cornicing. 'Do you mind if I record the conversation?' you start to say; 'There's a consent form...'

But he cuts you off. 'I really don't think that will be necessary here, do you?'

'I suppose not, no.'

'Now, what seems to be the problem? Your dreams perhaps? Or is it that you suffer from anxiety?'

'Well, yes, actually, I suppose it is anxiety.' A pencil scratches and you fear a misunderstanding: 'But not like that—*an* anxiety, I mean, about women.'

'A-ha!' An eager tensing behind your head.

'No! That's not what I mean! It's an anxiety about women's travel writing, and women travel writers—about talking to them.'

'You don't like talking to girls?'

Is he being deliberately obtuse? Is this some analytical technique to draw you out? Perhaps you should make a note and try it yourself, on a travel writer. 'Of course I like talking to girls!' you snap. 'It's just that I was anxious about the *topic*; and about talking to a woman travel writer about it. And now I'm worried I might have gone about it the wrong way.'

'I see.' There is a long pause. Muffled voices come through the ceiling, and further off the dulled thunder of a passing Tube train. His chair creaks and there is a soft rustle of cloth. You have a feeling that he has folded his thin fingers into a steeple beneath his downcast nose. 'Tell me,' he says; 'do you feel that you attempted to undercut your own authority and competence simply as a rhetorical strategy in the depiction of your conversation with Sara Wheeler?'

Startled, you twist your head and see, from a skewed angle, that his fingers are indeed joined beneath his nose. He parts them briefly. 'Answer the question.'

'No! It really *was* like I told it,' you say. 'I was less assured there than with anyone else. To be honest, I actually thought it'd gone much worse until I listened back to the recording.'

'Are you quite certain? This appears to be the first time you've deployed Eric Newby-style self-deprecation. You are aware, of course, that the trope of bumbling incompetence in travel writing has been identified as an authorial strategy—an excuse, if you like, a way to dodge ethical culpability in all manner of issues? And that a self-deprecating performance in a text could well be read as emanating from a position of great security and authority?' There's a faint whinnying tone to his voice, as if he is ascending on a thermal.

'Of course I am—but no!' Your ankles ache where they project from the end of the couch, and you wonder how he could possibly know who Eric Newby is. 'It's just that I felt anxious and inadequate, discussing gender in travel writing. I kept putting it off. I felt like Sara Wheeler was the only person I'd met so far that I could reasonably talk to about it. But then there was something she said—about her being able to dress up as a man and sneak onto Mount Athos if she wanted to...'

He coughs gently. Papers rustle, and when he speaks again you know by the flattened tone that he is reading from his notes. '"Gender, it is now recognized, is a factor that affects men's as well as women's travel writing."'

This sounds familiar. The walls of the room seem to be coming apart, sliding back, fading into a pale fog. 'Who said that?' you say with a certain dread.

He coughs again and says, in the same flat tone, 'Dúnlaith Bird, 2016, page 35.'

'Shit. I *met* her...'

'May I continue? "Gender norms and expectations affect men, and men's writing, just as much as women."'

You grimace. You sense that he is looking sternly over his glasses at the top of your head. He clears his throat and reads the attribution: 'Carl Thompson, 2011, page 173.'

All you can do is offer a small, pained groan.

He lets you lie there for a moment, and when he speaks again he is no longer reading from his notes. 'You have been a very silly boy, haven't you?' he says.

'I suppose I have.'

'You confused "gender" with "women".'

'Yep.'

'May I suggest that if you wish to discuss gender and travel writing again, you try doing it with a man?'

'It's a bit late now, but okay.'

'Excellent. Now I'm afraid this consultation is over.'

'Thank you.' You breathe out and wriggle your toes. And then, before you get up, you say brightly, 'Do you know, I have a feeling that this conversation will be much easier to get down on paper than the one with Sara Wheeler.'

He leans forward sharply so that his mouth is right beside your ear. A faint scent of cigars, not unpleasant. Sharp bristles touch momentarily against your cheek.

'You know why *that* is, don't you?' he hisses furiously. '*It's because you made me up...*'

216

15

JOURNALISM BETWEEN EQUALS

I met Samanth Subramanian in a pub in Dublin 4. It was an upscale pub in this upscale section of the city, with blond woodwork and fancy floor tiles. Its long shopfront was lined with hundreds of old medicine bottles, and the headlights of the cars passing along Donnybrook Road came through a matrix of blue and yellow glass. We sat in high-backed leather armchairs beneath the wall of bottles and ordered pints of Guinness from a barmaid with an Eastern European accent.

I'd been going back through Subramanian's books on the train ride from Galway to Dublin that morning, checking the passages I'd already underlined, scribbling new notes. But I kept looking up from the page. Columns of cold rain marched across the country as far as Athlone. Then the weather cleared and coppery sunlight came in low over the fields. The blocks of forestry had a wind-burnt auburn tint. There was a dissonance to the journey; the dissonance of strong travel writing read in a contrasting landscape: the books, when I looked back down, gave off the yellow, deadening heat of Sri Lanka and the Indian coast.

But here in the pub there was no dissonance at all. An Indian journalist with a British passport, a degree from an Ivy League university and two books about South Asia to his name, living in the Irish capital: Subramanian was effortlessly at home.

'We moved here partly because we'd taken a holiday here in 2015, and we loved it,' he said. 'We were here for three weeks, and we were figuring out ways to come back, essentially, and we engineered our way here, one way or another.' His wife was completing her master's at Trinity College, and Subramanian was using the library there while he worked on his next book.

The barmaid brought our pints across from the bar. Her blondish hair was scraped back in a tight ponytail. Subramanian nodded up at her. 'Thank you, thank you very much.'

He was a small man in his mid-thirties, with a neatly trimmed black beard, thin-rimmed glasses and a broad forehead. Sitting in the oversized leather chair, he had the look of a child genius. He wore a black tee shirt emblazoned with the name of his alma mater, Columbia University, in white letters. From my own seat across the table I saw two black pints with inch-deep white heads, then the black and white of his tee shirt; a clean two-tone against the coloured bottles to my right.

'So apart from Guinness, what was it that you loved about Ireland so much?'

'I mean, I don't know if you've been to India? You have? Okay, so you know this is a big contrast in several ways. It's less hot, which I love; I mean, I *love* the cold. It's less crowded; it feels like a more relaxed life than we were living back home. We were living in Delhi, and as you may have read in the papers, the air in Delhi is just *foul*.' His speech was full of deep emphases, but where Dervla Murphy had stressed the adverbs, Samanth Subramanian pressed down on verbs and adjectives. His sentences were more cleanly formed and properly punctuated than those of anyone I had met since Robin Hanbury-Tenison. He threw a rhetorical 'right?' into many of his statements, and occasionally asked himself a question—'what does that mean?'—as if to check that his thoughts were in proper order, which they invariably were.

He was, he told me, working on a biography of the eccentric British scientist J. B. S. Haldane.[1] It was a subject far removed from his previous South Asian beat.

'In my mind it feels perfectly natural,' he said. 'There have been people from outside India writing about India for many centuries, so why shouldn't an Indian person write about a British scientist? In my mind it makes perfect sense.'[2]

* * *

Samanth Subramanian was born in Bromley in Kent in 1981—hence the British passport. His parents had been living in the UK while his father was on temporary deputation for a state-owned Indian trading company.

'They were expats,' Subramanian said; 'they were always planning to go back.' Two years later the family returned to India, where Subramanian spent most of his childhood and teens—except for four years when his father took another overseas posting, this time in Indonesia. After school he went to the US to study at Pennsylvania State University. He signed up for the journalism course on a whim, half-expecting to shift to some other major before his college days were over. But he discovered that the subject suited him.

'It played into everything, every quality, that I thought should feature in what I considered a working career, which is that it should be interesting on a day-to-day basis, and different; it should allow me to read a lot; it should allow my own natural curiosity for things; it should provide avenues for that.'

After graduation he returned to India and began work as a cricket correspondent, travelling widely to cover test matches. Later, he went back to the US, to Columbia for his master's. Then he moved to Delhi to continue his career as a journalist. The style of journalism he had taken to was the committed, long-form tradition of the *New Yorker*. 'My platonic ideal of journalism', he called it: 'to spend three months just reading about something and talking to people about something, and then spending another month writing and rewriting, and then put together something that is definitive, at least from the point of view of journalism, even if not academia.' And now he was in Dublin.

Along the way he had published two books. The first, *Following Fish*, had appeared in India in 2010, and then internationally two years later. It was a sprightly book that worked its way, east to west, around the coast of India with a fishy theme—encountering fishermen, sampling fish-based cuisine, looking at fish in local cultures. His second book, *This Divided Island*, published in India in 2014 and internationally the following year, was bigger in every sense. It was an account of the aftermath of the Sri Lankan civil war, sketching the contexts of the conflict and encountering those affected by its violence. It had been shortlisted for the Samuel Johnson Prize for Non-Fiction.

I was, I suppose, stretching the parameters I had fixed for myself at the start of my journey in coming to speak to Samanth Subramanian. It wasn't so much that he was Indian (he was a British citizen, after all; he was published in London, and I'd already included Irish Dervla Murphy and Canadian Rory MacLean in my survey of travel writers). Rather it was my two-travel-books rule.

Following Fish, with its journey narrative and its linking theme was, unmistakably, a travel book. Its UK publisher, Atlantic, had tagged it as such on the back cover. The same publisher, however, had branded Subramanian's second book, *This Divided Island*, as something different: 'reportage'. But I couldn't really see the difference. It met all the criteria of my scholarly definitions of travel writing perfectly. It evoked place; it was an account of a journey; it was written in the first person; I supposed that what it described had taken place in reality and assumed that its 'author, narrator and principal character were but one or identical'.[3] This, in particular, was why I had wanted to speak to him—to discuss the curious connection between travel writing and journalism. And after my recent forays into the liminal space between the fact and aesthetic conventions, it was something of a relief to talk to someone who was professionally concerned with reporting 'the facts'.

* * *

I asked Subramanian to tell me more about the links between travel writing and journalism.

He took a sip of his Guinness. Black-and-white pint. Black-and-white tee shirt.

'Who do we think of as the first travel writer?' he said. 'Herodotus maybe? I'm not sure.'

'Herodotus is always cited,' I said. We were dealing with *facts* here; I wasn't going to let John Mandeville into *this* conversation.

He nodded. All his movements were neat and precise. 'Yes, and also the first historian, so I guess he has a lot to answer for. But what did Herodotus do, right? He told stories of things that happened far away and he brought them home, and he gave them to his audience and gave them a view of the world. It was *his* view of the world in particular, because as we know not everything he wrote was true and accurate. The Persians saw everything he wrote about from a very different perspective. But it was *his* view of the world that he then brought to the Greeks. We think of him as a historian now only because we see *him* now as history and the events he wrote about as history. But if we were living contemporaneously we'd be thinking of him as a journalist; he would be a war correspondent, in a sense. Maybe these events weren't happening in front of his eyes, but there was a version. They say journalism is the first draft of history, and I think this is what Herodotus was doing, in one sense. It was a marriage of these two genres, and maybe the reason people call it travel writing is only because these events happened so far away from where they were, right? I mean, that's the essence.'

I said that I'd always been a little uneasy about the idea of Herodotus as a travel writer, because of the absence of that obvious authorial 'I'. Mandeville was still hanging around somewhere, cradling his own pint in the gloomy back room behind the bar. I did my best to ignore him.

'Except for the fact that Herodotus is distilling all these events through himself,' Subramanian said. 'That's maybe the most personal aspect of the *Histories*. So... where was I going with all this? What I used to think earlier was that travel writing had nothing to do with journalism, in the classic way that it was practised, whether you want to think about Robert Byron or even Patrick Leigh Fermor, all these classics of travel writing—Mark Twain's *The Innocents Abroad* [1869]. You don't look at them as journalism in the sense that we think of journalism now, right? And so where these two genres converge is through the twentieth century particularly. The kind of work that Byron did or that Mark Twain did, the internet does fairly well for you now, right? It paints a picture of what a faraway place is like. Better than that: it gives you a picture of what it's *actually* like. For example, if you want to see what Petra is like, you would call it up on Google Images rather than reading a description of it. So the sense of lyrically, evocatively writing about a place and describing it for a reader who will never see it, that function seems to have been stripped away. What else is there? The adventure in getting to Afghanistan, to Oxiana—that isn't there anymore because it's very easy just to take a plane and go there, so therefore the caravanserais across Central Asia and so on, these are all a thing of the past as well.

'So one by one I think a lot of those functions of classic travel writing have fallen away. The one that *does* remain, I think, is that however much the internet tells you about the world and about a country or a city or a place, it can't tell you about the individual, intimate details of somebody's life, right? So if I were to go to Kerala and talk to a toddy shop owner about what his life is like and about the kind of customers he has, and what he does and where he came from, *that* is still not available online or in a picture or anywhere else. And each person's life is unique and each person's life has something to say.

'So that function of travel writing is still really strong. And that is a *journalistic* function, because that's what journalists do—journalists go and talk to people about their lives and about their problems and about their views on the world.'

This was a rather rousing new line. The idea that travel writing's informational aspect was now defunct was common enough, with the suggestion often following that highly personal inner journeys—or perhaps experiments with fiction—were the only remaining possibilities for the genre. But Subramanian had, with a certain meticulousness, broken the informational aspect into its constituent parts and identified those that still mattered most—and what mattered most, he seemed to be saying, was travel writing's capacity to make space for the travellee.

* * *

There is a moment in *The Places in Between* by Rory Stewart—the same Rory Stewart who had summoned up the spirits of the British Empire during his debate on truth and travel writing with Rory MacLean at the Royal Society of Literature—where the author, walking across northwest Afghanistan in 2002 just after the US-led invasion, is stopped by a journalist, blazing around in a jeep and looking for copy. Stewart— who just a couple of pages earlier has responded with a testy 'no' when his local guide asks if he is, himself, a journalist—portrays the encounter as a sort of clash of civilisations. The travel writer waxes lyrical about the 'Prussian blue sky' and says that he feels he has 'been preparing for this all my life'. But the uncomprehending journalist simply scribbles observations about his daily mileage and wispy beard.[4] The two figures met on the road are *not* fellow travellers, it seems. And there's no question about who sits above whom in Stewart's hierarchical positioning of the two species of writer.

This was by no means a universal take, of course. During my conversation with Patrick Barkham—like Subramanian, a professional, time-served journalist—he had mentioned, with a certain air of insecurity, his sense that to call a travel book 'journalistic' was 'kind of an insult'. But then Dervla Murphy, a respected travel writer for more than half a century, had called her own books 'journalistic records' and herself 'a sort of commentator, and to that extent a journalist'.

Some strange tussle seemed to be going on here. For a writer with literary aspirations, the word 'journalist' seemed to suggest relegation to the lower divisions, to hint at the harsh, half-voiced slur: *hack*. But on the other hand, for a writer with established literary credentials, eager to claim the kudos of empiricism, 'journalist' might appear a higher designation than 'travel writer'. Then there was another, contrary tension. If a writer who *was* happy to be called a journalist dared to display literary tendencies, to fling in a little too much colour, to start talking of Prussian blue skies, then he or she might be mocked for pretentiousness, or, worse yet, judged unreliable, suspected of straying into *fiction*. Meanwhile, if travel writers started deploying the signals of journalistic practice—Dictaphones, shorthand, formal interviews with officials—then whatever literary credentials they possessed might be stripped away.

What this speaks to, I think, is the curious inferiority complex of nonfiction in general. According to the scholar Catherine Mee, both journalism and travel writing are genres 'that have suffered a lack of critical attention because of their uncertain status as literature'.[5] And what made that status uncertain was 'their referential nature'. A commitment to representing facts, Mee wrote, 'restricts the writer's creative talents, conferring a minor status on these genres'.[6] Sara Wheeler, herself blithely unbothered, had talked of the same thing: the perceived hierarchy and the desire of the big boys of travel writing to be taken seriously as novelists.

None of this made sense. The idea that *A Time of Gifts*, say, was by simple dint of its claim to the fact convention inferior to a piece of outright fiction seemed ludicrous. Was it supposed to be an absolute distinction? Was it inferior to *all* fiction? To *Fifty Shades of Grey* and *The Da Vinci Code*? And if not, then how; where; and, most importantly of all, *why* did you mark the cut-off point? Geoffrey Moorhouse, himself

223

a veteran newspaperman who'd also produced fine and serious works of travel writing, had, I think, got to the bottom of all this: 'it is the result of a simple failure—or perhaps a reluctance—to distinguish between imagination and invention'.[7]

So where did this leave journalism? As so often, it depended on your point of departure. In Rory Stewart's account of his meeting on the road in Afghanistan—a passage spotted and identified as 'a critical commentary on journalistic writing' by the scholar Corinne Fowler[8]—Stewart describes the photographer who accompanies the interrogating reporter talking admiringly of Jon Krakauer's *Into the Wild* (1996). It is, the photographer says, '"a great piece of journalism"'.[9] This is the closing line of the scene, and the page-break that follows contains the unvoiced inference: the man moving slowly on foot, the travel writer, has the high ground—certainly aesthetic and probably moral too. But I get the feeling that Stewart had never read *Into the Wild*. If he went to look for it in the bookshop he'd find it in the travel section. And between the covers he'd discover meticulous research, often subsumed to the point of invisibility in an elegantly forged narrative. The book reads—and I'm aware that in saying this I am myself internalising the assumed hierarchy—*like a novel*.

* * *

Jon Krakauer belongs to the venerable tradition of long-form narrative journalism forged and finessed by the likes of Truman Capote and Tom Wolfe, big literary beasts in their own right. It is a distinctly North American approach, largely alien to British newsrooms. And it is an approach seemingly untroubled by insecurities about its position on some spurious slide rule. This was Samanth Subramanian's own tradition of journalism. And this, perhaps, was why he seemed to suffer no inferiority complex, and no discomfort with either designation. Journalist or travel writer—he could be both.

'So in literary travel writing we can separate that into the journalistic part and the travel writing part,' Subramanian said. 'And the journalistic part is how while the book is being researched the writer relates to the world around him, how he relates to the people around him in terms of the ethics of reporting and the soundness of it. But then in one sense—and this is a very strange thing to say—the actual travel writing part happens when you're at home, because what you're doing is actually sitting down and distilling everything that you've seen and heard onto the page. And that distillation, because it's happening through your own mind and voice, is the really personal part of the journey. That's the really personal part of the entire travel writing process and that happens at your desk, it doesn't happen outside. I mean, the travel has happened, but the travel *writing* is happening at your desk.'

There was a confidence about Samanth Subramanian. He moved through all these topics with a sureness of step and a clarity of speech—great, unbroken blocks of speech, without the usual mumbling and fumbling; without nudges and interjections from his interlocutor. I simply sat there, listening, looking across two slowly diminishing black-and-white pints of Guinness towards a small man in a black-and-white tee shirt, sitting in a huge armchair with one leg folded up beneath him.

I had enjoyed *Following Fish*, but it was *This Divided Island* that had really caught my attention, made me eager to seek out its author. It had the feel of a travel book of the most serious sort, with its crowding mass of testimonies. It reminded me of Dervla's books on Palestine and Northern Ireland.

The most arresting moment in *This Divided Island* comes when Subramanian meets a man named Ismail in the town of Kattankudy. Ismail, who has lost many friends during the recently ended conflict and has seen his six-year-old nephew killed by the Tamil Tigers, has met inquisitive journalists before. He is happy to talk, but first he wants to ask Subramanian a question:

> 'Of course,' I said. He wanted to know what kind of book I was writing, I thought.
> 'What good will this conversation do for me?' he asked.[10]

It was the ultimate question to be asked of every travel writer and every journalist, far more pointed and pressing than the solipsistic, 'What am I doing here?' Here was the travellee, seeing the traveller, recognising his agenda and interrogating it. It was not, I was quite certain, a moment that could ever have occurred in a fictionalised evocation of a life, no matter how sensitively done, no matter how effective at 'establishing solidarity with the travellee'. It existed here because

Subramanian was trying to report the actuality, and in doing so he had made space for the travellee to issue a challenge. When Rory Stewart lays out his 'critical commentary on journalistic writing' in *The Places in Between*, he is in supreme control, reinforcing his own superior standing and that of the book that he is writing. But *this* critical commentary came surging back, out of and against the text.

In response to the unanswerable question, Subramanian, deeply discomfited, can only talk weakly of the importance of stories being recorded. Ismail, it seems, has heard it all before. He agrees to the interview, 'with a shrug of immense politeness', on the promise of nothing more than a copy of the book in which he will appear. The moment—which unfolds on page 171 of the UK paperback edition—is a questioning of the writer's entire project. And yet, its very survival in the text seemed like the most compelling ethical justification of travel writing that I had encountered on my entire journey. Travel writing of the sort that featured in *This Divided Island*—and it *was* a travel book, whatever its publisher thought—could allow someone other than its own author to speak, and to speak *against* the author if needs be. That chance might only be offered through a haze, or through the tiniest of cracks. But it existed.

Subramanian told me that he still thought frequently about Ismail's challenge.

'This is the perennial journalistic problem, just to justify to yourself your intrusiveness in other people's lives, particularly at moments of distress, or to ask about moments of distress,' he said. 'And it's not something I've solved for myself at all.'

Outside the grey afternoon was fading fast, and the lights of the passing buses made a lurid kaleidoscope of the massed medicine bottles in the window. Fleetwood Mac's 'Little Lies' was on the pub stereo.

'In this day and age there's a lot of discussion, rightly so, about things like agency and appropriation and who should be the right person to tell whose stories,' Subramanian was saying. 'And there's all sorts of degrees of difference to this, right? I mean, for somebody from the UK or sitting in New York, for an Indian Tamil to go to Sri Lanka and tell the story of Sri Lankan Tamils, it seems pretty fine. I mean, you're all speaking the same language; this is good. But this was *very* problematic in Sri Lanka, because it really felt as if a journalist from the neighbouring "Big Brother" country was coming down into their little country and talking to people and telling their stories to the outside world. So that was bad enough. But I suppose if you were a Sinhalese journalist in Colombo going out to tell the stories of Tamils there would be a further degree of appropriation there.

'The ultimate ideal is, of course, for everyone to tell their own stories, but the world is just not built like that; it's just not practical. So what are you going to do? There's always going to be some overlap, so the only thing you can do is to try to be as sensitive as possible, to make sure that you get permissions from everyone that you talk to and make sure that they're comfortable with the way that they're being portrayed and what they're saying and so on. But it's endless; it's a spectrum, and you just have to try to be as honest and accurate as possible.'

* * *

I asked Subramanian if he ever had any slight unease about travel writing's dubious heritage. For centuries, India in particular had fallen under the gaze of European travel writers who—as far as Edward Said was concerned, in any case—were intimately involved in the colonial project. I had an idea that he'd provide a well-considered answer.

'The problem was not the travel writing,' he said; 'the problem was the larger culture of colonialism that fostered the travel writing. So you can't sort of decide that you won't read the great colonial travel writers—because they can be very good literature. And so I don't look upon that as a problem in any way.

'I mean, there are plenty of problems with me doing the kind of books I do myself, even within India. There are directions of power and dynamics of power. I'm an elite, English-speaking, foreign-educated Brahmin at the top of the caste system. There could be plenty of problems with me writing the kinds of books and articles that I do, and me having the kind of power and agency that I have that echo some of these colonial dynamics as well. So it's not for me to find fault with one but to be comfortable with the other. The only thing that I can do is to say, look, you didn't choose where you were born; the only thing you can do is write a book that's as sensitive as possible. And are some books less sensitive than others? Sure; you don't read those; that's fine.'

227

He paused for a second. 'I was going somewhere with this! Oh yes! What I *can* do, and what I really do want to do, is to sort of reverse, in whatever little way I can, the assumption that has been held for many centuries that if there's any part of the world that should be writing about any other part it's that the First World should be writing about the Second and Third; the Americans and the Brits and so on writing about India and Africa and Asia. I feel that not only is it possible for Indians to write about other parts of Asia, but it's also possible for Indians to write about the West, and it can be done with the same kind of rigour and standards and analysis that the West claims it holds dear. These are the big values of Western journalism—objectivity and fact-checking and all these things. *We* can play that game, and it's a worthy game to be played. I mean, I feel like there's huge value in it, otherwise I wouldn't be doing it. But I feel like the direction of the writer and the written, those two poles can shift and *have* shifted, and I'm trying to shift them, and many other people are trying to do that too, and I think it is slowly starting to happen.'

It was fully dark outside now. The traffic on Donnybrook Road had thickened to an ooze of yellow embers. I had a brief sense of déjà vu. I seemed to have been in this situation before: sitting across a table from a travel writer of my own generation while a cold city night came on beyond big windows. The glasses and the neat black hair and beard were familiar. It was Nicholas Jubber I was thinking of, ten months earlier, in London, in a different winter. But age, glasses and facial hair were about the only things that he and Subramanian had in common.

What was it that Jonathan Raban had said about earlier generations of English travel writers? Four centuries of imperial existence had given them a sense of precisely where they stood in the world—'bang at its moral centre'.[11] But Jubber *hadn't* seemed to possess such a confidence, and nor had Patrick Barkham. Quite the opposite really, in their different ways. But Subramanian... An idea was forming.

Pulp's 'Disco 2000' was on the stereo. There were only frothy inches of Guinness left in the bottom of our glasses, and Subramanian was talking about power.

'You can go from Delhi, which is a capital and major world city with the kind of incomes you wouldn't dream of in some of the small villages where I went for *Following Fish*. So there's a very big power dynamic that exists there,' he said. 'London to the imperium is not the only power dynamic that exists.'

'It makes me wonder,' I said hesitantly. The thought hadn't come together yet, and I went on carefully, trying to put the pieces in place as I spoke. 'The location of the power isn't necessarily a former or current imperial centre; it's just a position of relative wealth and literacy, isn't it?'

I hadn't quite managed to get the idea out yet, but Subramanian was off in a flash. 'And it changes, from article to article! If you're considering it as a journalist, from article to article it changes. There have been times when I've been at the opposite side.' He told me about his experiences interviewing politicians and EU commissioners. 'There's no such thing as journalism between equals,' he said.

* * *

It was getting late, and if I wanted to catch the last train back to Galway I would need to leave soon. But I still wanted to work out the half-formed idea—and to work out how to ask the question it suggested.

Most of *This Divided Island* takes place in Sri Lanka. But there are interludes where Subramanian goes to talk to Sri Lankans in exile—in London and New York and Toronto. And in each of these places he moves effortlessly. These do not appear to be foreign cities to him. There is no moment of astonished arrival; no entry into the contact zone. And now he was in Dublin, and what I'd slowly realised over the course of our conversation was that he didn't seem like a foreigner here, in this pub with its Guinness and its old medicine bottles—certainly less so than the Eastern European barmaid who had served us our pints; maybe less so than me. But if Subramanian had come to interview *me*, living in Delhi or Chennai, or Kuala Lumpur or Jakarta…

I mentioned the effortless international movement in *This Divided Island*.

'Ah!' He raised a finger. 'But you must remember my British passport!'

'Okay.'

'It made things much easier. Oh, I cannot tell you how much easier it made it! It would be much more difficult for an Indian writer with an Indian passport to go to Canada.'

It was a very fair point, but somehow that wasn't quite what I was getting at. 'Even without the British passport, there's an ease of intellectual movement,' I said.

That Subramanian speaks Tamil to his interviewees in northern Sri Lanka is a given, in his English-language book about the island. And as he moves around the Indian coast in *Following Fish* it requires no explanation that he is switching from English to Hindi to Tamil and back again as he meets his travellees.

The older scholarly critiques of travel writing did sometimes seem to suggest that 'London to the imperium' was the only direction of travel. This was clearly no longer true; it had never really been true at all, as long as there were Chinese monks at large and travellee-polemicists polishing their ripostes. And if the most important sort of power when it came to travel writing was simply the power to be able to *go*, and to *write*, well then—'I wondered,' I said, 'if someone like yourself is kind of at the pinnacle…'

Subramanian angled his head sharply, and for a moment I had an impression of new data being processed at incredible speed. 'Well!' he said, blinking swiftly behind his glasses. 'I had *never* thought of that! But you're completely right! If you strip away the practical aspect of ease of movement itself, yeah… You could—I—*I* could go to Toronto and I could walk around and nobody would look at me a second time, and I could access academia and ranks of the experts in the West and also do reporting in the East, or vice versa—just to use these overbroad categories of "West" and "East" for the moment.' He smiled and tilted his head again. 'I hadn't thought of that! It's very true, ya!'

So, I wondered aloud, might there be new challenges, new ethical difficulties to be considered for a writer like Subramanian?

He didn't need to think about the question for long—barely long enough to finish the final mouthful of his pint. 'In a couple of ways,' he said. 'One way is something that I need to engage with even now. I am in this fortunate space, but it's a product of privilege and I always have to negotiate that even when I'm doing the kind of work that I'm doing now. It's fine when I'm writing about subjects that come to me from the UK or Europe, because in that case I feel that in so far as there is a power dynamic there's some sort of balance or equity to it. But when I do go back home and when I do write magazine stories from India or

South Asia, I realise that, if anything, since I wrote *Following Fish* that power dynamic has been tilted even further. With *Following Fish*, I was a writer living in Delhi and writing a book meant to be read by Indian readers. Now, in an even more extreme case, I'd be a writer living in Dublin and writing a magazine article that will be read primarily by readers in the US. I mean, there are all these problems—problems in the sense that an editor in the US, however diligent she may be'—That meticulous use of the female pronoun! Subramanian moved very carefully, no matter how fast he spoke—'will never actually know the ground realities of what I'm dealing with, and therefore I could get away with simplification and elision and essentialisation. I would hate to do all of that, but there's no doubt about it I *could* do it if I wanted to; she would never know.

'The other problem is if a culture grows up—whether in China or Africa or anywhere else—where people feel that the only way to get a kind of writerly agency is to follow into the same fortunate space: this mobility, this space of mobility where it is informed by an education overseas, and by the literary culture overseas, where you read and write for the kind of magazines that I read and write for. Now, I didn't choose to do this, and I don't think there was a model when I started doing it; it just so happened. But for people to assume that that's the only way you can get into the space where you can write, and the only manner and technique that you can employ is this kind of *New Yorker* writing—that's a terrible mistake, and it would be terrible. It works for me and I like it, but it shouldn't be a default setting at all, and there should equally be other literary cultures which engage with India or any other territory being written about from the point of view of that territory itself, or from another point of view that isn't exclusively Western.'

One private criticism he'd heard of *This Divided Island*, he said, was that in its structure and approach, it followed too closely in the traditions of American journalism. This didn't seem very fair to me—a journalist from America would be less likely to be able to talk to people in Tamil for a start. Subramanian didn't think it was entirely fair either. But it was the book's form, he said, that had prompted the accusation.

'Now, I can't do anything about that because that's a form that I've either grown to love or have trained myself on, and it's very difficult

231

to break out of it, even if I wanted to—and I'm not sure I do. I think the form works for certain things. But I don't think that everybody should follow the same form. This kind of genre will only be enriched if there's a diversity of forms. And I'm worried, now that you've brought it up, that people will assume that this is the only form to gravitate to. That could be a problem.'

'I didn't mean to worry you,' I said.

'No, no; it's a fair question,' he said. 'You know there must be other ways of looking at the world; there must be other forms that a book can take—even travel writing. There must be other forms that travel writing can take.'

* * *

It was sharply cold outside. Subramanian headed home, moving swiftly, effortlessly. Bundled in a black winter coat, he seemed even smaller and neater. I clambered aboard a packed city bus heading in the opposite direction and wriggled my way to the top deck as it lurched through the manic streets of central Dublin. Glimpses of Christmas lights around St Stephen's Green, then tall shop fronts, flat as stage props, beyond the black stripe of the Liffey. Somewhere across the aisle, through the tangled limbs of standing passengers, a girl's voice: 'I like living in the city more than I'd expected.'

Subramanian was unlike any of the other people I'd met on my journeys. The scholar Catherine Mee had suggested that the journalist and the travel writer—the two figures that meet uneasily on the road in Rory Stewart's Afghanistan book, neither quite so exalted as the novelist or the poet—had something to teach one another. Travel writers, she thought, should follow the journalists' lead and pay more attention to the here and now: 'Attention to the present can cut short the cycle of travellers who arrive at their destination clutching an out-of-date classic of the genre and are disappointed to find that the local culture has not been preserved under glass.'[12]

One thing was certain: there were few traces of such belatedness in Subramanian's books, and whenever he strayed in that direction he caught himself. In *Following Fish* there is a moment where he almost—*almost*—expresses disappointment that a 'traditional' boat-builder on the coast of Gujarat is now using power tools, before he spots his own hypocrisy: the boat builder is as much a part of the twenty-first century as a metropolitan journalist, and 'the power saw is, in that sense, now a part of the natural order of things'.[13] And then, in *This Divided Island*, wandering the crumbling alleys of Jaffna, he thinks for a moment that he is exploring a city fixed in the past. Then he remembers: it looks this way because of the war. 'Jaffna was not suspended in amber; it had been prevented from renewing itself in the ways that a town normally would.'[14]

For Catherine Mee, the journalist could take something from the travel writer's example too: the longer, slower, deeper view that the pressing deadline disallowed. The 'book-length format and the extended period of travel, writing and publication allow space and time for greater elaboration than is possible in most forms of journalism'.[15] But as far as I could make out, Samanth Subramanian had no need of either of these lessons.

There was something else too. I hadn't asked him the one question that always—*always*—arose elsewhere: is it okay to make stuff up? It had never even occurred to me.

I got down from the bus at Heuston Station. Passengers stood around on the concourse waiting for their platforms. I ate a burger at Supermac's. A man in a heavy green jacket was moving between the tables, begging for change. Then I boarded the last train westwards, back into the cold darkness of the countryside.

16

LETTING THE SCHOLAR SPEAK

It was the question that I should have asked at the academic conference in Berlin: 'What was the first travel book you ever read?'

Carl Thompson frowned. 'I can answer much more clearly how I got into *studying* travel writing,' he said.

Back in Dorset, when Rory MacLean had had his giggling fit at my lapse into academic jargon—'traveller and travellee'; 'affective iden-tification'—I'd asked him if he knew anything of the scholarly business of travel writing studies.

'I've sort of *heard* about it,' he'd said; 'but it's like hearing about this very strange clique which lives probably somewhere on Bodmin Moor; a strange group that has strange rituals. But it's not a world I know.'

In this he was entirely normal. Right at the start, Nicholas Jubber—a man with an English degree from Oxford—had asked, incredulously, '*Is* there a lot of scholarship on travel writing?' And no one else I'd spoken to—other than Colin Thubron, who by his own account had only encountered the scholarship via his wife's university connec-tions—had anything more than the vaguest awareness that there might be whole legions of academics, somewhere out there, poring over travel texts. This, I'd realised, was having an unforeseen and unfortu-nate consequence. As my journey progressed, the travel writers—the object of study, sometimes treated, as Thubron had pointed out, as texts rather than people—had been *speaking*. I had given them *agency*, as the scholars would say. Colin Thubron had once been a foot-long section on my bookshelf; now he was a generous man in carpet slippers. Dervla Murphy had been a ragtag array of multihued paperbacks; now she was the maker of the best soup in the world.

But as the writers took fuller form, the very opposite fate had befallen the scholars. Travel writing studies had begun to feel like some fiendish doctrine, forged by distant desert fathers. When I mentioned a scholar by name in conversation with a travel writer, it was as if I was quoting a catechism, not speaking of a human being. The scholars were becoming *the other*. I wanted to do something to put that right. Also, having covered a lot of ground on my journey so far, I wanted to take stock, to see where the scholarship of travel writing, as well as the genre itself, might be heading. And so I'd contacted Carl Thompson, the scholar who'd given the opening keynote at the Berlin conference.

* * *

I'd arranged to meet him over lunch in the British Library where he was working on an edited collection of eighteenth- and nineteenth-century women's travel writing about India, adding scholarly footnotes to the texts of Jemima Kindersley's letters from her journey to India in the 1760s, and Maria Graham's 1812 *Journal of a Residence in India*. Perhaps at some point he'd sat across a desk from Nicholas Jubber, each unaware of what the other was about. We met outside Rare Books and went downstairs to find a seat in the noisy restaurant at the back of the building.

Thompson's clothes had the same slightly crumpled quality that I'd noticed in Berlin. He wore black-rimmed glasses at the end of his nose, and looked out over them with tired eyes. He really did look like a cabinetmaker or a blacksmith rather than an academic. He reminded me of people I knew from home who worked in sheds that smelt of sawdust and cold metal. He talked at an almighty pace, and sometimes a little tangle of tics and markers would come out at the start of his sentences: 'Asiwassayingitslikesorryexactly...' But he could hold onto a thread that led back to the original question through any number of wandering digressions, long after I'd forgotten what it was I had asked.

While we were waiting for lunch I asked him about the beginnings of his lifelong professional engagement with travel writing. When the travel writers I met talked about the origins of their vocation, the story was usually the obvious one: a youthful hankering for travel; an early passion for the books of their predecessors; or both thrown together in potent combination. My own obsession with the genre had the same beginnings: a flurry of books and backpacking in my late teens and early twenties, with the reading eventually outgrowing and outlasting the wanderlust. But when it came to the scholar there was a certain mystery: how did *they* get into *this*? And a further puzzlement: did they actually *like* travel writing?

Carl Thompson had to think about it for a minute. 'I suppose the travel book that I can first remember reading—I can't remember when that would be, but I'd certainly read it by the time I settled on doing travel writing studies for my master's thesis, so it must have been late teenage—was Charles Nicholl's *The Fruit Palace* [1985],' he said. 'I don't know if you know that?'

I didn't.

'It's really great, actually!'

The book was, as Thompson told it, a piece of 1980s travel writing in the classical mode: an account of a journey investigating the cocaine trade in South America, replete with literary references, and Redmond O'Hanlon-style self-deprecation. It was thirty years since he had read the thing, but it had clearly made an impression. 'It's very nicely done. It's well worth looking out.'

So that answered that, then: he *did* like travel writing, at the outset at least.

Thompson had also read Bruce Chatwin's *The Songlines* (1987) as a student, and had loved it. Coming back to it later he'd spotted all the problems—the questionable exoticism, the troublesome traces of old tropes about 'noble savages', the absence of Aboriginal voices, the blithe appropriation of a marginalised culture as a platform for the author's own big idea. But at first encounter there had only been the same excitement I recalled from my own first reading.

'I hadn't really thought through the sort of Orientalism side of it,' he said, 'but I was quite dazzled by the experimentation.'

'That's how he got away with it.'

'Exactly.'

'You look at it now and think why were people not howling with outrage?' I said. I'm not sure if I wasn't trying to ingratiate myself here, merrily scoffing at the ethical problems of the travel genre in scholarly company.

But Thompson frowned. 'Well, it's complicated,' he said. 'I'm sort of a little bit with Thomas Keneally about this—you know what Thomas Keneally said? And actually this takes us through to the interest in travel writing as a genre, because travel writing is quite consistently a popularising, middlebrow genre. And don't get me wrong, I think all of the criticism and qualifications and eye-rolling has to happen. But on the other hand, actually *making* that eye-rolling happen, in a sense, is quite a useful thing, because a lot of people wouldn't be having those debates if Chatwin hadn't put that out there. It's like someone like Clapton introducing you a little bit to reggae, and then you go and find real reggae.

'So Keneally's point—I quote it somewhere—he makes the point that, yes, you have to criticise these things, but on the other hand if Chatwin hadn't put it out there then many people would never have heard of songlines. It would have been a long time before *I* heard of songlines, and of course all the dot paintings, if Chatwin hadn't put it out there. And yes, you need to take it apart where he's gone wrong, but perhaps you should acknowledge also the way he's found an audience for this. And then, if you like, more nuanced and accurate scholars and critics can correct the picture and point out the obvious deficiencies.'[1]

Something rather unexpected had happened: *I* had set out looking to condemn a notoriously problematic travel writer, and Carl Thompson, the travel writing scholar, had stepped in to defend him. This was certainly not a scenario I could ever have imagined at the outset of my journey.

'That's a good defence of travel writing in general,' I said.

'Well, it is.'

* * *

Carl Thompson's academic involvement with travel writing had begun in his early twenties, when, as a postgraduate at Oxford, he'd found himself needing to come up with a topic for an MPhil thesis in a hurry.

'I had left it quite late, and I had to make that decision in about the middle of 1990. I had read Chatwin before that, so I knew Chatwin; I had liked Chatwin. I had read *The Fruit Palace*; I must have read something else. But certainly what I had also seen, as you can imagine, is that at that point there had been a sort of wave of newspaper articles, and ideas I must have picked up, about what had happened to travel writing in the 1980s. So I saw that and thought this is an interesting thing, and had liked *The Songlines*; and thought I'll do something on that, because it was very up to date and it just seemed an interesting topic. So in some ways it was just finding a topic quite quickly. It was something I was a little bit interested in, but I hadn't really given it too much thought. So that's literally how I came to it. And then to some extent carrying on doing it also probably becomes a matter of expediency.'

After the MPhil he'd lived in London and worked in IT for a few years, before returning to Oxford. To get the necessary funding for a PhD, he'd had to pick up the thread of his earlier research.

'And so then I sort of said I was going to do something that took the themes of the MPhil thesis, which was about 1980s travel writing, back to the Victorian period—notions of travel, what's a traveller, what's a tourist,' he said. 'But as I dug into the things that interested me they all led back to the Romantic period, so I sort of slipped back by accident to become a Romanticist. So in a sense carrying on with it is a sequence of slightly accidental, rather provisional things that happened through expedience at the time.'

It was like any other career, then.

Since completing his PhD at Oxford, Thompson had worked at Nottingham Trent University, St Mary's University in London, and now at the University of Surrey. His own research focus had remained the Romantic period of the eighteenth and early nineteenth centuries.

I wanted to know more about 'voyages and travels'—the older designation for what we might now call travel writing that he had mentioned back in Berlin. I was curious to know how it differed from the sort of modern travel writing produced by the writers I'd spoken to. Lunch had arrived, and as Thompson munched at his mushroom and halloumi sandwich, he explained. There was, he thought, a clear distinction. The older 'voyages and travels' had been a 'knowledge genre'—not just *a* vehicle, but *the* vehicle for presenting serious scientific, geographical, political, even philosophical findings and arguments. Think of Captain Cook; think of Charles Darwin and Alfred Russel Wallace.

Later, scribbling notes on my way home, I realised that it went back way beyond the eighteenth century—certainly as far as John Mandeville. And it applied to the other, parallel paths too. It had been a while since I'd thought about Yijing, the seventh-century Chinese monk. He'd brought back a first-person narrative of his travels in India and Southeast Asia, but the great bulk of his text—and the great purpose of his journey—was to gather authoritative information about Buddhism. Perhaps it was in the 'voyages and travels' mode that travel writing had been at its most universal. But then, about a century ago, something had shifted.

'I think, personally, that something really quite qualitatively different starts to happen once you get to early twentieth-century travel writing,' Thompson said, 'where you definitely much more have the ones that aren't reportage, they're not fact-finding.'

Sometime in the late Victorian era, the purely informational aspects began to peel away into professional scholarship he explained between mouthfuls of sandwich. Botanists, geographers and anthropologists stopped publishing first-person travelogues aimed at the reading public. The term 'voyages and travels'—which had been around since at least the sixteenth century—fell out of use; and 'travel writing' as we recognise it today came into being.

This new thing was what Thompson called a 'primarily aesthetic mode of travel writing'. It was true that much of the travel writing of the twentieth and twenty-first centuries retained some informational imperative—Philip Marsden digging into the story of the Armenian diaspora; Patrick Barkham plotting the natural histories of badgers and butterflies. But the order of precedence had been inverted. In the era of 'voyages and travels' any aesthetic qualities that the text might possess were secondary, even incidental, to the importance of the discoveries it described. But in the age of 'travel writing', the book seldom claimed the status of proper scholarship. It was meant, first and foremost, to be *read*. Thinking back, I realised that I could just about trace the shift in the travelogues about Cornwall that I'd read, back in the Penzance public library. At the start of the nineteenth century, Richard Warner's account had been sternly informational; when Wilkie Collins came rambling through in mid-century, entertainment was becoming a clear imperative; and by the first decade of the twentieth century,

Charles Lewis Hind was, unmistakably, a travel writer as I knew it a hundred years later.

But somehow, the vital aesthetic characteristic of modern travel writing hardly ever came up for discussion in the annals of travel writing studies. At the Berlin conference, just one presenter—Elizabeth Robertson, an American woman working on Wilfred Thesiger—had talked about the 'literary' qualities of the text. It seemed like a curious oversight, I thought, but according to Thompson it went beyond the study of travel writing. Since the 1980s, he said, scholars had been generally wary of debating the essential aesthetic merits of any writing.

'So you don't have people sort of weighing in that Wordsworth is a better poet than Byron; we just don't have those debates anymore, and that's probably by and large to the good.' I lifted my hand to raise an objection, but he went on. 'But whereas with Wordsworth and Byron, you probably wouldn't set them up against each other, you would still discuss, "Well, what's the aesthetic effect of this text?" And there isn't as much of *that* in travel writing studies.'

I lowered my hand. 'That's what I was going to say.'

'I suspect that for a lot of what we're calling the "travel writing" side of it—the twentieth century—there almost needs to be a way of weaving that back in a bit. Because they *are* aesthetically constructed texts.'

Of course they were. When trying to explain which sort of travel books I loved best I had always struggled to express it clearly: 'creative'; 'finely written'; 'literary'—they were all nebulous and hopelessly subjective categorisations. But 'aesthetically constructed' was perfect; a case of academic terminology cutting through with clarity. And naturally, an aesthetically constructed text might be less bound to the 'fact convention'. Was it simply that Rory MacLean better recognised travel writing's proper status in the post-'voyages and travels' world, while most of his peers—not least Rory Stewart—were still stuck in the past?

* * *

When I first dipped into scholarly critiques of travel writing, years earlier, my earliest impression had been of a righteous postcolonial crusade. There seemed to be legions of earnest critics pointing out the clear complicity of older travel writing—or 'voyages and travels'—in

Europe's imperial projects, and highlighting examples of more recent books keeping alive outdated notions of 'here and there', 'us and them'. But since I'd begun my concerted quest in search of travel writing I'd dug deeper into the more recent scholarship, the latest issues of *Studies in Travel Writing*, the most up-to-date collections of essays. As I did so I'd realised that travel writing studies had, in some ways, moved on. Sometime in the early 2000s, the crusade had come to a natural climax. The point had been made, and there wasn't a great deal more to say about it. Since then, scholarship of travel writing seemed to have become less hostile, more diffuse. Questions of power, the 'construction of difference', traveller and travellee, remained important. But few people now seemed to be trying to prove that there was something universally *wrong* with travel writing. Certainly no one in Berlin had made that claim.

I should have been relieved. But somehow the idea that a zealous endeavour had come to a close was disappointing. Was this a new facet of belatedness? If the last great commercial boom for travel writing had fizzled out at the turn of the twenty-first century, perhaps I'd arrived too late for the excitement of the scholarly onslaught too. Was I wandering around an empty battlefield? And if the scholarship of travel writing was no longer driven forward by such a forceful critique— well, where did it go from here? It was the same sort of question people were always posing about travel writing itself.

Carl Thompson seemed like a good person to ask. Alongside his research on the Romantic period, he'd conducted a number of grand surveys—of both travel writing and its scholarship.

He made a brief show of being daunted—'Hmm, let me think!'— then plunged in. 'So, in terms of where it goes, I think you're quite right that you hit a logical endpoint with the very radical critique, even though it's very important never to forget that critique. All that must not be forgotten. But it's maybe not the only thing that needs talking about in travel writing.

'It's like all those big radical, reforming shake-ups of these disciplines in the 70s and 80s, whether it's feminism or postcolonialism; all these things had to happen, massively important. But then what happens, if you like, is that certain polemical positions which had to be said get nuanced, refined, qualified—often in the spirit of the polemic, but also more complicated, because the world is always more complicated. And that can feel like it's losing a certain force. You get this debate in modern postcolonial studies or feminist studies—have we overqualified and nuanced the exchanges between either side of the imperial divide so much that we forget there is an inequality? So I think that can feel like it's happening with travel writing studies. But for me it's always about dialogue; you need to keep a rigorous, quite hardcore postcolonial view, while also perhaps acknowledging the more complex things that travel writing did and the more positive things which travel writing does.'

There was, he said, plenty of scope for imaginative scholars to consider the aesthetics of travel writing, old and new. The economies of its production, its reception amongst readers—historical and contemporary—deserved investigation. Discussions of gender and 'difference' were by no means exhausted, and there were always confounding texts written from unexpected angles to be uncovered—or to be written.

'Issues of mobility, migration and refugees at one end; privileged tourists at the other—those sorts of things aren't going to go away,' he said. 'So obviously travel writing gives us all sorts of reflections on those. I think we are all now very aware of what can be the pitfalls of travel writing and the necessary scepticism you have to have about any piece of travel writing. What was it achieving, and what did it contribute positively as well as negatively? There is that thing where any sort of representation is problematic, but there are some situations where you *have to* represent other people.'

I'd heard this before somewhere. 'That's always it,' I said. 'If you take it to the extreme, you're not allowed to represent, and that's not a positive outcome.'

'Yeah, and there are lots of situations in the world that need drawing attention to.' He mentioned Norman Lewis' reports from the Amazon—the reports of the oppression of Indigenous peoples that had provided the publicity necessary for Robin Hanbury-Tenison to kickstart Survival International.

'Obviously it would have been great if they could have represented themselves to us,' Thompson said, 'but in a world where they can't do that, you sometimes need intermediaries. And then you have to acknowledge all the faults of the intermediary but still acknowledge what they're doing positively as well. I have this with students often when you're talking about any sort of historical figure connected with empire or women's rights. Often they're not being a feminist as we would like them to be a feminist, say; but sometimes in the positive things that they *are* doing they are shifting the debate on a little bit. And people connected with empire—all sorts of problematic things they take for granted, but in some little area they are trying to change things, so you have both points of view. Like Chatwin, with *The Songlines*.'

'Carl, thank you so much,' I said, as the waitress cleared away our plates. It had been a lot like talking to a travel writer. And it had quietened at least some of my old anxieties about the genre.

17

UPSTREAM, DOWNSTREAM

I got down onto the pathway at the head of Hammersmith Bridge and walked west, upstream. To my left the river rolled uneasy through the night. On the far bank, it seemed as though a slice of the city had fallen away. A single light shone wanly in a wall of vegetation. The temperature was near zero, but I thought of other rivers—the Musi, the Kapuas and the Batang Hari, bending coffee-coloured through green. The lonely light across the water suggested a fisherman's hut: bamboo, blackened cooking pots and chickens.

I was straying into dangerous territory here—conflating the Thames in darkness with the rivers of Sumatra and Borneo. I'd end up in the Congo if I wasn't careful, declaring brightly that to go upstream was to travel back in time—'Conradian atavism', as the scholar Rob Nixon called it.[1]

But then a Deliveroo cyclist clipped past and a woozy blast of seasonal song emerged from a waterside pub: Paul McCartney had saved me. True, the same song was probably ringing from the PA in Mega Mall in Pontianak on the banks of the Kapuas right at this very moment. But I was safely back in London, an hour after nightfall and a week before Christmas.

But if I kept on along the Thames Path I really would be travelling backwards. Sixteen miles upstream I'd find myself, standing on the bridge between Eton and Windsor, watching the planes coming up out of Heathrow in the gloaming. And if I went on upriver beyond that—well, I might actually end up in Southeast Asia.

* * *

I need to come clean. I may have been a little coy on this point, so I'll state it plainly now, though not without embarrassment: when I was in my early twenties, I wanted very much to *be* a travel writer.

At first I imagined writing of long journeys on foot—along the Atlantic coastline of Europe, maybe. Or of portentous transcontinental trips—perhaps the supremely well-beaten overland track between India and Europe, done east to west in a weak attempt at originality. But soon the synopses that I conceived beneath the extractor fans of Cornish restaurant kitchens took on historical and cultural themes. Eventually I came up with an idea that I thought might actually be achievable on a tight budget. And so, at the age of twenty-four, I flew to Indonesia. I'd been there before, on a winter surf trip with friends a couple of years earlier. Now I returned as an aspiring travel writer. My 'theme' was the intersection of world religions and 'traditional belief systems'. I'd read very little serious literature on the subject, and I spoke only a rudimentary backpacker's pidgin of the Indonesian language. But I set out with perfect confidence. It was an unremarkable journey, east from Bali towards Timor, done inside seven weeks. But back in Cornwall that summer, I wrote the thing up between the kitchen shifts.

At the start of *this* journey, before I went to speak to Nicholas Jubber and Colin Thubron, I excavated the manuscript and looked at it for the first time in well over a decade. It was not a comfortable experience. There was anti-tourism aplenty, and any number of crude attempts to overcome belatedness. Complex contemporary Indonesia got no mention; all I was interested in was picturesque villages of wood and thatch, firmly fixed in a rhetorical past. I presented unchecked historical detail, newly cribbed from guidebooks, as if it were my own authoritative scholarship, and spliced in episodes from the earlier surf trip as if they were all part of a single journey. I did talk to plenty of travellees. But I only recorded the conversations when, at my prompting, they discussed ghosts and black magic—the stuff that made their lives seem as exotic, as different, as *other* as possible. And in the written dialogue there was no hint of the strangled questions or imperfectly understood answers that must have resulted from my inadequate language skills. I never countenanced the possibility that any Indonesians might ever be able to read what I had written—still less considered what they might make of it. The whole thing was a tissue of original travel writing sin. It was also very, very boring. The narrative plodded relentlessly from one island to another, from each predictable and unenlightening encounter to the next—though I hadn't been able to see any of that at the time.[2]

In the year that followed the trip to Indonesia, I sent the manuscript to a dozen publishers and literary agents. Most posted it straight back with a form rejection slip. But I did get one personal response. I think it may have opened with a token compliment about 'effectiveness'. This was followed by a gentle explanation of the fact that travel writing was 'currently a very difficult market'—quite simply, there was no popular demand for this sort of thing any more. It was the last time I sent the manuscript out. I had had a lucky escape.

By this stage I was back in Indonesia, teaching English at US$500 a month, making a concerted effort to learn to speak Indonesian properly, and reading enthusiastically about the country's history. I had also started submitting articles to Indonesia's main English-language newspaper, and to the clutch of glossy magazines which, in those days, still emerged from Jakarta and Bali each month. Most of my articles were travel pieces, based on the trips I took at weekends and school holidays. Later, I moved on to edit copy for a rickety, understaffed news weekly based in Bali. This paid even less than teaching, but I made up the difference with freelance travel pieces. After that, I started working on guidebooks.

This is the stuff that people who've never heard of Freya Stark or Wilfred Thesiger generally seem to think of as 'travel writing'. But when I decided, a few years later, to have another go at a longer writing project—a successful one, as it turned out—it was a biography of a nineteenth-century explorer. I then wrote a couple of books about Indonesia's past. A good deal of travel went into their making, and I smuggled bits of first-person narrative into the prefaces and epilogues. But they certainly weren't 'travel books'; they were narrative histories. If anyone ever asked me which writers in *that* genre I particularly

247

admired, I always mentioned William Dalrymple, thinking of his hulking accounts of nineteenth-century South Asia. But of course, before the history books, Dalrymple had been one of the most successful travel writers of his generation. I was on my way to talk to him now, heading upriver along the banks of the Thames, into the past. If I'd turned around and gone downstream a couple of miles, I would have come to the future. But of course, I couldn't know that yet.

* * *

Dalrymple's first book, *In Xanadu*, was published in 1989. It was an account of a journey he had made with a couple of university friends along the time-honoured overland route between Europe and Asia. It was very, very funny, but its engagement with the matter of history elevated it well above standard backpacker fare. Its engagement with its own antecedents was something out of the ordinary too. Robert Byron, Peter Fleming, Eric Newby—Dalrymple didn't so much as fall back on older texts as frolic with them. He wrote the book when he was just twenty-two. (Youth was no excuse, then, for the execrable Indonesia manuscript which I had now returned, with a shudder, to its bottom drawer.)

Later, there was more serious travel writing: *From the Holy Mountain* (1997), about a journey on the theme of Middle Eastern Christianity; *The Age of Kali* (1998), a collection of journalistic travel pieces from the Indian subcontinent. Then in 2002 came *White Mughals*, the first of the big narrative histories, exploring the hybridism and acculturation that was sometimes a feature of British involvement in India in the eighteenth and early nineteenth centuries, before the disengaged hubris of the Raj properly kicked in. But the book that had placed Dalrymple near the top of my own list of favourite travel writers was his second, *City of Djinns* (1993). It was a travel book of the sort that does not include a map of the 'author's route': an account of an extended sojourn in a single place. Notionally, it was a memoir of the first year that the young Dalrymple and his wife Olivia spent living in Delhi, and an account of his own wanderings there. But he used this form as a framework for a history of the city, spun backwards into the deep past. Reading *City of Djinns* certainly gave me something to fall back hard on when I first visited India. But it also gave me a sense that serious research in libraries and archives was not just a complement to travel writing; it could be the *object*, and even a sort of crypto-travel writing in its own right. I suppose the fact that I ended up writing narrative history books myself has something to do with that.

* * *

'Have some wine!'

A deluge of red sloshed into my glass, and a block of cheese collapsed under wild single-handed assault. 'Have some Stilton!' He pushed the plate across, tossing fistfuls of pistachios into his mouth with his free hand at the same time.

A West London A-road roared just beyond the kitchen door, but the cottage seemed to belong to the Cotswolds. It was cosy, low-ceilinged, though it had the unmistakable desiccation of a place occupied for only part of the year.

Getting to meet William Dalrymple had proven a tricky. He still lived mainly in India, and though he was usually in Britain during the summer and at Christmas, he seemed seldom actually to be at this, his second home in London. He always responded with merry generosity when I got in touch—*Sure! Welcome! Come any time you like!* But in the end I'd only been able to pin him down to a passing hour between a visit to family in Scotland and a London restaurant booking.

'I *literally* just arrived from Edinburgh a moment ago,' he said, spilling pistachio shells over the scrubbed kitchen table. Three days earlier he'd been in Delhi.

As in every photograph of him I'd ever seen, he was wearing a crumpled collarless shirt. Fins of brown hair rose on either side of a balding crown, and he scratched at his peppery beard as he talked. He had an air of jolly disorder, but there was something unexpectedly imposing in his physical presence. He could have been a retired rugby player.

'Have some pistachios!'

Making a list of Dalrymple's books ahead of this visit, I had realised that as great a temporal distance now separated *In Xanadu*'s publication from the present in one direction, as from the 1950s in the other. Its language certainly seemed badly dated in places. The student author wrote of travelling in 'virgin territory' and tossed out alarming comments about 'sinister, swarthy Turks'.[3] Unsurprisingly, in recent interviews Dalrymple had talked of having 'more or less completely disowned' *In Xanadu*,[4] and reflecting on the twenty-fifth anniversary of the book's publication he had described it as a record of 'the impressions, prejudices and enthusiasms of a very young, naïve and deeply Anglocentric undergraduate [...] quick to judge and embarrassingly slow to hesitate before stereotyping entire nations'.[5]

I wondered if the 1980s had actually been *closer* to the 1950s, in terms of a British travel writer's place in the world, than to the twenty-first century.

Dalrymple chuckled softly—though I'm not sure whether it was at my idea, or simply as he remembered that his own literary debut was now thirty years old.

'It's an interesting thought,' he said, scratching his beard. 'I think it was a period, funnily enough, on the cusp between the two worlds, very much, because it was already a postcolonial world, with academic studies of travel writing...'

'But then the 1950s were also partly postcolonial,' I cut in; 'sure, there was no postcolonial studies...'

'But there *was* in the 1980s. The principal criticisms of travel writing, particularly from an academic point of view, were already there. And the idea, in its more crude form, that the white travel writer was a sort of outlier of colonialism, the last of the Wilfred Thesigers, was in a sense probably closer on target in the 1980s, in that a lot of stuff was going on in that period which put itself within the crosshairs of that school of criticism. But I think that period straddled the two worlds, in a sense. There is a massive gap in perceptions of the world, particularly in this country, pre-1980s and post-1980s. I mean, I travelled it myself, in a sense, in fast forward, between *In Xanadu* and *From the Holy Mountain*. The ghost of the old colonial travel writing was still very much around, and yet the new world was very much there. By the time I had written *In Xanadu*, Pico Iyer had already written *Video Night in Kathmandu*.' This was the book, published in 1988, that travel writing scholars always seemed to cite as the exemplar of 'cosmopolitan' travel writing.

Dalrymple went on. 'The possibilities of travel writing being about modernity and about development and about a new world—rather than just about history, or indeed just nostalgic romps through old imperial territories—was already there. So I think it was an interesting moment to be writing, in that the battleground—the critical battleground—was already there.'

The doorbell rang. It was a bevy of young relatives who tumbled into the kitchen in a welter of striped scarves and Christmas cheer. Dalrymple's wife, the artist Olivia Fraser, came downstairs and evicted us from the kitchen to make space for the visitors.

We carried our wine glasses through to the living room and Dalrymple attacked the gas heater with the same force he had brought to bear on the block of Stilton.

'I can't remember how to turn this fire on here. Maybe it's not fixed up any more...' He called back to the kitchen: 'Olive, do we still have our gas fire working? No? They chopped it all off?'

He shrugged, sloshed more wine into my glass, then sprawled on the sofa, propping himself on one elbow like an odalisque in an Orientalist painting.

He talked about the apparent shift in his own authorial persona from *In Xanadu* in 1989, to the deeply engaged and culturally sensitive reporter of *From the Holy Mountain*, less than a decade later.

'I think the transition that you're seeing is not just that I'm reading different books and getting the hang of how to write; it's also just growing up. I was born into a sort of extraordinary fragment of Edwardian Scotland. I grew up with people who still had governesses—one of whom is now the queen of chic, by the way; Tilda Swinton had a governess; she was very much around in my childhood. And looking back, the fragment of that world that I grew up in in the late 60s and 70s and early 80s, was a kind of now vanished fragment of Chekhovian existence, a sort of Turgenev world. I suppose it still just continues in some way, but it's certainly less Edwardian than the world that I grew up in. And I think that what you see in those books, the difference between *In Xanadu* and *Holy Mountain* is just someone who's got out a bit! And talked to some people!' He roared with laughter.

He'd raised the subject of his own rather rarefied background himself. Did a certain point of departure, a certain sort of education (Dalrymple had been at Ampleforth and Cambridge) lend itself to travel writing, I wondered? But he'd heard all this before, and didn't have much time for it.

251

'Well, I don't think you necessarily need to be white and British! I mean if you look at the persona of Vikram Seth in *From Heaven Lake* [1983], or the persona of Amitav Ghosh in *In an Antique Land* [1992], those are both books of travel which are deeply bookish. Now, admittedly, you could say that both of those guys came out of an Indian education system that was modelled on the British one, so it's not a million miles away. But equally, Nicolas Bouvier, who was from a very different world...'

I loved Nicolas Bouvier's *The Way of the World*, originally published in French in 1963 as *L'Usage du monde*. It was another account of an overland journey towards India, but it was palpably different in style and sensibility from most British travel writing. 'He doesn't parade knowledge of Classics in the way that British travel writers might do,' I said.

'I've certainly never made a classical reference in my life!' Dalrymple said sharply. He had, I realised, an ability to be decidedly robust, combative even, in conversation, while never seeming less than cheerfully garrulous.

'No,' I countered, 'but there's a sense of education...' But he cut me off.

'I don't buy this idea. I mean, I think that British white upper-class males have written some terrific travel books, but I don't buy this idea.'

He talked about the annual Jaipur Literature Festival, of which he was co-director with Namita Gokhale. The festival always featured a travel writing panel, he said, and the assorted travel writers invariably got on with one another—unlike the sometimes fractious biographers who took part in another regular festival session.

'I think if you put Peter Hessler and Paul Theroux next to Robert Macfarlane and me, what we all have in common, and what binds us, is that we all like getting out of the house and being off and immersing ourselves in other cultures. And we all have very diverse backgrounds. And so I feel extremely uncomfortable, and I think it's just plain wrong, the postcolonial criticism that this is a white man's genre that is only done by British public schoolboys.'

I wasn't entirely convinced that the list of names he'd cited in making this point (Seth, Ghosh, Hessler, Theroux, Macfarlane) was all *that* diverse, differing nationalities notwithstanding—though he did also mention Pankaj Mishra, Sara Wheeler and Robyn Davidson. But I liked the idea that travel writers, wherever they came from, were all bound by a shared interest in the world. I'd certainly enjoyed the company of everyone I'd met on my own journey.

* * *

I'd been keen to speak to Dalrymple in part because he was one of the few travel writers who ever seemed to make direct reference to scholarly critiques during interviews. And he had a tendency to give short shrift to the more simplistic postcolonial assaults. In the introduction to *The Last Mughal* he'd satirised the prose style of scholarly articles, 'invariably given titles with a present participle and a fashionable noun of obscure meaning'.[6] Elsewhere, he had spoken scathingly of 'unthinking sheep tumbling along in the wake of Edward Said's flock'.[7]

And yet I didn't think this was simply a defensive pose—a travel writer returning insults with insults, fighting off those who might attack his own work. Beyond *In Xanadu*, with its eyebrow-raising anachronisms, Dalrymple's books sometimes seemed like a direct— and successful—attempt to surmount the problems that critical scholars might identify in much 'Western' writing about 'the Orient'. His histories made an impressive job of giving prominence to local voices, dredging up contemporary sources in Persian and Urdu of the sort that seldom feature in ripping pop-history yarns of the British Empire. His 2009 book, *Nine Lives*, meanwhile, seemed like a concerted attempt to 'let the subaltern speak', as certain scholars might put it—to hand as much of the narrative as possible over to the travellee. And the themes he'd often explored—of hybridity, transculturation, the crossing of borders—were the regular obsessions of postcolonialism. The scholar Paul Smethurst had noticed this. Dalrymple's work, he'd written, 'sometimes shows affiliation with postcolonial theory, while, at the same time, opposing Said'.[8]

I asked Dalrymple why it was that he occupied this seemingly contradictory position.

'So, first of all,' he said, 'I like Said, admire Said, and Said liked *From the Holy Mountain*; I've got a fan letter from him somewhere. So it's nothing about Said. But there was a moment in the late 80s when all sorts of rubbish imitation travel books were being written, when sort of cheap imitations of Chatwin and Theroux were gushing out, which became very boring because they were all less good than the originals and just dull. *Orientalism* was written, when?'

'1978,' I said.

'It's a very long time ago!' he laughed. 'Ideas move on. And so when someone just churns that out in a slightly new form, one just yawns, which is my real reason, I suppose, for irritation.'

'But you must be aware,' I said, 'that you have—whether consciously or not—engaged with some of the ideas that came out of postcolonial studies, and you have kind of actioned them. The idea of hybridity...' I had a sense that I wouldn't get too far with this.

Dalrymple scratched his beard and took another slug of his wine. 'I think the ideas in those books, and in a sense the theoretical underpinning behind them, come more from my experience of just living in Delhi and engaging with that world and trying to work out how to tell that story. If you're someone who's living in that world and immersed in it properly, as I've been now for thirty years, it's impossible that you could write a book that only gives British accounts; it's bonkers.'

'But people still do.'

'Not anyone who lives there! It only happens when you've got people coming in for a week and doing it. For anyone who lives and immerses themselves in that world, that's just a basic human fact. Whether you're Amitav Ghosh immersing yourself in Egypt or Jonathan Raban settling down in Seattle—you do become sensitive to the world you're living in, unless you're a block of ice. And so, yes, I think these are natural human tendencies that are there in human history. They're not a product of postcolonial criticism.'

* * *

We had talked well beyond the promised hour. The young relatives had already departed, and Olivia Fraser came in to try to extricate her husband to honour the dinner booking. I grimaced apologetically over my ever-refilled wine glass.

'Look!' Dalrymple grinned, pointing at his wife's leg wear from his firmly entrenched position on the sofa—'hybrid trousers!'

Fraser, a slim, dark-haired woman, glanced down, briefly confused. She was wearing a pair of harem pants in green check. 'Yes,' she said vaguely, 'hybrid trousers; Indian style, Fraser tartan—but we need to *go*…'

Dalrymple's sons, Sam and Adam, appeared from upstairs, and he asked them about their own favourite travel writers. Sam, who was making a start in journalism himself, loved Patrick Leigh Fermor but was troubled by Robert Byron ('he doesn't really interact with anyone, unless it's for a joke').

Dalrymple twisted in his seat towards his other son, a tall young man, leaning against a bookshelf. 'Adam, what have you read?'

'Travel writing? Nothing really.' Adam was much more interested in history.

'Leigh Fermor? No?'

'No. I've read *In Xanadu*, that's about it.'

Everyone laughed. This was a very merry household—but they did need to go to dinner.

'Five minutes!' Dalrymple threw up his hand. His pose now was more Mughal than odalisque.

I mouthed 'sorry' at Olivia Fraser.

The others went to get their coats, while I sculled the last of my wine and hurriedly asked if he thought he'd ever write another travel book. Quite possibly, he said, though he had no immediate plans, and it would have to be very different from anything he'd done before.

'One of the things I was very aware of from the very beginning was the slightly sad thing of a one-trick travel writer repeating it. Much as I love him, Eric Newby in a sense remained a totem for me. I remember reading *Round Ireland in Low Gear* [1987] and thinking I never, ever, *ever* want to be in my seventies on a *fucking* bike in the rain and writing another *fucking* travel book! I've always been very keen that I don't play the same trick twice, and all my travel books are very different, more so than the history books. I think Eric Newby was not only crucial in showing me how to do *In Xanadu*; he was also crucial in showing me how not to do the rest of my career.'

Olivia Fraser coughed pointedly from behind the kitchen door. 'Huppity-hup!'

I was going to be the cause of a domestic incident in a minute. The restaurant booking had been for eight o'clock. It was now nearly half past.

'It wasn't my fault!' I whispered as I collected my coat from the kitchen.

'I know; he doesn't stop!' she said with a grin, then to her husband, 'Put your shoes on! Hurry up! I'm not going to say anything more unless you get in the car!'

But Dalrymple was still on the sofa. I think he was checking Twitter.

* * *

I've no idea whether the Dalrymple family lost their restaurant booking that night. But I do know that the following day an email appeared in my inbox.

'Sitting with a brilliant British female travel writer who has strong views on white males dominating travel writing,' it read; 'I think you two should meet...'

William Dalrymple, a writer whose own subject matter was the past, was sending me downstream, into the future.

* * *

Two months later, six miles down the Thames.

A cold hard wind from the east was pushing angry wavelets back upriver, beneath London Bridge. At a pedestrian crossing near Borough Market, a thin young man with pointed shoes bounced on his heels and rolled his jaw, a single rose in his hand. It was Valentine's Day.

I met Monisha Rajesh outside a café on Bermondsey Street. A young woman with very straight hair and a tiny stud glittering in the side of her nose, she arrived pushing a pram. She hoisted the baby to her hip, collapsed the pram single-handed, and shunted it over the threshold of the café.

'Do you need a hand?'

'I've got it,' she said merrily.

The baby was dressed in a red romper suit. She was nine months old. Her name was Ariel—'After *The Tempest*, not *The Little Mermaid*!'

The café was all pale wood, scrubbed brickwork and noise. We squeezed in at a tiny table in the corner.

I had already thought of Monisha Rajesh, back at the start; trying to identify younger travel writers I might try to meet, I'd put her on the list. But then I'd crossed her off as ineligible. She was a widely published freelance journalist, but she'd only written one travel book, *Around India in 80 Trains* (2012). But, as it turned out, she had just delivered the follow-up to her publisher a few days before we met. So she did have two travel books to her name after all.

The new book was called *Around the World in 80 Trains* (2019). This time she'd travelled with her fiancé—now her husband—through Europe, across Asia and around North America.

'So here's a question then,' I said, 'are you now trapped as a train writer?' Paul Theroux had managed more than three decades of train-based travel writing.

'No, *nooo!*' she said. 'In fact, I discussed this with my agent at length...' Ariel was looking at me over the top of her mother's cup of almond hot chocolate with huge dark eyes.

Rajesh's first book hadn't really been *about* trains, though. It was a busy account of a journey around India in the somewhat awkward company of a Norwegian photographer. But it was also a memoir of an unhappy spell during her childhood when her parents had taken the family away from England to live for a couple of years in Chennai. Rajesh's parents had come originally from India themselves, but Rajesh was born in King's Lynn.

'Did you grow up in Norfolk?'

'No, no, *nooo!*' she laughed. Something about those stressed and rounded vowels made me think of wedding receptions, book launches. 'Very much *nooo*, not in Norfolk. So, I was born in King's Lynn; my parents were doctors and we moved every three years; they did rotations and wherever a job came up they just went. They came to England, in 1975 I think it was. They came to Newcastle then moved to Hull—all the really glamourous spots!—then Norfolk where I was born, and then we moved back to Hull, and then Sheffield for three years. In fact, I largely grew up in Yorkshire. So we went from Sheffield to India when I was nine, then India back to Hull, Hull to Sheffield, then Sheffield to Birmingham. And Birmingham, my parents have been there since I was fifteen, so that's probably been the longest that they've been anywhere. They've been there twenty-one years now, which for us is quite something!'

If she had a home town, she said, it was London, where she'd lived and worked—when not travelling—since doing her master's in the city fifteen years earlier. 'For me England is home, in a sort of broad scheme of things. But a home town, I guess London is the closest that would come to it.'

Ariel let out a sudden scream, and Rajesh grimaced and nodded at my digital recorder. 'Sorry; that's going to be on there, isn't it?'

'That's alright,' I said; 'I can edit it out, pretend it didn't happen...'

She talked more about her peripatetic childhood while the café clattered around us.

'I think that's why I find travel quite, not easy...' she paused for a moment, then nodded, 'Actually, yeah, I probably do find it easy, because we were so used to being in different places all the time that we never had a sense of wanting to go back anywhere. And also just meeting people, chatting to people, making friends very quickly, just being able to adapt very quickly to different situations—that was probably because of the way we had to adapt as kids. Every time you'd made really good friends at school and you'd think "I'm settled now", mum would be like, "We're moving"...'

'The reason I'm curious about it,' I said, 'is the question of who *are* travel writers, typically? And historically they have been...'

'Posh white men!'

I hadn't meant to go to that subject so soon in the conversation. I'd actually been thinking of Rajesh's fellow Norfolk-born travel writing journalist, Patrick Barkham—his sense of rootedness there; of Dervla Murphy, embedded in Lismore; and of Robin Hanbury-Tenison's comment about the importance of a 'taproot'. But posh white men came into this too. Being utterly anchored in a single place didn't, on the face of it, look like a great qualification for a travel writer—unless, of course, the travel writing was to be done with a certain patrician confidence, and the anchor-point was bang at the perceived moral centre of the universe. Rajesh's qualifications for the job—the accustomed ease of movement, the adaptability—seemed more solidly practical.

'I think that's what it is,' she said, when I tried to explain this idea.

She could see her own privilege though—and in that she perhaps wasn't so different from the earlier generations of British travel writers. 'You can go to a private school, and you have parents who will pay for your postgrad, and yes I'm sure that did very much lend itself to me going off and doing what I did.' But this, she said, was actually part of what she'd wanted to describe in *Around India in 80 Trains*. The stories told in the novels and memoirs of other British writers whose parents and grandparents had come from South Asia—writers like Meera Syal and Sathnam Sanghera—were entirely alien to her own experiences.

'I just couldn't relate to where they lived or the idea of having parents they couldn't communicate with in English and being so frightened about telling them about partners who were white and stuff, which is just something we didn't ever have as kids. So I used to read all those books thinking there's something in there that's different and I know I can do something different with this.

'My parents were working economic migrants; they came to do postgrads and then never went back. It was a very different kind of diaspora. So I thought, there's a gap here for people like me, whose parents all came as lawyers and doctors and accountants and all drive BMWs and live in big houses and their kids all go to private school— which I know is probably not very interesting to other people who don't want to read about the upper-middle-class existence. But it's a totally different perspective. After *Around India in 80 Trains* a lot of people got in touch, who I guess were of a similar kind of background to me, who said it's quite fun reading this, kind of from a British-Indian perspective.'

There is a striking scene towards the end of *Around India in 80 Trains*: a priest and an official forbid Rajesh entry to a temple, telling her that she cannot be 'a real Hindu'—a judgement they base on her nationality, dress and their mistaken belief that she is married to a white man. An argument ensues, during which Rajesh condemns their hypocrisy and religious attitude.[9] The specific scenario arises from her own Indian heritage, of course. But beyond that, there is the assurance with which she describes the confrontation—it wasn't a scene I could ever imagine William Dalrymple writing. *I* certainly would have lacked the confidence to pass the critical judgement if I had been describing such an incident in India; I'd probably have produced something equivocating, apologetic, or, perhaps more likely, avoided writing about it at all.

'I can't watch TV programmes on India now,' Rajesh said, 'because it drives me crazy, even Joanna Lumley. Invariably they all wear a bindi and a shawl and go to a wedding and say how sweet and lovely the people are, and you think, "Oh *God!*"'

I didn't make the connection until much later, but this was exactly Roslyn's complaint about travel writing at the Globetrotters Club.

Rajesh went on. 'And also I think when you're white and middle class and you're going somewhere like India there's always that sort of nervousness about being critical about the country, in a way that I could do, and I could say whatever I wanted about the country. But then, I knew that I'd have a lot of Indian people saying in reviews, "Ugh, here she is; the non-resident Indians, the NRIs, the *not-real-Indians*, come over here and criticise our country and then swan off back to their home in London". You're never going to please everybody, but being an "insider-outsider", as one of my friends called me, it was great.'

Insider-outsider... there was something here, some important quality. Way back towards the beginning of my journey, in another part of London, when I'd asked Barnaby Rogerson to define travel writing he'd spoken of the need for the author to be 'sufficiently an outsider'. *Sufficiently* an outsider—not *absolutely* an outsider. And there was something of this in the arguments of scholars like Sara Mills about women travel writers of the colonial era: they saw things differently because, although they were part of colonial society, they were not quite at its secure masculine centre.

'I noticed in *Around India in 80 Trains*,' I said, 'that sometimes you use "we", and you mean Indians, and sometimes you use "they".' These words—'we' and 'they'—seemed to be essential to the ideas of here and elsewhere, home and abroad, insider and outsider, that had underpinned so much travel writing for so long.

'A few people have said that to me,' Rajesh said. 'There were times when I wasn't sure do I say "we" or do I say "they", because I'm talking about *those* Indians there who are very different from *we* Indians *here*— and then there's a blurry bit.'

I was beginning to wonder if that blurry bit might be the best place for flexible, reflexive twenty-first-century travel writing to operate...

Ariel, who seemed to know very well when her presence was being overlooked, suddenly swept a short arm across the table and sent hot chocolate slopping out of its cup.

'Oh God!' Rajesh rolled her eyes. 'You! Shall we keep you quiet with some food? I think we might do that!' She took out a tube of baby food. 'I'm glad I did the journey when I did because now I can't even go out for a coffee without causing a trouble.'

* * *

It had been essential, Rajesh said, to make the round-the-world trip for her new book as a single, committed journey.

'If I'd just sort of stopped and flown home in between, showered, taken stock of where I was, repacked, gone out, it just wouldn't have been the same at all,' she said. 'Also there'd have been a sort of cheating element as well, because the whole point was to get round as far as we could and to come back to London. I have a lot of problems with nonfiction writers who do it for the sake of the book, and factually it's correct, but actually they did things in between. I think if you're going to call your book nonfiction you have to make it nonfiction. A lot of people feel very differently about it, but I'm really quite rigid on that. Even with quotes from people I've chatted to on the trains, I'd transcribe everything, even with bad grammar and things, I'd just put it in anyway, because I don't really think you've got a right to change people's grammar and spelling and pronunciation and stuff.'

Like Patrick Barkham and Samanth Subramanian, Rajesh was a trained journalist. And looking back, what linked all three was obvious: this professional commitment to representing the plain facts of what people said—and how they said it. It struck me again: this gave the travellee a particular chance for agency, even to resist. But even here, there was a certain ambiguity.

'One thing I did do a bit with the first book,' Rajesh said, 'is I didn't make anything up, but I did do a bit of shifting for the sake of the narrative. Like if I had a train journey, a seventy-two-hour journey where I'd talked to nobody, and then I had a journey where I'd talked to three or four different people at once and couldn't fit it all in the same chapter, I would just move the conversation to another train, to make sure that that did go in but to make sure there wasn't an overload.'

Sara Wheeler had spoken of the same practice of bringing a dialogue from elsewhere to lift a section of the text—'like yeast'.

'Do you not think having crossed that frontier there's suddenly...' I began hesitantly.

'You start moving loads of things! Yes!' Rajesh laughed. 'But I never did anything else. I'd certainly never make up conversations, or anything like that; I think that you certainly can't do. And in fact, with a lot of people I'd spoken to who I'd kept in touch with, I often sent it to them saying are you alright with what I've said about you?'

Here it was again—that daunting process that Patrick Barkham had gone through with the draft chapters for *Islander*. And I found out later from Nicholas Jubber that he too sometimes did the same thing. All three—Barkham, Jubber and Rajesh—were travel writers of a younger, and maybe more ethically engaged, generation.

'So did any of the people that you did that with come back with any problems?' I asked.

'No they were absolutely fine with it,' she said. 'And I've done it with this book as well.'

* * *

A few months before I went to meet Monisha Rajesh, the writer and TV presenter Benedict Allen had been reported missing in Papua New Guinea. He was supposedly attempting a solo trek to visit a community excitedly described in the UK press as 'a lost tribe of headhunters'.[10] He was picked up by rescuers at a jungle airstrip a few days later, by which time there had been a predictable kerfuffle on social media. Allen had had plenty of enthusiastic defenders, but others had suggested that escapades of this sort were intimately connected to 'colonial nostalgia'.[11] It certainly looked like the sort of thing 'which put itself within the crosshairs of that school of criticism', as Dalrymple had said. But he had been talking of the more troublesome travel writing of the 1980s. We were two decades into the twenty-first century now.

Rajesh herself had been involved in a brief digital skirmish, when she defended one of the critical commentators on Twitter. She took this sort of stuff in her stride with a certain weary, eye-rolling humour.

'It was just such an odd thing,' she said. 'I looked at the websites of all the people defending Benedict Allen, and they all called themselves "adventurers" and "explorers" and "vagabonds". And I thought, why do women travel writers never call themselves that? *I* don't; we're *not*. I'm a *travel writer*. I'm not a *vagabond*, or an explorer, or any of these really look-at-me things!'

'But how does that make you feel, seeing as this is your genre?' I asked. As with so many of the questions I'd been asking of the writers

I'd met, this was really angled, with some anguish, at myself. It was *my* genre too—the one I'd been pursuing closely for the last year, the one I'd been obsessed with since late adolescence, the one I'd sometimes felt queasy, uneasy, even guilty about. We weren't in the 1930s anymore, or in the 1980s, but there *were* still plenty of travel books 'that have a fit young man with his shirt off on the cover, doing something tough in the jungle', as Barnaby Rogerson had put it.

But Monisha Rajesh's answer, coming through the noise of the café, the burbling babies, the hissing coffee machine, the clattering door and the cold wind on the street outside, had the quality of an unexpected absolution.

'Well, do you know what?' she said, 'I *don't* really see myself as in the same genre. I think it's quite a different thing.'

* * *

A few months after we met, Rajesh's publisher sent me an advance copy of her new travel book, *Around the World in 80 Trains*. It was fast-paced and funny, and full of human encounters—and it turned out to be one of the best-selling British travel books of the year. It was also, plainly, the record of two well-educated young Britons from privileged backgrounds on a transcontinental jaunt. It wasn't so very different from *In Xanadu*, thirty years earlier, then. Except...

At one point, Rajesh and her fiancé, Jem, who is half-Malaysian, are singled out for a search by security guards on a Russian train:

> Returning our passports, the first guard gave us both one last look, then tugged at the dog and moved to the next carriage.
> 'We're the only people they checked,' whispered Jem.
> 'We're the only brown people on board,' I whispered back.[12]

Later, unnerved in a creepy Canadian motel, Rajesh points out that '"We're literally the only brown people for miles."'[13] This was a nice inversion of the old 'first white man they'd ever seen' cliché. It certainly gave me pause, made me consider my own complacency—not so much in how I'd read travel writing itself, but in how I'd taken the academic critique. At first encounter with the postcolonial scholarship, years earlier—and even more recently, at the start of this journey—I'd been halfway inclined to accept the most extreme proposition: that there was something fundamentally *wrong* with travel writing. The idea pained me, but it had been hard to get around. But it was an idea, I now suspected, that rested on a misconception: that travel writing always journeyed from the same immovable centre; that its dominance by a certain set of people was intrinsic rather than incidental; that the only possible counterblast was a 'writing back', a reversal along the same one-way street. But Monisha Rajesh wasn't 'writing back'. She went out in exactly the same direction as Colin Thubron and all the rest—*from* England. It was what she came home with that was different.

Until very recently, British travel writing had certainly lacked diversity (I might have agonised over the gender imbalance on my own journey, but just how many writers of colour had I spoken to?). But if the genre was a raffish open house, then it surely had to operate an open-door policy. People from any background, any angle could, should, *would* one day cross the threshold. As Samanth Subramanian had said of problematic colonial-era travel writing, the books that had something *wrong* with them were just a symptom of bigger issues, not the problem.

There was something else about *Around the World in 80 Trains* too: it was supremely unbothered by any sense of belatedness. There was no melancholy hankering for the past, no narrowly defined search for 'authenticity' and I couldn't remember ever reading another travel book so entirely at ease with the practical realities of modern travel. Rajesh watches Netflix on sleeper trains, FaceTimes her mother for medical advice, uses translation apps to argue with Italian laundromat attendants, and links up with Buddhist nuns on WeChat. None of this was described with the faintly ironic 'too-cool-for-school post-modernism' of Pico Iyer's 'cosmopolitan' travel books.[14] It was just an unbothered account of the way of the modern world.

At one point in the book, a self-styled 'traveller', met in Ulaanbaatar, tells Rajesh that "'You can't say you've been to Mongolia if you've not been riding on the steppe.'" But Rajesh, whose own experience of the country has been exclusively urban, is unconcerned:

> In a year, even six months, neither truth would be valid: here in the city, hotels would multiply, bars would open, business would thrive, pollution would choke, and the population would explode. Meanwhile

on the steppe, climate change would dominate, temperatures would rise, grass would dry up, livestock would die, and herders would migrate to the city. If we ever returned, this Mongolia would no longer exist, and another would be waiting.[15]

I found myself thinking of John Mandeville yet again—he was always loitering somewhere nearby. There was something he'd written, towards the end of his *Travels*:

> [T]here are many marvels which I have not spoken of, for it would be too long to tell of them all. And also I do not want to say any more about marvels that there are there, so that other men who go there can find new things to speak of which I have not mentioned. For many men have great delight and desire in hearing of new things; and so I shall cease telling of the different things I saw in those countries, so that those who desire to visit those countries may find enough new things to speak of for the solace and recreation of those whom it pleases to hear them.[16]

Disregarding the ultimately fraudulent nature of the text, it was a gesture of striking magnanimity. Mandeville was both signalling the way for the travel writers of the future, and making sure that there was plenty left for them to write about. But this rested on an idea of the world as fixed, knowable in its entirety, containable, *controllable*—the very idea that would underpin the colonial knowledge-project in the centuries to come. But Mandeville needn't have held back: the supply of new things downstream was limitless.

* * *

I was moving into the final stages of my journey now, and between what I had heard from Samanth Subramanian and Monisha Rajesh, I was feeling optimistic about the future of travel writing. I had one last contemporary writer to meet—a writer who, I had a feeling, would help to fix that optimism. But the old ghosts were still with me; I had bookshelves full of them, and a lingering uncertainty: could I still read them, and if so, *how* should I read them? En route to my final encounter there would be a chance for a detour to the archives, and, perhaps, a chance to answer those questions.

18

WINTERREISE I

Edinburgh in darkness. On the bus from the airport: rain-blurred traffic lights; the sound of heavy tyres on wet tarmac; and through a wide window, an image of a woman angling a remote control at an unseen television and a man bowed over a jigsaw puzzle. I got down at Waverley Bridge.

This was the last part of my journey—a two-part foray into the deep north. I stood for a moment in the middle of the bridge beneath streetlights haloed with fine rain. To the west the traffic pulsed along Princes Street, past the Scott Monument and the stolid blocks of the New Town. To the east the Old Town rose, as dense and sheer as a pine plantation. That's where I was headed. I crossed the bridge and began the steep climb through the strata of the city.

It was February and it was raining, but somehow there was nothing miserable about the evening. The stonework glittered and the buildings were lit from below as if for a performance. As I tugged my trolley case up the wet steps I let Edinburgh's Gothic turrets and dormers transmogrify, to become the clock towers and cupolas of Vienna and Prague, with the fields and forests of 1930s Mitteleuropa sliding in to replace the unseen Scottish Lowlands in the darkness beyond. Of course. I had come to Edinburgh in search of Patrick Leigh Fermor.

* * *

I don't remember exactly where or when I first read Patrick Leigh Fermor's *A Time of Gifts*, but I do remember my reaction. It was a Penguin paperback with a blue spine and the iconic cover illustration by John Craxton: a young man with a knapsack and walking stick, facing a rising sun across a wintery landscape of castles, rivers and mountains. That image, and the book's title, seemed to promise strange and wonderful things, but they were inadequate preparation for what lay within. The American writer Ben Downing described his own awestruck first encounter: 'I began reading straight away, but after a few pages stopped and rubbed my eyes in disbelief. It couldn't be this good.'[1] My response was much the same. I must have been in my early twenties, already moderately well-steeped in travel writing. But this was something entirely out of the ordinary.

The book was a belated reconstruction, published more than four decades after the fact, of the first part of a journey on foot across Europe, 'from the Hook of Holland to Constantinople', begun in December 1933 when Leigh Fermor was just eighteen. The language provided the first, delighted shock. At the time, I was still barely recovered from an adolescent Hemingway fixation—something that Thesiger's restrained prose style had done little to counteract. But *A Time of Gifts* was an irresistible spate of words, sweeping away any lingering conviction that short, declarative sentences were the only way to go. Leigh Fermor could send paragraphs spiralling skywards like mad fireworks—and he could get away with it. Sometimes, sketching a landscape or a building, he seemed simply to set a sentence running at the bottom corner of the scene and let it worm its way across every detail before it ever reached a full stop. A description of vineyards on the banks of the Rhine could leave you giddy:

> Pruned to the bone, the dark vine-shoots stuck out of the snow in rows of skeleton fists which shrank to quincunxes of black commas along the snow-covered contour lines of the vineyards as they climbed, until the steep waves of salients and re-entrants faltered at last and expired over-head among the wild bare rocks.[2]

It wasn't really the sort of thing you ought to try and emulate—though people often did: Colin Thubron conjuring up historical banquets in Moscow in *Among the Russians*; Jason Elliot climbing aboard an imaginary phoenix for a historical overview of Afghanistan in *An Unexpected*

Light.[3] But, by God, it was intoxicating! I didn't even know what a quincunx was, but that hardly mattered. The same applied to the great gouts of arcane knowledge. The classical references, the history of obscure princedoms, the fragments of Latin, the fragments of Greek: it was *all* Greek to me, but you could just let it wash over you like a symphony. Above all else, the book was full, not only of promise, but also of *joy*—the joy of a journey, and of its memory, and of its writing.

There was something else too. When it came to the romantic image of the travel writer, no one—not even Thesiger—could top Patrick Leigh Fermor. He was a hard-partying war hero with a woman in every port. He spoke half the languages of Europe, and was as arrestingly handsome in old age as he had been at eighteen. He drank like a fish and smoked like a chimney but lived to the age of ninety-six, charming all and sundry to the very last. William Dalrymple had written that 'it was really he who created the persona of the bookish wanderer [...] the footloose scholar in the wilds, scrambling through remote mountains, a knapsack full of good books on his shoulder'.[4] With Leigh Fermor you could have your cake and eat it: a man of outdoors action with the contents of entire libraries locked up in his head. The image was particularly seductive to post-adolescent boys, certainly; but its hold was rather harder to escape than that of Hemingway. Without Leigh Fermor's model, Dalrymple himself surely wouldn't have travelled or written in quite the same way. More recently, Robert Macfarlane's authorial persona in *Mountains of the Mind* (2003) and *The Wild Places* (2007)—the hardy outdoorsman with limitless literary references, the 'lone enraptured male' in Kathleen Jamie's famous critique—seemed to owe a good deal to Leigh Fermor's precedent.[5] And without Leigh Fermor, I certainly wouldn't have been shaking off my umbrella and collecting a dorm key and a pillowcase from a French-accented receptionist called Sammy in a backpackers' hostel just off the Royal Mile on a wet February evening.

* * *

Patrick Leigh Fermor was born in London in 1915. Like Thesiger—his senior by just five years, though he seemed to belong to another century altogether—he grew up knowing very little of his father, away working for the British Empire. During childhood and teens Leigh Fermor rattled between various homes—some in deep rural England, some within roaring distance of the lions at London Zoo—and between various fee-paying educational establishments. He was kicked out of more than one boarding school—in the final instance (by his own account) for having been caught holding hands with a greengrocer's daughter. Famously (and also by his own account), an alarmed housemaster once described him as 'a dangerous mixture of sophistication and recklessness'.[6] Getting into Oxford or Cambridge was likely to prove a challenge, so Leigh Fermor's father sent word from his post in India that the boy should aim for Sandhurst instead. But before he turned eighteen—the minimum age of entry for Sandhurst cadets—he had fallen in with London's well-heeled bohemians, the aging 'Bright Young People', still eking out the end of the 1920s party in a new and darker decade. He read Norman Douglas' *Old Calabria* (1915), lost his virginity to a glamorous thirty-something divorcee, met a drunk Robert Byron in a nightclub and gave up on the army. And then, two months short of his nineteenth birthday, he boarded a ship bound for Holland, aiming to cross the continent 'like a pilgrim or a palmer, an errant scholar, a broken knight'.[7] He had only a monthly allowance forwarded to various post offices along the way and certain letters of introduction to schloss-dwelling Mitteleuropean aristocrats to aid his passage...

Leigh Fermor made it to Istanbul, more than a year later, and then moved on to Greece where he fell in love with a Romanian princess sixteen years his senior. His language skills got him into the Intelligence Corps during World War II. He served alongside local guerrillas in Crete, and took part in the infamous kidnapping of a German general on the island. In Cairo, at the end of the war, he met Joan Raynor, the daughter of a Conservative Chief Whip and an industrial heiress. They eventually married—though only after Raynor had spent the best part of a quarter-century picking up Leigh Fermor's bar tabs and overlooking his infidelities. By this time the couple had settled in Greece, in a house built on a low promontory among the dark cypresses a short way south of the village of Kardamyli. And Leigh Fermor was already a renowned travel writer.

His first book, *The Traveller's Tree*, about a journey through the Caribbean, had appeared in 1950. Two books about Greece had followed, *Mani* (1958) and *Roumeli* (1966), in which his baroque style, ostentatious scholarship and flights of historical fancy had properly emerged. There was also *A Time to Keep Silence* (1953), a slim and beautiful account of time spent in French monasteries, and a forgettable novella called *The Violins of Saint-Jacques* (1953). And by the time of his marriage to Joan in 1968, Leigh Fermor was finally making proper progress on an old project of writing up his teenage odyssey across pre-war Europe. It was an endeavour that consumed the rest of his writing life, and which he never properly completed.

Patrick Leigh Fermor died in 2011, eight years after Joan. His collected manuscripts and the voluminous correspondence between the author and his lifelong publisher, John Murray, had ended up at the National Library of Scotland in Edinburgh.

* * *

In the morning the dormitory came awake with a muffled dawn chorus of digital notifications. Upstairs in the breakfast room young Australians sat hunched over bowls of cereal with mobile phones cradled at eye level in their left hands. Was this anything like the *Jugendherberge* in Munich where Patrick Leigh Fermor had his backpack stolen in 1933? Outside, the day was still and the sky was the colour of a dirty mop. Below the castle, tour guides stood around, slapping their sides and waiting for their charges in the cold. The city had lost its nocturnal glitter.

The National Library of Scotland stood a short way south of the Royal Mile. The reading room was on the top floor, higher than the surrounding rooftops; a glass-walled space set among ventilation ducts and chimneypots. A mile to the southeast, Arthur's Seat pushed blackly out of the morning mist.

I took a seat by the window. There were foam book supports and page holders like white rosary beads at each workstation, and on the wall by the collection desk a large image of Patrick Leigh Fermor's passport from his 1930s travels. There was none of the barely supressed mania of the British Library here. The archivists moved softly over the carpets as if in stockinged feet, and there were only ever two or three researchers at work. For a little while a young man in a woollen waistcoat came and sat across the table from me, tenderly unloading back issues of *Gay Scotland* magazine from a cardboard box.

I wanted to do the same thing that I had done with Wilfred Thesiger's papers, back in the spring: to sift through the correspondence and the manuscripts, searching for something of the writer's process—and maybe even some sense of the man himself. But this time the sense of jeopardy I had felt at Eton was absent. I was just as excited to approach these fabled materials, but there was little apprehension about what I might find. Perhaps it was simply because I was approaching the end of my journey. During the last few encounters with living writers, there had been a dimly perceptible slackening of the tension, a faint intimation that some hidden conflict was moving towards resolution. Or perhaps it was simply because Patrick Leigh Fermor was a less enigmatic, less disturbing figure than Thesiger.

I collected the first boxes from the desk and returned to my seat. Across the rooftops, Arthur's Seat had now emerged in full beneath the seal-grey sky: a ragged cliff face; a patchy pelt of lion-coloured grass.

There were decades of correspondence between John 'Jock' Murray, sixth scion of the Murray publishing dynasty, and Leigh Fermor. (I just couldn't bring myself to call him 'Paddy'; in my notes he was always 'PLF'.) The letters from Murray's side often had the same cajoling, faintly patronising tone that had marked the missives from Thesiger's agent—the sort of language you might use to an extremely bright but thoroughly lazy and decidedly volatile child. Extracting from the author even a few hundred words to introduce a new edition of *A Time to Keep Silence* seemed to require months, even years of delicate flattery and wheedling—though Leigh Fermor was ever prolific on the question of how to avoid paying income tax in either Britain or Greece. Any royalties accrued in America were to be sent straight to a Swiss bank account. There were memorandums of agreement—in terms little changed in fifty years—for books that had eventually emerged, and for books that never materialised in their promised form. One, undated, was for a work provisionally named 'Of No Fixed Abode'.[8] Was this the earliest suggested title for what eventually became *A Time of Gifts*?

The story of how Leigh Fermor's 'great trudge' across Europe eventually came to be recorded in print was almost as remarkable as that of the journey itself. During the late 1930s there was apparently some brief effort to write an account.[9] But the partying and the travelling got in the way. Then came the war, and afterwards there were other writing projects to hold his attention. But in 1962 the American travel magazine *Holiday* approached the already esteemed author and asked for a 2,000-word article under the heading 'The Pleasures of Walking'. *Holiday*'s editors may not have been entirely familiar with Leigh Fermor's standard working practices: it would be over two years before they took delivery of the commissioned piece. And instead of five pages of type—a morning's work for any diligent hack—what they received was an 84,000-word manuscript. In the end they filleted a standalone piece from the mass—'A Cave on the Black Sea'—and ran it in May 1965. In the meantime, Leigh Fermor had begun the endless toing and froing with Jock Murray about what was obviously the raw beginnings of a book—his own letters flying in from all corners; the publisher's responses reliably addressed from Albemarle Street in London. Leigh Fermor gave the new project the working title 'Parallax'; Murray preferred the more prosaic 'A Youthful Journey'.

Leigh Fermor tinkered with the work throughout the late 60s, tweaking sentences, redrafting chapters, adding new sections. Then, sometime around 1971, he seems to have changed tack. The first part of the manuscript, he now recognised, was artificially compressed— written before he'd entirely forgotten that he was supposed to be producing a magazine article. Now he went back to the beginning and started again, with all fetters cast off. In London, Jock Murray realised that what was emerging could never be contained within a single volume. The crucial step would be to get Leigh Fermor over the line with volume one. The author eventually delivered a finished draft in 1975. The title shifted again, to 'A Winter Journey', and then, finally, to *A Time of Gifts*, a line borrowed from a poem by Louis MacNeice. It was published in September 1977 when Leigh Fermor was sixty-two, well over four decades after he set out on the journey that the book described.

A Time of Gifts carried readers only as far as the Czechoslovak–Hungarian frontier, ending with the words 'TO BE CONTINUED'. Another volume, *Between the Woods and the Water*, emerged nine years later, but the density and digressiveness of Leigh Fermor's writing style meant that the job was *still* not done. The second book ended on the approach to the border of Bulgaria, with the insistent promise

'TO BE CONCLUDED'. But the fact was that by this stage Leigh Fermor, now in his seventies and still ensconced on his Greek promontory with new villas sprouting on the hillside above, was monumentally and incurably blocked.

For the rest of his life, talk of 'Volume Three' tended to elicit vague assurances and discomfited apologies—though he was reportedly still tinkering with various drafts to the very last. Three years after his death a final instalment of sorts did emerge. It had been edited by Colin Thubron and Artemis Cooper, Leigh Fermor's official biographer. Its title was *The Broken Road* (2013). To complete the trilogy the editors had, in fact, gone back to its very beginning: the feral manuscript that emerged from the *Holiday* magazine commission. It was—almost—a satisfactory conclusion. The prose wasn't quite as flamboyantly wrought as that of volumes one and two. But the *joy* was there, alright. There was no definitive finale, however: the work-in-progress had ended abruptly—mid-sentence, like Egeria's account of her fourth-century pilgrimage to Jerusalem—a few day's short of Istanbul.

* * *

I called up the original 1960s manuscript from the archives. It was written longhand in black ink on loose sheets of card, and it made a pleasing stack on the table beside my laptop. I sat there, looking at it for a long moment, unsure quite what I was supposed to do. I took out my own paperback copy of *A Time of Gifts* and laid it alongside. The two texts were roughly the same depth.

Leigh Fermor's handwriting was both looser and spikier than Thesiger's. It looked like a mass of small black tacks, spilled onto a greyish surface. At the top of the first page of the manuscript the original title, 'The Pleasures of Walking', was underscored with three wobbly lines. The words had later been blocked out and 'A Youthful Journey' written in above in blue, with the author's name below. At top-right another note—in the same hand, but shakier, suggestive of old age— read 'Later called A Time of Gifts'. The whole thing had been densely worked over—not by an editor, as had been the case with the drafts of Thesiger's *Arabian Sands*, but by the author himself. On virtually every line a word had been added, a clause crossed out, a new sentence squeezed in. The narrative began, 'I struck the board and cry'd "No more; I will abroad'"—from the George Herbert poem that would eventually make an epigraph for *A Time of Gifts*. And a thick line of black felt-tip had been drawn at a diagonal across the first section and topped with a rough 'C'—presumably meaning 'cut'.[10]

I turned over the page. The opening was certainly condensed. By the sixth sheet of card he was already in Munich. A third of *A Time of Gifts* would have to pass before he got this far, and what filled twelve pages of the 'Winterreise' chapter in the book—including my very favourite scene, a virtuoso vision of a German beer house at full capacity—was covered in just 130 words:

> Here, on the first night, I must have succumbed to vast quantities of beer in the Hofbrauhaus, where, among giant Nibelungenlied pillars, a thousand Bavarian peasants were smoking pipes with painted china bowls and long cherry wood stems, and swilling from lidded stone mugs; for I woke up in the suburbs next day in a kind cobbler's house, where he and his wife had brought me in a cart. Returning to the centre of town, I discovered that someone in the Jungendherberge where I had left my stuff had stolen my rucksack. A charming old Baltic Russian, for whom I had a letter, re-equipped me from his own supply, and, after a cheerful stay, I set off southeastwards through Lower Bavaria, saddened by the loss of my notes and sketches.[11]

As the manuscript progressed you could sense the original intention to produce a short piece for a magazine steadily slipping from the author's view. He slowed up, began to breath more deeply. And then, perhaps a quarter of the way in, he found the right pace, and what would eventually be published as *The Broken Road*, was suddenly there on the table before me.

I leafed my way onwards, building a pile of overturned pages to the left. The tinkering was incessant, on every page. I had the feeling that some of the edits had been inked in many years after the manuscript was first written. Sometimes he had added a whole new passage in blue on the reverse, marking the point of insertion with a long, wavering line. The thing ended on page 354—and just as in the posthumously published book, the cut-off came mid-sentence: 'and yet, in another sense, although'.

But there was surely something significant here. It struck me the moment I saw that final page: the last line ran all the way to the bottom right-hand corner. There was no faltering, no bunching up of the worlds, no sense of a tiring hand. I actually flipped the sheet over and scanned the blank reverse, flipped it back, and then flipped it over again, as if I could make the missing page flicker into being. *The missing page*... Mid-sentence, bottom right: no one stops writing there. A sudden and fierce conviction: he *must* have written on. A few lines, at very least, perhaps a few pages, maybe all the way to the end of the narrative in Istanbul.

'And yet, in another sense, although...' Bottom right: that's where you reach for another sheet; or, if you're all out of paper, you squeeze the words down, cram them in, pack the thing like a suitcase and never slide the zip closed until you've thumbed in a full stop. Either that, or you simply turn the page over and write on the reverse, at least until paragraph's end. I was quite certain of it. *The Broken Road* was perhaps not 'unfinished', then; it was *incomplete*.

In the margin, at the bottom left of page 354, was a scribbled note in blue ink: 'T.B.C.' It was dated 10 December 1997. So he really had considered this old manuscript a working draft of volume three, at least a decade after the publication of *Between the Woods and the Water*. The final pages—if indeed they existed—must have gone missing sometime between the mid-1960s and the late 1990s.

* * *

At lunchtime I left the library and walked south. I bought a toasted sandwich and a cup of coffee and went and sat for a while on a bench in Greyfriars Kirkyard. The cloying dampness of the morning had lifted. The sky was high and blank now, with no hint of a breeze. I could hear birdsong and drilling, bagpipes drifting in from the Royal Mile, and the sudden cascade of empty bottles poured into a bin in a back alley behind a pub. A cavity seemed to be opening in the fabric of the winter—one of those interludes of absolute stillness a few hours or days long, when the turning earth seems to creak to a halt.

Little groups of tourists wandered between the gravestones, looking for famous names. Asian families in puffa jackets; skinny thirty-something American couples with striped scarves. They moved like dignitaries inspecting the aftermath of a disaster.

I was eager to get back to the library, but I stayed on the bench for a while, thinking of youthful journeys.

In the summer of 1935, while Leigh Fermor was partying in Athens at the end of his great walk, another young Englishman, of almost exactly the same age but of very different social background, got down from a steamer in Vigo to begin his own pedestrian odyssey in mainland Europe. There was no pocket money waiting for him poste restante on the way ahead, and no letters of introduction to barons. But he travelled across Spain with a similar youthful joy—and with a similar propensity for romantic dalliances. And like Leigh Fermor, he would make no effort properly to put the journey down on paper until the 1960s.

I'd often wondered whether it was the publication of Laurie Lee's *As I Walked Out One Midsummer Morning* in 1969 that gave Patrick Leigh Fermor the final impetus to finish the job on *A Time of Gifts*; whether its sudden appearance prompted a jolt of professional jealousy. There were such close parallels between the two projects. I'd also often wondered why it was Leigh Fermor rather than Lee who had such a hold on my imagination.

Laurie Lee's background and upbringing in rural Gloucestershire were much closer to my own experiences. His ultimate rootedness in the place from which he hailed—rather than on some hot Greek foreshore—was personally familiar too. And I loved his books, the glorious lack of restraint in their prose, the virtuoso conjuring of a sense of place. So why didn't Laurie Lee occupy the permanent seat at the head of the council of writers inside my head? And why was the man who did, in truth, so alien to me?

Somerset Maugham supposedly once described Leigh Fermor as a 'middle-class gigolo for upper-class women'.[12] It was a particularly vicious barb, but there might well have been something in it. Romanian princesses aside, his writing career had been incubated under the warming beneficence of his wife's 'private income'. For years before they settled in Greece she sent him regular allowances, as his parents had once forwarded pound notes to European post offices. But the use of the term 'middle class' to describe men like Patrick Leigh Fermor always brought me up short. The prep schools and parties with Bright Young People; the correspondence with duchesses and the supremely plummy diction—none of this had any connection to my own naive West Cornwall conception of what it meant to be 'middle class'. And when it came to the 'belatedness' that the travel writing scholars so often impugned, Leigh Fermor was surely more unashamedly belated than any of them. *A Time of Gifts* and *Between the Woods and the Water* had given him an exalted position among the younger travel writers of the 1980s—and had given them a model to emulate. But he was by then a man in his seventies writing about a journey that had taken place in his teens, and which itself seemed to have been self-consciously angled at a mythic and exclusive past of baronial piles and leather-bound libraries. The Greek and the Latin and the rote-learnt verse that larded the books signified another world.

But there it was: another world.

I don't know why it had never struck me before. I don't know why it hadn't come to me back on the bridge at Eton. Travel writing was *supposed* to be about other worlds. You didn't need to *identify* with writers to find them fascinating; you didn't need to share with them a class or a gender or an ethnicity. You just needed to be *interested*. And nothing was more interesting than the exotic.

* * *

Back in the reading room I called up the 'Green Diary'. This was the one surviving journal from Leigh Fermor's teenage journey. The first had been lost when his pack was stolen from the Munich youth hostel. This second journal too had vanished for many years. After completing the walk, Leigh Fermor had left it at Baleni, the ancestral pile of his Romanian princess, Balasha. He'd expected to return, but never did, and the diary ended up as flotsam adrift on the uneasy currents of post-war Europe. Remarkably, Leigh Fermor eventually got it back—though not until 1965, when he had already begun the interminable process of properly describing the old adventure.

The diary sat in a bolstered green box. It had fallen apart, and the original cover lay beneath it in a cellophane envelope, strapped with silver tape and penned with red felt-tip: 'VITAL DIARY KEEP IN 2ND LEFTHAND DRAWER'. Beneath that, in another cellophane envelope, was the original cloth binding from the spine, looking like some sacred relic, a fragment from a saintly shroud. The words 'Mount Athos' were barely traceable across its frayed fibres. The main body of the diary had been loosely rebound with creamy paper. On the first page, a list of 'Countries passed through' ran from Holland to Greece. A child's touch, that, and a reminder of just how young Leigh Fermor had been when he set out. He'd written his name—calling himself by his middle name, 'Michael', at first, and then adding 'Patrick' later. He'd also written, 'If lost, please give to nearest British consul.'[13]

At the back there were childish cartoons of Mexican bandits, rough sketches of musical instruments, a recipe for Turkish coffee, an inaccurate translation of the Muslim prayer call, fragments of vocabulary in several languages, an attempt to write his own middle name—*Mihaal*—in Arabic script and a note-to-self: 'Books to get at home, Seton-Watson's "History of Rumania" Steven Runciman's "History of 1st Bulgarian Empire" Hobhouse's "Albania"...' These scraps and doodles were startlingly familiar: I'd find much the same stuff at the back of my own journals from early backpacking trips in India and Southeast Asia.

The diary was chaotic and inconsistent. It began with a run of densely pencilled pages, written in full narrative form. But these entries covered only twelve days of walking, and they were followed by long gaps—one lasting a full four months. When he took up the diary again it was in a cursory note form that carried him all the way to Istanbul. 'Got up late'; 'excellent luncheon'; 'read papers in bed all morning'; 'lay in bed late reading P. G. Wodehouse'. There wasn't much mystique here. I leafed through to the end, then went back to the beginning, the fulsome entries which started as he left Bratislava on 19 March 1934, and began to read properly.

The young Leigh Fermor wandered across open, level country, lost his way for a while, and at nightfall was approaching a town called Nagy-Magyar:

> I was surprised to see hundreds of swarthy black haired children in coloured blankets, old brown skinned hags with strands of greasy hair under their head cloths, and tall dark shifty-eyed, loose-limbed young men, and realised that these were the Zigeuner folk, the Hungarian gypsies I had heard so much about—they are the most amazing people and completely eastern—Metternich said "east of Vienna, the Orient begins" and he was right.[14]

This was so very different from Thesiger's staccato diary entries. Leigh Fermor was walking in the past tense, treading out full sentences as he went. You could almost see him spotting things as he moved along and thinking, 'I'll write that later.' In other places the diary unfolded in real time—moments of sudden connection as he described exactly what he saw as he wrote at breakfast or dinner. At one point, sitting over his diary in a crowded tavern, he spots a girl making eyes at him across the room, and starts to create a sketch from life. You can sense him glancing up and down, from girl to page and back again: 'Her face is slightly Mongolian in type, her high cheeks pushing up the corners of her huge black eyes [...] She has cast some very come-nearer glances over here, and I can't quite place her.'[15]

This was where the jeopardy should have been. Leigh Fermor had begun writing the later narrative of what the Green Diary described three decades later. The idea that *A Time of Gifts* and *Between the Woods and the Water* and *The Broken Road* were really an accurate record of what had actually happened was patently ridiculous. People seemed to recognise this, but, as with Laurie Lee, they didn't really seem to mind. Dervla Murphy, reviewing *A Time of Gifts* in the *Irish Times*, had written: 'it doesn't matter a damn whether he is describing it as he remembers it in 1934 or in 1964 or simply as he fancies it might have been in 1634'.[16] Even later, when the extent of his fictionalising tendencies began to be revealed, Leigh Fermor didn't seem to stir up the consternation prompted by other fabricating travel writers. Artemis Cooper's biography had appeared a year after his death. Précising the books, she made unbothered references to the way he had 'elaborated'[17] and 'combined' and 'fused together'.[18] Even the author's private revelation that Malek, the horse upon which he rode in *Between the Woods and the Water*, was an invention, introduced in case the reader 'might be getting bored of me just plodding along' didn't seem to trouble her: 'This is what novelists do every day.'[19]

But Patrick Leigh Fermor was *not* a novelist, and *A Time of Gifts* deployed the same cunning signals of truth-telling that all travel writers since John Mandeville have used. Indeed, the most effective of all were the frequent references to the deficiencies of his own memory, scattered through the published books: 'Except for the snow-covered landscape and the clouds and the tree-bordered flow of the Merwede, the next two days have left little behind them but the names of the towns I slept in'; 'Nothing remains from that first day in Germany but

a confused memory of woods and snow.'[20] What this generated, I
think, was a sort of collusion between the writer and the reader—
unconscious on the reader's part, probably: a well-received request to
suspend all critical judgement, and to accept that the astonishing detail
elsewhere was the product of total recall.

He did have the diary for reference, though. At the start of the
penultimate chapter of *A Time of Gifts*, Leigh Fermor makes reference
to its recent recovery (he got it back during a late reunion with the
Romanian princess, who had guarded it for almost three decades), and
begins to quote from it as he moves towards the end of the book. The
twelve days detailed in the proper entries at the start of the Green
Diary covered exactly the same ground as the two final chapters.

* * *

The light outside was already failing. I could pick out a crusting of
figures on the skyline at the top of Arthur's Seat now. The diary was
propped on the foam book supports in front of me. With the leaded
holder draped across the open pages, it looked like a Bible in a country
church. I took out my copy of *A Time of Gifts*, turned to page 261, and
began to read the two texts, one against the other. It felt like stepping
onto a tightrope.

For the most part, it seemed, Leigh Fermor had gone where he said
he'd gone, though there were little discrepancies here and there, and
the odd sign of a blatant insertion: there was no trace in the diary of
the lavish account of a church service in a village called Kobolkut, as
described in the book. But elsewhere you could see where the direct
observations of the teenager had gone straight into the text of the
middle-aged man. In a description on page 273 of the book, of log-rafts
drifting down to the Danube at dusk, every detail—the red reflections
of the raftsmen's cooking fires, their knee-high leather boots, their
shouted greeting across the water—came straight from the diary.

What was most arresting, however, was the way Leigh Fermor, in
the eventual book, had fictionalised the diary entries themselves.
Introducing the first excerpt, he declared that 'I have not interfered
with the text except for cutting and condensing and clearing up obscur-
ities.'[21] But this was nonsense. He'd fiddled with every single excerpt.
Here was the supposedly original diary entry about the Gypsies on the
outskirts of Nagy-Magyar, as it appeared in *A Time of Gifts*:

The whole village teemed with swarthy black-haired children in coloured blankets. There were dark-skinned hags with strands of greasy hair hanging out of their headcloths and tall, dark, loose-limbed and shifty-eyed young men. Zigeunerfolk! Hungarian Gipsies, like the ones I saw in Pozony. Amazing! *Östlich von Wien fängt der Orient an!*[22]

Not only had he gone to work on the style; the inserted mention of Pozony looked suspiciously like a cover for an invention earlier in the book. He'd also thrown the Metternich quote into the original German, and dropped the citation. Was he doing this to make his teenaged self seem more sophisticated? To cast a pall of befuddling learnedness?

He did it again and again—threw in scraps of non-English vocabulary to the supposedly authentic excerpts where the real diary featured none, corrected a fumbled (and uncited) reference to Alfred, Lord Tennyson, tossed in an unattributed line from Dante Gabriel Rossetti's 'The Blessed Damozel'.[23] Elsewhere he simply invented diary passages—counterfeiting his own text! Leigh Fermor was constructing an authorial persona—not for the man doing the writing, but for the boy doing the walking. He made him more bookish, more erudite; awarded him a greater stock of literary references than he had ever possessed.

But somehow I felt no sense of outrage or betrayal here. It seemed less like a con than a hearty joke, openly shared with his readers. I found myself carried along with it. Here was the passage I'd noted about the girl in the bar. In the Green Diary itself, the entry for 28 March 1935 had ended, 'When I look up, she stares me full in eyes, turning coyly away after a moment. I am going to sit down here a bit before finding a bed.'

A bowdlerised version of this, claiming to be a straight excerpt from the diary, appears in *A Time of Gifts*, along with what purports to be the next diary entry. In this the denouement is revealed. The girl sends a message with a waiter to the handsome foreign boy across the room: would he like an 'interview'? Leigh Fermor declines, and she disgruntledly redirects her charms towards other drinkers. A few moments later another customer advises the young stranger that he has made a wise decision in steering clear of the girl. Her name, the man says, is Mancsi, and 'she'd been with everyone in Nové Zamky; *quicumque vult*, in fact'.[24] This was supposedly as written on the morning of 29 March 1934.

What the hell did *qui-cumque vult* mean? I looked to Google on my laptop. It was the opening of the Athanasian Creed, apparently. It meant 'whosoever wishes'. I pushed the computer aside and leafed back through the Green Diary to see if either the young traveller or his well-wisher had really declaimed in Latin in a village bar in Czechoslovakia in 1934. Here was the actual entry: 'She was a proper wrong 'un, and had been had by everyone in Nové Zamky...'[25]

I laughed out loud, then caught myself in the silence of the reading room, crammed my fist up under my nose, and sat there, rocking with unexpected delight.

* * *

Outside, dusk was falling. The cloud over the city had thinned, and a few shards of lapis-blue showed high over Arthur's Seat. I could still pick out figures on the summit.

I swung back and forth between the two texts, the one of 1934 and the other from 1977, watching the dual narrative leapfrogging itself, the book now jumping ahead, the diary now vaulting forward. I knew exactly where I was heading.

A Time of Gifts closes at nightfall on a bridge over the Danube, with Leigh Fermor suspended between Czechoslovakia and Hungary. As he stands there in the sunset, delaying his entry into a new country, storks appear, winging their way northwards, out of Africa, drawing all the places he has already seen—and all those he has yet to visit—into a magical, monarch-of-all-I-survey arc, while across the water in the Hungarian frontier town of Esztergom, Easter celebrations unfold in a fabulous frieze.

I was tacking between the two texts every few lines now, and I didn't really need to ask; I already knew the answer. But I let the diary reach the finish line first: 'At about five o'clock, I reached Parkan, and soon crossed the iron bridge into Hungary.'

That was it. No enchanted pause midstream. No old shepherd. No heron crossing the water to the far bank in the failing light. And definitely no storks. I knew too that if I went on through the later, more cursory section of the diary, I'd find no mention of the same storks, reversing their journey over the Great Balkan Range as recorded in *The Broken Road*.[26] But I'd already known that too, really, and I couldn't care less. I pushed the diary back on the foam supports, let the actual nineteen-year-old hurry off in search of his first Hungarian bed, and went with the book, went with its joyous uplift, went with all its light and colour, and didn't stop reading until I reached the final, fabulous promise: 'To be continued'.

There was only the faintest trace of light in the sky outside now. The glass walls were reflecting the reading room back at itself, but when I leant close I could still see the Edinburgh rooftops. There was probably a pigeon or two amongst the chimney pots, perhaps a seagull. But there might as well have been great skeins of storks, swooping low over the library, twisting around the dome of the Old College, wheeling upwards over Arthur's Seat, trailing their red legs over the darkening land with everything from a Monaco apartment to a compound in Lismore laid out along their flight path.

TO BE CONTINUED

19

WINTERREISE II

Waverley Bridge again, this time in hard morning sunlight.

I had passed another day in the library. Working through the remaining letters and manuscripts was effortless, inconsequential, like riding a bicycle down a gentle slope, though I kept drifting away from the papers in the box files, back to my copy of *A Time of Gifts* itself. Outside, the sky—empty of storks—came clear and a small triangle of cobalt-blue sea showed beyond the shoulder of Arthur's Seat. I'd spent a third night in the hostel, and now I had a train to catch.

The sun was just up over the black cliff of the Old Town where the crown steeple of St Giles' Cathedral rose like an upended Tibetan *dorje*. At the other end of the bridge the New Town was open-faced to the morning, with white buses passing the Royal British Hotel. I found a bench, up against the parapet, and sat for a while, avoiding a small puddle of last night's vomit that was drying on the slats. A woman with a South Asian accent and a large pink suitcase stood nearby, talking into her mobile phone: 'Actually, this is the first night we've slept more than four or five hours.'

I closed my eyes for a moment. I was headed northwards, into the Highlands. One last writer to meet. And then—what had Samanth Subramanian said? Travel *writing* happens at your desk. I still wasn't sure where *that* would take me.

Perhaps I had made too long a halt on the bridge: I hurried down the slipway into the station and boarded the train.

* * *

I had a table seat by the window. I'd meant to reread *Between the Woods and the Water* on the way north, the second part of Patrick Leigh Fermor's trans-European trilogy, but the book lay unopened, and I pressed my forehead to the glass as the short day unfurled outside.

We crossed the Firth of Forth and the water was smooth and blue, fading yellow to seaward. A ship moved upstream towards the bridge, its bow wave breaking far behind in slivers of blinding silver. The tide was low and there were dark figures out on the sand flats. A glimpse of tinder-dry gorse specked with yellow flowers brought a sudden stab of homesickness. I took out my notebook and let the flashing images unspool onto the page in real-time. Two men clearing ivy from a tree beside the track; one hacking with a small axe from above, the other tugging from below; the midriff of the tree naked and pale. Freighters moored at odd angles in the mouth of the Firth, empty of cargo and high in the water like cathedrals on a great blue plain. Just outside Kirkcaldy, a single cluster of snowdrops in the deep shade of an embankment: a first symptom of spring like a hidden malignance.

It was a long time since I had drunk in a journey as thirstily as this. I began to fantasise about walking the same route, stretching the single day into an unreal season; a scent of pine sap and woodsmoke and the sound of hard frost breaking underfoot, then a breathless ascent to a high pass.

The train was climbing into the Cairngorms now, with deep blue snow on either side of the track and red deer hinds on a ridge. An off-kilter eighth of a moon rode high in the thin blue. Then we were through Dalwhinnie and the sunlight took on a northern thinness. The mountains locked together behind the train, and a little while later the blue bight of the Moray Firth opened ahead and we rolled through the gorse to Inverness.

She picked me up from the station in a blue convertible with a faulty nearside window.

* * *

For a long while I had wondered how to end my journey. I could have gone on, tracking down travel writer after travel writer, going into archives, attending conferences, meeting readers. But if I was ever to get to my desk and properly to begin the other journey, then the process had to come to a close. I had to choose a final writer.

It seemed only right to look for someone who might claim to be a travel writer of the moment, of the future even. I could perfectly well have ended with Samanth Subramanian or Monisha Rajesh. But somehow there'd always been a few more questions to ask. So who else?

If popularity with readers and esteem amongst peers were the most important measures, then I might have sought out Robert Macfarlane for my last encounter. He had been partly responsible for establishing the 'new nature writing' as a popular genre. But I was quite certain that the 'generic heritage' of his oeuvre lay as much in travel writing as in any older nature writing tradition. He'd written of the inspiration he'd found in *A Time of Gifts*, and had called *In Patagonia* his 'book of a lifetime'.[1] He was surely the direct successor of those writers: he had the exuberant scholarliness, literariness, interest in ideas; he had the star quality, unmistakable prose style and the legions of pale imitators.

Almost every writer I'd met had sung Macfarlane's praises. (As Olivia Fraser was attempting to get him to end our conversation, William Dalrymple had said, 'Robert Macfarlane is called "our husband", by the way, by our children, because we talk of him with such reverence!') There was little doubt that for well over a decade he had, in the words of the scholar Paul Smethurst, 'been re-energizing the tradition of British pedestrian travel writing'.[2] I loved his books myself, reread them frequently—precisely *because* they felt so much a part of the travel writing tradition I'd been reading into since my teens. But if I'd gone to him, wouldn't I have ended up making no progress whatsoever? Another Oxbridge-educated, middle-class Englishman. It wouldn't have done much for the anxieties I'd been trying to ease. The 'ancient pattern' of travel writing might have been 'departure, adventure, return', but wasn't some sort of transformation supposed to have taken place along the way?[3] If not, then you might as well stay at home.

But then, fortuitously, an alternative name came forth. And just as it had been Dalrymple who sent me to Monisha Rajesh, the suggestion here came from a member of an older travel writing generation. I'd bumped into Philip Marsden at a talk about exploration in an old schoolhouse back in Cornwall. He'd asked about my project, who I'd met already, where I was headed next.

'Have you spoken to Kapka Kassabova?' he asked. 'She has a new book out, *Border*; it's just...'; and he offered a wordless wince of admiration, just as when he'd talked about Turgenev on the flight from Newquay to Dublin.

* * *

Kapka Kassabova grew up in Sofia, but after the fall of the Iron Curtain her family emigrated—first, briefly, to England, and then, when Kassabova was eighteen, to New Zealand. She studied French at university in Wellington, and then published three poetry collections and two novels, in English. In her twenties she spent time in Marseilles and Berlin and Argentina. Later she'd moved to Edinburgh and shifted her focus from fiction and poetry to nonfiction. And now she lived with her partner in the Highlands, beyond Inverness.

After Philip Marsden's prompt I read her three published nonfiction books in short succession and wondered why I hadn't come to them before. There was *Street Without a Name* (2008), in its first half a memoir of childhood in Sofia, in its second half a travelogue about a return to Bulgaria, fourteen years after her departure to New Zealand. There was *Twelve Minutes of Love* (2011), an effortlessly cool account of the author's pursuit of tango, in clubs and dancehalls from Germany to Argentina. And then, most recently, there was *Border* (2017), an exploration of the edge-lands of Europe, full of personal testimonies from the uneasy region where the political frontiers of Bulgaria, Turkey and Greece come together. Each book was strikingly different from the next in form and subject matter—no fear of bicycles in the rain in Ireland here. But a distinctive sensibility seemed to unite them. They were shot through with irony and melancholy, and they were plainly *not* the work of a writer with a secure point of departure, bang at the moral centre of the universe. Kassabova's prose had a clean, precise elegance, and this in her fourth—*fourth!*—language. Her name on the page looked like a hilltop city of minarets and cupolas.

Scholars had started to notice Kapka Kassabova. One, discussing her earlier poetry and fiction, claimed that she had constructed 'a poetics of exile'.[4] Another declared that her travel writing embodied 'some of the ethico-political ambiguities of a genre that is moving away from its imperialist legacy towards rearticulations of cosmo-politanism and wider recognition of the claims of the other'.[5] As far as I could make out through the academic verbiage, that seemed to mean that she was about as far from a dispiriting return to the start as was possible to imagine.

* * *

The cottage was tucked away in a long valley that ran deep into the Highlands. It faced a lumpy meadow and a double rank of conifers with a bank of snow-barred hills beyond. There were faded Tibetan prayer flags strung from the eaves, and an upturned green canoe, weighted down with a growbag, at the back of the parking space. Kassabova's partner, Tony, appeared from the side of the house. He was a Scotsman with straggly iron-grey hair, and he moved with the slight forward tilt of one habituated to being outdoors in wild weather. He'd been work-ing in the garden, and he held up earth-stained hands with a wry chuckle to ward off a handshake. He was an art dealer, but meeting him you might have marked him for a forester or a drystone-waller. It was this observation that prompted a first flicker of the peculiar sense of familiarity, déjà vu almost, that would come ever stronger, until finally it made sense, much later that evening. A manic black-and-white span-iel called Globbie ran out and thrashed around my legs. It could have been litter-mate to the spaniel that had greeted me at the door when I went to interview Philip Marsden, a lifetime ago.

Kassabova's workspace was a little two-room outbuilding. An incense stick smouldered in a corner of the outer room. The books against the walls—in English and French and Bulgarian—were arranged by category, each shelf marked with a hand-written sticker: 'Balkans'; 'Soviet Empire'. The inner room was where she wrote, a built-in desk facing a window looking out to the trees. Rebecca West's *Black Lamb and Grey Falcon* (1941) lay amongst the papers. A map of the Balkans was pinned to the wall on the right.

Kassabova found a stool for me to sit on, gave me bitter dark choc-olate to nibble as we talked, and boiled a kettle for green tea. She had thick black hair and very dark eyes. She was in her forties, but—this again!—she looked much younger. She wore funny elbow-length fingerless gloves that she pushed up and down her arms from time to time. She spoke quietly, with a faint trace of a New Zealand accent.

She asked me to explain my own journey. Somehow, this task had been much easier at the outset, but I did my best. She listened keenly, with occasional interjections—'Oh! That's interesting.' When I mentioned Eland Books she smiled brightly. 'Oh, they're brilliant; I just love everything they publish! But no, I haven't met the great Barnaby.'

Then it was my turn. 'Are you a travel writer?' I asked.

She smiled, the way people do when a half-expected trick question arrives. But it seemed a necessary query. Kassabova was also an established poet and novelist, and I'd noticed that she bracketed 'travel' and 'memoir' together on her own bookshelves.

She thought for a moment. 'It's always difficult to label what it is that you're doing, because you may not be the best judge of that, but it feels as if it's more about journeying, not in the strictly geographical sense, but in many other ways. And more and more it seems that in these journeys, these pilgrimages—I suppose *Border* was a form of pilgrimage, as is this new book that I'm writing now, even more so—it seems as if I'm more and more in search of pattern, of metaphor, of a unifying vision—perhaps *not* unifying; perhaps a fractured vision. More and more in search of symbol rather than movement. Having said that my main...' She paused, privately checking a detail, then went on: 'Yes; I'm always sparked off by specific places. I think my obsession always begins with a specific physical or geographical place. And when I establish contact with it, through some kind of writerly instinct, I think amazing material begins to come out of it.'

She preferred, ultimately, to place her work under the broad designation of 'creative nonfiction'. It was certainly far removed from any clichéd conception of the generic travelogue. But it closely fitted the academic understanding of travel writing that I'd been working with from the very start: Jonathan Raban's 'raffish open house', with its space for everything from memoir to reportage; and then the core first-person form, in which author and protagonist appear as one, narrating a journey or journeys, or an interaction with a place. And the matter of Kassabova's work—especially *Border*—was the stuff from which travel writing's most pressing ethical anxieties arose: engagement with the lives, the stories, the voices of the travellee. She handled *that* better than almost anyone else I'd read in recent years.

'But the first-person mode of narration seems to be what you've come to?' I asked.

'Yes, yes. I think the first-person journey seems necessary; it feels necessary for what I am trying to do, which is a kind of exploration which is not purely an observer's viewpoint. And I think all of these decisions that we make about perspective, and how much you figure in the narrative, all of those decisions in my case are made quite intuitively, quite instinctively, rather than in any preconceived way. But now I'm beginning to see the reason behind it and the mechanism behind it, and I think it boils down to authenticity, to finding the most authentic way into your subject. And in my case obviously the subject is tied in with a certain region, or with a certain psychogeography if you like, because in the case of *Border* and in the case of this book that I'm writing now, called *To the Lake*, it's very much a sort of psychogeography matrix. I'm not setting off into an unknown landscape that I have no previous connection to.'

Psychogeography. It wasn't a term that had arisen before in my conversations with travel writers—though it occasionally appeared in scholarly discussions of nature writing.

'So,' I asked, 'do you make a distinction then between psychogeography and travel writing?'

'I don't know. I don't really know the theory of travel writing; I haven't studied it; I've just read lots of books. But it strikes me that what I'm interested in—on the ground, but also as a writer and as a reader of other people's work—is human geography, is the impact of a place on its people, but also on the journeyman, on the journeywoman. I don't know whether *Border* is an example of a human geographical approach, but it seems to me that I am not a nature writer, in the sense that I am drawn to wildernesses more and more, but I am not going to write about badgers—*ever*, I don't think! Because I am far too angry and in love with human stories. I guess I am fundamentally an emotionally driven writer, so the curiosity, the intellectual curiosity... Globbie!'

The dog had burst in through the unlatched door and was bouncing merrily on the rumpled rug between our seats.

* * *

Kassabova boiled the little kettle on her desk for more tea. Outside the valley had already turned blue ahead of the long northern night.

I asked why she had become a writer in English, rather than Bulgarian, or Russian, or French.

'Because I was living in an English-speaking country, and would be for the foreseeable future!' she said. 'It was a totally pragmatic decision.' She had, though, worked on the Bulgarian-language version of *Border*, after the translator had made a rough first draft—'to make it sound like me in Bulgarian'.

She told me about the new book she was working on—the reason for the Balkan map on the wall and the Rebecca West on the desk. It was again an exploration of an actual place, lakes on the Macedonia–Albania border, combined with memoir and drawing on her own Balkan heritage.[6]

From time to time she reached for a pen and made a note of something on a pad that lay on her desk to the left—a name I had mentioned (Egeria, Ella Maillart), or a concept hauled over from travel writing studies. She'd never heard the term 'travellee', and her response when I used it was much the same as Rory MacLean's: 'Oh God! Oh, for God's sake! Oh, *please*! Travellee! The one who's being travelled upon, as it were?'

The dog burst in again several times. Kassabova chased it out, but the latch on the outer door wouldn't catch, and a little while later it would return, wagging its tail manically.

Between the canine interruptions, I asked about her influences. Influence, she said, was an instinctive, subconscious thing—'unless you are consciously copying someone'. But she did say that as a child reading in Bulgarian and Russian, and then later as a young woman reading in French and English, she had always been attracted to stories of journeys. And she mentioned Paul Bowles.

'He did say, I think this is from his memoir *Without Stopping* [1972], "Like any romantic, I had always been vaguely certain that sometime during my life I should come into a magic place which in disclosing its secrets would give me wisdom and ecstasy—perhaps even death." Very well said.'

'That's the ultimate commitment,' I said.

'It is, isn't it?' She laughed softly. 'Whatever it takes!'

What she wanted in a book, she said, was some kind of emotional jeopardy. 'I guess what I'm saying is that I'm aware that in my books, I want my journeys, the journeys of my books, to transform me every time. Maybe that's a big ask. Can you keep it up? How many times can you be transformed? But I want that. I want that depth of experience. And I also want it as a reader. Those are the books that I love; where I sense that something is at stake for the traveller, for the travel writer; that they are not entirely safe; that they are not just a privileged observer among the natives, who can then safely return to their privileged existence in the First World.'

* * *

Safe return—the final part of the 'ancient pattern', after departure and adventure, implicit in almost every travel book I had ever read, growing up. Even when a writer did not depart or return literally, a trace of their origin–destination was palpable. Thesiger might have lived in the Iraqi Marshes; Patrick Leigh Fermor might have settled on a Greek foreshore. But their style, their perspective, their sensibility—it all looped out from and back to England, and a very particular England at that, bang at the moral centre.

But this, I'd realised as I prepared to travel to Scotland, was where Kapka Kassabova stood apart. In both *Street Without a Name* and *Twelve Minutes of Love* there was no clear point of departure or return. There was simply the middle component: adventure, unanchored and adrift. It gave the books a compellingly strange quality.

I might have expected to find a similar quality in the books of some other writers I'd met. But when I went back to check, it wasn't there. In Samanth Subramanian's work there was still an implicit sense of an anchor-point—less a physical place, perhaps, than a social position; but solid, nonetheless. And though she sometimes used that slippery 'we' when talking about 'Indians', in person and on the page Monisha Rajesh was solidly English, *from England*.

No; it was with Kapka Kassabova's work that I'd first properly encountered this curious new quality. I wasn't the first person to notice. The scholar Ludmilla Kostova had called *Street Without a Name* a 'migrant's narrative', which, 'it would seem, has to violate what is (arguably) the most enduring convention of traditional representations of travel and tourism'—and that convention, of course, was *departure, adventure, return.*[7]

Kassabova called herself a 'global soul' in both *Street Without a Name* and *Twelve Minutes of Love.*[8] That term was originally Pico Iyer's.[9] But Iyer himself seemed to have the same point of departure and return that Subramanian had inherited; diffuse and disembodied, yet perfectly assured. Kassabova's claim was somehow more convincing.

I did my best to explain this, talking about the curious lacuna between the two parts of *Street Without a Name*—the memoir of a Bulgarian childhood, and the adult travelogue.

'The point of departure isn't really there,' I said; 'it's not clear where you're going back to, it's not clear where the point of departure is.'

'I can see that,' she said. 'I wasn't really aware of it when I was writing it. I was not aware of it, but now that you say it I can see that that was a reflection of the fact that I belonged nowhere at that point in time. I had just moved from New Zealand to Scotland; I didn't know anyone. I was in the new place, and I was trying to reconnect with something, with anything. I felt disconnected. So maybe in a sense that flawed and fractured form that *Street Without a Name* took is a reflection of my psychological state at the time.'

And then in *Twelve Minutes of Love*, the point of departure was not simply unclear, obscured, but plainly absent.

'You're decentred in it,' I said. 'And the thing that you're travelling to, tango, the object of the quest, is decentred too—because it's everywhere.'

'I guess I am part of my subject, in that sense, my very uprootedness,' she said. 'I guess really this is not up to me to be analysing this, but it does strike me as important that I am an émigrée, and I think the condition of the émigrée probably informs my approach to my writing. The tango is the dance of immigrants, so in that sense it is my very condition that reflects the nature of tango in that book.'

It was also a book in which it was largely impossible to make a distinction between traveller and travellee. The other people that Kassabova describes are Europeans in Argentinian tango classes, Latin Americans in the dance clubs of Paris and Berlin, Antipodeans in Edinburgh. 'It sort of disrupts conventions,' I said, 'but also gets over that core ethical problem of travel writing, which is representing and constructing difference...'

'The other,' she cut in with a polite nod.

'The other, yeah! There's no other—maybe centred, settled people are the other in *Twelve Minutes of Love*, but you don't really have anything to do with them.'

'I suppose I *am* the other,' she said. Well, yes—but then, for me, as I'd realised in the Greyfriars Kirkyard, so was Patrick Leigh Fermor. That was another story, though.

Kassabova went on: 'The search for tango is the search for what everyone else was trying to say through tango. It is the condition of the displaced, the very condition of being other. I mean, that's what tango is about.'

But in *Border*, I'd thought I could sense a subtle shift. Somehow, the decentred quality of the earlier books was less obvious; there might even have been a faintest implicit suggestion of departure, adventure, return. It had been a puzzle, but now a likely explanation seemed obvious. At the very end of the previous book, *Twelve Minutes of Love*, after various ill-fated tango-based relationships, Kassabova had described meeting Tony, by chance, at a Scottish roadside in the dusk. And now here we were, in her office beside a cottage hunkered low in the Highlands.

'The book you're working on now,' I said; 'I wonder if you can identify your point of departure.'

'I wonder too! If we're talking in terms of literal point of departure it's the same as in *Border*; it's Scotland…'

* * *

I had read somewhere that there had been some hostile responses in Bulgaria to *Street Without a Name*. I'd worried that this might be an awkward subject, but Kassabova was untroubled.

'Sure, sure,' she said; 'there was some hostility towards it. I mean, I never really think about whether people are going to like or dislike what I write; it's not really why you write. So I don't mind if people dislike my work for personal reasons.'

'But why? What was their complaint with it?'

'It was an emotional kind of response. The satirical element in the book was seen as unkindness by some, and the fact that there is a gently mocking, but on the whole, I thought, compassionate kind of tone was

not understood. And it is very much not in the Bulgarian literary tradition to write about one's family and one's country in a satirical way.
So it was lost in translation, in a way.'

Thinking back, I realised that I'd unconsciously assumed that the
travellee-reader always had the ethical high ground, was always right.
But maybe not; maybe the travellee-reader could get things bluntly
wrong. Maybe I'd sometimes missed the point too, reading travellers'
accounts of Cornwall.

Did she think it was ever entirely possible, I asked, to write about
Bulgaria for an English-reading audience, and to make the account
wholly palatable for a Bulgarian audience at the same time?

'No,' she said; 'but that's okay; you don't have to make it
palatable.'

'Palatable is the wrong word,' I said; 'I mean so it's not instantly
going to press some wrong buttons.'

'Well, that's why I had to make some small tweaks in the Bulgarian
Border. But that wasn't along the line of pleasing or displeasing the
reader, but cultural know-how, that some things are culturally a given
to the home audience.' Samanth Subramanian had mentioned something similar, about the Indian and international editions of his books,
all published in a single language.

'Borders are very fraught things in the book,' Kassabova said; 'and
very emotionally charged, almost taboo. There is almost this sense
that... yeah... writing with equanimity about a triple border in the
Balkans can only be done if you've been educated in a culture which is
non-Balkan, which is my case. That's what has enabled me to write
Border, because I don't live in the Balkans. So in that sense it's a very
un-Balkan book, even though it is suffused even with Balkan words.'

There was some link here to what Monisha Rajesh had said about
her being an 'insider-outsider' in India.

'It's a question about the validity of the outsider eye,' I said. 'And
it's that question of whether it's ever possible to produce travel writing
that will not feel a bit odd to the people being written about.'

She nodded. 'It's one of many ethical questions surrounding this
genre, isn't it?'

'It's the central one, really.'

I wasn't sure if Kassabova entirely surmounted this issue by writing
about the Balkans as an insider-outsider, but she certainly 'problema-

tised' it (I was getting worryingly fond of this sort of academese). She helpfully blurred the old binary distinction between traveller and travellee. But this left me ever so slightly uneasy. Patrick Barkham had said, 'If the only person who can write about Eigg is someone who lives on Eigg—we're screwed at that point, aren't we?' But if the only person who could write about Eigg—or about the Balkans, or India, or Cornwall—was some kind of insider-outsider, then weren't we similarly limited?

'Could you imagine your voice, your approach, your mode of— we'll call it travel writing—working anywhere outside the Balkans?' I asked. I'd asked Barkham the same question, more or less, but Kassabova's answer was very different.

'Yeah, I can see myself writing a journey anywhere that I find imaginatively exciting, where I can establish some kind of deep connection.'

'I did wonder if you would become a writer specifically about the Balkans.'

'I hope not,' she said. 'I hope I don't limit myself, or pigeonhole myself, imaginatively above all. You have to remain imaginatively alive, and that means completely open.'

'That's nice.' I said it very meekly and very quietly. But there was a great relief. Patrick Barkham had told me that he would struggle with the daunting ethical challenges of writing beyond British shores. Maybe he embodied a necessary, long-overdue crisis of confidence at the old, fragmenting centre of the travel writing universe. But Kapka Kassabova, Bulgarian-Kiwi-Highlander and global soul—whether she had a point of departure or not—was willing to journey anywhere. Travel writing wasn't dead.

Kassabova was still talking: 'That was one of the things with *Border* that I found most daunting: this is so complex, this is so important, it's so under-told; how am I going to do it justice? It became my only worry, almost. How can I do justice to the enormity of this, and the specificity of these people and their worries? How do I do this honourably?'

'And do you think you succeeded?'

'Yes!' she said, with a sharp nod.

* * *

Afterwards we went across to the cottage. It was dark now, with a smear of stars overhead.

'Do you know what the travellee is?' Kassabova said to Tony as we crossed the threshold. He gave a snort of laughter when she explained, and I grinned sheepishly. Again, a sudden wash of familiarity. Tony had appeared briefly in *Twelve Minutes of Love*, of course, but there was none of that uncanniness I'd experienced on coming face to face with Rory MacLean's wife, Katrin. I felt as though I'd met him somewhere before—but not in a book.

The cottage was small, open through and through on the ground floor. The upper level seemed to have been dropped clumsily atop the original crofter's homestead, a cumbersome appendage with creaking, off-true floors. There were blankets and low sofas and a wood-burner. They didn't have a microwave.

Tony laid the table for dinner. I'd brought a bottle of New Zealand wine. I said I hadn't been able to find anything from Bulgaria in the supermarket. 'Probably safer that way,' Kassabova smiled.

After we'd eaten we moved to the other end of the room and drank whisky and homemade ginger tea.

The familiarity: it was as if I already knew this house. William Dalrymple had said that travel writers simply tended to get on with one another, regardless of their backgrounds. Certainly, there was no one I'd met on this journey whose company I hadn't enjoyed. But this was something else.

We gave contemporary nature writing a bit of a hard time. Kassabova and I had talked a little about this earlier. I'd wondered if British nature writers might one day start to look beyond British shores.

'And beyond birds? Do you think we've had enough birds? I mean...' She'd shaken her head, baffled. 'I don't want to come across as being negative; I'm not at all negative about it; please don't make me sound negative. I'm just astonished.'

I asked Tony about the artists he worked with. It turned out he knew someone I knew from home, a man who made fantastical sculptures from old junk and industrial cast-offs. He was the father of one of my best friends at primary school. My other best friend had been the son of a tin miner, but I don't think any of us noticed a distinction. Both men had power tools and drove old pickup trucks.

'David, yeah, good old David...' said Tony, and suddenly I understood why this household, these people, seemed familiar, why I felt so comfortable here: we could have been in West Cornwall. I *knew* houses like this: little pockets of ramshackle construction and unaffected bohemia, beyond the radars of prowling second-homers, inhabited by people who spoke without class signifiers and might as easily have been fishermen or artists—or quite possibly both at the same time.

It was a very, very old cliché of the journey narrative: I'd come to the ends of the earth—and from *my* point of departure, this Highland valley really did feel that way—to find something that was just like home.

* * *

It was too late and too far to travel back to Edinburgh, so I slept on a pull-down bed in the outer room of Kassabova's office, under the 'travel and memoir' shelf. It was very dark and very silent, and I could feel the cold pressing in close around the building.

I woke early and stood outside and watched the sun come up over the pines. The view was framed by pylons and swooping wires. Somehow I'd missed them the day before. A woodpecker fired off a short rattle in the trees. Another still bright day.

Globbie came skittering across the gravel to greet me, and a moment later Tony came past from the house, heading out early to work.

'Go for a walk if you like,' he called; 'the dog'll show you the way.'

I cut out along the front of the house, past weedy winter vegetable beds, and found my way to a river. The dog ran on ahead, tail thrashing at the fallen leaves. There was frost on the grass. The river ran dark and muscular, and beyond it were bare trees with grey trunks and port-coloured branches, then a deep wall of conifers. I could have walked on and on this way, between the woods and the water.

This was Scotland, of course, but I couldn't help associating the pine-thick, river-carved landscape with the Balkan ranges that Kassabova had written about in *Border*—and that Patrick Leigh Fermor had passed through, more than seven decades earlier. Both writers had an equally valid view of the place. There weren't, and there never should be, any qualifications, identifiable in advance, for good travel writers. You simply had to let them go out, travel, write. *Then* you could scrutinise. And it really didn't matter whether they departed from Eton, or from a street without a name in Sofia.

I threw a stick for the dog. There was a cold scent off the water: moss and stones and wet wood.

Still though—insider-outsider, if that's what you happened to be, seemed a particularly useful status. You could see things from new angles, like Kapka Kassabova, or say things that others might not feel able to say, like Monisha Rajesh...

And then a sudden idea, beside the cold dark water with the dog foraging for the stick in the scrub somewhere ahead and a limning of frost on the stones at the bank. Could I make *myself* an insider-outsider—to both travel writing and travel writing studies? Was that, in fact, what I already was? I'd be at my desk very soon, with no further opportunity for diversion. Was this a way to get the thing done?

* * *

When I got back to the house, Kassabova was standing outside the door in knitted boots, holding a steaming travel mug.

'Do you want to walk down to the river with me?'

We went in the other direction this time, upstream, along a track towards a point where the river narrowed between high banks.

We leant against the fence by the track, facing into the sun, squinting and shielding our eyes. Kassabova sipped her coffee. I asked if she'd ever write about this place (and privately wondered whether she could be an insider-outsider here too). Maybe, she said, but definitely not as a nature writer!

In Bulgaria, as in Britain, she said, a middle-class fascination with the countryside, and a literary interest in villages and old ways, had become more obvious in recent years. She wondered if it somehow fed, both from and into, a rise of nativist sentiment.

'We seem to want to know *more* about the things that we already know. There is this addictive, almost narcissistic desire to be told more and more about the things that we identify with,' she said. 'Give me *more* villages, give me *more* birds.'

Travel writing could certainly be wearyingly repetitive too, particularly when it deliberately followed its own footsteps. And it often got things horribly wrong when it encountered difference. But *wanting* to encounter difference instead of turning inwards—surely that was an honourable aim.

We walked back. When we were near the house, Kassabova said, emphatically, repeating a point from the previous day, 'I want something to be at *stake* for the writer.'

EPILOGUE

THE DEATH OF THE AUTHOR

The young couple at the café table hear the taxi coming up the road from Sparta before they see it, the crunch of the gear changes and the rattle of the exhaust disturbing the still evening air. It stops right in front of their place on the terrace under the shade trees. A passenger clambers out, a shaven-headed man in his late thirties. He thanks the driver in English, shoulders a blue backpack, and jogs up the steps of the small hotel across the way. A few minutes later he appears again, on a first-floor balcony, and stands, hands planted on the railing, breathing deeply. The woman looks up as her partner pours tarry red wine from a carafe, and briefly catches the stranger's eye. He smiles and nods in friendly acknowledgement, but she looks quickly back down to her mobile phone. The couple do not see him again, and when he returns to the street half an hour later the café terrace is empty.

He wanders through the village towards the castle, hands in pockets, looking at the purple bougainvillea spilling over pocked masonry, and up to the high dark wall of the Taygetos range. The mountains have already lowered a soft summer twilight onto the village, but a pale glory along the uppermost ridge shows that in the west the sun still hangs above a hidden Messenian horizon.

After a while he turns back, and finds a seat outside a bar on the little village plaza. Four old men sit against the bolted wooden doors of the building opposite, glasses of ouzo at their sides and slim, yellow-eyed cats around their feet. Two tables down, a middle-aged English couple are picking at their dinner. The woman says something about 'the universality of tourism', and he half turns his head to catch the phrase. A waiter comes out, and he orders a beer and an omelette with feta cheese. A bell tolls somewhere: nine o'clock.

He bends in his seat for a moment to brush away the mosquitoes gathering at his bare ankles, then takes out a notebook with a hard, burgundy cover. It is already three-quarters full with pencilled jottings, the page edges grubby. He flicks through to the first blank sheet and begins to write:

1 June, Mystras, Greece—At a table on the little village square with the dusk coming in...

* * *

Since late winter I had sat at a desk in a white upstairs room near the market square in a small town off the M6 motorway in County Galway. I had three hardback A5 notebooks now, stacked neatly at the back of the desk. Two had black covers, and were full of notes from my reading, and outlines of the questions I had planned to ask the writers I met. The other had a burgundy cover. I'd used it as a journal to write up each individual trip, each encounter. There were fifty-one blank pages remaining at the end.

To begin with, there were many hours of recorded conversation to transcribe. I'd start each morning, earphones in, poised over the keyboard like a swimmer waiting for a starting pistol. I'd press play and dive forward, and I was usually still at it, brain and fingers numb, when Cara got home from work. Eventually, the transcripts amounted to a massed 200,000 words. Then I had to begin again with each individual block of unmediated dialogue. This was how I imagined a sculptor must feel facing a lumpen mass of unhewn marble: sometimes you could already see the outline of the figure within; sometimes you just had to start chiselling to find out what would emerge.

I usually worked through the weekends, but if the weather was clear we went walking—in the woods at Monivea; or on the low foreshore at Tawin where hares got up amongst the stones and raced away over the tide-wrack, and the Burren showed pewter-coloured across the water. A fierce winter gave way to an uncommonly hot summer.

EPILOGUE

The insider-outsider stuff seemed to come of its own accord. And when I was more than halfway through, I realised that I'd unconsciously done a little decentring of my own. Nothing to compete with Kapka Kassabova, naturally; but I found that I'd made my own point of departure and return ambiguous—was it a stony parish in West Cornwall, a university library in the English Midlands, or an old walled town in the west of Ireland? Perhaps anyone could make themselves a global soul on a small scale if they put their mind to it.

This was the second part of the travel writing journey—the one that Rory MacLean and Samanth Subramanian had both described, and at times I struggled to read the route map. In the early stages of the actual journey—the one on the ground, rather than the page—I had been casting about, uncertain of my own trajectory. Now, with hindsight, I could see the path clearly, and sometimes it suggested a rearrangement of the pieces. Sitting at my desk, I found myself moving the encounters back and forth between the order of the actuality and that suggested by narrative logic. Here was the inherent tension of travel writing practice, the tension revealed in the conversations with Sara Wheeler and the readers at the Globetrotters Club. In the end I went with the reordering, but I combed through the chapters carefully, trying to douse any resultant smoulder of artifice at their edges, excising any reflection on an apparently 'earlier' encounter that had really belonged to the future of the actuality I described. I wasn't actually fictionalising *anything* here, but some latent trace of fictionality seemed to linger nonetheless. That's travel writing, I suppose…

For what it's worth, I really did begin as I have begun: down a long white track in Cornwall, then the library and the cathedral. But I spoke to Nicholas Jubber and Colin Thubron *before* Barnaby Rogerson, then went on to Patrick Barkham, then Nick Danziger. And the Berlin conference, as I hope its telling suggests, happened at another time entirely. Beyond that, the narrative unfolds in the same order as the actual journey, with two exceptions: the conversation with the Globetrotters readers and the lunch with Carl Thompson happened at the very end, after everything else—but before what I am about to relate here. So, there you have it.

A few times, just for fun, I went right across the fictional frontier, following MacLean's lead and signalling frantically ('Fictional elements here, dear reader!'). This was somehow less fraught, but even so, I always retreated rapidly, back to the resistant matter of the transcripts and the notebooks. What scared me was not *losing* control, but its opposite: assuming a novelist's absolute power.

There was no right or wrong way to go about these things, I'd long since realised. But for myself, I was still convinced that the simplest, least ethically fraught approach for a travel writer was to keep a firm anchor in the actuality. Not in some nebulous 'truth' or 'greater truth', whatever that meant; but in the plain stuff confirmed by a digital recording or a note scribbled in the moment: 'The Englishwoman just said something about "the universality of tourism", and the mosquitoes are needling my ankles...'

It still had to come filtered through the fickle tissue of memory, of course, warped by every book the writer had read since childhood. The scholar James Clifford—discussing ethnography, though he could as easily have been talking of travel writing—wrote of 'serious true fictions' and how 'Power and history work through them, in ways their authors cannot fully control.'[1] But there was something else that authors couldn't fully control, and that was what actually *happened* to them along the road, who they met, what their interlocutors said. A few well-signalled diversions were all well and good—and a lot of fun—and perhaps some reordering of the pieces too. But in the end, knocking repeatedly against the hard, resistant actuality of the journey seemed the only obvious counterbalance to that almighty weight of power and history. It allowed at least a possibility of other voices hissing through the cracks of the text: *What good will this conversation do for me?* It also seemed like the best way to avoid the disapproval of readers.

I'd promised myself one final journey when the bulk of the work was done. It would be a reward, and a chance to fill those blank pages at the back of the burgundy notebook. But there was also, I knew, some unfinished business. There was one final writer to consider, more slippery than any other, and yet more firmly, and disquietingly, installed within my head than even Patrick Leigh Fermor.

I'd packed a sleeping bag and trekking pole, a couple of travel books, two large-scale maps of the Taygetos Mountains, and the burgundy notebook. Then I had flown to Greece.

* * *

EPILOGUE

The village of Anavryti in the airless late afternoon; a clutch of white-walled, red-roofed houses strung along a green ridge almost 3,000 feet up on the eastern flank of the Taygetos. The lanes are empty and the windows shuttered. The only people out of doors are a woman and a man, sitting left and right of the dark doorway of the little taverna at the heart of the village. There are vines over the taverna terrace, hydrangeas growing in halved oil drums, and cool spring-water spouting from pipes set into the surrounding walls. The man wears a grubby green tee shirt with short sleeves that show the swollen pink of his upper biceps. He rests a half-drunk bottle of Amstel beer on his knee. The woman is slim, in her forties, with greying blond hair. Her name is Aglaia.

They know that someone is coming up the lane from the left before they see him. His passing has set all the village dogs barking on this quiet afternoon. He comes into view by the war memorial under its limp Greek flag: a man with a blue backpack and a trekking pole. He lifts a stained cap to mop the sweat from his brow, showing a closely shaven head; a foreigner. He looks up uncertainly at the taverna terrace. The tatty white plastic chairs are tilted against the tables. Aglaia smiles from her seat by the door.

'Welcome to our village!' She speaks more than enough English to deal with foreign tourists.

'Are you open?'

'Of course.' She rises and pulls down a chair for him. 'What would you like?'

He drops his pack heavily and the trekking pole clatters to the floor. He seems uncertain, almost shy. Perhaps he is uncomfortably conscious of the fact that he speaks no Greek. 'Umm... something to eat? An omelette?'

'With cheese?'

'Please. And an iced coffee—a frappé?'

As she turns to the kitchen she sees him lifting a battered plastic bottle from his pack, so she fetches a jug and fills it from the nearest waterspout. 'Better you drink this,' she says with a smile. 'The freshest in the world!' It's an English line she has used plenty of times when hikers from overseas come through Anavryti. When she returns with the coffee she notices that his left arm is scratched and bleeding above the elbow.

307

'What happened?' she asks, concerned.

He glances at the scratches and makes to cover them, abashed. 'Oh, it was... on the path...' He motions in the direction from which he appeared a few minutes earlier. He means the last overgrown stretch of the trail below the village, where it is thick with nettles and brambles. Aglaia goes inside and comes back with cotton wool and antiseptic and gently wipes the blood from his arm.

'You must be careful,' she says, and he nods shyly.

'Thank you.'

The omelette she makes is as yellow as fresh turmeric, and specked with mountain herbs. When he has eaten he unfolds a map across the table and bends over it for a long while. Aglaia clears the plate away and asks where he is going. He gestures, half to the map and half to the landscape, and seems to be saying that he has walked from Mystras, up the deep Lagada Gorge, and that he is heading on towards the summit of Profitis Ilias, high point of the Taygetos. Then he'll cross the watershed and follow a beetling valley that meets the Vyros Gorge, which will lead him to the village of Chora—an elevated western counterpart to Anavryti across the range. Finally, he'll descend to the coast at Kardamyli. This is certainly much further than anyone could walk in a single day.

'Where do you sleep?' Aglaia asks. He motions vaguely towards the mountain.

He sits for half an hour, writing in a notebook with a burgundy cover. Then he rises, wearily, fills his bottle from a waterspout and hoists his pack onto his shoulders. Aglaia points the way to the uphill path. He manages an awkwardly accented 'thank you' and 'goodbye' in Greek. The fading click of his pole against the stones is audible for a few moments above the sound of running water. The man in the green tee shirt has never moved, though a fresh bottle of Amstel now rests on his knee.

Several hours later, towards nightfall, two men hurrying down from the upper slopes with bags of wild herbs see the same foreigner labouring up through the pines. They offer cheery greetings as they pass, and he raises a weary hand and leans heavily on his pole.

A little further up the mountain, he cuts off the trail and finds a patch of soft earth. He hangs his boots on a branch and wriggles into his sleeping bag. Darkness comes with the suddenness of a tidal bore. An owl hoots in the trees. A church bell tolls the hour, very faint from a village below. He lies on his back, cushioning his head on the pack, and scribbles a few lines in his notebook with the last of the daylight: 'A church bell below, an owl hooting... An idea for the final chapter— a dream sequence...'

* * *

A dream sequence:

I awoke with a start—someone was shaking me by the collar and shouting. As soon as I was fully awake, I made out two men...

... one dark-haired, one fair.

'Get up, get up! We're taking you up the mountain!'

They loomed over me. The dark-haired man was older, with a downcast nose and a slight pout. The blond was younger, with a wide forehead under a straw-coloured fringe. His eyes were very blue. They were both extremely good-looking, but you could tell by the way they carried themselves that they knew it all too well. Their English accents were excessively rarefied.

I stumbled from my sleeping bag. 'Who *are* you?'

'Call me Paddy,' said the brunet.

'Call me Bruce,' said the blond.

I groaned. This had to happen eventually. 'Oh God... I'd really rather not...' I began, but they were already striding away uphill.

'Come on!'

I pulled on my boots, and floundered after them. They had already cleared the treeline and were striking for the summit at an impossible diagonal. Their rucksacks—the brunet's of faded canvas; the blond's of expensive-looking leather—appeared to be completely empty. Mine was laden with maps and books and processed cheese and tinned sardines.

'Wait for me!' I shouted—then paused. A little way off, in the shadows beneath the last pine tree, were two women. Again, one was dark-haired, one fair. They were huddled together, speaking in undertones, but I caught a snatch of accents: one English, one American. They were scribbling urgently in what looked like chequebooks.

'Hold on a moment!' I muttered, and strode towards them. A furious yell came from above but I ignored it. 'I need to ask those women something...' But as I neared the pine tree they vanished, and another still more forceful yell echoed down the slope: 'Hurry *up!*'

It was impossible to keep up. They leapt from rock to rock like mountain goats, pausing only to shout down an occasional encouragement: '*Solvitur ambulando!*' Soon they were distant dots, surging towards the summit in the light of the rising sun. But when finally I made it to the top, at least half an hour behind them, I found them unexpectedly crestfallen.

'What's wrong?'

'Someone got here before us,' the brunet muttered.

'Who?'

He nodded towards the uppermost crag. A jet was passing, far above, and I heard a new voice, every bit as primly accented, but with a certain gravelly rasp: 'One abominates the internal combustion engine...'

I knew that voice! Was Robin Hanbury-Tenison here? But of course not: it was the original. He sat cross-legged at the very top of the mountain, monarch of all he surveyed, dressed as the Sheik of Araby: Thesiger himself.

The others stared sulkily at their toes. 'He always gets there first,' said the blond.

I left the three of them to it and wandered off to the side, seeking a place to sit out of the wind. Below me the western valleys of the range were still deep in shadow, but I caught a flicker of movement where another path descended steeply from the summit. There was someone there, far ahead of us and travelling on. I shaded my eyes and squinted. I couldn't be certain at such a distance, but it was either a Chinese monk, a Galician nun or an Irishwoman on a bicycle.

Back at the summit the blond and the brunet were fumbling with pieces of tarpaulin.

'Paddy! Bruce!' I said sternly (and why the hell not?) 'What on earth are you doing?'

'We want to rest.'

The blond was trying to fix the corners of the tangled tarps to upended rocks, but they kept slipping loose. 'Snake-proof groundsheets,' he said, as if that explained everything. 'Someone showed me once, but I can't remember how to do it.'

EPILOGUE

I looked quizzically at Thesiger, still cross-legged on the highest crag. He was staring down the length of his great nose with an expression of pure disgust.

'God,' he said; 'you must be a couple of pansies...'

* * *

This is what I remember:

A steep hillside in a high-walled valley to the west of Profitis Ilias, with a bare twenty minutes of daylight to spare. The unease that has nagged since the pass gives way to jittery fear, mixed with self-reproach—and also embarrassment. The rotten thread of the path I have been struggling to follow has finally snapped. Ahead, a sheer yellow mountainside. Two hundred feet below, the pale stones in the bed of the gorge. There is no way on, and no way down.

* * *

I had woken at six-thirty from an entirely dreamless sleep. The sun was just up through the pines and a sound of bells and whistles drifted in from the mountainside above. I thought it must be a shepherd. But when I started along the trail I saw that it was two hunters, drawing the slopes for hares with a pack of skinny black-and-tan hounds. Each hound had a little cowbell tied to its collar.

It was after midday by the time I reached the summit of Profitis Ilias. Sickle-winged swifts sliced at the cold air, and Sparta showed white on the plain to the northeast like a city in a dream. There was a roofless chapel at the summit, squalid with candlewax and icons in broken frames. I took out my mobile phone, but there was no signal. I descended to a pass marked with patches of snow-in-summer flowers, ate a lunch of tinned sardines and Laughing Cow cheese, crossed the watershed, and ran into trouble.

On the eastern flank of the Taygetos Range—which runs from the heart of the Peloponnese to the southernmost terminus of the Mani—the map had matched the ground reality of clear trails and regular water sources. But it was very different here. I came to dead-ends in airless gullies, followed the false promise of paths that turned out to lead back up the mountain, and took two hours to cover a meagre map-kilometre. Once, I startled a family of wild pigs at close quarters: three black-faced adults and a clutch of gingery babies. They stared at me, huffing in outrage for a full minute, then trotted prissily into the scrub below; and a little while later I came to a strange open place, sheeny with mica and scattered with cattle bones. Eventually, I scrambled down into a maze of tiny terraces and foundation walls in the valley head. The terraces were long abandoned, thick with waist-high bracken and young pines. I filled my bottles at a spring under a boulder. A queasy intimation suggested that this was the last water I would see.

For the next three hours I tried to follow the line of the trail indicated by the map, along the left wall of the valley through dense stands of pine and dwarf oak. There *had* been a path here, once. Sometimes I could trace its shadow along the slope, and occasionally there were faded dabs of red paint on stones, indicating a ghostly trajectory. But they were too infrequent to serve as a useful guide, and their sporadic appearance took on a mocking quality—proof that no one had been foolish enough to walk this way for a very long time.

The valley was airless, and the narrow band of sky above was paling towards evening. I noticed, with some concern, that the phantom path was edging me higher and higher above the valley floor as it dropped away below. I emerged in a sloping patch of wild pasture, ringed with thorny bushes. I circled it seeking a way out, a faint metallic taste of panic at the back of my throat, then struck out manically down the darkly forested slope below. Another mocking red dot, and an old rubber boot sticking out of the leaf-litter; then a gasping ascent, and finally there was no way forward at all.

The sensible thing to do, I knew, was to retrace my steps to the clearing above, make camp there, and in the morning, rested and clear-headed, seek a safe route down. But the idea of sleeping on the slope, essentially trapped, was a miserable prospect. An awful claustrophobia had set in, and with it an irrational conviction: I *had* to reach the bed of the ravine, dust-dry below, a long white track through the mountains. Then, at least, the next day's march would be clear.

And so, knowing that I was making a very rash decision even as I started, I began to climb down a sheer, 200-foot cliff, unbalanced by my laden pack, encumbered by my trekking pole and exhausted by some fourteen hours of walking.

EPILOGUE

At first there were ledges and outcrops that gave an illusion of security. But from halfway down, the cliff was horribly exposed. The strap connecting the trekking pole to my wrist gave way. The pole clattered below. Proper panic hit, with a sudden tremor in my knees where they braced against the rock. I knew from the map how little progress I'd made. I had less than a litre of water remaining. There was not a hint of a mobile phone signal in this deep mountain cleft; and I understood now that this was no well-beaten route where I could expect swift discovery by a fellow hiker. A twisted ankle, let alone some more serious injury—it didn't bear thinking about.

What was I doing here? Really: what on earth was I doing here? Kapka Kassabova had said that something should be at stake for the writer, but this was ridiculous. The reason for this journey was exclusive and quixotic, with no space for the travellee. Imagine that some ill-equipped foreigner tumbled to injury or death from the cliffs below my home-place in Cornwall, and we found out later that he'd come to commune with—I don't know, the spirit of D. H. Lawrence, or something. Imagine the scorn! Imagine the howling travellee-polemic I'd produce in response to *that*...

On a cliff face in a gorge in the Taygetos Mountains at dusk, I think it must have been shame that overcame panic and saw me safely to the bottom: just imagine if you *died* doing this!

* * *

From the notebook:

> *4 June. Grim and frightening descent of the valley—to write up properly later. Bedded down in the gorge. Stony, but I actually slept surprisingly well.*
>
> *Hot and white on the further descent. No springs despite what was marked on the map, and path mostly non-existent.*
>
> *Eventually, a glimpse of a church, perched on a precipice ahead, and then a proper marked path. I sat amongst heather and looked out. The sea, framed by the gorge, was oily and flat.*

* * *

I shambled into Chora in a scorching midday. There was a tap set into a niche in a wall near the church at the road-head. The water that

313

spluttered out was hot, but I downed grateful mouthfuls then filled my empty bottles.

If I'd followed the narrow lane straight down through the houses I'd have come directly to my destination. But, still shaken by my experience in the gorge the previous evening, I was perversely resentful—as if it had all been *his* fault, not my own. I needed to rest and to compose myself first.

I walked out along a strip of sweating tarmac to the next village, Exchori. Far below, the coast swept north past Kalamata. There was a white taverna above the empty road with vines clambering to an upper terrace. A woman in white trousers brought me iced coffee and a glass of cold water. I drank it in a single draught, then sat limply, feeling the fluid slowly refilling my veins.

After half an hour I got up heavily and walked back to Chora. The place was shuttered and silent. Beyond the last house, a path ran between olive trees and through tall yellow grass, shifting in the gusts of wild, herb-scented heat. At the end of the path: a little chapel of pitted stone, set on a promontory with a fig tree bursting below. This was it, then.

Patrick Leigh Fermor had lived for almost half a century on the coast below this spot, of course. But I wasn't here for Patrick Leigh Fermor; I'd dealt with him back in Edinburgh. I'd walked three days across the mountains because of Bruce Chatwin.

* * *

Travel writing aficionados are generally expected to laud Bruce Chatwin's 1977 debut, *In Patagonia*, perhaps above all other travel books. But for me it has always been his later work, *The Songlines* (1987), which has the greatest hold. It was the first of his books that I read, when I was perhaps twenty-one: a sparsely written account of a journey through Central Australia, interspersed with a sort of postmodern memoir of a travelling life in shards and fragments, and the bravura performance of a wholly unscientific theory about the origins of language, nomadism and human 'restlessness'. (It is also, plainly, an exercise in wishful thinking by a frightened dying man—but you need biographical details, which I was missing at first reading, to recognise that.) *The Songlines* was quite unlike anything else I'd yet encountered in the travel genre.

At the time I wanted very much to be a travel writer myself—and the narrator of *this* book was the travel writer I most wanted to be. The brief biography inside the front cover revealed little, but the text itself suggested a hardy aesthete with an impossible array of literary references and the ability to rig up a snake-proof groundsheet. In the portrait on the back cover Chatwin looked like a professional surfer. He'd taken Patrick Leigh Fermor's 'footloose scholar in the wilds' model and given it an irresistible shot of contemporary cool. It was the snake-proof groundsheet that really got me. I was very impressed. I noted the technique carefully—corners tied to branches to lift the edges clear and stop anything slithering in—in case I should ever need to sleep out in the Australian bush.

By the time I read *The Songlines*, Bruce Chatwin had been dead for a decade. I knew nothing about his life, nothing about the literary controversies of the 1980s. My paperback copy had the word 'travel' alongside the barcode on the back. The name on the spine was 'Bruce Chatwin' and the name of the narrator appeared to be 'Bruce Chatwin' too. I assumed, as you do, that they were 'but one or identical'.[2] I read with fact convention fully engaged.

It was only later I discovered that things weren't quite so simple, that Chatwin had ordered the book withdrawn from the Thomas Cook Travel Book Award, claiming it wasn't a travel book at all, that both he and his defenders had insisted it was a 'novel'. Later, too, I found out a little about postcolonial theory and saw just how blithely Chatwin had trampled his way in, with all the confidence of one departing from the centre of the universe, allowing space for scarcely a single Aboriginal voice. Almost everything *The Songlines* had to say about Aboriginal culture came mediated by other books, or by the author's white Australian informants. Even if you *did* accept that this was a novel—and its main characters were all plainly identifiable as actual people living in and around Alice Springs, people that Chatwin had met—there was something very troublesome going on.

Later, I read Nicholas Shakespeare's 1999 biography of Chatwin, and picked up the mentions of his name in the memoirs of other people. The more I learnt about the man, the less attractive he became. Everyone who had known him personally seemed to insist that he was wonderful, but whenever they tried to describe him on the page he came across as a braggart and a bore—a thoroughly careless person who used others very readily.

I was certainly not the only person to feel this way. Shakespeare's biography, published a decade after Chatwin's death, received many effusive reviews for the work itself, but a good few harsh notices for its subject. Nigel Barley, writing in the *Times Higher Education Supplement*, described Chatwin as 'a mix of Jay Gatsby and Princess Diana with a designer rucksack'.[3] Sara Wheeler, customarily forthright, called him 'a monster'.[4] I'd asked about this when I went to speak to her that winter afternoon in London. Why, I'd wanted to know, did Chatwin earn more of her ire than the more straightforwardly monstrous V. S. Naipaul? She thought about it for a while, then said that it was because Naipaul at least *knew* he was a monster.

And then there was that snake-proof groundsheet. In the biography, Nicholas Shakespeare speaks to Toly Sawenko, the man whose image and family history Chatwin appropriated for the figure of Arkady in *The Songlines*, and who provided the author with his one, very brief experience of travel in the Central Australian bush. Sawenko recalls the author's terror of snakes during their second overnight halt. No one else was worried, but the two Aboriginal men they were travelling with set up a secure sleeping place for the nervous Englishman, before bedding down on the ground themselves. In the book Chatwin shamelessly inverts this. It is 'Arkady' and the Aboriginal men who are spooked by the possibility of snakes, while 'For myself, I rigged up a "snakeproof" groundsheet to sleep on, tying each corner to a bush so its edges were a foot from the ground.'[5]

Shakespeare records Sawenko rereading this passage, then saying— and you can sense the dry sniff, the twisted smile, the sad arching of the eyebrows—'How impressed people must have been.'[6]

* * *

Bruce Chatwin died of AIDS in Nice on 18 January 1989. He was forty-eight. He had made great efforts to disguise the real cause of his illness, and had fled back at the end to the American wife whose inherited wealth he had drawn on for two decades while he gallivanted about the globe.

He had published five books in his lifetime, two of them very slim novellas and only one of them—the first, *In Patagonia*—nonfiction by his own reckoning.[7] He hated being called a travel writer, but he would never escape the designation. One of the doctors who treated him during his final illness described him in his medical notes as 'a very nice 47-year-old travel writer with AIDS'.[8] He might at least have appreciated the 'very nice' part.

A month after his death, Chatwin's wife, Elizabeth, took his ashes to Greece, to Kardamyli. He had first visited the place—and had first met Patrick Leigh Fermor—in the early 1970s, while trying and failing to complete a proposed book about nomadism. He'd returned in 1985 and spent seven months in a hotel up the hill from Leigh Fermor's house, working on the first draft of *The Songlines*. Walking in the hills with the older writer one day, Chatwin had come across the tiny, tenth-century Byzantine chapel of St Nicholas, just below the village of Chora. It was here, in February 1989, that Elizabeth, accompanied by Patrick and Joan Leigh Fermor, buried the ashes.[9] And it was here, three decades later, that I shucked off my filthy backpack, sat down on the hot steps, and realised that I *had* ended up right back where I'd started after all—at the memorial-place of a travel writer 'not so much dead [...] as deeply and probably irretrievably encrypted'.[10] John Mandeville had had the last laugh in the end.

* * *

Now that I was actually here, I wasn't quite sure what to do. The chapel had stood on this promontory for a thousand years. If I spoke Greek, took the time, asked, I'd surely find that it had its own stories, among which the burial of an Englishman's ashes did not rank. The weathered wooden door was held closed with a stick. I lifted it carefully and went inside. Dark, faded frescoes; a few broken altar stones; a family of bats roosting in the dome—quivering yellow pompoms mantled with papery black. I stepped back outside.

It was fiercely hot, and the mountainside was noisy with cicadas. I still had several miles to go, down to Kardamyli where I'd try to find a cheap room for the night. But it would be foolish to walk on in this heat. Better to wait a few hours until the sun was lower in the sky. The front of the chapel was catching the glare, but along the northern wall there was a strip of shade. I stretched myself out on the hard ground, propped my head on my backpack, and opened a book: 'In Alice

Springs—a grid of scorching streets where men in long white socks were forever getting in and out of Land Cruisers—I met a Russian who was mapping the sacred sites of the Aboriginals.'[11]

The theorising seemed thinner than ever—the sort of stuff that a pompous twenty-one-year-old might expound over banana pancakes on the Southeast Asian backpacker circuit. The intellectual posturing was ridiculous. Rilke! Bishop Berkeley's Refutation of Matter! And the strained signalling of uncomplicated heterosexuality, the locker-room bragging of visits to African brothels, the ostentatious admiration of the breasts and hips of Australian women—it suddenly seemed desperately sad, so sad that something small turned over inside my chest: an unexpected pity, not for the 'Bruce' of the book, but for the encrypted author behind him.

But the style of his prose; the way he could call up a place in its entirety with just a few, apparently inconsequential details (the catch of sunlight on glass; a woman's arm in a plaster-cast); the distilled anecdotes and character sketches; the sheer joy of being at large in the world with eye and brain engaged—all of that remained. I couldn't care less what the author thought: it was *my* prerogative as *reader* to say whether this was a travel book—and a travel book it most certainly was.

That, in the end, was where this journey had led me. I would probably always want to write around travel, and to travel around writing. But I wasn't sure that I really wanted to be a 'travel writer'. It wasn't because, like Chatwin, Raban and Leigh Fermor, I thought that travel writing was somehow a disreputable, sub-literary genre. Quite the opposite, in fact, and I wasn't sure that I had what it took. I wasn't sure I'd ever really want to be a 'travel writing scholar' either, at least not without serious caveats and qualifications (though I hoped I'd go to many more conferences, read through many more journals before I was done). But 'travel writing reader', the thing I'd been before all else—that was what I wanted to remain forever. 'John Mandeville' and 'Bruce Chatwin' existed within *my* head, because I read—and read hopefully. And if I could still be gone from a Greek hillside, away to Australia for a few hours on a hot afternoon, then I'd lost nothing coming over the mountains.

* * *

At one point I heard voices among the olive trees and sat up, fearful of being caught reading by a local. Another bloody tourist, down at the chapel, looking for the dead English writer. But the voices drifted away.

As the sun swung down, the strip of shade narrowed. By three o'clock it was no longer wide enough to cover me, so I got up. Twigs and dirt had stuck to the backs of my legs. I put the book away in my pack, and as I straightened up I noticed a niche in the chapel wall. There was something inside—a clear plastic box, wedged in place with a stone. I knew what it was as soon as I reached it out. I'd chanced upon these things before, crammed beneath granite outcrops or tucked inside Bronze Age barrows on the moors at home. A geocache: a symbolic prize for digital treasure-hunters guided by the GPS coordinates posted online by the cache's creator. There was a sticker on the lid: 'This is an official game piece. Refer to geocaching.com for details. Cache name: SONGLINES'.

I looked inside. There was a logbook, and a few of the little trinkets that dedicated geocachers leave to trade—plastic Disney figurines; a hairclip; an earring. I leafed through the logbook. I wasn't the first to come upon the cache by chance. Twelve months earlier 'Robin and Carol' had found it 'whilst looking for Bruce'. So had 'Francisco and Corinne' from Italy, the previous autumn.

I added my own note, then returned the contents to the box. But I didn't close the lid. I'd taken something away from this place, so I ought to leave something in trade. But I didn't have much with me— no plastic toys, and certainly no hairclips or earrings. A coin seemed unimaginative; a battery from my head-torch likewise. And an empty sardine tin or a folded Laughing Cow wrapper would look like vandalism. The only thing I could think of was my pencil. It was much chewed, sharpened to a mere three inches, the rubber hanging off the end. I placed it inside and returned the cache to its niche.

Ahead lay a sweltering descent and a weary entry into Kardamyli. Later there would be the sea, and a view back to Profitis Ilias, impossibly distant, a single speck of snow showing beneath the summit. Later still, there'd be a café table in Kalamata, a bus back to Athens and everything that would ever follow. But I had nothing with which to write myself off the mountain.

AFTERWORD

TRAVEL WRITING IN THE AGE OF COVID-19

In late February 2020—after the journey described here was complete, and after the bulk of the writing was done—I found myself at the Edward Stanford Travel Writing Awards ceremony. It was held at the London Transport Museum, just around the corner from the Crown Court Church in Covent Garden—though this was a rather more glamourous affair than a Globetrotters meeting, with fancy finger food and plenty of wine. Philip Marsden was there, and Nicholas Jubber and Monisha Rajesh. They all had books on the various shortlists, as did Rory MacLean and Sara Wheeler, though in the end the main Stanford Dolman Travel Book of the Year prize went to Robert Macfarlane for *Underland*. During one of the acceptance speeches an alarming thought struck me, and I whispered to the person beside me, 'This is probably all a bit risky, given the circumstances—a room full of travel writers. You'd never know where they've just come back from.' At the airport next morning, waiting for my own flight back to Ireland, I spotted, for the first time, a few travellers wearing face masks.

As it turned out, the Travel Writing Awards was one of the last literary gatherings of the year. There'd be no busy calendar of academic conferences either, and precious few long-distance journeys.

The COVID-19 coronavirus pandemic has had an immediately devastating effect on the global travel industry, and on its attendant media too. Several long-established travel magazines went to the wall in 2020; Lonely Planet was stripped of its editorial staff and sold off, and other guidebook publishers found themselves at the brink of bank-ruptcy. Stanfords bookstore in Covent Garden had to turn to crowd-funding to get its business through the second lockdown. But when it comes to travel *books* of the sort I've looked at here, those 'aesthetically constructed texts', the impact has been more complex. For sure, any travel writers planning research trips in 2020 will have had to change their plans. But for the travel books already on the shelves (and, fortuitously, there had been an unusually rich run of new titles in 2019), the crisis might actually have worked in their favour. During the first lockdown in early 2020, articles began to appear listing favou-rite travel books, and championing their reading as a form of armchair travel. It's too early to tell whether this will have an impact on the decisions of commissioning editors in the years to come, but the vener-able publisher John Murray, working with author Nick Hunt, has already combed its archives to launch a new list of reissued 'Travel Classics' in 2021—the first direct competition for Eland Books since the turn of this century. And why not? If the ready availability of cheap air travel really was a factor in the earlier decline of travel writing as a commercial genre, then a period of enforced immobility must surely have revived a readerly hankering for vicarious journeys.

There have been other developments of significance for travel writ-ing too. The COVID-19 pandemic coincided with a hugely increased global awareness of the Black Lives Matter movement, and with high-profile debates around colonialism and decolonisation. Those debates, clearly, have great relevance to the travel genre, given its heritage, its challenges and its postcolonial critique. During 2020, the British Guild of Travel Writers held a series of panel discussions—online, of course—on 'Decolonising Travel Writing', organised by the journalist Meera Dattani, which reached a new audience of practitioners and readers. Debates once confined to academic conferences, or to the more radical fringes of travel writing practice, suddenly seem to have a lot more traction. Again, it's impossible to know exactly what impact this will have on the future of the genre, though it seems likely that at very least there will be a better effort to seek out more diverse travel writing voices—hopefully with some 'insider-outsiders' and people with unstable points of departure amongst them. And surely ignorance will no longer be a sufficient excuse for the problems that still sometimes pop up when writers encounter difference—and when readers read of those encounters.

As for the immediate future of the form itself, it may be that there is a resurgent demand for grand tales of transcontinental adventures and voyages to far-off lands, for vicarious journeys of the old, romantic sort. Or it may be that there is an accelerated turn towards deeper engagement with narrower spaces—what the scholar Charles Forsdick calls 'vertical travel writing'. Perhaps it's most likely that we'll see an uptick in both approaches, and they may, at long last, need to expand the 'travel' section in the bookshop once more.

None of this is any sort of meaningful consolation for all the deaths, the bereavements, the disrupted lives. But people will always want to read about journeys, and were I to place a wager, I'd say that ultimately the COVID-19 pandemic may turn out to have been good for travel writing—in more ways than one.

Tim Hannigan, Cornwall/Galway, January 2021

NOTES

1. THE LONG WHITE TRACK

1. Debbie Lisle, *The Global Politics of Contemporary Travel Writing* (Cambridge: Cambridge University Press, 2006), p. xi.
2. Evelyn Waugh, *When the Going was Good* (London: Duckworth Overlook, 1946), p. xi.
3. The book that Marsden wrote about this journey, *The Summer Isles: A Voyage of the Imagination*, was published by Granta in October 2019.
4. The article I originally wrote based on the interview with Philip Marsden appeared in the now defunct *My Cornwall* magazine, issue 30 (Summer 2015).

2. NAMING FATHERS

1. Herbert Mason, *Gilgamesh: A Verse Narrative* (New York: Signet, 1972), p. 61.
2. Jonathan Raban, *For Love and Money* (London: Picador, 1987), p. 253.
3. Tim Youngs, *The Cambridge Introduction to Travel Writing* (Cambridge: Cambridge University Press, 2013), p. 3.
4. Paul Fussell, *Abroad: British Literary Travelling Between the Wars* (Oxford: Oxford University Press, 1980), p. 202.
5. Carl Thompson, *Travel Writing* (Abingdon: Routledge, 2011), p. 26.
6. Jan Borm, 'Defining Travel: On the Travel Book, Travel Writing and Terminology', in Glenn Hooper and Tim Youngs (eds), *Perspectives on Travel Writing* (Aldershot: Ashgate, 2004), pp. 13–26: 17.
7. Mary Baine Campbell, *The Witness and the Other World: Exotic European Travel Writing, 400–1600* (Ithaca: Cornell University Press, 1988), p. 27.
8. M. L. McClure and C. L. Feltoe (eds), *The Pilgrimage of Etheria* (London: Macmillan, 1919), p. 1.

9. Michael Harbsmeier, 'Spontaneous Ethnographies: Towards a Social History of Travellers' Tales', *Studies in Travel Writing* 1(1) (1997), pp. 216–38: 226.
10. I-Tsing [Yijing], *A Record of the Buddhist Religion as Practised in India and the Malay Archipelago*, trans. Junjiro Takakusu (Oxford: Clarendon Press, 1896), p. xxxii.
11. Steve Clark, 'Introduction', in Steve Clark (ed.), *Travel Writing and Empire: Postcolonial Theory in Transit* (London: Zed Books, 1999), p. 3.
12. Iain Macleod Higgins, *Writing East: The 'Travels' of Sir John Mandeville* (Philadelphia: University of Pennsylvania Press, 1997), p. 6.
13. C. W. R. D. Moseley (trans.), *The Travels of Sir John Mandeville* (London: Penguin, 2005), p. 169.
14. Ibid., p. 184.
15. Cited in Campbell, *The Witness and the Other World*, p. 136.
16. Campbell, *The Witness and the Other World*, p. 127.
17. Ibid., p. 149.
18. Higgins, *Writing East*, p. 8.
19. Giles Milton, *The Riddle and the Knight: In Search of Sir John Mandeville* (London: Allison & Busby Ltd, 1996), p. 62.

3. A LETTER TO THE EDITOR

1. Richard Hakluyt, *The Principal Navigations, Voyages, Traffiques and Discoveries of the English Nation*, 16 vols. (Edinburgh: E. and G. Goldsmid, 1885), Vol. 1, p. 4.
2. Nicolas Bouvier, *The Way of the World*, 2nd edn (London: Eland Books, 2007), p. 12.
3. Hakluyt, *Principal Navigations*, p. 4.
4. Ibid., p. 5.
5. In Spring 2021, John Murray—a venerable publisher of travel writing—launched a new 'Travel Classics' list, perhaps suggesting a renewed interest in the genre's back catalogue.
6. Barnaby Rogerson, 'Where Travel Writing is Now', *Errant Magazine*, 18 September 2015. Available at: http://www.errantmagazine.ca/where-travel-writing-is-now/ [accessed 5 June 2019].

4. IN BERLIN

1. Edward W. Said, *Orientalism*, 3rd edn (London: Penguin Books, 2003), p. 3.
2. Ibid., p. 63.
3. Peter Hulme, *Colonial Encounters: Europe and the Native Caribbean, 1492–1797* (London: Methuen, 1986), p. 2.

4. Said, *Orientalism*, p. 93.
5. Syed Hussein Alatas, *The Myth of the Lazy Native* (Frank Cass & Co.: London, 1977).
6. Mary Louise Pratt, *Imperial Eyes: Travel Writing and Transculturation*, 2nd edn (Abingdon: Routledge, 2008), p. 8.
7. Ibid., p. 197.
8. Charles Sugnet, 'Vile Bodies, Vile Places: Traveling with *Granta*', *Transition* 51 (1991), pp. 70–85: 85.
9. Carl Thompson, 'Beyond Gender? Gendering and Ungendering Early Nineteenth-Century Travel Writing' (conference paper), *Encounters with Difference: A Conference on Travel Writing and Gender*, Freie Universität Berlin, 27–28 October 2017.
10. Lucas Tromly, 'Echotourism and Masculinity: The African Travelogues of Tim Butcher, H. M. Stanley, and Graham Greene', *Studies in Travel Writing* 23(2) (2019), pp. 158–74.
11. Churnjeet Mahn, 'Intercourses: Sexuality and Dissent in Travel Writing' (conference paper), *Encounters with Difference: A Conference on Travel Writing and Gender*, Freie Universität Berlin, 27–28 October 2017.

5. BELATED TRAVELLERS

1. *Epic Continent*, Nicholas Jubber's book about the epic literature of Europe, was published by John Murray in May 2019.
2. Tabish Khair, 'An Interview with William Dalrymple and Pankaj Mishra', in Justin D. Edwards and Rune Graulund (eds), *Postcolonial Travel Writing* (Basingstoke: Palgrave Macmillan, 2011), pp. 173–84: 176.
3. Nicholas Jubber, *The Timbuktu School for Nomads* (London: Nicholas Brealey, 2016), p. 298.
4. Patrick Holland and Graham Huggan, 'Varieties of Nostalgia in Contemporary Travel Writing', in Glenn Hooper and Tim Youngs (eds), *Perspectives on Travel Writing* (Aldershot: Ashgate, 2004), pp. 139–52: 142.
5. Evelyn Waugh, *Labels: A Mediterranean Journey* (London: Duckworth Overlook, 1930), p. 44.
6. James Buzard, *The Beaten Track* (Oxford: Oxford University Press, 1993), p. 8.
7. Debbie Lisle, *The Global Politics of Contemporary Travel Writing* (Cambridge: Cambridge University Press, 2006), p. 3.
8. Robert Byron, *The Road to Oxiana* (London: Macmillan, 1937), p. 83.
9. Sara Mills, *Discourses of Difference: An Analysis of Women's Travel Writing and Colonialism* (London: Routledge, 1991), p. 140.
10. Nicholas Jubber, *Drinking Arak Off an Ayatollah's Beard* (Boston: Da Capo Press, 2010), p. 274.

11. In fact, the title was 'I Am Not Cosmophobic; I'm Just English: Space and Spaciousness in Colin Thubron's Travel Writings'; the presenter was Jim Schramer of Youngstown State University.

12. As it turns out, despite having already signalled his own exit, Theroux couldn't leave the foreign journey alone: his latest travel book, *On the Plain of Snakes: A Mexican Journey*, was published by Hamish Hamilton in October 2019.

13. Thubron's *The Amur River* is due for publication by Chatto & Windus in September 2021.

14. William Dalrymple, 'In the Footsteps of Marco Polo: The Journey that Changed William Dalrymple's Life', *The Spectator*, 24 June 2015. Available at: https://www.spectator.co.uk/article/in-the-footsteps-of-marco-polo-the-journey-that-changed-william-dalrymple-s-life [accessed 20 September 2019].

6. THE TRAVEL WRITER WHO DISAPPEARED

1. Peter Moore, *The Wrong Way Home* (London: Bantam Books, 1999), p. 194.

2. An edited transcript of the interview with Nick Danziger which forms the basis of this chapter was published as: Tim Hannigan, 'Interview with Nick Danziger', *Studies in Travel Writing* 22(2) (2018), pp. 215–25.

3. The specific quotes in question being from the third stanza of 'Arithmetic on the Frontier'—'A scrimmage in a Border Station, / A canter down some dark defile…'—and the final stanza of 'The Young British Soldier': 'When you're wounded and left on Afghanistan's plains, / And the women come out to cut up what remains…'.

4. Corinne Fowler, *Chasing Tales: Travel Writing, Journalism and the History of British Ideas about Afghanistan* (Amsterdam: Rodopi, 2007), p. 32.

5. Danziger's most recent book project has continued this approach. *Another Life* (2020), for which he collaborated again with Rory MacLean, follows individuals in India, Cambodia, Zambia, Uganda, Niger, Honduras, Bolivia and Armenia across a decade, from 2005 to 2015, tracing their stories against the United Nations Millennium Development Goals.

6. Danziger is also co-director of Picture People, a UK-registered charity which provides training and support for filmmakers and activists to document and challenge social injustice in communities across the world.

7. A CLASS OF THEIR OWN

1. Wilfred Thesiger, *Arabian Sands* (London: Longmans, 1959), p. xiii.

2. Eton College Collection, MS 433 06 01 01.

3. Ibid.

4. Ibid.

5. Eton College Collection, MS 433 06 03 01.

6. Ibid.

7. Thesiger, *Arabian Sands*, p. 55.

8. Michael Asher, *Thesiger* (London: Viking, 1994), p. 278.

9. Thesiger, *Arabian Sands*, p. 56.

10. Alexander Maitland, *Wilfred Thesiger: The Life of the Great Explorer* (London: HarperPress, 2006), p. 60.

11. Wilfred Thesiger, *The Life of My Choice* (New York: W. W. Norton, 1980), p. 73.

12. Eric Newby, *A Short Walk in the Hindu Kush* (London: Secker and Warburg, 1958), p. 269.

13. Eton College Collection, MS 433 06 04 15.

14. I later wrote to Thesiger's biographer and literary executor, Alexander Maitland, to ask if he knew anything about the apparent omission in the diary sequence. He told me that a sixth Arabian diary—for 1946–7, and presumably covering the crossings of the Empty Quarter—had been lost. Thesiger claimed to have no idea when or where the loss had occurred, so we do not know if it had vanished before or after the writing of *Arabian Sands*. Perhaps it is out there somewhere, squirrelled away in a loft or basement.

15. Eton College Collection, MS 433 02 02 26.

16. Eton College Collection, MS 433 07 01 12.

17. Ibid.

18. Eton College Collection, MS 433 07 01 13.

19. Ibid.

20. Ibid.

21. Thesiger, *Arabian Sands*, p. 219.

22. This and subsequent quotes from the manuscript are from the Eton College Collection, MS 433 07 01 02.

23. Maitland, *Wilfred Thesiger*, p. 223.

24. Eton College Collection, MS 433 07 01 09.

25. Ibid.

26. Ibid.

27. Thesiger, *Arabian Sands*, p. 166.

8. LUCKY MAN

1. James Robert Enterline, *Erikson, Eskimos, and Columbus: Medieval European Knowledge of America* (Baltimore: Johns Hopkins University Press, 2002), p. 220. In the original, Columbus referred to a '*tierra firme grandíssima*', which might be better translated as 'vast mainland' rather than 'continent'.

2. Mary Baine Campbell, *The Witness and the Other World: Exotic European Travel Writing, 400–1600* (Ithaca: Cornell University Press, 1988), p. 27.

3. Ibid., p. 209.

4. Jonathan Raban, *For Love and Money* (London: Picador, 1987), p. 254.

5. The idea that 'gentlemen didn't write books' was certainly not unusual in the age of imperial exploration. Apsley Cherry-Garrard, who travelled with Scott to the Antarctic and wrote the magnificent *The Worst Journey in the World* (London: Constable, 1922), declared that 'When I went South, I never meant to write a book; I rather despised those who did so as being of an inferior brand to those who did things and said nothing about them' (p. v). It was, supposedly, George Bernard Shaw who eventually convinced him to put pen to paper.

6. Mason was killed in 1961, during another expedition in Brazil (without Hanbury-Tenison), apparently by a group of Panará—a so-called 'uncontacted tribe' at the time. His travelling companions found his body on a forest trail, surrounded by dozens of ceremonially arranged arrows and clubs.

7. Hanbury-Tenison's book on Sarawak, *Finding Eden*, was published by I. B. Tauris in 2017.

8. Philip Marsden, *Rising Ground* (London: Granta, 2014), p. 221.

9. THE TRAVELLEE-READER

1. Carl Thompson, *Travel Writing* (Abingdon: Routledge, 2011), p. 4.

2. Steve Clark, '"Bang at its moral center": Ideologies of Genre in Butor, Fussell, and Raban', *Studies in Travel Writing* 4(1) (2000), pp. 106–25: 108.

3. Mary Louise Pratt, 'Arts of the Contact Zone', *Profession* (1991), pp. 33–40: 35.

4. Wendy Bracewell, 'The Travellees' Eye: Reading European Travel Writing, 1750–1850', in Julia Kuehn and Paul Smethurst (eds), *New Directions in Travel Writing Studies* (Basingstoke: Palgrave Macmillan, 2015), pp. 215–27: 218.

5. Ibid., p. 221.

6. Ibid., p. 216.

7. Bernard Deacon, *Cornwall: A Concise History* (Cardiff: University of Wales Press, 2007), p. 2.

8. Ella Westland, 'The Passionate Periphery: Cornwall and Romantic Fiction', in Ian A. Bell (ed.), *Peripheral Visions: Images of Nationhood in Contemporary British Fiction* (Cardiff: University of Wales Press, 1995), pp. 153–72: 157.

9. Elements of this chapter featured in my article: Tim Hannigan,

"'A Hideous and a Wicked Country": Cornwall under the Travel Writer's Gaze, and Receiving Travelers' Texts as a "Travelee-Reader"', *Terrae Incognitae* 51(2) (2019), pp. 113–52.

10. Richard Warner, *A Tour through Cornwall in the Autumn of 1808* (Bath: Richard Cruttwell, 1809), p. 346.

11. Quoted in W. H. Hudson, *The Land's End* (New York: Appleton and Company, 1908), p. 30.

12. Warner, *A Tour through Cornwall*, p. 174.

13. Johannes Fabian, *Time and the Other: How Anthropology Makes its Object*, 3rd edn (New York: Columbia University Press, 2014), p. 35.

14. Ali Behdad, *Belated Travelers: Orientalism in the Age of Colonial Dissolution* (Durham: Duke University Press, 1994), pp. 6–7.

15. Walter White, *A Londoner's Walk to the Land's End* (London: Chapman and Hall, 1855), p. 1.

16. Ibid., p. 167.

17. Ibid., p. 202.

18. Wilkie Collins, *Rambles Beyond Railways* (London: Richard Bentley, 1851), p. 7.

19. Ibid., p. 3.

20. Charles Lewis Hind, *Days in Cornwall* (London: Methuen, 1907), p. 1.

21. Ibid., pp. 4, 11.

22. Ibid., p. 12.

23. Bernard Deacon, '"The hollow jarring of the distant steam engines": Images of Cornwall between West Barbary and Delectable Duchy', in Ella Westland (ed.), *Cornwall: The Cultural Construction of Place* (Newmill: Patten Press, 1997), pp. 7–24: 8–9.

24. Collins, *Rambles Beyond Railways*, pp. 227–8.

10. BESIDE THE BLACKWATER

1. Dervla Murphy, *Wheels Within Wheels* (London: John Murray, 1979), p. 13.

2. Sara Mills, *Discourses of Difference: An Analysis of Women's Travel Writing and Colonialism* (London: Routledge, 1991), p. 104.

3. Carl Thompson, *Travel Writing* (Abingdon: Routledge, 2011), p. 28.

11. FLYING PIGS

1. Percy G. Adams, *Travelers and Travel Liars, 1660–1800* (Berkeley: University of California Press, 1962).

2. Daniel Carey, 'Truth, Lies and Travel Writing', in Carl Thompson (ed.), *The Routledge Companion to Travel Writing* (Abingdon: Routledge, 2016), pp. 3–14.

3. Kirsten Sandrock, 'Truth and Lying in Early Modern Travel Narratives: Coryat's *Crudities*, Lithgow's *Totall Discourse* and Generic Change', *European Journal of English Studies* 19(2) (2015), pp. 189–203: 189, 191.

4. Peter Hulme and Tim Youngs, *Talking about Travel Writing: A Conversation Between Peter Hulme and Tim Youngs* (Leicester: English Association Issues in English, 2007), p. 7.

5. Robert Macfarlane, 'Introduction', in Rory MacLean, *Falling for Icarus*, 2nd edn (London: Tauris Parke Paperbacks, 2011), p. viii.

6. Claire Lindsay, *Contemporary Travel Writing of Latin America* (Abingdon: Routledge, 2010), p. 99.

7. Corinne Fowler, 'Fiction and Affect: Anglophone Travel Writing and the Case of Paraguay', in Corinne Fowler, Charles Forsdick and Ludmilla Kostova (eds), *Travel and Ethics: Theory and Practice* (Abingdon: Routledge, 2014), pp. 52–76: 66.

8. MacLean has since published a new travel book, *Pravda Ha Ha: Truth, Lies and the End of Europe* (London: Bloomsbury, 2019), which retraces the route of *Stalin's Nose* in reverse, thirty years on, beginning in Russia and ending in Britain.

12. COLLATERAL DAMAGE

1. Wilfred Thesiger, *Desert, Marsh and Mountain* (London: HarperCollins, 1979), p. 182.

2. Jan Borm, 'Defining Travel: On the Travel Book, Travel Writing and Terminology', in Glenn Hooper and Tim Youngs (eds), *Perspectives on Travel Writing* (Aldershot: Ashgate, 2004), pp. 13–26: 17.

3. Tim Youngs, *The Cambridge Introduction to Travel Writing* (Cambridge: Cambridge University Press, 2013), p. 163.

4. Patrick Holland and Graham Huggan, *Tourists with Typewriters: Critical Reflections on Contemporary Travel Writing* (Ann Arbor: University of Michigan Press, 1998), p. viii.

5. Debbie Lisle, *The Global Politics of Contemporary Travel Writing* (Cambridge: Cambridge University Press, 2006), p. 7.

6. Robin Jarvis, 'Travel Writing: Reception and Readership', in Carl Thompson (ed.), *The Routledge Companion to Travel Writing* (Abingdon: Routledge, 2016), pp. 89–98: 89.

7. Jonathan Rose, 'Rereading the English Common Reader: A Preface to a History of Audiences', *Journal of the History of Ideas* 53(1) (1992), pp. 47–70: 49.

8. Jarvis, 'Travel Writing: Reception and Readership', p. 89.

9. Amazon, Customer review of *The Old Patagonian Express* by Paul Theroux, 2015: https://www.amazon.com/gp/customer-reviews/R1E99AH7

2HETPG/ref=cm_cr_arp_d_rvw_ttl?ie=UTF8&ASIN=0140861084 [accessed 10 June 2019].

10. Amazon, Customer review of *The Happy Isles of Oceania* by Paul Theroux, 1999: https://www.amazon.de/gp/customer-reviews/R2LR2R5MSS TV7Q?ASIN=B00AH37F2Q [accessed 10 June 2019].

11. Amazon, Customer review of *The Happy Isles of Oceania* by Paul Theroux, 2004: https://www.amazon.com/gp/customer-reviews/R2O1R1Y C7VNC34/ref=cm_cr_getr_d_rvw_ttl?ie=UTF8&ASIN=B00AH 37F2Q [accessed 10 June 2019].

12. Amazon, Customer review of *The Happy Isles of Oceania* by Paul Theroux, 2016: https://www.amazon.com/gp/customer-reviews/RDMW28J WTE3X0/ref=cm_cr_getr_d_rvw_ttl?ie=UTF8&ASIN=B00 AH37F2Q [accessed 10 June 2019].

13. Amazon, Customer review of *The Happy Isles of Oceania* by Paul Theroux, 2002: https://www.amazon.com/gp/customer-reviews/R3U1IPLN YBV1S4/ref=cm_cr_getr_d_rvw_ttl?ie=UTF8&ASIN=B00AH37F2Q [accessed 10 June 2019].

14. Edward W. Said, *Orientalism*, 3rd edn (London: Penguin Books, 2003), p. 93.

15. Ziauddin Sardar, *Orientalism* (Buckingham: Open University Press, 1999), p. 71.

13. TO THE EAST

1. T. C. McLuhan (ed.), *Touch the Earth: A Self-Portrait of Indian Existence* (Victoria: Promontory Press, 1992).

2. An edited transcript of the interview with Patrick Barkham which forms the basis of this chapter was published as: Tim Hannigan, 'Interview with Patrick Barkham', *Studies in Travel Writing* 21(4) (2017), pp. 429–40.

3. The book that arguably began the 'new nature writing' trend was Roger Deakin's *Waterlog*, which appeared in 1999, nine years head of *Granta 102: The New Nature Writing*. Paul Theroux's *The Great Railway Bazaar*, which kicked off the earlier travel writing boom, appeared eight years ahead of *Granta 10*. The similar pattern is notable.

4. Jan Borm, 'Defining Travel: On the Travel Book, Travel Writing and Terminology', in Glenn Hooper and Tim Youngs (eds), *Perspectives on Travel Writing* (Aldershot: Ashgate, 2004), pp. 13–26: 17.

5. *Islander* was published by Granta in October 2017. Barkham's fifth book, *Wild Child*, appeared in 2020.

6. Patrick Barkham, *Coastlines* (London: Granta, 2015), p. 149.

7. Steve Clark, '"Bang at its moral center": Ideologies of Genre in Butor, Fussell, and Raban', *Studies in Travel Writing* 4(1) (2000), pp. 106–25: 108.

14. ON THE COUCH

1. Sara Wheeler, *Terra Incognita* (London: Jonathan Cape, 1996), p. 1.
2. This book, *Mud and Stars*, was published by Jonathan Cape in July 2019.
3. Sara Wheeler, 'Where Have All the Female Travel Writers Gone?', *The Guardian*, 28 February 2017. Available at: https://www.theguardian.com/books/2017/feb/28/where-female-travel-writers-gone-sara-wheeler [accessed 9 June 2019].
4. Wheeler, *Terra Incognita*, p. 196.
5. Peter Hulme, 'Travelling to Write (1940–2000)', in Peter Hulme and Tim Youngs (eds), *The Cambridge Companion to Travel Writing* (Cambridge: Cambridge University Press, 2002), pp. 87–102: 97; Yaël Schlick, *Feminism and the Politics of Travel after the Enlightenment* (Lewisburg: Bucknell University Press, 2012), p. 177; Tim Youngs, *The Cambridge Introduction to Travel Writing* (Cambridge: Cambridge University Press, 2013), p. 136.
6. Wheeler, *Terra Incognita*, p. 196.
7. Sara Mills, *Discourses of Difference: An Analysis of Women's Travel Writing and Colonialism* (London: Routledge, 1991) p. 3.
8. Ibid., p. 174.
9. Ibid., p. 3.
10. Debbie Lisle, *The Global Politics of Contemporary Travel Writing* (Cambridge: Cambridge University Press, 2006), p. 99.
11. The books in question were Lucretia Stewart's *The Weather Prophet: A Caribbean Journey* (London: Chatto & Windus, 1995) and Dea Birkett's *Serpent in Paradise* (London: Picador, 1997).
12. This whole question inevitably brings to mind another venerable travel writing figure: Jan Morris, who began her writing career in the 1950s as James Morris, but who underwent gender reassignment in 1972. Towards the end of my conversation with Sara Wheeler I mentioned Morris: would Wheeler include her if she were editing a collection of 'women's travel writing'? 'Without any caveats,' she replied, 'she's a woman and that's that.'
13. Colin Thubron, *Behind the Wall* (London: Heinemann, 1987), p. 191.
14. Ibid., p. 194.

15. JOURNALISM BETWEEN EQUALS

1. Samanth Subramanian's *A Dominant Character: The Radical Science and Restless Politics of J. B. S. Haldane* was published by Atlantic Books in 2020.
2. An edited transcript of the interview with Samanth Subramanian which forms the basis of this chapter was published as: Tim Hannigan, 'Interview with Samanth Subramanian', *Studies in Travel Writing* 23(1) (2019), pp. 70–85.

3. Jan Borm, 'Defining Travel: On the Travel Book, Travel Writing and Terminology', in Glenn Hooper and Tim Youngs (eds), *Perspectives on Travel Writing* (Aldershot: Ashgate, 2004), pp. 13–26: 17.

4. Rory Stewart, *The Places in Between* (London: Picador, 2004), p. 30.

5. Catherine Mee, 'Journalism and Travel Writing: From *grands reporters* to Global Tourism', *Studies in Travel Writing* 13(4) (2009), pp. 305–15: 305.

6. Ibid., p. 306.

7. Geoffrey Moorhouse, 'The Inward Journey, the Outward Passage: A Literary Balancing Act', *Studies in Travel Writing* 3(1) (1999), pp. 17–26: 17.

8. Corinne Fowler, *Chasing Tales: Travel Writing, Journalism and the History of British Ideas about Afghanistan* (Amsterdam: Rodopi, 2007), p. 148.

9. Stewart, *The Places in Between*, p. 30.

10. Samanth Subramanian, *This Divided Island* (London: Atlantic Books, 2016), p. 171.

11. Jonathan Raban, *For Love and Money* (London: Picador, 1987), p. 254.

12. Mee, 'Journalism and Travel Writing', p. 309.

13. Samanth Subramanian, *Following Fish* (London: Atlantic Books, 2012), p. 199.

14. Subramanian, *This Divided Island*, p. 98.

15. Mee, 'Journalism and Travel Writing', p. 310.

16. LETTING THE SCHOLAR SPEAK

1. What Thomas Keneally said about *The Songlines* was this: '[White] Australians were raised to think that at the heart of Australia there was a dead heart [...] It's a dangerous thing to say, but I think [Chatwin] did Aboriginal Australia a service. If there were ten books I had to set every [Australian] to read not for the sake of nationalism but for the sake of coming to terms with who we are on earth, *The Songlines* would be one of them.' Quoted in Nicholas Shakespeare, *Bruce Chatwin* (London: Harvill Press, 1999), p. 488.

17. UPSTREAM, DOWNSTREAM

1. Rob Nixon, 'Preparations for Travel: The Naipaul Brothers' Conradian Atavism', *Research in African Literatures* 22(2) (1991), pp. 177–90.

2. I published an article based on my examination of this old manuscript: Tim Hannigan, 'Counting Up the Lies: A Self-Reflexive Investigation of Craft and Fictionalization in a Modern Travel Book', *Journeys* 19(2) (2018), pp. 1–22.

3. William Dalrymple, *In Xanadu* (London: Collins, 1989), pp. 74, 112.

4. Tim Youngs, 'Interview with William Dalrymple', *Studies in Travel Writing* 9(1) (2005), pp. 37–63: 40.

5. William Dalrymple, 'In the Footsteps of Marco Polo: The Journey that Changed William Dalrymple's Life', *The Spectator*, 24 June 2015. Available at: https://www.spectator.co.uk/article/in-the-footsteps-of-marco-polo-the-journey-that-changed-william-dalrymple-s-life [accessed 9 September 2020].

6. William Dalrymple, *The Last Mughal: The Fall of Delhi, 1857* (London: Bloomsbury, 2006), p. 13.

7. Tabish Khair, 'An Interview with William Dalrymple and Pankaj Mishra', in Justin D. Edwards and Rune Graulund (eds), *Postcolonial Travel Writing* (Basingstoke: Palgrave Macmillan, 2011), pp. 173–84: 178.

8. Paul Smethurst, 'Post-Orientalism and the Past-Colonial in William Dalrymple's Travel Histories', in Justin D. Edwards and Rune Graulund (eds), *Postcolonial Travel Writing* (Basingstoke: Palgrave Macmillan, 2011), pp. 156–72: 168.

9. Monisha Rajesh, *Around India in 80 Trains* (London: Nicholas Brealey Publishing, 2012), pp. 217–19.

10. Sam Greenhill, 'Family of missing British explorer who ventured into the Papua New Guinea jungle with no GPS while searching for a lost tribe fear he could have been "robbed and left for dead" by drug barons', *The Daily Mail*, 14 November 2017. Available at: https://www.daily-mail.co.uk/news/article-5082983/British-explorer-missing-remote-headhunters-jungle.html [accessed 10 June 2019].

11. Charlie Brinkhurst-Cuff, 'The White Man's Blunders of "Explorer" Benedict Allen Feed Racist Myths', *The Guardian*, 17 November 2017. Available at: https://www.theguardian.com/commentisfree/2017/nov/17/benedict-allen-explorer-racist-british-colonial [accessed 10 June 2019].

12. Monisha Rajesh, *Around the World in 80 Trains* (London: Bloomsbury, 2019), p. 15.

13. Ibid., p. 124.

14. Graham Huggan, *Extreme Pursuits: Travel/Writing in an Age of Globalization* (Ann Arbor: University of Michigan Press, 2009), p. 16.

15. Rajesh, *Around the World in 80 Trains*, pp. 37–8.

16. C. W. R. D. Moseley (trans.), *The Travels of Sir John Mandeville* (London: Penguin, 2005), p. 188.

18. WINTERREISE I

1. Ben Downing, 'A Visit with Patrick Leigh Fermor', *The Paris Review* 165 (2003). Available at: https://www.theparisreview.org/letters-essays/

264/a-visit-with-patrick-leigh-fermor-ben-downing [accessed 11 June 2019].

2. Patrick Leigh Fermor, *A Time of Gifts* (London: John Murray, 1977), pp. 63–4.

3. Colin Thubron, *Among the Russians* (London: Heinemann, 1983), p. 32; Jason Elliot, *An Unexpected Light* (London: Picador, 1999), p. 218.

4. William Dalrymple, 'Introduction', in James O'Reilly, Larry Habegger and Sean O'Reilly (eds), *The Best Travel Writing 2010* (Palo Alto: Traveler's Tales, 2010), pp. xvii–xxvii: xvii.

5. Kathleen Jamie, 'A Lone Enraptured Male', *London Review of Books*, 6 March 2008, pp. 25–7.

6. Leigh Fermor, *A Time of Gifts*, p. 17.

7. Ibid., p. 20.

8. Sir Patrick Leigh Fermor Archive, National Library of Scotland, MS Acc.13338/123.

9. Artemis Cooper, *Patrick Leigh Fermor: An Adventure* (London: John Murray, 2012), p. 116.

10. Sir Patrick Leigh Fermor Archive, National Library of Scotland, MS Acc.13338/162.

11. Ibid.

12. Cooper, *Patrick Leigh Fermor*, p. 298.

13. Sir Patrick Leigh Fermor Archive, National Library of Scotland, MS Acc.13338/471.

14. Ibid.

15. Ibid.

16. Quoted in Cooper, *Patrick Leigh Fermor*, p. 364.

17. Cooper, Patrick Leigh Fermor, p. 74.

18. Ibid., p. 90.

19. Ibid., p. 65.

20. Leigh Fermor, *A Time of Gifts*, pp. 36, 42.

21. Ibid., p. 261.

22. Ibid., p. 263.

23. Ibid.

24. Ibid., p. 277.

25. Sir Patrick Leigh Fermor Archive, National Library of Scotland, MS Acc.13338/471.

26. Patrick Leigh Fermor, *The Broken Road* (London: John Murray, 2013), pp. 55–8.

19. WINTERREISE II

1. Robert Macfarlane, *The Gifts of Reading* (London: Penguin, 2017); Robert Macfarlane, 'Book of a Lifetime: In Patagonia, by Bruce Chatwin', *The*

Independent, 21 June 2012, available at: https://www.independent.co.uk/arts-entertainment/books/reviews/book-of-a-lifetime-in-patagonia-by-bruce-chatwin-7873053.html [accessed 11 June 2019].

2. Paul Smethurst, '"Habits of a landscape": The Geocritical Imagination in Robert Macfarlane's *The Wild Places* and *The Old Ways*', in Julia Kuehn and Paul Smethurst (eds), *New Directions in Travel Writing Studies* (Basingstoke: Palgrave Macmillan, 2015), pp. 97–110: 103.

3. Casey Blanton, *Travel Writing: The Self and the World* (London: Routledge, 2002), p. 2.

4. Paloma Fresno Calleja, 'Migration, Travel and Identity in Kapka Kassabova's *Reconnaissance*', *Journal of Postcolonial Writing* 42(1) (2006), pp. 18–31: 19.

5. Ludmilla Kostova, 'Writing Across the Native/Foreign Divide: The Case of Kapka Kassabova's Street Without a Name', in Corinne Fowler, Charles Forsdick and Ludmilla Kostova (eds), *Travel and Ethics: Theory and Practice* (Abingdon: Routledge, 2014), pp. 165–82: 178.

6. Kassabova's *To the Lake* was published by Granta in February 2020.

7. Kostova, 'Writing Across the Native/Foreign Divide', pp. 173–4.

8. Kapka Kassabova, *Twelve Minutes of Love* (London: Granta, 2011), p. 171.

9. Pico Iyer, *The Global Soul* (New York: Alfred A. Knopf, 2000).

EPILOGUE: THE DEATH OF THE AUTHOR

1. James Clifford, 'Introduction: Partial Truths', in James Clifford and George E. Marcus (eds), *Writing Culture: The Poetics and Politics of Ethnography* (Los Angeles: University of California Press, 1986), pp. 1–26: 7.

2. Jan Borm, 'Defining Travel: On the Travel Book, Travel Writing and Terminology', in Glenn Hooper and Tim Youngs (eds), *Perspectives on Travel Writing* (Aldershot: Ashgate, 2004), pp. 13–26: 17.

3. Nigel Barley, 'The Fake with the Pert Rump', *The Times Higher Education Supplement*, 4 June 1999. Available at: https://www.timeshighereduca-tion.com/books/the-fake-with-the-pert-rump/160681.article [accessed: 6 October 2019].

4. Sara Wheeler, *Access All Areas* (London: Jonathan Cape, 2011), p. 128.

5. Bruce Chatwin, *The Songlines* (London: Franklin Library, 1987), p. 104.

6. Nicholas Shakespeare, *Bruce Chatwin* (London: Harvill Press, 1999), p. 420.

7. Ibid., p. 313.

8. Elizabeth Chatwin and Nicholas Shakespeare (eds), *Under the Sun: The Letters of Bruce Chatwin* (London: Jonathan Cape, 2010), p. 507.

9. Artemis Cooper, *Patrick Leigh Fermor: An Adventure* (London: John Murray, 2012), p. 373.

10. Iain Macleod Higgins, *Writing East: The 'Travels' of Sir John Mandeville* (Philadelphia: University of Pennsylvania Press, 1997), p. 8.

11. Chatwin, *The Songlines*, p. 1.

SELECT BIBLIOGRAPHY

Adams, P. G. (1962) *Travelers and Travel Liars, 1660–1800*. Berkeley: University of California Press.

Asher, M. (1994) *Thesiger*. London: Viking.

Barker, F., Hulme, P. and Iversen, M. (eds) (1994) *Colonial Discourse / Postcolonial Theory*. Manchester: Manchester University Press.

Bassnett, S. (1998) 'When is a Translation not a Translation?', in Bassnett, S. and Lefevere, A. (eds), *Constructing Cultures: Essays on Literary Translation*. Clevedon: Multilingual Matters, pp. 25–40.

———— (1999) 'Travel Writing within British Studies', *Studies in Travel Writing* 3(1), pp. 1–16.

Behdad, A. (1994) *Belated Travelers: Orientalism in the Age of Colonial Dissolution*. Durham: Duke University Press.

Blanton, C. (2002) *Travel Writing: The Self and the World*. London: Routledge.

Borm, J. (2004) 'Defining Travel: On the Travel Book, Travel Writing and Terminology', in Hooper, G. and Youngs, T. (eds), *Perspectives on Travel Writing*. Aldershot: Ashgate, pp. 13–26.

Burton, S. (2014) *Travel Narrative and the Ends of Modernity*. Cambridge: Cambridge University Press.

Buzard, J. (1993) *The Beaten Track*. Oxford: Oxford University Press.

Campbell, M. B. (1988) *The Witness and the Other World: Exotic European Travel Writing, 400–1600*. Ithaca: Cornell University Press.

Chatwin, E. and Shakespeare, N. (eds) (2010) *Under the Sun: The Letters of Bruce Chatwin*. London: Jonathan Cape.

Chatwin, J. (2012) *Anywhere Out of the World: The Work of Bruce Chatwin*. Manchester: Manchester University Press.

Clark, S. (2000) '"Bang at its moral center": Ideologies of Genre in Butor, Fussell, and Raban', *Studies in Travel Writing* 4(1), pp. 106–25.

———— (ed.) (1999) *Travel Writing and Empire: Postcolonial Theory in Transit*. London: Zed Books.

Clifford, J. and Marcus, G. E. (eds) (1986) *Writing Culture: The Poetics and Politics of Ethnography*. Los Angeles: University of California Press, pp. 1–26.

Cocker, M. (1992) *Loneliness and Time: British Travel Writing in the Twentieth Century*. London: Secker & Warburg.

Cocking, B. (2011) 'Newby and Thesiger: Humour and Lament in the Hindu Kush', *Studies in Travel Writing* 15(1), pp. 93–109.

———. (2013) 'Truth and Travel Writing: Staging Authenticity in Redmond O'Hanlon's *Into the Heart of Borneo* (1984) and *Congo Journey* (1996)', *JOMEC Journal* 4, pp. 1–16.

Cooper, A. (2012) *Patrick Leigh Fermor: An Adventure*. London: John Murray.

Couser, G. T. (2012) *Memoir: An Introduction*. New York: Oxford University Press.

Das, N. and Youngs, T. (eds) (2019) *The Cambridge History of Travel Writing*. Cambridge: Cambridge University Press.

Duncan, J. and Gregory, D. (eds) (1999) *Writes of Passage: Reading Travel Writing*. London: Routledge.

Edwards, J. D. and Graulund, R. (eds) (2011) *Postcolonial Travel Writing*. Basingstoke: Palgrave Macmillan.

Fabian, J. (2014) *Time and the Other: How Anthropology Makes its Object*. 3rd edn. New York: Columbia University Press.

Forsdick, C. (2009) 'Peter Fleming and Ella Maillart in China: Travel Writing as Stereoscopic and Polygraphic Form', *Studies in Travel Writing* 13(4), pp. 293–303.

Fowler, C. (2007) *Chasing Tales: Travel Writing, Journalism and the History of British Ideas about Afghanistan*. Amsterdam: Rodopi.

Fowler, C., Forsdick, C. and Kostova, L. (eds) (2014) *Travel and Ethics: Theory and Practice*. Abingdon: Routledge.

Fussell, P. (1980) *Abroad: British Literary Travelling Between the Wars*. Oxford: Oxford University Press.

Harbsmeier, M. (1997) 'Spontaneous Ethnographies: Towards a Social History of Travellers' Tales', *Studies in Travel Writing* 1(1), pp. 216–38.

Higgins, I. M. (1997) *Writing East: The 'Travels' of Sir John Mandeville*. Philadelphia: University of Pennsylvania Press.

Holland, P. and Huggan, G. (1998) *Tourists with Typewriters: Critical Reflections on Contemporary Travel Writing*. Ann Arbor: University of Michigan Press.

Hooper, G. and Youngs, T. (eds) (2004) *Perspectives on Travel Writing*. Aldershot: Ashgate.

Howard, D. R. (1980) *Writers and Pilgrims: Medieval Pilgrimage Narratives and Their Posterity*. London: University of California Press.

Huggan, G. (2009) *Extreme Pursuits: Travel / Writing in an Age of Globalization*. Ann Arbor: University of Michigan Press.

Hulme, P. (1986) *Colonial Encounters: Europe and the Native Caribbean, 1492–1797*. London: Methuen.

Hulme, P. and Youngs, T. (2007) *Talking about Travel Writing: A Conversation Between Peter Hulme and Tim Youngs*. Leicester: English Association Issues in English.

———— (eds) (2002) *The Cambridge Companion to Travel Writing*. Cambridge: Cambridge University Press.

Islam, S. M. (1996) *The Ethics of Travel: From Marco Polo to Kafka*. Manchester: Manchester University Press.

Jamie, K. (2008) 'A Lone Enraptured Male', *London Review of Books*, 6 March, pp. 25–7.

Jarvis, Robin (2005) 'Self-discovery from Byron to Raban: The Long Afterlife of Romantic Travel', *Studies in Travel Writing* 9(2), pp. 185–204.

Korte, B. (1996) *English Travel Writing from Pilgrimages to Postcolonial Explorations*. Basingstoke: Palgrave Macmillan.

Kowalewski, M. (ed.) (1992) *Temperamental Journeys: Essays on the Modern Literature of Travel*. Athens: University of Georgia Press.

Kuehn, J. and Smethurst, P. (2009) *Travel Writing, Form, and Empire: The Poetics and Politics of Mobility*. Abingdon: Routledge.

———— (eds) (2015) *New Directions in Travel Writing Studies*. Basingstoke: Palgrave Macmillan.

Lindsay, C. (2010) *Contemporary Travel Writing of Latin America*. Abingdon: Routledge.

Lisle, D. (2006) *The Global Politics of Contemporary Travel Writing*. Cambridge: Cambridge University Press.

Maitland, A. (2006) *Wilfred Thesiger: The Life of the Great Explorer*. London: HarperPress.

Marfè, L. (2012) 'Chatwinesque, or Travel Writing as a Narrative Genre', *Arcadia International Journal of Literary Culture* 46(2), pp. 444–53.

Mason, H. (1972) *Gilgamesh: A Verse Narrative*. New York: Signet.

McClure, M. L. and Feltoe, C. L. (eds) (1919) *The Pilgrimage of Etheria*. London: Macmillan.

Mee, C. (2009) 'Journalism and Travel Writing: From *grands reporters* to Global Tourism', *Studies in Travel Writing* 13(4), pp. 305–15.

Mills, S. (1991) *Discourses of Difference: An Analysis of Women's Travel Writing and Colonialism*. London: Routledge.

Milton, G. (1996) *The Riddle and the Knight: In Search of Sir John Mandeville*. London: Allison & Busby Ltd.

Moorhouse, G. (1999) 'The Inward Journey, the Outward Passage: A Literary Balancing Act', *Studies in Travel Writing* 3(1), pp. 17–26.

Moseley, C. W. R. D. (trans.) (2005) *The Travels of Sir John Mandeville*. London: Penguin.

Moynagh, M. (2008) *Political Tourism and its Texts*. Toronto: University of Toronto Press.

Nixon, R. (1991) 'Preparations for Travel: The Naipaul Brothers' Conradian Atavism', *Research in African Literatures* 22(2), pp. 177–90.

Pratt, M. L. (1991) 'Arts of the Contact Zone', *Profession*, pp. 33–40.

———— (2008) *Imperial Eyes: Travel Writing and Transculturation*. 2nd edn. Abingdon: Routledge.

Purchas, S. (1905) *Hakluytus Posthumus or, Purchas his Pilgrimes*. London: Hakluyt Society.

Raban, J. (1987) *For Love and Money*. London: Picador.

Rose, J. (1992) 'Rereading the English Common Reader: A Preface to a History of Audiences', *Journal of the History of Ideas* 53(1), pp. 47–70.

Said, E. W. (2003) *Orientalism*. 3rd edn. London: Penguin Books.

Sandrock, K. (2015) 'Truth and Lying in Early Modern Travel Narratives: Coryat's *Crudities*, Lithgow's *Totall Discourse* and Generic Change', *European Journal of English Studies* 19(2), pp. 189–203.

Sardar, Z. (1999) *Orientalism*. Buckingham: Open University Press.

Schlick, Y. (2012) *Feminism and the Politics of Travel after the Enlightenment*. Lewisburg: Bucknell University Press.

Shakespeare, N. (1999) *Bruce Chatwin*. London: Harvill Press.

Sugnet, C. (1991) 'Vile Bodies, Vile Places: Traveling with *Granta*', *Transition* 51, pp. 70–85.

Thompson, C. (2011) *Travel Writing*. Abingdon: Routledge.

———— (ed.) (2016) *The Routledge Companion to Travel Writing*. Abingdon: Routledge.

Tromly, L. (2019) 'Echotourism and Masculinity: The African Travelogues of Tim Butcher, H. M. Stanley, and Graham Greene', *Studies in Travel Writing* 23(2), pp. 158–74.

Youngs, T. (2013) *The Cambridge Introduction to Travel Writing*. Cambridge: Cambridge University Press.

———— (ed.) (2006) *Travel Writing in the Nineteenth Century*. London: Anthem Press.

ACKNOWLEDGEMENTS

First thanks must of course go to all the travel writers, scholars, readers and others who agreed to talk to me. They were all incredibly generous with their time—and brave enough to put themselves in the position of travellee. Particular thanks to Philip Marsden, with whom the journey began, and whose support for the project has meant a great deal. Following Patrick Barkham's lead, I sent my draft chapters out to each of the writers described therein. It was decidedly nerve-wracking: what *would* I do if one of them raised a serious objection? But as it turned out, I needn't have worried. Everyone took things in the best possible spirit—though they saved me from myself in any number of small details, from inaccurate years of publication to misidentified tree species. The process unquestionably improved the final manuscript.

I am grateful for the permissions to include material from the archives of two of the twentieth century's most significant travel writers. The excerpts from the Patrick Leigh Fermor Archive, held at the National Library of Scotland, are reproduced courtesy of the Patrick Leigh Fermor Estate. The excerpts from the papers of Wilfred Thesiger are reproduced with permission of the Provost and Fellows of Eton College, and with permission of Curtis Brown Group Ltd, London, on behalf of The Beneficiaries of the Estate of Wilfred Thesiger. I am also grateful to Eland Publishing for the permission to use the quote from Nicolas Bouvier's *The Way of the World* as an epigraph. The quote from Graham Greene's *Ways of Escape* (Vintage, 1999, p. 47) appears courtesy of David Higham Associates.

ACKNOWLEDGEMENTS

As described in the first chapter, the genesis of this journey was a magazine assignment to interview Philip Marsden. But before I had a chance to make a book proposal of that rudimentary idea, I got the opportunity to turn it into a PhD. That opportunity came about through an introduction—for which I am very grateful indeed—by Charlie Mansfield of the University of Plymouth to Corinne Fowler and Harry Whitehead of the University of Leicester. Corinne and Harry went on to become my PhD supervisors for three wonderful years at Leicester, with further supervision from Sharon Ouditt of Nottingham Trent University. I could not have asked for three better supervisors—unfailingly supportive, open-minded and generous with their time, but always ready to nudge me in the right direction. This book couldn't have been written without them. At the University of Leicester, thanks also to Nick Everett and Mark Rawlinson for their thoroughgoing interrogations to make sure that I was on the right track. Thanks particularly to Nick for the detailed discussions of the work in progress, well beyond the call of duty. At the final stage of its academic journey, the project was examined by Peter Hulme and Jonathan Taylor; very many thanks to both of them for their detailed reading, with comments which have informed this ultimate version, and for making the examination such a pleasurable experience.

My PhD research was funded by the AHRC through the brilliant Midlands4Cities Doctoral Training Partnership (M4C), to which I'm eternally grateful. Many thanks to Susanna Ison and the rest of the central M4C team, and to the University of Leicester's M4C site directors, Neil Christie, Phil Shaw and Martin Halliwell, for approving my various research funding applications, and to Louise Taylor for speeding those applications on their way. Thanks also to my fellow M4C researchers across the DTP, especially Aly Stoneman, Sofia Aatkar and Zee Oliver for their friendship, solidarity and discussions of travel writing over the years.

Beyond the campus, sincere thanks to the librarians and archivists of Eton College, the National Library of Scotland and the Bodleian Library, in particular Stephie Coane at Eton for the warm welcome and generous assistance with Thesiger's papers. Thanks too to Alexander Maitland on that front. Thanks to all my friends and colleagues in the world of travel writing studies whose research and discussions have fed

ACKNOWLEDGEMENTS

into and greatly enriched this project—in particular the Borders and Crossings network and the members of SELVA (Société d'Étude de la Littérature de Voyage du monde Anglophone). I endeavour to remain an insider-outsider, but this is surely one of the most welcoming and supportive of all scholarly communities. Particular thanks to Tim Youngs for many helpful insights, and for publishing some of the raw material of the project in *Studies in Travel Writing*.

Beyond the bounds of academia, thanks to Robert Dudley for his efforts and advice. Very many thanks to Michael Dwyer at Hurst for commissioning the project as a book for readers in the real world, to Lara Weisweiller-Wu for skilfully guiding it to publication, and to Rose Bell for her meticulous copyediting, which saved me from many embarrassing errors. Thanks, of course, to my family. And finally, but most importantly, many thanks and much love to Cara for her endless patience and support.

INDEX

INDEX

INDEX

INDEX

INDEX

INDEX